NOTES ON NOVELISTS
WITH SOME OTHER NOTES

NOTES ON NOVELISTS

WITH SOME OTHER NOTES

BY

HENRY JAMES

BIBLO and TANNEN
NEW YORK
1969

Printed in U.S.A. by
NOBLE OFFSET PRINTERS, INC.
NEW YORK 3, N. Y.

CONTENTS

v

vi CONTENTS

NOTES ON NOVELISTS
WITH SOME OTHER NOTES

NOTES ON NOVELISTS

ROBERT LOUIS STEVENSON

IT was the happy fortune of Robert Louis Stevenson to
have created beyond any man of his craft in our day a
body of readers inspired with the feelings that we for
the most part place at the service only of those for
whom our affection is personal. There was no one
who knew the man, one may safely assert, who was
not also devoted to the writer—conforming in this respect to a general law (if law it be) that shows us many
exceptions; but, naturally and not inconveniently, it
had to remain far from true that all devotees of the
writer were able to approach the man. The case was
nevertheless that the man somehow approached *them*,
and that to read him—certainly to read him with the
full sense of his charm—came to mean for many persons much the same as to "meet" him. It was as if
he wrote himself outright and altogether, rose straight
to the surface of his prose, and still more of his happiest verse; so that these things gave out, besides whatever else, his look and motions and voice, showed his
life and manners, all that there was of him, his "tremendous secrets" not excepted. We grew in short to
possess him entire, and the example is the more curious and beautiful as he neither made a business of
"confession" nor cultivated most those forms through
which the *ego* shines. His great successes were sup-

posititious histories of persons quite different from himself, and the objective, as we have learned to call it,
was the ideal to which he oftenest sacrificed.

The effect of it all none the less was such that his
Correspondence has only seemed to administer delightfully a further push to a door already half open
and through which we enter with an extraordinary
failure of any sense of intrusion. We feel indeed that
we are living with him, but what is that but what we
were doing before? Through his Correspondence certainly the *ego* does, magnificently, shine—which is
much the best thing that in any correspondence it can
ever do. But even the "Vailima Letters," published
by Mr. Sidney Colvin in 1895, had already both established that and allayed our diffidence. "It came
over me the other day suddenly that this diary of mine
to you would make good pickings after I am dead, and
a man could make some kind of book out of it without
much trouble. So, for God's sake, don't lose them."

Being on these terms with our author, and feeling as
if we had always been, we profit by freedoms that seem
but the consecration of intimacy. Not only have we
no sense of intrusion, but we are so prepared to penetrate further that when we come to limits we quite
feel as if the story were mutilated and the copy not
complete. There it is precisely that we seize the
secret of our tie. Of course it was personal, for how
did it operate in any connection whatever but to make
us live with him? We had lived with him in "Treasure
Island," in "Kidnapped" and in "Catriona," just as
we do, by the light of these posthumous volumes, in
the South Seas and at Vailima; and our present con-

fidence comes from the fact of a particularly charming continuity. It is not that his novels were "subjective," but that his life was romantic, and in the very same degree in which his own conception, his own presentation, of that element touches and thrills. If we want to know even more it is because we are always and everywhere in the story.

To this absorbing extension of the story then the two volumes of Letters[1] now published by Mr. Sidney Colvin beautifully contribute. The shelf of our library that contains our best letter-writers is considerably furnished, but not overcrowded, and its glory is not too great to keep Stevenson from finding there a place with the very first. He will not figure among the writers—those apt in this line to enjoy precedence —to whom only small things happen and who beguile us by making the most of them; he belongs to the class who have both matter and manner, substance and spirit, whom life carries swiftly before it and who signal and communicate, not to say gesticulate, as they go. He lived to the topmost pulse, and the last thing that could happen was that he should find himself on any occasion with nothing to report. Of all that he may have uttered on certain occasions we are inevitably not here possessed—a fact that, as I have hinted above, affects us, perversely, as an inexcusable gap in the story; but he never fails of the thing that we most love letters for, the full expression of the moment and the mood, the actual good or bad or middling, the thing in his head, his heart or his house.

[1] "The Letters of Robert Louis Stevenson to his Family and Friends. Selected and Edited, with Notes and Introduction, by Sidney Colvin," 1899.

Mr. Colvin has given us an admirable "Introduction"
—a characterisation of his friend so founded at once on
knowledge and on judgment that the whole sense of
the man strikes us as extracted in it. He has eluci-
dated each group or period with notes that leave nothing to be desired; and nothing remains that I can
think of to thank him for unless the intimation that we
may yet look for another volume—which, however
much more free it might make us of the author's mystery, we should accept, I repeat, with the same absence
of scruple. Nothing more belongs to our day than
this question of the inviolable, of the rights of privacy
and the justice of our claim to aid from editors and
other retailers in getting behind certain eminent or
defiant appearances; and the general knot so presented
is indeed a hard one to untie. Yet we may take it for
a matter regarding which such publications as Mr.
Colvin's have much to suggest.

There is no absolute privacy—save of course when
the exposed subject may have wished or endeavoured
positively to constitute it; and things too sacred are
often only things that are not perhaps at all otherwise
superlative. One may hold both that people—that
artists perhaps in particular—are well advised to cover
their tracks, and yet that our having gone behind, or
merely stayed before, in a particular case, may be a
minor question compared with our having picked up a
value. Personal records of the type before us can at
any rate obviously be but the reverse of a deterrent to
the urged inquirer. They are too happy an instance—
they positively make for the risked indiscretion.
Stevenson never covered his tracks, and the tracks
prove perhaps to be what most attaches us. We fol-

low them here, from year to year and from stage to
stage, with the same charmed sense with which he has
made us follow some hunted hero in the heather.
Life and fate and an early catastrophe were ever at his
heels, and when he at last falls fighting, sinks down in
the very act of valour, the "happy ending," as he calls
it for some of his correspondents, is, though precipitated and not conventional, essentially given us.

His descent and his origin all contribute to the picture, which it seems to me could scarce—since we speak
of "endings"—have had a better beginning had he
himself prearranged it. Without prearrangements indeed it was such a cluster of terms as could never be
wasted on him, one of those innumerable matters of
"effect," Scotch and other, that helped to fill his
romantic consciousness. Edinburgh, in the first place,
the "romantic town," was as much his "own" as it
ever was the great precursor's whom, in "Weir of
Hermiston" as well as elsewhere, he presses so hard;
and this even in spite of continual absence—in virtue
of a constant imaginative reference and an intense intellectual possession. The immediate background
formed by the profession of his family—the charge of
the public lights on northern coasts—was a setting that
he could not have seen his way to better; while no less
happy a condition was met by his being all lonely in
his father's house—the more that the father, admirably
commemorated by the son and after his fashion as
strongly marked, was antique and strenuous, and that
the son, a genius to be and of frail constitution, was (in
the words of the charming anecdote of an Edinburgh
lady retailed in one of these volumes), if not exactly
what could be called bonny, "pale, penetrating and in-

teresting." The poet in him had from the first to be pacified—temporarily, that is, and from hand to mouth, as is the manner for poets; so that with friction and tension playing their part, with the filial relation quite classically troubled, with breaks of tradition and lapses from faith, with restless excursions and sombre returns, with the love of life at large mixed in his heart with every sort of local piety and passion and the unjustified artist fermenting on top of all in the recusant engineer, he was as well started as possible toward the character he was to keep.

All this obviously, however, was the sort of thing that the story the most generally approved would have had at heart to represent as the mere wild oats of a slightly uncanny cleverness—as the life handsomely reconciled in time to the common course and crowned, after a fling or two of amusement, with young wedded love and civic responsibility. The actual story, alas, was to transcend the conventional one, for it happened to be a case of a hero of too long a wind and too well turned out for his part. Everything was right for the discipline of Alan Fairford but that the youth *was* after all a phœnix. As soon as it became a case of justifying himself for straying—as in the enchanting "Inland Voyage" and the "Travels with a Donkey" —how was he to escape doing so with supreme felicity? The fascination in him from the first is the mixture, and the extraordinary charm of his letters is that they are always showing this. It is the proportions moreover that are so admirable—the quantity of each different thing that he fitted to each other one and to the whole. The free life would have been all his dream if so large a part of it had not been that love of letters, of expression and form, which is but another name for the life of service. Almost the last word about him, by the same law, would be that he had at any rate consummately written, were it not that he seems still better characterised by his having at any rate supremely lived.

Perpetually and exquisitely amusing as he was, his ambiguities and compatibilities yielded, for all the wear and tear of them, endless "fun" even to himself; and no one knew so well with what linked diversities he was saddled or, to put it the other way, how many horses he had to drive at once. It took his own delightful talk to show how more than absurd it might be, and, if convenient, how very obscurely so, that such an incurable rover should have been complicated both with such an incurable scribbler and such an incurable invalid, and that a man should find himself such an anomaly as a drenched yatchsman haunted with "style," a shameless Bohemian haunted with duty, and a victim at once of the personal hunger and instinct for adventure and of the critical, constructive, sedentary view of it. He had everything all round— adventure most of all; to feel which we have only to turn from the beautiful flush of it in his text to the scarce less beautiful vision of the great hilltop in Pacific seas to which he was borne after death by islanders and chiefs. Fate, as if to distinguish him as handsomely as possible, seemed to be ever treating him to some chance for an act or a course that had almost nothing in its favour but its inordinate difficulty. If the difficulty was in these cases not *all* the beauty for him it at least never prevented his finding in it—or our finding, at any rate, as observers—so much beauty as comes from a great risk accepted either for an idea or for simple joy. The joy of risks, the more personal the better, was never far from him, any more than the excitement of ideas. The most important step in his life was a signal instance of this, as we may discern in the light of "The Amateur Emigrant" and "Across the Plains," the report of the conditions in which he fared from England to California to be married. Here as always the great note is the heroic mixture—the thing he *saw*, morally as well as imaginatively; action and performance at any cost, and the cost made immense by want of health and want of money, illness and anxiety of the extremest kind, and by unsparing sensibilities and perceptions. He had been launched in the world for a fighter with the organism say of a "composer," though also it must be added with a beautiful saving sanity.

It is doubtless after his settlement in Samoa that his letters have most to give, but there are things they throw off from the first that strike the note above all characteristic, show his imagination always at play, for drollery or philosophy, with his circumstances. The difficulty in writing of him under the personal impression is to suggest enough how directly his being the genius that he was kept counting in it. In 1879 he writes from Monterey to Mr. Edmund Gosse, in reference to certain grave symptoms of illness: "I may be wrong, but . . . I believe I must go. . . . But death is no bad friend; a few aches and gasps, and we are done; like the truant child, I am beginning to grow weary and timid in this big, jostling city, and could run to my nurse, even although she should have to whip me before putting me to bed." This charming renunciation expresses itself at the very time his talent was growing finer; he was so fond of the sense of youth and the idea of play that he saw whatever happened to him in images and figures, in the terms almost of the sports of childhood. "Are you coming over again to see me some day soon? I keep returning, and now hand over fist, from the realms of Hades. I saw that gentleman between the eyes, and fear him less after each visit. Only Charon and his rough boatmanship I somewhat fear."

The fear remained with him, sometimes greater, sometimes less, during the first years after his marriage, those spent abroad and in England in health resorts, and it marks constantly, as one may say, one end of the range of his humour—the humour always busy at the other end with the impatience of timidities and precautions and the vision and invention of essentially open-air situations. It was the possibility of the open-air situation that at last appealed to him as the cast worth staking all for—on which, as usual in his admirable rashnesses, he was extraordinarily justified. "No man but myself knew all my bitterness in those days. Remember that, the next time you think I regret my exile. . . . Remember the pallid brute that lived in Skerryvore like a weevil in a biscuit."

He found after an extraordinarily adventurous quest the treasure island, the climatic paradise that met, that enhanced his possibilities; and with this discovery was ushered in his completely full and rich period, the time in which—as the wondrous whimsicality and spontaneity of his correspondence testify—his genius and his character most overflowed. He had done as well for himself in his appropriation of Samoa as if he had

done it for the hero of a novel, only with the complications and braveries actual and palpable. "I have no
more hope in anything"—and this in the midst of magnificent production—"than a dead frog; I go into
everything with a composed despair, and don't mind—
just as I always go to sea with the conviction I am to be
drowned, and like it before all other pleasures." He
could go to sea as often as he liked and not be spared
such hours as one of these pages vividly evokes—those
of the joy of fictive composition in an otherwise pros-
trating storm, amid the crash of the elements and with
his grasp of his subject but too needfully sacrificed, it
might have appeared, to his clutch of seat and ink-
stand. "If only I could secure a violent death, what a
fine success! I wish to die in my boots; no more Land
of Counterpane for me. To be drowned, to be shot,
to be thrown from a horse—aye, to be hanged rather
than pass again through that slow dissolution."

He speaks in one of the "Vailima Letters," Mr. Colvin's publication of 1895, to which it is an office of
these volumes promptly to make us return, of one of
his fictions as a "long tough yarn with some pictures
of the manners of to-day in the greater world—not the
shoddy sham world of cities, clubs and colleges, but
the world where men still live a man's life." That is
distinct, and in the same letter he throws off a summary of all that in his final phase satisfied and bribed
him which is as significant as it is racy. His correspondent, as was inevitable now and then for his friends
at home, appears to have indulged in one of those
harmless pointings of the moral—as to the distant
dangers he *would* court—by which we all were more or
less moved to relieve ourselves of the depressed con-

sciousness that he could do beautifully without us and
that our collective tameness was far (which indeed was
distinctly the case) from forming his proper element.
There is no romantic life for which something amiable
has not to be sweepingly sacrificed, and of *us* in our
inevitable category the sweep practically was clean.

Your letter had the most wonderful "I told you so" I ever heard
in the course of my life. Why, you madman, I wouldn't change
my present installation for any post, dignity, honour, or advantage
conceivable to me. It fills the bill; I have the loveliest time.
And as for wars and rumours of wars, you surely know enough of
me to be aware that I like that also a thousand times better than
decrepit peace in Middlesex. I do not quite like politics. I am too
aristocratic, I fear, for that. God knows I don't care who I chum
with; perhaps like sailors best; but to go round and sue and sneak
to keep a crowd together—never.

His categories satisfied him; he had got hold of "the
world where men still live a man's life"—which was
not, as we have just seen, that of "cities, clubs and
colleges." He was supremely suited in short at last—
at the cost, it was to be said, of simplifications of view
that, intellectually, he failed quite exactly (it was one
of his few limitations) to measure; but in a way that
ministered to his rare capacity for growth and placed
in supreme relief his affinity with the universal romantic.
It was not that anything could ever be for him plain
sailing, but that he had been able at forty to turn his
life into the fairytale of achieving, in a climate that he
somewhere describes as "an expurgated heaven," such
a happy physical consciousness as he had never known.
This enlarged in every way his career, opening the
door still wider to that real puss-in-the-corner game of
opposites by which we have critically the interest of
seeing him perpetually agitated. Let me repeat that

these new volumes, from the date of his definite ex-
patriation, direct us for the details of the picture constantly to the "Vailima Letters;" with as constant an
effect of our thanking our fortune—to say nothing of
his own—that he should have had in these years a
correspondent and a confidant who so beautifully drew
him out. If he possessed in Mr. Sidney Colvin his
literary chargé d'affaires at home, the ideal friend and
alter ego on whom he could unlimitedly rest, this is a
proof the more—with the general rarity of such cases
—of what it was in his nature to make people wish to
do for him. To Mr. Colvin he is more familiar than to
any one, more whimsical and natural and frequently
more inimitable—of all of which a just notion can be
given only by abundant citation. And yet citation
itself is embarrassed, with nothing to guide it but his
perpetual spirits, perpetual acuteness and felicity,
restlessness of fancy and of judgment. These things
make him jump from pole to pole and fairly hum, at
times, among the objects and subjects that filled his
air, like a charged bee among flowers.

He is never more delightful than when he is most
egotistic, most consciously charmed with something he
has done.

And the papers are some of them up to dick, and no mistake.   I
agree with you, the lights seem a little turned down.

When we learn that the articles alluded to are those
collected in "Across the Plains" we quite assent to this
impression made by them after a troubled interval, and
envy the author who, in a far Pacific isle, could see
"The Lantern Bearers," "A Letter to a Young Gentleman" and "Pulvis et Umbra" float back to him as a
guarantee of his faculty and between covers constitut-

ing the book that is to live. Stevenson's masculine wisdom moreover, his remarkable final sanity, is always—and it was not what made least in him for happy intercourse—close to his comedy and next door to his slang.

And however low the lights are, the stuff is true, and I believe the more effective; after all, what I wish to fight is the best fought by a rather cheerless presentation of the truth. The world must return some day to the word "duty," and be done with the word "reward." There are no rewards, and plenty duties. And the sooner a man sees that and acts upon it, like a gentleman or a fine old barbarian, the better for himself.

It would perhaps be difficult to quote a single paragraph giving more than that of the whole of him. But there is abundance of him in this too:

How do journalists fetch up their drivel? . . . It has taken me two months to write 45,500 words; and, be damned to my wicked prowess, I am proud of the exploit! . . . A respectable little five-bob volume, to bloom unread in shop windows. After that I'll have a spank at fiction. And rest? I shall rest in the grave, or when I come to Italy. If only the public will continue to support me! I lost my chance not dying; there seems blooming little fear of it now. I worked close on five hours this morning; the day before, close on nine; and unless I finish myself off with this letter I'll have another hour and a half, or *aiblins twa*, before dinner. Poor man, how you must envy me as you hear of these orgies of work, and you scarce able for a letter. But Lord! Colvin, how lucky the situations are not reversed, for I have no situation, nor am fit for any. Life is a steigh brae. Here, have at Knappe, and no more clavers!

If he talked profusely—and this is perfect talk—if he loved to talk above all of his work in hand, it was because, though perpetually frail, he was never inert, and did a thing, if he did it at all, with passion. He was not fit, he says, for a situation, but a situation overtook him inexorably at Vailima, and doubtless at last indeed swallowed him up. His position, with differences, comparing in some respects smaller things to greater, and with fewer differences after all than likenesses, his position resembles that of Scott at Abbotsford, just as, sound, sensible and strong on each side in spite of the immense gift of dramatic and poetic vision, the earlier and the later man had something of a common nature. Life became bigger for each than the answering effort could meet, and in their death they were not divided. Stevenson's late emancipation was a fairytale only because he himself was in his manner a magician. He liked to handle many matters and to shrink from none; nothing can exceed the impression we get of the things that in these years he dealt with from day to day and as they came up, and the things that, as well, almost without order or relief, he planned and invented, took up and talked of and dropped, took up and talked of and carried through. Had I space to treat myself to a clue for selection from the whole record there is nothing I should better like it to be than a tracking of his "literary opinions" and literary projects, the scattered swarm of his views, sympathies, antipathies, *obiter dicta*, as an artist—his flurries and fancies, imaginations, evocations, quick infatuations, as a teller of possible tales. Here is a whole little circle of discussion, yet such a circle that to engage one's self at all is to be too much engulfed.

His overflow on such matters is meanwhile amusing enough as mere spirits and sport—interesting as it would yet be to catch as we might, at different moments, the congruity between the manner of his feeling a fable in the germ and that of his afterwards handling it.

There are passages again and again that light strikingly what I should call his general conscious method in this relation, were I not more tempted to call it his conscious—for that is what it seems to come to—negation of method. A whole delightful letter—to Mr. Colvin, February 1, 1892—is a vivid type. (This letter, I may mention, is independently notable for the drollery of its allusion to a sense of scandal—of all things in the world—excited in some editorial breast by "The Beach of Falesà;" which leads him to the highly pertinent remark that "this is a poison bad world for the romancer, this Anglo-Saxon world; I usually get out of it by not having any women in it at all." Then he remembers he had "The Treasure of Franchard" refused as unfit for a family magazine and feels—as well he may— "despair weigh upon his wrists." The despair haunts him and comes out on another occasion. "Five more chapters of David. . . . All love affair; seems pretty good to me. Will it do for the young person? I don't know: since the Beach, I know nothing except that men are fools and hypocrites, and I know less of them than I was fond enough to fancy.") Always a part of his physiognomy is the play, so particularly salient, of his moral fluctuations, the way his spirits are upset by his melancholy and his grand conclusions by his rueful doubts.

He communicates to his confidant with the eagerness of a boy confabulating in holidays over a Christmas charade; but I remember no instance of his expressing a subject, as one may say, *as* a subject—hinting at what novelists mainly know, one would imagine, as the determinant thing in it, the idea out of which it springs. The form, the envelope, is there with him,

headforemost, *as* the idea; titles, names, that is, chapters, sequences, orders, while we are still asking ourselves how it was that he primarily put to his own mind
what it was all to be about. He simply *felt* this, evidently, and it is always the one dumb sound, the stopped
pipe or only unexpressed thing, in all his contagious
candour. He finds none the less in the letter to which
I refer one of the problems of the wonderful projected
"Sophia Scarlet" "exactly a Balzac one, and I wish I
had his fist—for I have already a better method—the
kinetic—whereas he continually allowed himself to be
led into the static." There we have him—Stevenson,
not Balzac—at his most overflowing, and after all
radiantly capable of conceiving at another moment that
his "better method" would have been none at all for
Balzac's vision of a subject, least of all of *the* subject,
the whole of life. Balzac's method was adapted to
his notion of presentation—which we may accept, it
strikes me, under the protection of what he presents.
Were it not, in fine, as I may repeat, to embark in a
bigger boat than would here turn round I might note
further that Stevenson has elsewhere—was disposed in
general to have—too short a way with this master.
There is an interesting passage in which he charges
him with having never known what to leave out, a
passage which has its bearing on condition of being
read with due remembrance of the class of performance
to which "Le Colonel Chabert," for instance, "Le
Curé de Tours," "L'Interdiction," "La Messe de
l'Athée" (to name but a few brief masterpieces in a
long list) appertain.

These, however, are comparatively small questions;
the impression, for the reader of the later letters, is

simply one of singular beauty—of deepening talent, of happier and richer expression, and in especial of an ironic desperate gallantry that burns away, with a finer and finer fire, in a strange alien air and is only the more touching to us from his own resolute consumption of the smoke. He had incurred great charges, he sailed a ship loaded to the brim, so that the strain under which he lived and wrought was immense; but the very grimness of it all is sunny, slangy, funny, familiar; there is as little of the florid in his flashes of melancholy as of the really grey under stress of his wisdom. This wisdom had sometimes on matters of art, I think, its lapses, but on matters of life it was really winged and inspired. He has a soundness as to questions of the vital connection, a soundness all liberal and easy and born of the manly experience, that it is a luxury to touch. There are no compunctions nor real impatiences, for he had in a singular degree got what he wanted, the life absolutely discockneyfied, the situation as romantically "swagger" as if it had been an imagination made real; but his practical anxieties necessarily spin themselves finer, and it is just this production of the thing imagined that has more and more to meet them. It all hung, the situation, by *that* beautiful golden thread, the swinging of which in the wind, as he spins it in alternate doubt and elation, we watch with much of the suspense and pity with which we sit at the serious drama. It is serious in the extreme; yet the forcing of production, in the case of a faculty so beautiful and delicate, affects us almost as the straining of a nerve or the distortion of a feature.

I sometimes sit and yearn for anything in the nature of an income that would come in—mine has all got to be gone and fished for with the immortal mind of man. What I want is the income that really comes in of itself, while all you have to do is just to blossom and exist and sit on chairs. . . . I should probably amuse myself with works that would make your hair curl, if you had any left.

To read over some of his happiest things, to renew one's sense of the extraordinarily fine temper of his imagination, is to say to one's self "What a horse to have to ride every week to market!" We must all go to market, but the most fortunate of us surely are those who may drive thither, and on days not too frequent, nor by a road too rough, a ruder and homelier animal. He touches in more than one place—and with notable beauty and real authority in that little mine of felicities the "Letter to a Young Gentleman"—on the conscience for "frugality" which should be the artist's finest point of honour; so that one of his complications here was undoubtedly the sense that on this score his position had inevitably become somewhat false. The literary romantic is by no means necessarily expensive, but of the many ways in which the practical, the active, has to be paid for this departure from frugality would be, it is easy to conceive, not the least. And we perceive his recognising this as he recognised everything— if not in time, then out of it; accepting inconsistency, as he always did, with the gaiety of a man of courage— not being, that is, however intelligent, priggish for logic and the grocer's book any more than for anything else. Only everything made for keeping it up, and it was a great deal to keep up; though when he throws off "The Ebb-Tide" and rises to "Catriona," and then again to "Weir of Hermiston," as if he could rise to almost anything, we breathe anew and look longingly forward. The latest of these letters contain such admirable things, testify so to the reach of his intelligence and in short vibrate so with genius and charm, that we feel him at moments not only unexhausted but replenished, and capable perhaps, for all we know to the contrary, of new experiments and deeper notes. The intelligence and attention are so fine that he misses nothing from unawareness; not a gossamer thread of the "thought of the time" that, wafted to him on the other side of the globe, may not be caught in a branch and played with; he puts such a soul into nature and such human meanings, for comedy and tragedy, into what surrounds him, however shabby or short, that he really lives in society by living in his own perceptions and generosities or, as we say nowadays, his own atmosphere. In this atmosphere—which seems to have had the gift of abounding the more it was breathed by others—these pages somehow prompt us to see almost every object on his tropic isle bathed and refreshed.

So far at any rate from growing thin for want of London he can transmit to London or to its neighbourhood communications such as it would scarce know otherwise where to seek. A letter to his cousin, R. A. M. Stevenson, of September 1894, touches so on all things and, as he would himself have said, so adorns them, brimming over with its happy extravagance of thought, that, far again from our feeling Vailima, in the light of it, to be out of the world, it strikes us that the world has moved for the time to Vailima. There is world enough everywhere, he quite unconsciously shows, for the individual, the right one, to be what we call a man of it. He has, like every one not convenienced with the pleasant back-door of stupidity, to make his account with seeing and facing more things, seeing and facing everything, with the unrest of new impressions and ideas, the loss of the fond complacencies of youth.

But as I go on in life, day by day, I become more of a bewildered child; I cannot get used to this world, to procreation, to heredity, to sight, to hearing; the commonest things are a burthen. The prim obliterated polite face of life, and the broad, bawdy and orgiastic—or mænadic—foundations, form a spectacle to which no habit reconciles me; and "I could wish my days to be bound each to each" by the same open-mouthed wonder. They *are* anyway, and whether I wish it or not. . . . I remember very well your attitude to life—this conventional surface of it. You have none of that curiosity for the social stage directions, the trivial *ficelles* of the business; it is simian; but that is how the wild youth of man is captured.

The whole letter is enchanting.

But no doubt there is something great in the half success that has attended the effort of turning into an emotional region Bald Conduct without any appeal, or almost none, to the figurative, mysterious and constitutive facts of life. Not that conduct is not constitutive, but dear! it's dreary! On the whole, conduct is better dealt with on the cast-iron "gentleman" and duty formula, with as little fervour and poetry as possible; stoical and short.

The last letter of all, it will have been abundantly noted, has, with one of those characteristically thrownout references to himself that were always half a whim, half a truth and all a picture, a remarkable premonition. It is addressed to Mr. Edmond Gosse.

It is all very well to talk of renunciation, and of course it has to be done. But for my part, give me a roaring toothache! I do like to be deceived and to dream, but I have very little use for either watching or meditation. I was not born for age. . . . I am a childless, rather bitter, very clear-eyed, blighted youth. I have, in fact, lost the path that makes it easy and natural for you to descend the hill. I am going at it straight. And where I have to go down it is a precipice. . . . You can never write another dedication that can give the same pleasure to the vanished Tusitala.

Two days later he met his end in the happiest form, by the straight swift bolt of the gods. It was, as all his readers know, with an admirable unfinished thing in hand, scarce a quarter written—a composition as to which his hopes were, presumably with much justice and as they were by no means always, of the highest. Nothing is more interesting than the rich way in which, in "Weir of Hermiston" and "Catriona," the predominant imaginative Scot reasserts himself after gaps and lapses, distractions and deflections superficially extreme. There are surely few backward jumps of this energy more joyous and à *pieds joints*, or of a kind more interesting to a critic. The imaginative vision is hungry and tender just in proportion as the actual is otherwise beset; so that we must sigh always in vain for the quality that this purified flame, as we call it, would have been able to give the metal. And how many things for the critic the case suggests—how many possible reflections cluster about it and seem to take light from it! It was "romance" indeed, "Weir of Hermiston," we feel, as we see it only grow in assurance and ease when the reach to it over all the spaces becomes more positively artificial. The case is *literary* to intensity, and, given the nature of the talent, only thereby the more beautiful: he embroiders in silk and silver—in defiance of climate and nature, of every near aspect, and with such another antique needle as was nowhere, least of all in those latitudes, to be bought—in the intervals of wondrous international and insular politics and of fifty material cares and complications. His special stock of association, most per-

sonal style and most unteachable trick fly away again
to him like so many strayed birds to nest, each with
the flutter in its beak of some scrap of document or
legend, some fragment of picture or story, to be retouched, revarnished and reframed.

These things he does with a gusto, moreover, for
which it must be granted that his literary treatment of
the islands and the island life had ever vainly waited.
Curious enough that his years of the tropics and his
fraternity with the natives never drew from him any
such "rendered" view as might have been looked for
in advance.   For the absent and vanished Scotland he
has the image—within the limits (too narrow ones we
may perhaps judge) admitted by his particular poetic; but the law of these things in him was, as of
many others, amusingly, conscientiously perverse.   The
Pacific, in which he materially delighted, made him
"descriptively" serious and even rather dry; with his
own country, on the other hand, materially impossible, he was ready to tread an endless measure.   He
easily sends us back again here to our vision of his
mixture.   There was only one thing on earth that he
loved as much as literature—which was the total absence of it; and to the present, the immediate, whatever
it was, he always made the latter offering.   Samoa was
susceptible of no "style"—none of that, above all,
with which he was most conscious of an affinity—save
the demonstration of its rightness for life; and this
left the field abundantly clear for the Border, the Great
North Road and the eighteenth century.   I have been
reading over "Catriona" and "Weir" with the purest
pleasure with which we can follow a man of genius—
that of seeing him abound in his own sense.   In "Weir"

especially, like an improvising pianist, he superabounds
and revels, and his own sense, by a happy stroke, appeared likely never more fully and brightly to justify
him; to have become even in some degree a new sense,
with new chords and possibilities. It is the "old game,"
but it is the old game that he exquisitely understands.
The figure of Hermiston is creative work of the highest order, those of the two Kirsties, especially that of
the elder, scarce less so; and we ache for the loss of a
thing which could give out such touches as the quick
joy, at finding herself in falsehood, of the enamoured
girl whose brooding elder brother has told her that as
soon as she has a lover she will begin to lie (" 'Will I
have gotten my jo now?' she thought with secret rapture"); or a passage so richly charged with imagination
as that in which the young lover recalls her as he has
first seen and desired her, seated at grey of evening
on an old tomb in the moorland and unconsciously
making him think, by her scrap of song, both of his
mother, who sang it and whom he has lost, and

of their common ancestors now dead, of their rude wars composed, their weapons buried with them, and of these strange change-
lings, their descendants, who lingered a little in their places and
would soon be gone also, and perhaps sung of by others at the gloam-
ing hour. By one of the unconscious arts of tenderness the two
women were enshrined together in his memory. Tears, in that hour
of sensibility, came into his eyes indifferently at the thought of
either; and the girl, from being something merely bright and
shapely, was caught up into the zone of things serious as life and
death and his dead mother. So that, in all ways and on either side,
Fate played his game artfully with this poor pair of children. The
generations were prepared, the pangs were made ready, before the
curtain rose on the dark drama.

It is not a tribute that Stevenson would at all have
appreciated, but I may not forbear noting how closely

such a page recalls many another in the tenderest manner of Pierre Loti. There would not, compared, be a pin to choose between them. How, we at all events ask ourselves as we consider "Weir," could he have kept it up ?—while the reason for which he didn't reads itself back into his text as a kind of beautiful rash divination in him that he mightn't have to. Among prose fragments it stands quite alone, with the particular grace and sanctity of mutilation worn by the marble morsels of masterwork in another art. This and the other things of his best he left; but these things, lovely as, on rereading many of them at the suggestion of his Correspondence, they are, are not the whole, nor more than the half, of his abiding charm. The finest papers in "Across the Plains," in "Memories and Portraits," in "Virginibus Puerisque," stout of substance and supremely silver of speech, have both a nobleness and a nearness that place them, for perfection and roundness, above his fictions, and that also may well remind a vulgarised generation of what, even under its nose, English prose can be. But it is bound up with his name, for our wonder and reflection, that he is something other than the author of this or that particular beautiful thing, or of all such things together. It has been his fortune (whether or no the greatest that can befall a man of letters) to have had to consent to become, by a process not purely mystic and not wholly untraceable—what shall we call it ?—a Figure. Tracing is needless now, for the personality has acted and the incarnation is full. There he is—he has passed ineffaceably into happy legend. This case of the figure is of the rarest and the honour surely of the greatest. In all our literature we can count them, sometimes with the work and sometimes without. The work has often been great and yet the figure *nil*. Johnson was one, and Goldsmith and Byron; and the two former moreover not in any degree, like Stevenson, in virtue of the element of grace. Was it this element that fixed the claim even for Byron? It seems doubtful; and the list at all events as we approach our own day shortens and stops. Stevenson has it at present—may we not say?—pretty well to himself, and it is not one of the scrolls in which he least will live.

ÉMILE ZOLA

IF it be true that the critical spirit to-day, in presence of the rising tide of prose fiction, a watery waste out of which old standards and landmarks are seen barely to emerge, like chimneys and the tops of trees in a country under flood—if it be true that the anxious observer, with the water up to his chin, finds himself asking for the *reason* of the strange phenomenon, for its warrant and title, so we likewise make out that these credentials rather fail to float on the surface. We live in a world of wanton and importunate fable, we breathe its air and consume its fruits; yet who shall say that we are able, when invited, to account for our preferring it so largely to the world of fact? To do so would be to make some adequate statement of the good the product in question does us. What does it do for our life, our mind, our manners, our morals —what does it do that history, poetry, philosophy may not do, as well or better, to warn, to comfort and command the countless thousands for whom and by whom it comes into being? We seem too often left with our riddle on our hands. The lame conclusion on which we retreat is that "stories" are multiplied, circulated, paid for, on the scale of the present hour, simply because people "like" them. As to why people *should* like anything so loose and mean as the preponderant mass of the "output," so little indebted for the magic of its action to any mystery in the making, is more than the actual state of our perceptions enables us to say.

This bewilderment might be our last word if it were
not for the occasional occurrence of accidents especially
appointed to straighten out a little our tangle. We
are reminded that if the unnatural prosperity of the
wanton fable cannot be adequately explained, it can at
least be illustrated with a sharpness that is practically
an argument. An abstract solution failing we encounter it in the concrete. We catch in short a new impression or, to speak more truly, recover an old one. It
was always there to be had, but we ourselves throw off
an oblivion, an indifference for which there are plenty
of excuses. We become conscious, for our profit, of a
case, and we see that our mystification came from the
way cases had appeared for so long to fail us. None of
the shapeless forms about us for the time had attained
to the dignity of one. The one I am now conceiving
as suddenly effective—for which I fear I must have
been regarding it as somewhat in eclipse—is that of
Émile Zola, whom, as a manifestation of the sort we
are considering, three or four striking facts have lately
combined to render more objective and, so to speak,
more massive. His close connection with the most
resounding of recent public quarrels; his premature and
disastrous death; above all, at the moment I write, the
appearance of his last-finished novel, bequeathed to
his huge public from beyond the grave—these rapid
events have thrust him forward and made him loom
abruptly larger; much as .if our pedestrian critic,
treading the dusty highway, had turned a sharp corner.

It is not assuredly that Zola has ever been veiled or
unapparent; he had, on the contrary been digging his
field these thirty years, and for all passers to see, with
an industry that kept him, after the fashion of one of

the grand grim sowers or reapers of his brother of the brush, or at least of the canvas, Jean-François Millet, duskily outlined against the sky. He was there in the landscape of labour—he had always been; but he was there as a big natural or pictorial feature, a spreading tree, a battered tower, a lumpish round-shouldered useful hayrick, confounded with the air and the weather, the rain and the shine, the day and the dusk, merged more or less, as it were, in the play of the elements themselves. We had got used to him, and, thanks in a measure just to this stoutness of his presence, to the long regularity of his performance, had come to notice him hardly more than the dwellers in the marketplace notice the quarters struck by the town-clock. On top of all accordingly, for our skeptical mood, the sense of his work—a sense determined afresh by the strange climax of his personal history—rings out almost with violence as a reply to our wonder. It is as if an earthquake or some other rude interference had shaken from the town-clock a note of such unusual depth as to compel attention. We therefore once more give heed, and the result of this is that we feel ourselves after a little probably as much enlightened as we can hope ever to be. We have worked round to the so marked and impressive anomaly of the adoption of the futile art by one of the stoutest minds and stoutest characters of our time. This extraordinarily robust worker has found it good enough for him, and if the fact is, as I say, anomalous, we are doubtless helped to conclude that by its anomalies, in future, the bankrupt business, as we are so often moved to pronounce it, will most recover credit.

What is at all events striking for us, critically speaking, is that, in the midst of the dishonour it has gradually harvested by triumphant vulgarity of practice, its pliancy and applicability can still plead for themselves. The curious contradiction stands forth for our relief— the circumstance that thirty years ago a young man of extraordinary brain and indomitable purpose, wishing to give the measure of these endowments in a piece of work supremely solid, conceived and sat down to Les Rougon-Macquart rather than to an equal task in physics, mathematics, politics or economics. He saw his undertaking, thanks to his patience and courage, practically to a close; so that it is exactly neither of the so-called constructive sciences that happens to have had the benefit, intellectually speaking, of one of the few most constructive achievements of our time. There then, provisionally at least, we touch bottom; we get a glimpse of the pliancy and variety, the ideal of vividness, on behalf of which our equivocal form may appeal to a strong head. In the name of what ideal on its own side, however, does the strong head yield to the appeal? What is the logic of its so deeply committing itself? Zola's case seems to tell us, as it tells us other things. The logic is in its huge freedom of adjustment to the temperament of the worker, which it carries, so to say, as no other vehicle can do. It expresses fully and directly the whole man, and big as he may be it can still be big enough for him without becoming false to its type. We see this truth made strong, from beginning to end, in Zola's work; we see the temperament, we see the whole man, with his size and all his marks, stored and packed away in the huge hold of Les Rougon-Macquart as a cargo is packed away on a ship. His personality is the thing that finally pervades and prevails, just as so often on a vessel the presence of the cargo makes itself felt for the assaulted senses. What has most come home to me in reading him over is that a scheme of fiction so conducted is in fact a capacious vessel. It can carry anything—with art and force in the stowage; nothing in this case will sink it. And it is the only form for which such a claim can be made. All others have to confess to a smaller scope—to selection, to exclusion, to the danger of distortion, explosion, combustion. The novel has nothing to fear but sailing too light. It will take aboard all we bring in good faith to the dock.

An intense vision of this truth must have been Zola's comfort from the earliest time—the years, immediately following the crash of the Empire, during which he settled himself to the tremendous task he had mapped out. No finer act of courage and confidence, I think, is recorded in the history of letters. The critic in sympathy with him returns again and again to the great wonder of it, in which something so strange is mixed with something so august. Entertained and carried out almost from the threshold of manhood, the high project, the work of a lifetime, announces beforehand its inevitable weakness and yet speaks in the same voice for its admirable, its almost unimaginable strength. The strength was in the young man's very person— in his character, his will, his passion, his fighting temper, his aggressive lips, his squared shoulders (when he "sat up") and overweening confidence; his weakness was in that inexperience of life from which he proposed not to suffer, from which he in fact suffered on the surface remarkably little, and from which he was never to suspect, I judge, that he had suffered at all. I may mention for the interest of it that, meeting him during his first short visit to London—made several years before his stay in England during the Dreyfus

trial—I received a direct impression of him that was
more informing than any previous study. I had seen
him a little, in Paris, years before that, when this impression was a perceptible promise, and I was now to
perceive how time had made it good. It consisted,
simply stated, in his fairly bristling with the betrayal
that nothing whatever had happened to him in life but
to write Les Rougon-Macquart. It was even for that
matter almost more as if Les Rougon-Macquart had
written *him*, written him as he stood and sat, as he
looked and spoke, as the long, concentrated, merciless
effort had made and stamped and left him. Something very fundamental was to happen to him in due
course, it is true, shaking him to his base; fate was not
wholly to cheat him of an independent evolution. Re-
calling him from this London hour one strongly felt
during the famous "Affair" that his outbreak in connection with it was the act of a man with arrears of
personal history to make up, the act of a spirit for
which life, or for which at any rate freedom, had been
too much postponed, treating itself at last to a luxury
of experience.

I welcomed the general impression at all events—
I intimately entertained it; it represented so many
things, it suggested, just as it was, such a lesson. You
could neither have everything nor be everything—you
had to choose; you could not at once sit firm at your
job and wander through space inviting initiations.
The author of Les Rougon-Macquart had had all
those, certainly, that this wonderful company could
bring him; but I can scarce express how it was implied
in him that his time had been fruitfully passed with
them alone. His artistic evolution struck one thus as,

in spite of its magnitude, singularly simple, and evidence of the simplicity seems further offered by his last production, of which we have just come into possession. "Vérité" truly does give the measure, makes the author's high maturity join hands with his youth, marks the rigid straightness of his course from point to point. He had seen his horizon and his fixed goal from the first, and no cross-scent, no new distance, no blue gap in the hills to right or to left ever tempted him to stray. "Vérité," of which I shall have more to say, is in fact, as a moral finality and the crown of an edifice, one of the strangest possible performances. Machine-minted and made good by an immense expertness, it yet makes us ask how, for disinterested observation and perception, the writer had used so much time and so much acquisition, and how he can all along have handled so much material without some larger subjective consequence. We really rub our eyes in other words to see so great an intellectual adventure as Les Rougon-Macquart come to its end in deep desert sand. Difficult truly to read, because showing him at last almost completely a prey to the danger that had for a long time more and more dogged his steps, the danger of the mechanical all confident and triumphant, the book is nevertheless full of interest for a reader desirous to penetrate. It speaks with more distinctness of the author's temperament, tone and manner than if, like several of his volumes, it achieved or enjoyed a successful life of its own. Its heavy completeness, with all this, as of some prodigiously neat, strong and complicated scaffolding constructed by a firm of builders for the erection of a house whose foundations refuse to bear it and that is unable therefore to rise—its very betrayal of a method and a habit more than adequate, on past occasions, to similar ends, carries us back to the original rare exhibition, the grand assurance and grand patience with which the system was launched.

If it topples over, the system, by its own weight in these last applications of it, that only makes the history of its prolonged success the more curious and, speaking for myself, the spectacle of its origin more attaching. Readers of my generation will remember well the publication of "La Conquête de Plassans" and the portent, indefinable but irresistible, after perusal of the volume, conveyed in the general rubric under which it was a first instalment, Natural and Social History of a Family under the Second Empire. It squared itself there at its ease, the announcement, from the first, and we were to learn promptly enough what a fund of life it masked. It was like the mouth of a cave with a signboard hung above, or better still perhaps like the big booth at a fair with the name of the show across the flapping canvas. One strange animal after another stepped forth into the light, each in its way a monster bristling and spotted, each a curiosity of that "natural history" in the name of which we were addressed, though it was doubtless not till the issue of "L'Assommoir" that the true type of the monstrous seemed to be reached. The enterprise, for those who had attention, was even at a distance impressive, and the nearer the critic gets to it retrospectively the more so it becomes. The pyramid had been planned and the site staked out, but the young builder stood there, in his sturdy strength, with no equipment save his two hands and, as we may say, his wheelbarrow and his trowel. His pile of material—of stone, brick and rubble or whatever—was of the smallest, but this he apparently felt as the least of his difficulties. Poor, uninstructed, unacquainted, unintroduced, he set up his subject wholly from the outside, proposing to himself wonderfully to get into it, into its depths, as he went.

If we imagine him asking himself what he knew of the "social" life of the second Empire to start with, we imagine him also answering in all honesty: "I have my eyes and my ears—I have all my senses: I have what I've seen and heard, what I've smelled and tasted and touched. And then I've my curiosity and my pertinacity; I've libraries, books, newspapers, witnesses, the material, from step to step, of an *enquête*. And then I've my genius—that is, my imagination, my passion, my sensibility to life. Lastly I've my method, and that will be half the battle. Best of all perhaps even, I've plentiful lack of doubt." Of the absence in him of a doubt, indeed of his inability, once his direction taken, to entertain so much as the shadow of one, "Vérité" is a positive monument—which again represents in this way the unity of his tone and the meeting of his extremes. If we remember that his design was nothing if not architectural, that a "majestic whole," a great balanced façade, with all its orders and parts, that a singleness of mass and a unity of effect, in fine, were before him from the first, his notion of picking up his bricks as he proceeded becomes, in operation, heroic. It is not in the least as a record of failure for him that I note this particular fact of the growth of the long series as on the whole the liveliest interest it has to offer. "I don't know my subject, but I must live into it; I don't know life, but I must learn it as I work"—that attitude and programme represent, to my sense, a drama more intense on the worker's own part than any of the dramas he was to invent and put before us.

It was the fortune, it was in a manner the doom, of Les Rougon-Macquart to deal with things almost always in gregarious form, to be a picture of *numbers*, of classes, crowds, confusions, movements, industries— and this for a reason of which it will be interesting to attempt some account. The individual life is, if not wholly absent, reflected in coarse and common, in generalised terms; whereby we arrive precisely at the oddity just named, the circumstance that, looking out somewhere, and often woefully athirst, for the taste of fineness, we find it not in the fruits of our author's fancy, but in a different matter altogether. We get it in the very history of his effort, the image itself of his lifelong process, comparatively so personal, so spiritual even, and, through all its patience and pain, of a quality so much more distinguished than the qualities he succeeds in attributing to his figures even when he most aims at distinction. There can be no question in these narrow limits of my taking the successive volumes one by one—all the more that our sense of the exhibition is as little as possible an impression of parts and books, of particular "plots" and persons. It produces the effect of a mass of imagery in which shades are sacrificed, the effect of character and passion in the lump or by the ton. The fullest, the most characteristic episodes affect us like a sounding chorus or procession, as with a hubbub of voices and a multitudinous tread of feet. The setter of the mass into motion, he himself, in the crowd, figures best, with whatever queer idiosyncrasies, excrescences and gaps, a being of a substance akin to our own. Taking him as we must, I repeat, for quite heroic, the interest of detail in him is the interest of his struggle at every point with his problem.

The sense for crowds and processions, for the gross and the general, was largely the *result* of this predicament, of the disproportion between his scheme and his material—though it was certainly also in part an effect of his particular turn of mind. What the reader easily discerns in him is the sturdy resolution with which breadth and energy supply the place of penetration. He rests to his utmost on his documents, devours and assimilates them, makes them yield him extraordinary appearances of life; but in his way he too improvises in the grand manner, the manner of Walter Scott and of Dumas the elder. We feel that he *has* to improvise for his moral and social world, the world as to which vision and opportunity must come, if they are to come at all, unhurried and unhustled— must take their own time, helped undoubtedly more or less by blue-books, reports and interviews, by inquiries "on the spot," but never wholly replaced by such substitutes without a general disfigurement. Vision and opportunity reside in a personal sense and a personal history, and no short cut to them in the interest of plausible fiction has ever been discovered. The short cut, it is not too much to say, was with Zola the subject of constant ingenious experiment, and it is largely to this source, I surmise, that we owe the celebrated element of his grossness. He was *obliged* to be gross, on his system, or neglect to his cost an invaluable aid to representation, as well as one that apparently struck him as lying close at hand; and I cannot withhold my frank admiration from the courage and consistency with which he faced his need.

His general subject in the last analysis was the nature of man; in dealing with which he took up, obviously, the harp of most numerous strings. His business was to make these strings sound true, and there were none that he did not, so far as his general economy permitted, persistently try. What happened then was that many —say about half, and these, as I have noted, the most silvered, the most golden—refused to give out their music. They would only sound false, since (as with all his earnestness he must have felt) he could command them, through want of skill, of practice, of ear, to none of the right harmony. What therefore was more natural than that, still splendidly bent on producing his illusion, he should throw himself on the strings he might thump with effect, and should work them, as our phrase is, for all they were worth? The nature of man, he had plentiful warrant for holding, is an extraordinary mixture, but the great thing was to represent a sufficient part of it to show that it was solidly, palpably, commonly the nature. With this preoccupation he doubtless fell into extravagance— there was clearly so much to lead him on. The coarser side of his subject, based on the community of all the instincts, was for instance the more practicable side, a sphere the vision of which required but the general human, scarcely more than the plain physical, initiation, and dispensed thereby conveniently enough with special introductions or revelations. A free entry into this sphere was undoubtedly compatible with a youthful career as hampered right and left even as Zola's own.

He was in prompt possession thus of the range of sympathy that he *could* cultivate, though it must be added that the complete exercise of that sympathy might have encountered an obstacle that would somewhat undermine his advantage. Our friend might have found himself able, in other words, to pay to the instinctive, as I have called it, only such tribute as protesting taste (his own dose of it) permitted. Yet there it was again that fortune and his temperament served him. Taste as he knew it, taste as his own constitution supplied it, proved to have nothing to say to the matter. His own dose of the precious elixir had no perceptible regulating power. Paradoxical as the remark may sound, this accident was positively to operate as one of his greatest felicities. There are parts of his work, those dealing with romantic or poetic elements, in which the inactivity of the principle in question is sufficiently hurtful; but it surely should not be described as hurtful to such pictures as "Le Ventre de Paris," as "L'Assommoir," as "Germinal." The conception on which each of these productions rests is that of a world with which taste has nothing to do, and though the act of representation may be justly held, as an artistic act, to involve its presence, the discrimination would probably have been in fact, given the particular illusion sought, more detrimental than the deficiency. There was a great outcry, as we all remember, over the rank materialism of "L'Assommoir," but who cannot see to-day how much a milder infusion of it would have told against the close embrace of the subject aimed at ? "L'Assommoir" is the nature of man—but not his finer, nobler, cleaner or more cultivated nature; it is the image of his free instincts, the better and the worse, the better struggling as they can, gasping for light and air, the worse making themselves at home in darkness, ignorance and poverty. The whole handling makes for emphasis and scale, and it is not to be measured how, as a picture of conditions, the thing would have suffered from timidity. The qualification of the painter was precisely his stoutness of stomach, and we scarce exceed in saying that to have taken in and given out again less of the infected air would, with such a resource, have meant the waste of a faculty.

I may add in this connection moreover that refinement of intention did on occasion and after a fashion of its own unmistakably preside at these experiments; making the remark in order to have done once for all with a feature of Zola's literary physiognomy that appears to have attached the gaze of many persons to the exclusion of every other. There are judges in these matters so perversely preoccupied that for them to see anywhere the "improper" is for them straightway to cease to see anything else. The said improper, looming supremely large and casting all the varieties of the proper quite into the shade, suffers thus in their consciousness a much greater extension than it ever claimed, and this consciousness becomes, for the edification of many and the information of a few, a colossal reflector and record of it. Much may be said, in relation to some of the possibilities of the nature of man, of the nature in especial of the "people," on the defect of our author's sense of proportion. But the sense of proportion of many of those he has scandalised would take us further yet. I recall at all events as relevant —for it comes under a very attaching general head— two occasions of long ago, two Sunday afternoons in

Paris, on which I found the question of intention very curiously lighted. Several men of letters of a group in which almost every member either had arrived at renown or was well on his way to it, were assembled under the roof of the most distinguished of their number, where they exchanged free confidences on current work, on plans and ambitions, in a manner full of interest for one never previously privileged to see artistic conviction, artistic passion (at least on the literary ground) so systematic and so articulate. "Well, I on my side," I remember Zola's saying, "am engaged on a book, a study of the *mœurs* of the people, for which I am making a collection of all the 'bad words,' the *gros mots*, of the language, those with which the vocabulary of the people, those with which their familiar talk, bristles." I was struck with the tone in which he made the announcement—without bravado and without apology, as an interesting idea that had come to him and that he was working, really to arrive at character and particular truth, with all his conscience; just as I was struck with the unqualified interest that his plan excited. It was *on* a plan that he was working—formidably, almost grimly, as his fatigued face showed; and the whole consideration of this interesting element partook of the general seriousness.

But there comes back to me also as a companion-piece to this another day, after some interval, on which the interest was excited by the fact that the work for love of which the brave license had been taken was actually under the ban of the daily newspaper that had engaged to "serialise" it. Publication had definitively ceased. The thing had run a part of its course, but it had outrun the courage of editors and the curiosity

of subscribers—that stout curiosity to which it had
evidently in such good faith been addressed. The
chorus of contempt for the ways of such people, their
pusillanimity, their superficiality, vulgarity, intellectual platitude, was the striking note on this occasion; for the journal impugned had declined to proceed and the serial, broken off, been obliged, if I am
not mistaken, to seek the hospitality of other columns,
secured indeed with no great difficulty. The composition so qualified for future fame was none other,
as I was later to learn, than "L'Assommoir"; and my
reminiscence has perhaps no greater point than in
connecting itself with a matter always dear to the
critical spirit, especially when the latter has not too
completely elbowed out the romantic—the matter of
the "origins," the early consciousness, early steps,
early tribulations, early obscurity, as so often happens,
of productions finally crowned by time.

Their greatness is for the most part a thing that has
originally begun so small; and this impression is particularly strong when we have been in any degree
present, so to speak, at the birth. The course of the
matter is apt to tend preponderantly in that case to
enrich our stores of irony. In the eventual conquest of
consideration by an abused book we recognise, in
other terms, a drama of romantic interest, a drama
often with large comic no less than with fine pathetic
interweavings. It may of course be said in this particular connection that "L'Assommoir" had not been
one of the literary things that creep humbly into the
world. Its "success" may be cited as almost insolently
prompt, and the fact remains true if the idea of success be restricted, after the inveterate fashion, to the

idea of circulation. What remains truer still, however,
is that for the critical spirit circulation mostly matters
not the least little bit, and it is of the success with which
the history of Gervaise and Coupeau nestles in *that*
capacious bosom, even as the just man sleeps in Abra-
ham's, that I here speak.   But it is a point I may better
refer to a moment hence.

Though a summary study of Zola need not too
anxiously concern itself with book after book—always
with a partial exception from this remark for "L'Assommoir"—groups and varieties none the less exist in
the huge series, aids to discrimination without which
no measure of the presiding genius is possible.   These
divisions range themselves to my sight, roughly speaking, however, as scarce more than three in number—
I mean if the ten volumes of the Œuvres Critiques
and the Théâtre be left out of account.   The critical
volumes in especial abound in the characteristic, as
they were also a wondrous addition to his sum of
achievement during his most strenuous years.   But I
am forced not to consider them.   The two groups
constituted after the close of Les Rougon-Macquart
—"Les Trois Villes" and the incomplete "Quatre
Évangiles"—distribute themselves easily among the
three types, or, to speak more exactly, stand together
under one of the three.   This one, so comprehensive
as to be the author's main exhibition, includes to my
sense all his best volumes—to the point in fact of producing an effect of distinct inferiority for those outside
of it, which are, luckily for his general credit, the less
numerous.   It is so inveterately pointed out in any
allusion to him that one shrinks, in repeating it, from
sounding flat; but as he was admirably equipped from
the start for the evocation of number and quantity, so

those of his social pictures that most easily surpass
the others are those in which appearances, the appearances familiar to him, are at once most magnified and
most multiplied.

To make his characters swarm, and to make the
great central thing they swarm about "as large as life,"
portentously, heroically big, that was the task he set
himself very nearly from the first, that was the secret
he triumphantly mastered. Add that the big central
thing was always some highly representative institu-
tion or industry of the France of his time, some seated
Moloch of custom, of commerce, of faith, lending itself to portrayal through its abuses and excesses, its
idol-face and great devouring mouth, and we embrace
the main lines of his attack. In "Le Ventre de Paris"
he had dealt with the life of the huge Halles, the general markets and their supply, the personal forces,
personal situations, passions, involved in (strangest of
all subjects) the alimentation of the monstrous city,
the city whose victualling occupies so inordinately
much of its consciousness. Paris richly gorged, Paris
sublime and indifferent in her assurance (so all unlike
poor Oliver's) of "more," figures here the theme itself, lies across the scene like some vast ruminant
creature breathing in a cloud of parasites. The book
was the first of the long series to show the full freedom
of the author's hand, though "La Curée" had already
been symptomatic. This freedom, after an interval,
broke out on a much bigger scale in "L'Assommoir,"
in "Au Bonheur des Dames," in "Germinal," in "La
Bête Humaine," in "L'Argent," in "La Débâcle,"
and then again, though more mechanically and with
much of the glory gone, in the more or less wasted

energy of "Lourdes," "Rome," "Paris," of "Fécondité," "Travail" and "Vérité."

"Au Bonheur des Dames" handles the colossal
modern shop, traces the growth of such an organisation as the Bon Marché or the Magasin-du-Louvre,
sounds the abysses of its inner life, marshals its population, its hierarchy of clerks, counters, departments,
divisions and sub-divisions, plunges into the labyrinth
of the mutual relations of its staff, and above all traces
its ravage amid the smaller fry of the trade, of all the
trades, pictures these latter gasping for breath in an
air pumped clean by its mighty lungs. "Germinal"
revolves about the coal-mines of Flemish France, with
the subterranean world of the pits for its central presence, just as "La Bête Humaine" has for its protagonist a great railway and "L'Argent" presents in terms
of human passion—mainly of human baseness—the
fury of the Bourse and the monster of Credit. "La
Débâcle" takes up with extraordinary breadth the first
act of the Franco-Prussian war, the collapse at Sedan,
and the titles of the six volumes of The Three Cities
and the Four Gospels sufficiently explain them. I
may mention, however, for the last lucidity, that
among these "Fécondité" manipulates, with an amazing misapprehension of means to ends, of remedies to
ills, no less thickly peopled a theme than that of the
decline in the French birth-rate, and that "Vérité"
presents a fictive equivalent of the Dreyfus case, with
a vast and elaborate picture of the battle in France
between lay and clerical instruction. I may even
further mention, to clear the ground, that with the
close of Les Rougon-Macquart the diminution of
freshness in the author's energy, the diminution of in-

tensity and, in short, of quality, becomes such as to render sadly difficult a happy life with some of the later volumes. Happiness of the purest strain never indeed, in old absorptions of Zola, quite sat at the feast; but there was mostly a measure of coercion, a spell without a charm. From these last-named productions of the climax everything strikes me as absent but quantity ("Vérité," for instance, is, with the possible exception of "Nana," the longest of the list); though indeed there is something impressive in the way his quantity represents his patience.

There are efforts here at stout perusal that, frankly, I have been unable to carry through, and I should verily like, in connection with the vanity of these, to dispose on the spot of the sufficiently strange phenomenon constituted by what I have called the climax. It embodies in fact an immense anomaly; it casts back over Zola's prime and his middle years the queerest grey light of eclipse. Nothing moreover—nothing "literary"—was ever so odd as in this matter the whole turn of the case, the consummation so logical yet so unexpected. Writers have grown old and withered and failed; they have grown weak and sad; they have lost heart, lost ability, yielded in one way or another —the possible ways being so numerous—to the cruelty of time. But the singular doom of this genius, and which began to multiply its symptoms ten years before his death, was to find, with life, at fifty, still rich in him, strength only to undermine all the "authority" he had gathered. He had not grown old and he had not grown feeble; he had only grown all too wrongly insistent, setting himself to wreck, poetically, his so massive identity—to wreck it in the very waters in which he had formally arrayed his victorious fleet. (I say "poetically" on purpose to give him the just benefit of all the beauty of his power.) The process of the disaster, so full of the effect, though so without the intention, of perversity, is difficult to trace in a few words; it may best be indicated by an example or two of its action.

The example that perhaps most comes home to me is again connected with a personal reminiscence. In the course of some talk that I had with him during his first visit to England I happened to ask him what opportunity to travel (if any) his immense application had ever left him, and whether in particular he had been able to see Italy, a country from which I had either just returned or which I was luckily—not having the Natural History of a Family on my hands—about to revisit. "All I've done, alas," he replied, "was, the other year, in the course of a little journey to the south, to my own *pays*—all that has been possible was then to make a little dash as far as Genoa, a matter of only a few days." "Le Docteur Pascal," the conclusion of Les Rougon-Macquart, had appeared shortly before, and it further befell that I asked him what plans he had for the future, now that, still *dans la force de l'âge*, he had so cleared the ground. I shall never forget the fine promptitude of his answer—"Oh, I shall begin at once Les Trois Villes." "And which cities are they to be?" The reply was finer still—"Lourdes, Paris, Rome."

It was splendid for confidence and cheer, but it left me, I fear, more or less gaping, and it was to give me afterwards the key, critically speaking, to many a mystery. It struck me as breathing to an almost tragic degree the fatuity of those in whom the gods stimulate that vice to their ruin. He was an honest man—he had always bristled with it at every pore; but no artistic reverse was inconceivable for an adventurer who, stating in one breath that his knowledge of Italy consisted of a few days spent at Genoa, was ready to declare in the next that he had planned, on a scale, a picture of Rome. It flooded his career, to my sense, with light; it showed how he had marched from subject to subject and had "got up" each in turn—showing also how consummately he had reduced such getting-up to an artifice. He had success and a rare impunity behind him, but nothing would now be so interesting as to see if he could again play the trick. One would leave him, and welcome, Lourdes and Paris—he had already dealt, on a scale, with his own country and people. But was the adored Rome also to be his on such terms, the Rome he was already giving away before possessing an inch of it? One thought of one's own frequentations, saturations—a history of long years, and of how the effect of them had somehow been but to make the subject too august. Was *he* to find it easy through a visit of a month or two with "introductions" and a Bædeker?

It was not indeed that the Bædeker and the introductions didn't show, to my sense, at that hour, as extremely suggestive; they were positively a part of the light struck out by his announcement. They defined the system on which he had brought Les Rougon-Macquart safely into port. He had had his Bædeker and his introductions for "Germinal," for "L'Assommoir," for "L'Argent," for "La Débâcle," for "Au

Bonheur des Dames"; which advantages, which re-
searches, had clearly been all the more in character for
being documentary, extractive, a matter of *renseigne-
ments*, published or private, even when most mixed
with personal impressions snatched, with *enquêtes sur
les lieux*, with facts obtained from the best authorities,
proud and happy to co-operate in so famous a connection. That was, as we say, all right, all the more that
the process, to my imagination, became vivid and was
wonderfully reflected back from its fruits. There *were*
the fruits—so it hadn't been presumptuous. Presumption, however, was now to begin, and what omen
mightn't there be in its beginning with such complacency ? Well, time would show—as time in due course
effectually did. "Rome," as the second volume of
The Three Cities, appeared with high punctuality a
year or two later; and the interesting question, an occasion really for the moralist, was by that time not to
recognise in it the mere triumph of a mechanical art,
a "receipt" applied with the skill of long practice, but
to do much more than this—that is really to give a
name to the particular shade of blindness that could
constitute a trap for so great an artistic intelligence.
The presumptuous volume, without sweetness, without
antecedents, superficial and violent, has the minimum
instead of the maximum of *value;* so that it betrayed
or "gave away" just in this degree the state of mind
on the author's part responsible for its inflated hollow-
ness. To put one's finger on the state of mind was to
find out accordingly what was, as we say, the matter
with him.

It seemed to me, I remember, that I found out as
never before when, in its turn, "Fécondité" began the

work of crowning the edifice. "Fécondité" is physiological, whereas "Rome" is not, whereas "Vérité" likewise is not; yet these three productions joined hands at a given moment to fit into the lock of the mystery the key of my meditation. They came to the same thing, to the extent of permitting me to read into them together the same precious lesson. This lesson may not, barely stated, sound remarkable; yet without being in possession of it I should have ventured on none of these remarks. "The matter with" Zola then, so far as it goes, was that, as the imagination of the artist is in the best cases not only clarified but intensified by his equal possession of Taste (deserving here if ever the old-fashioned honour of a capital) so when he has lucklessly never inherited that auxiliary blessing the imagination itself inevitably breaks down as a consequence. There is simply no limit, in fine, to the misfortune of being tasteless; it does not merely disfigure the surface and the fringe of your performance —it eats back into the very heart and enfeebles the sources of life. When you have no taste you have no discretion, which is the conscience of taste, and when you have no discretion you perpetrate books like "Rome," which are without intellectual modesty, books like "Fécondité," which are without a sense of the ridiculous, books like "Vérité," which are without the finer vision of human experience.

It is marked that in each of these examples the deficiency has been directly fatal. No stranger doom was ever appointed for a man so plainly desiring only to be just than the absurdity of not resting till he had buried the felicity of his past, such as it was, under a great flat leaden slab. "Vérité" is a plea for science, as science, to Zola, is *all* truth, the mention of any other kind being mere imbecility; and the simplification of the human picture to which his negations and exasperations have here conducted him was not, even when all had been said, credible in advance. The result is amazing when we consider that the finer observation is the supposed basis of all such work. It is not that even here the author has not a queer idealism of his own; this idealism is on the contrary so present as to show positively for the falsest of his simplifications. In "Fécondité" it becomes grotesque, makes of the book the most muscular mistake of *sense* probably ever committed. Where was the judgment of which experience is supposed to be the guarantee when the perpetrator could persuade himself that the lesson he wished in these pages to convey could be made immediate and direct, chalked, with loud taps and a still louder commentary, the sexes and generations all convoked, on the blackboard of the "family sentiment?"

I have mentioned, however, all this time but one of his categories. The second consists of such things as "La Fortune des Rougon" and "La Curée," as "Eugène Rougon" and even "Nana," as "Pot-Bouille," as "L'Œuvre" and "La Joie de Vivre." These volumes may rank as social pictures in the narrowest sense, studies, comprehensively speaking, of the manners, the morals, the miseries—for it mainly comes to that—of a bourgeoisie grossly materialised. They deal with the life of individuals in the liberal professions and with that of political and social adventures, and offer the personal character and career, more or less detached, as the centre of interest. "La Curée" is an evocation, violent and "romantic," of the extravagant appetites, the fever of the senses, supposedly fostered, for its ruin, by the hapless second Empire, upon which general ills and turpitudes at large were at one time so freely and conveniently fathered. "Eugène Rougon" carries out this view in the high colour of a political portrait, not other than scandalous, for which one of the ministerial *âmes damnées* of Napoleon III., M. Rouher, is reputed, I know not how justly, to have sat. "Nana," attaching itself by a hundred strings to a prearranged table of kinships, heredities, transmissions, is the vast crowded *epos* of the daughter of the people filled with poisoned blood and sacrificed as well as sacrificing on the altar of luxury and lust; the panorama of such a "progress" as Hogarth would more definitely have named — the progress across the high plateau of "pleasure" and down the facile descent on the other side. "Nana" is truly a monument to Zola's patience; the subject being so ungrateful, so formidably special, that the multiplication of illustrative detail, the plunge into pestilent depths, represents a kind of technical intrepidity.

There are other plunges, into different sorts of darkness; of which the esthetic, even the scientific, even the ironic motive fairly escapes us—explorations of stagnant pools like that of "La Joie de Vivre," as to which, granting the nature of the curiosity and the substance laboured in, the patience is again prodigious, but which make us wonder what pearl of philosophy, of suggestion or just of homely recognition, the general picture, as of rats dying in a hole, has to offer. Our various senses, sight, smell, sound, touch, are, as with Zola always, more or less convinced; but when the particular effect upon each of these is added to the

effect upon the others the mind still remains bewilderedly unconscious of any use for the total. I am not
sure indeed that the case is in this respect better with
the productions of the third order—"La Faute de
l'Abbé Mouret," "Une Page d'Amour," "Le Rêve,"
"Le Docteur Pascal"—in which the appeal is more
directly, is in fact quite earnestly, to the moral vision;
so much, on such ground, was to depend precisely on
those discriminations in which the writer is least at
home. The volumes whose names I have just quoted
are his express tribute to the "ideal," to the select
and the charming—fair fruits of invention intended to
remove from the mouth so far as possible the bitterness of the ugly things in which so much of the rest
of his work had been condemned to consist. The subjects in question then are "idyllic" and the treatment
poetic, concerned essentially to please on the largest
lines and involving at every turn that salutary need.
They are matters of conscious delicacy, and nothing
might interest us more than to see what, in the shock
of the potent forces enlisted, becomes of this shy element. Nothing might interest us more, literally, and
might positively affect us more, even very nearly to
tears, though indeed sometimes also to smiles, than to
see the constructor of Les Rougon-Macquart trying,
"for all he is worth," to be fine with fineness, finely
tender, finely true—trying to be, as it is called, distinguished—in face of constitutional hindrance.

The effort is admirably honest, the tug at his subject
splendidly strong; but the consequences remain of the
strangest, and we get the impression that—as representing discriminations unattainable—they are somehow the price he paid. "Le Docteur Pascal," for

instance, which winds up the long chronicle on the romantic note, on the note of invoked beauty, in order to sweeten, as it were, the total draught—"Le Docteur Pascal," treating of the erotic ardour entertained for each other by an uncle and his niece, leaves us amazed at such a conception of beauty, such an application of romance, such an estimate of sweetness, a sacrifice to poetry and passion so little in order. Of course, we definitely remind ourselves, the whole long chronicle is explicitly a scheme, solidly set up and intricately worked out, lighted, according to the author's pretension, by "science," high, dry and clear, and with each part involved and necessitated in all the other parts, each block of the edifice, each "morceau de vie," *physiologically* determined by previous combinations. "How can I help it," we hear the builder of the pyramid ask, "if experience (by which alone I proceed) shows me certain plain results—if, holding up the torch of my famous 'experimental method,' I find it stare me in the face that the union of certain types, the conflux of certain strains of blood, the intermarriage, in a word, of certain families, produces nervous conditions, conditions temperamental, psychical and pathological, in which nieces *have* to fall in love with uncles and uncles with nieces? Observation and imagination, for any picture of life," he as audibly adds, "know no light but science, and are false to all intellectual decency, false to their own honour, when they fear it, dodge it, darken it. To pretend to any other guide or law is mere base humbug."

That is very well, and the value, in a hundred ways, of a mass of production conceived in such a spirit can never (when robust execution has followed) be small.

But the formula really sees us no further. It offers a definition which is no definition. "Science" is soon said—the whole thing depends on the ground so covered. Science accepts surely *all* our consciousness of life; even, rather, the latter closes maternally round it—so that, becoming thus a force within us, not a force outside, it exists, it illuminates only as we apply it. We do emphatically apply it in art. But Zola would apparently hold that it much more applies *us*. On the showing of many of his volumes then it makes but a dim use of us, and this we should still consider the case even were we sure that the article offered us in the majestic name is absolutely at one with its own pretension. This confidence we can on too many grounds never have. The matter is one of appreciation, and when an artist answers for science who answers for the artist—who at the least answers for art? Thus it is with the mistakes that affect us, I say, as Zola's penalties. We are reminded by them that the game of art has, as the phrase is, to be played. It may not with any sure felicity for the result be both taken and left. If you insist on the common you must submit to the common; if you discriminate, on the contrary, you must, however invidious your discriminations may be called, trust to them to see you through.

To the common then Zola, often with splendid results, inordinately sacrifices, and this fact of its overwhelming him is what I have called his paying for it. In "L'Assommoir," in "Germinal," in "La Débâcle," productions in which he must most survive, the sacrifice is ordered and fruitful, for the subject and the treatment harmonise and work together. He describes what he best feels, and feels it more and more

as it naturally comes to him—quite, if I may allow
myself the image, as we zoologically see some mighty
animal, a beast of a corrugated hide and a portentous
snout, soaking with joy in the warm ooze of an African
riverside.   In these cases everything matches, and
"science," we may be permitted to believe, has had
little hand in the business.   The author's perceptions
go straight, and the subject, grateful and responsive,
gives itself wholly up.   It is no longer a case of an uncertain smoky torch, but of a personal vision, the
vision of genius, springing from an inward source.   Of
this genius "L'Assommoir" is the most extraordinary
record.   It contains, with the two companions I have
given it, all the best of Zola, and the three books together are solid ground—or would be could I now so
take them—for a study of the particulars of his power.
His strongest marks and features abound in them;
"L'Assommoir" above all is (not least in respect to
its bold free linguistic reach, already glanced at) completely genial, while his misadventures, his unequipped
and delusive pursuit of the life of the spirit and the
tone of culture, are almost completely absent.

It is a singular sight enough this of a producer of illusions whose interest for us is so independent of our
pleasure or at least of our complacency—who touches
us deeply even while he most "puts us off," who makes
us care for his ugliness and yet himself at the same
time pitilessly (pitilessly, that is, for *us*) makes a mock
of it, who fills us with a sense of the rich which is none
the less never the rare.   Gervaise, the most immediately "felt," I cannot but think, of all his characters,
is a lame washerwoman, loose and gluttonous, without
will, without any principle of cohesion, the sport of

every wind that assaults her exposed life, and who, rolling from one gross mistake to another, finds her end in misery, drink and despair. But her career, as presented, has fairly the largeness that, throughout the chronicle, we feel as epic, and the intensity of her creator's vision of it and of the dense sordid life hanging about it is one of the great things the modern novel has been able to do. It has done nothing more completely constitutive and of a tone so rich and full and sustained. The tone of "L'Assommoir" is, for mere "keeping up," unsurpassable, a vast deep steady tide on which every object represented is triumphantly borne. It never shrinks nor flows thin, and nothing for an instant drops, dips or catches; the high-water mark of sincerity, of the genial, as I have called it, is unfailingly kept.

For the artist in the same general "line" such a production has an interest almost inexpressible, a mystery as to origin and growth over which he fondly but rather vainly bends. How after all does it so get itself *done*? —the "done" being admirably the sign and crown of it. The light of the richer mind has been elsewhere, as I have sufficiently hinted, frequent enough, but nothing truly in all fiction was ever built so strong or made so dense as here. Needless to say there are a thousand things with more charm in their truth, with more beguilement of every sort, more prettiness of pathos, more innocence of drollery, for the spectator's sense of truth. But I doubt if there has ever been a more totally *represented* world, anything more founded and established, more provided for all round, more organised and carried on. It is a world practically workable, with every part as functional as every other,

and with the parts all chosen for direct mutual aid.
Let it not be said either that the equal constitution
of parts makes for repletion or excess; the air circulates
and the subject blooms; deadness comes in these matters only when the right parts are absent and there
is vain beating of the air in their place—the refuge of
the fumbler incapable of the thing "done" at all.

The mystery I speak of, for the reader who reflects
as he goes, is the wonder of the scale and energy of
Zola's assimilations. This wonder besets us above
all throughout the three books I have placed first.
How, all sedentary and "scientific," did he get so
near? By what art, inscrutable, immeasurable, in-
defatigable, did he arrange to make of his documents,
in these connections, a use so vivified? Say he was
"near" the subject of "'L'Assommoir" in imagination, in more or less familiar impression, in temperament and humour, he could not after all have been
near it in personal experience, and the copious personalism of the picture, not to say its frank animalism,
yet remains its note and its strength. When the note
had been struck in a thousand forms we had, by multiplication, as a kind of cumulative consequence, the
finished and rounded book; just as we had the same
result by the same process in "Germinal." It is not
of course that multiplication and accumulation, the
extraordinary pair of legs on which he walks, are
easily or directly consistent with his projecting himself morally; this immense diffusion, with its appropriation of everything it meets, affects us on the contrary as perpetually delaying access to what we may
call the private world, the world of the individual.
Yet since the individual—for it so happens—is simple

and shallow our author's dealings with him, as met and
measured, maintain their resemblance to those of the
lusty bee who succeeds in plumping for an instant, of a
summer morning, into every flower-cup of the garden.

Grant—and the generalisation may be emphatic—
that the shallow and the simple are *all* the population
of his richest and most crowded pictures, and that his
"psychology," in a psychologic age, remains thereby
comparatively coarse, grant this and we but get another view of the miracle. We see enough of the
superficial among novelists at large, assuredly, without
deriving from it, as we derive from Zola at his best,
the concomitant impression of the solid. It is in general—I mean among the novelists at large—the impression of the *cheap*, which the author of Les Rougon-
Macquart, honest man, never faithless for a moment
to his own stiff standard, manages to spare us even in
the prolonged sandstorm of "Vérité." The Common
is another matter; it is one of the forms of the superficial—pervading and consecrating all things in such a
book as "Germinal"—and it only adds to the number
of our critical questions. How in the world is it made,
this deplorable democratic malodorous Common, so
strange and so interesting ? How is it taught to receive
into its loins the stuff of the epic and still, in spite of
that association with poetry, never depart from its
nature ? It is in the great lusty game he plays with
the shallow and the simple that Zola's mastery resides,
and we see of course that when values are small it
takes innumerable items and combinations to make up
the sum. In "L'Assommoir" and in "Germinal," to
some extent even in "La Débâcle," the values are all,
morally, personally, of the lowest—the highest is poor

Gervaise herself, richly human in her generosities and follies—yet each is as distinct as a brass-headed nail.

What we come back to accordingly is the unprecedented case of such a combination of parts. Painters, of great schools, often of great talent, have responded liberally on canvas to the appeal of ugly things, of Spanish beggars, squalid and dusty-footed, of martyred saints or other convulsed sufferers, tortured and bleeding, of boors and louts soaking a Dutch proboscis in perpetual beer; but we had never before had to reckon with so literary a treatment of the mean and vulgar. When we others of the Anglo-Saxon race are vulgar we are, handsomely and with the best conscience in the world, vulgar all through, too vulgar to be in any degree literary, and too much so therefore to be critically reckoned with at all. The French are different—they separate their sympathies, multiply their possibilities, observe their shades, remain more or less outside of their worst disasters. They mostly contrive to get the *idea*, in however dead a faint, down into the lifeboat. They may lose sight of the stars, but they save in some such fashion as that their intellectual souls. Zola's own reply to all puzzlements would have been, at any rate, I take it, a straight summary of his inveterate professional habits. "It is all very simple—I produce, roughly speaking, a volume a year, and of this time some five months go to preparation, to special study. In the other months, with all my *cadres* established, I write the book. And I can hardly say which part of the job is stiffest."

The story was not more wonderful for him than that, nor the job more complex; which is why we must say of his whole process and its results that they constitute together perhaps the most extraordinary *imitation* of observation that we possess. Balzac appealed to "science" and proceeded by her aid; Balzac had *cadres* enough and a tabulated world, rubrics, relationships and genealogies; but Balzac affects us in spite of everything as personally overtaken by life, as fairly hunted and run to earth by it. He strikes us as struggling and all but submerged, as beating over the scene such a pair of wings as were not soon again to be wielded by any visitor of his general air and as had not at all events attached themselves to Zola's rounded shoulders. His bequest is in consequence immeasurably more interesting, yet who shall declare that his adventure was in its greatness more successful ? Zola "pulled it off," as we say, supremely, in that he never but once found himself obliged to quit, to our vision, his magnificent treadmill of the pigeonholed and documented—the region we may qualify as that of experience by imitation. His splendid economy saw him through, he laboured to the end within sight of his notes and his charts.

The extraordinary thing, however, is that on the single occasion when, publicly—as his whole manifestation was public—life did swoop down on him, the effect of the visitation was quite perversely other than might have been looked for. His courage in the Dreyfus connection testified admirably to his ability to live for himself and out of the order of his volumes —little indeed as living at all might have seemed a question for one exposed, when his crisis was at its height and he was found guilty of "insulting" the powers that were, to be literally torn to pieces in the

precincts of the Palace of Justice. Our point is that
nothing was ever so odd as that these great moments
should appear to have been wasted, when all was said,
for his creative intelligence. "Vérité," as I have intimated, the production in which they might most
have been reflected, is a production unrenewed and
unrefreshed by them, spreads before us as somehow
flatter and greyer, not richer and more relieved, by
reason of them. They really arrived, I surmise, too
late in the day; the imagination they might have vivified was already fatigued and spent.

I must not moreover appear to say that the power
to evoke and present has not even on the dead level of
"Vérité" its occasional minor revenges. There are
passages, whole pages, of the old full-bodied sort,
pictures that elsewhere in the series would in all likeli-
hood have seemed abundantly convincing. Their misfortune is to have been discounted by our intensified,
our finally fatal sense of the *procédé*. Quarrelling with
all conventions, defiant of them in general, Zola was
yet inevitably to set up his own group of them—as,
for that matter, without a sufficient collection, without
their aid in simplifying and making possible, how could
he ever have seen his big ship into port? Art wel-
comes them, feeds upon them always; no sort of form
is practicable without them. It is only a question of
what particular ones we use—to wage war on certain
others and to arrive at particular forms. The convention of the blameless being, the thoroughly "scientific" creature possessed impeccably of all truth and
serving as the mouthpiece of it and of the author's
highest complacencies, this character is for instance
a convention inveterate and indispensable, without

whom the "sympathetic" side of the work could never
have been achieved. Marc in "Vérité," Pierre Fro-
ment in "Lourdes" and in "Rome," the wondrous
representatives of the principle of reproduction in
"Fécondité," the exemplary painter of "L'Œuvre,"
sublime in his modernity and paternity, the patient
Jean Macquart of "La Débâcle," whose patience is as
guaranteed as the exactitude of a well-made watch,
the supremely enlightened Docteur Pascal even, as I
recall him, all amorous nepotism but all virtue too and
all beauty of life—such figures show us the reasonable
and the good not merely in the white light of the old
George Sand novel and its improved moralities, but
almost in that of our childhood's nursery and school-
room, that of the moral tale of Miss Edgeworth and
Mr. Thomas Day.

Yet let not these restrictions be my last word. I
had intended, under the effect of a reperusal of "La
Débâcle," "Germinal" and "L'Assommoir," to make
no discriminations that should not be in our hero's
favour. The long-drawn incident of the marriage of
Gervaise and Cadet-Cassis and that of the Homeric
birthday feast later on in the laundress's workshop,
each treated from beginning to end and in every item
of their coarse comedy and humanity, still show the
unprecedented breadth by which they originally made
us stare, still abound in the particular kind and degree
of vividness that helped them, when they appeared,
to mark a date in the portrayal of manners. Nothing
had then been so sustained and at every moment of
its grotesque and pitiful existence lived into as the
nuptial day of the Coupeau pair in especial, their
fantastic processional pilgrimage through the streets

of Paris in the rain, their bedraggled exploration of the halls of the Louvre museum, lost as in the labyrinth of Crete, and their arrival at last, ravenous and exasperated, at the *guinguette* where they sup at so much a head, each paying, and where we sit down with them in the grease and the perspiration and succumb, half in sympathy, half in shame, to their monstrous pleasantries, acerbities and miseries. I have said enough of the mechanical in Zola; here in truth is, given the elements, almost insupportably the sense of life. That effect is equally in the historic chapter of the strike of the miners in "Germinal," another of those illustrative episodes, viewed as great passages to be "rendered," for which our author established altogether a new measure and standard of handling, a new energy and veracity, something since which the old trivialities and poverties of treatment of such aspects have become incompatible, for the novelist, with either rudimentary intelligence or rudimentary self-respect.

As for "La Débâcle," finally, it takes its place with Tolstoi's very much more universal but very much less composed and condensed epic as an incomparably human picture of war. I have been re-reading it, I confess, with a certain timidity, the dread of perhaps impairing the deep impression received at the time of its appearance. I recall the effect it then produced on me as a really luxurious act of submission. It was early in the summer; I was in an old Italian town; the heat was oppressive, and one could but recline, in the lightest garments, in a great dim room and give one's self up. I like to think of the conditions and the emotion, which melt for me together into the memory

I fear to imperil. I remember that in the glow of my admiration there was not a reserve I had ever made that I was not ready to take back. As an application of the author's system and his supreme faculty, as a triumph of what these things could do for him, how could such a performance be surpassed? The long, complex, horrific, pathetic battle, embraced, mastered, with every crash of its squadrons, every pulse of its thunder and blood resolved for us, by reflection, by communication from two of the humblest and obscurest of the military units, into immediate vision and contact, into deep human thrills of terror and pity—this bristling centre of the book was such a piece of "doing" (to come back to our word) as could only shut our mouths. That doubtless is why a generous critic, nursing the sensation, may desire to drop for a farewell no term into the other scale. That our author was clearly great at congruous subjects—this may well be our conclusion. If the others, subjects of the private and intimate order, gave him more or less inevitably "away," they yet left him the great distinction that the more he could be promiscuous and collective, the more even he could (to repeat my imputation) illustrate our large natural allowance of health, heartiness and grossness, the more he could strike us as penetrating and true. It was a distinction not easy to win and that his name is not likely soon to lose.

GUSTAVE FLAUBERT

THE first thing I find to-day and on my very threshold [1] to say about Gustave Flaubert is that he has been reported on by M. Émile Faguet in the series of Les Grands Écrivains Français with such lucidity as may almost be taken to warn off a later critic. I desire to pay at the outset my tribute to M. Faguet's exhaustive study, which is really in its kind a model and a monument. Never can a critic have got closer to a subject of this order; never can the results of the approach have been more copious or more interesting; never in short can the master of a complex art have been more mastered in his turn, nor his art more penetrated, by the application of an earnest curiosity. That remark I have it at heart to make, so pre-eminently has the little volume I refer to not left the subject where it found it. It abounds in contributive light, and yet, I feel on reflection that it scarce wholly dazzles another contributor away. One reason of this is that, though I enter into everything M. Faguet has said, there are things—things perhaps especially of the province of the artist, the fellow-craftsman of Flaubert—that I am conscious of his not having said; another is that inevitably there are particular possibilities of reaction in our English-speaking consciousness that hold up a light of their own. Therefore I venture

[1] On the occasion of these prefatory remarks to a translation of "Madame Bovary," appearing in A Century of French Romance, under the auspices of Mr. Edmund Gosse and Mr. William Heinemann, in 1902.

to follow even on a field so laboured, only paying this
toll to the latest and best work because the author has
made it impossible to do less.

Flaubert's life is so almost exclusively the story of
his literary application that to speak of his five or six
fictions is pretty well to account for it all. He died
in 1880 after a career of fifty-nine years singularly
little marked by changes of scene, of fortune, of attitude, of occupation, of character, and above all, as
may be said, of mind. He would be interesting to the
race of novelists if only because, quite apart from the
value of his work, he so personally gives us the example
and the image, so presents the intellectual case. He
was born a novelist, grew up, lived, died a novelist,
breathing, feeling, thinking, speaking, performing
every operation of life, only as that votary; and this
though his production was to be small in amount and
though it constituted all his diligence. It was not
indeed perhaps primarily so much that he was born
and lived a novelist as that he was born and lived
literary, and that to be literary represented for him
an almost overwhelming situation. No life was long
enough, no courage great enough, no fortune kind
enough to support a man undeɪ the burden of this
character when once such a doom had been laid on
him. His case was a doom because he felt of his voca-
tion almost nothing but the difficulty. He had many
strange sides, but this was the strangest, that if we
argued from his difficulty to his work, the difficulty
being registered for us in his letters and elsewhere, we
should expect from the result but the smallest things.
We should be prepared to find in it well-nigh a complete
absence of the signs of a gift. We should regret that

the unhappy man had not addressed himself to something he might have found at least comparatively easy. We should singularly miss the consecration supposedly given to a work of art by its having been conceived in joy. That is Flaubert's remarkable, his so far as I know unmatched distinction, that he has left works of an extraordinary art even the conception of which failed to help him to think in serenity. The chapter of execution, from the moment execution gets really into the shafts, is of course always and everywhere a troubled one—about which moreover too much has of late been written; but we frequently find Flaubert cursing his subjects themselves, wishing he had not chosen them, holding himself up to derision for having done so, and hating them in the very act of sitting down to them. He cared immensely for the medium, the task and the triumph involved, but was himself the last to be able to say why. He is sustained only by the rage and the habit of effort; the mere *love* of letters, let alone the love of life, appears at an early age to have deserted him. Certain passages in his correspondence make us even wonder if it be not hate that sustains him most. So, successively, his several supremely finished and crowned compositions came into the world, and we may feel sure that none others of the kind, none that were to have an equal fortune, had sprung from such adversity.

I insist upon this because his at once excited and baffled passion gives the key of his life and determines its outline. I must speak of him at least as I feel him and as in his very latest years I had the fortune occasionally to see him. I said just now, practically, that he is for many of our tribe at large *the* novelist, intent and typical, and so, gathered together and foreshortened, simplified and fixed, the lapse of time seems to show him. It has made him in his prolonged posture extraordinarily objective, made him even resemble one of his own productions, constituted him as a subject, determined him as a figure; the limit of his range, and above all of his reach, is after this fashion, no doubt, sufficiently indicated, and yet perhaps in the event without injury to his name. If our consideration of him cultivates a certain tenderness on the double ground that he suffered supremely in the cause and that there is endlessly much to be learned from him, we remember at the same time that, indirectly, the world at large possesses him not less than the *confrère*. He has fed and fertilised, has filtered through others, and so arrived at contact with that public from whom it was his theory that he was separated by a deep and impassable trench, the labour of his own spade. He is none the less more interesting, I repeat, as a failure however qualified than as a success however explained, and it is as so viewed that the unity of his career attaches and admonishes. Save in some degree by a condition of health (a liability to epileptic fits at times frequent, but never so frequent as to have been generally suspected,) he was not outwardly hampered as the tribe of men of letters goes—an anxious brotherhood at the best; yet the fewest possible things appear to have ever succeeded in happening to him. The only son of an eminent provincial physician, he inherited a modest ease and no other incumbrance than, as was the case for Balzac, an over-attentive, an importunate mother; but freedom spoke to him from behind a veil, and when we have mentioned the few apparent facts of experience that make up his landmarks over and beyond his interspaced publications we shall have completed his biography. Tall, strong, striking, he caused his friends to admire in him the elder, the florid Norman type, and he seems himself, as a man of imagination, to have found some transmission of race in his stature and presence, his light-coloured salient eyes and long tawny moustache.

The central event of his life was his journey to the East in 1849 with M. Maxime Du Camp, of which the latter has left in his "Impressions Littéraires" a singularly interesting and, as we may perhaps say, slightly treacherous report, and which prepared for Flaubert a state of nostalgia that was not only never to leave him, but that was to work in him as a motive. He had during that year, and just in sufficient quantity, his revelation, the particular appropriate disclosure to which the gods at some moment treat the artist unless they happen too perversely to conspire against him: he tasted of the knowledge by which he was subsequently to measure everything, appeal from everything, find everything flat. Never probably was an impression so assimilated, so positively transmuted to a function; he lived on it to the end and we may say that in "Salammbô" and "La Tentation de Saint-Antoine" he almost died of it. He made afterwards no other journey of the least importance save a disgusted excursion to the Rigi-Kaltbad shortly before his death. The Franco-German War was of course to him for the time as the valley of the shadow itself; but this was an ordeal, unlike most of his other ordeals, shared after all with millions. He never married—he declared, toward the end, to the most comprehending of his confidants, that he had been from the first "afraid of life"; and the friendliest element of his later time was, we judge, that admirable comfortable commerce, in her fullest maturity, with Madame George Sand, the confidant I just referred to; which has been preserved for us in the published correspondence of each. He had in Ivan Turgenieff a friend almost as valued; he spent each year a few months in Paris, where (to mention everything) he had his natural place, so far as he cared to take it, at the small literary court of the Princess Mathilde; and, lastly, he lost toward the close of his life, by no fault of his own, a considerable part of his modest fortune. It is, however, in the long security, the almost unbroken solitude of Croisset, near Rouen, that he mainly figures for us, gouging out his successive books in the wide old room, of many windows, that, with an intervening terrace, overlooked the broad Seine and the passing boats. This was virtually a monastic cell, closed to echoes and accidents; with its stillness for long periods scarce broken save by the creak of the towing-chain of the tugs across the water. When I have added that his published letters offer a view, not very refreshing, of his youthful entanglement with Madame Louise Colet—whom we name because, apparently not a shrinking person, she long ago practically named herself—I shall have catalogued his personal vicissitudes. And I may add further that the connection with Madame Colet, such as it was, rears its head for us in something like a desert of immunity from such complications.

His complications were of the spirit, of the literary vision, and though he was thoroughly profane he was yet essentially anchoretic. I perhaps miss a point,

however, in not finally subjoining that he was liberally
accessible to his friends during the months he regularly
spent in Paris. Sensitive, passionate, perverse, not
less than *immediately* sociable—for if he detested his
collective contemporaries this dropped, thanks to his
humanising shyness, before the individual encounter—
he was in particular and superexcellently not *banal*,
and he attached men perhaps more than women, inspiring a marked, a by no means colourless shade of
respect; a respect not founded, as the air of it is apt to
be, on the vague presumption, but addressed almost in
especial to his disparities and oddities and thereby,
no doubt, none too different from affection. His friends
at all events were a rich and eager *cénacle*, among whom
he was on occasion, by his picturesque personality, a
natural and overtopping centre; partly perhaps because he was so much and so familiarly at home. He
wore, up to any hour of the afternoon, that long, col-
loquial dressing-gown, with trousers to match, which
one has always associated with literature in France—
the uniform really of freedom of talk. Freedom of
talk abounded by his winter fire, for the *cénacle* was
made up almost wholly of the more finely distinguished
among his contemporaries; of philosophers, men of
letters and men of affairs belonging to his own generation and the next. He had at the time I have in mind
a small perch, far aloft, at the distant, the then almost
suburban, end of the Faubourg Saint-Honoré, where on
Sunday afternoons, at the very top of an endless flight
of stairs, were to be encountered in a cloud of conversation and smoke most of the novelists of the general
Balzac tradition. Others of a different birth and complexion were markedly not of the number, were not
even conceivable as present; none of those, unless I

misremember, whose fictions were at that time "serial-
ised" in the Revue des Deux Mondes. In spite of
Renan and Taine and two or three more, the contributor to the Revue would indeed at no time have found
in the circle in question his foot on his native heath.
One could recall if one would two or three vivid allusions to him, not of the most quotable, on the lips
of the most famous of "naturalists"—allusions to him
as represented for instance by M. Victor Cherbuliez
and M. Octave Feuillet. The author of these pages
recalls a concise qualification of this last of his fellows
on the lips of Émile Zola, which that absorbed auditor
had too directly, too rashly asked for; but which is alas
not reproducible here. There was little else but the
talk, which had extreme intensity and variety; almost
nothing, as I remember, but a painted and gilded idol,
of considerable size, a relic and a memento, on the
chimney-piece. Flaubert was huge and diffident, but
florid too and resonant, and my main remembrance is
of a conception of courtesy in him, an accessibility to
the human relation, that only wanted to be sure of
the way taken or to take. The uncertainties of the
French for the determination of intercourse have often
struck me as quite matching the sharpness of their
certainties, as we for the most part feel these latter,
which sometimes in fact throw the indeterminate into
almost touching relief. I have thought of them at
such times as the people in the world one may have
to go more of the way to meet than to meet any other,
and this, as it were, through their being seated and
embedded, provided for at home, in a manner that
is all their own and that has bred them to the positive
preacceptance of interest on their behalf. We at least
of the Anglo-American race, more abroad in the world,

perching everywhere, so far as grounds of intercourse
are concerned, more vaguely and superficially, as well
as less intelligently, are the more ready by that fact
with inexpensive accommodations, rather conscious
that these themselves forbear from the claim to fasci-
nate, and advancing with the good nature that is the
mantle of our obtuseness to any point whatever where
entertainment may be offered us. My recollection is
at any rate simplified by the fact of the presence almost always, in the little high room of the Faubourg's
end, of other persons and other voices. Flaubert's
own voice is clearest to me from the uneffaced sense
of a winter week-day afternoon when I found him by
exception alone and when something led to his reading
me aloud, in support of some judgment he had thrown
off, a poem of Théophile Gautier's. He cited it as an
example of verse intensely˘and distinctively French,
and French in its melancholy, which neither Goethe
nor Heine nor Leopardi, neither Pushkin nor Tennyson nor, as he said, Byron, could at all have matched in
kind. He converted me at the moment to this perception, alike by the sense of the thing and by his large
utterance of it; after which it is dreadful to have to
confess not only that the poem was then new to me,
but that, hunt as I will in every volume of its author,
I am never able to recover it. This is perhaps after all
happy, causing Flaubert's own full tone, which was the
note of the occasion, to linger the more unquenched.
But for the rhyme in fact I could have believed him to
be spouting to me something strange and sonorous of
his own. The thing really rare would have been to
hear him do that—hear him *gueuler*, as he liked to
call it. Verse, I felt, we had always with us, and almost
any idiot of goodwill could give it a value. The value

of so many a passage of "Salammbô" and of "L'Éducation" was on the other hand exactly such as gained when he allowed himself, as had by the legend ever been frequent *dans l'intimité*, to "bellow" it to its fullest effect.

One of the things that make him most exhibitional and most describable, so that if we had invented him as an illustration or a character we would exactly so have arranged him, is that he was formed intellectually of two quite distinct compartments, a sense of the real and a sense of the romantic, and that his production, for our present cognisance, thus neatly and vividly divides itself. The divisions are as marked as the sections on the back of a scarab, though their distinctness is undoubtedly but the final expression of much inward strife. M. Faguet indeed, who is admirable on this question of our author's duality, gives an account of the romanticism that found its way for him into the real and of the reality that found its way into the romantic; but he none the less strikes us as a curious splendid insect sustained on wings of a different coloration, the right a vivid red, say, and the left as frank a yellow. This duality has in its sharp operation placed "Madame Bovary" and "L'Éducation" on one side together and placed together on the other "Salammbô" and "La Tentation." "Bouvard et Pécuchet" it can scarce be spoken of, I think, as having placed anywhere or anyhow. If it was Flaubert's way to find his subject impossible there was none he saw so much in that light as this last-named, but also none that he appears to have held so important for that very reason to pursue to the bitter end. Posterity agrees with him about the impossibility, but rather takes upon itself to break with the rest of the logic. We may perhaps, however, for symmetry, let "Bouvard et Pécuchet" figure as the tail—if scarabs ever have tails—of our analogous insect. Only in that case we should also append as the very tip the small volume of the "Trois Contes," preponderantly of the deepest imaginative hue.

His imagination was great and splendid; in spite of which, strangely enough, his masterpiece is not his most imaginative work. "Madame Bovary," beyond question, holds that first place, and "Madame Bovary" is concerned with the career of a country doctor's wife in a petty Norman town. The elements of the picture are of the fewest, the situation of the heroine almost of the meanest, the material for interest, considering the interest yielded, of the most unpromising; but these facts only throw into relief one of those incalculable incidents that attend the proceedings of genius. "Madame Bovary" was doomed by circumstances and causes—the freshness of comparative youth and good faith on the author's part being perhaps the chief—definitely to take its position, even though its subject was fundamentally a negation of the remote, the splendid and the strange, the stuff of his fondest and most cultivated dreams. It would have seemed very nearly to exclude the free play of the imagination, and the way this faculty on the author's part nevertheless presides is one of those accidents, manœuvres, inspirations, we hardly know what to call them, by which masterpieces grow. He of course knew more or less what he was doing for his book in making Emma Bovary a victim of the imaginative habit, but he must have been far from designing or measuring the total effect which renders the work so general, so complete an expression of himself. His separate idiosyncrasies, his irritated sensibility to the life about him, with the power to catch it in the fact and hold it hard, and his hunger for style and history and poetry, for the rich and the rare, great reverberations, great adumbrations, are here represented together as they are not in his later writings. There is nothing of the near, of the directly observed, though there may be much of the directly perceived and the minutely detailed, either in "Salammbô" or in "Saint-Antoine," and little enough of the extravagance of illusion in that indefinable last word of restrained evocation and cold execution "L'Éducation Sentimentale." M. Faguet has of course excellently noted this—that the fortune and felicity of the book were assured by the stroke that made the central figure an embodiment of helpless romanticism. Flaubert himself but narrowly escaped being such an embodiment after all, and he is thus able to express the romantic mind with extraordinary truth. As to the rest of the matter he had the luck of having been in possession from the first, having begun so early to nurse and work up his plan that, familiarity and the native air, the native soil, aiding, he had finally made out to the last lurking shade the small sordid sunny dusty village picture, its emptiness constituted and peopled. It is in the background and the accessories that the real, the real of his theme, abides; and the romantic, the romantic of his theme, accordingly occupies the front. Emma Bovary's poor adventures are a tragedy for the very reason that in a world unsuspecting, unassisting, unconsoling, she has herself to distil the rich and the rare. Ignorant, unguided, undiverted, ridden by the very nature and mixture of her consciousness, she makes of the business an inordinate failure, a failure which in its turn makes for Flaubert the most pointed, the most *told* of anecdotes.

There are many things to say about "Madame Bovary," but an old admirer of the book would be but half-hearted—so far as they represent reserves or puzzlements—were he not to note first of all the circumstances by which it is most endeared to him. To remember it from far back is to have been present all along at a process of singular interest to a literary mind, a case indeed full of comfort and cheer. The finest of Flaubert's novels is to-day, on the French shelf of fiction, one of the first of the classics; it has attained that position, slowly but steadily, before our eyes; and we seem so to follow the evolution of the fate of a classic. We see how the thing takes place; which we rarely can, for we mostly miss either the beginning or the end, especially in the case of a consecration as complete as this. The consecrations of the past are too far behind and those of the future too far in front. That the production before us *should* have come in for the heavenly crown may be a fact to offer English and American readers a mystifying side; but it is exactly our ground and a part moreover of the total interest. The author of these remarks remembers, as with a sense of the way such things happen, that when a very young person in Paris he took up from the parental table the latest number of the periodical in which Flaubert's then duly unrecognised masterpiece was in course of publication. The moment is not historic, but it was to become in the light of history, as may be said, so unforgettable that every small feature of it

yet again lives for him: it rests there like the backward
end of the span.   The cover of the old Revue de Paris
was yellow, if I mistake not, like that of the new, and
"Madame Bovary: Mœurs de Province," on the inside of it, was already, on the spot, as a title, mysteri-
ously arresting, inscrutably charged.   I was ignorant
of what had preceded and was not to know till much
later what followed; but present to me still is the act
of standing there before the fire, my back against the
low beplushed and begarnished French chimney-piece
and taking in what I might of that instalment, taking
it in with so surprised an interest, and perhaps as well
such a stir of faint foreknowledge, that the sunny little
salon, the autumn day, the window ajar and the cheerful
outside clatter of the Rue Montaigne are all now for
me more or less in the story and the story more or less
in them.   The story, however, was at that moment
having a difficult life; its fortune was all to make; its
merit was so far from suspected that, as Maxime Du
Camp—though verily with no excess of contrition—
relates, its cloth of gold barely escaped the editorial
shears.   This, with much more, contributes for us to
the course of things to come.   The book, on its appearance as a volume, proved a shock to the high propriety of the guardians of public morals under the
second Empire, and Flaubert was prosecuted as author
of a work indecent to scandal.   The prosecution in the
event fell to the ground, but I should perhaps have
mentioned this agitation as one of the very few, of
any public order, in his short list.   "Le Candidat"
fell at the Vaudeville Theatre, several years later, with
a violence indicated by its withdrawal after a performance of but two nights, the first of these marked by a
deafening uproar; only if the comedy was not to re-

cover from this accident the misprised lustre of the novel was entirely to reassert itself. It is strange enough at present—so far have we travelled since then—that "Madame Bovary" should in so comparatively recent a past have been to that extent a cause of reprobation; and suggestive above all, in such connections, as to the large unconsciousness of superior minds. The desire of the superior mind of the day—that is the governmental, official, legal—to distinguish a book with such a destiny before it is a case conceivable, but conception breaks down before its design of making the distinction purely invidious. We can imagine its knowing so little, however face to face with the object, what it had got hold of; but for it to have been so urged on by a blind inward spring to publish to posterity the extent of its ignorance, that would have been beyond imagination, beyond everything but pity.

And yet it is not after all that the place the book has taken is so overwhelmingly explained by its inherent dignity; for here comes in the curiosity of the matter. Here comes in especially its fund of admonition for alien readers. The dignity of its substance is the dignity of Madame Bovary herself as a vessel of experience—a question as to which, unmistakably, I judge, we can only depart from the consensus of French critical opinion. M. Faguet for example commends the character of the heroine as one of the most living and discriminated figures of women in all literature, praises it as a field for the display of the romantic spirit that leaves nothing to be desired. Subject to an observation I shall presently make and that bears heavily in general, I think, on Flaubert as a painter of life, subject to this restriction he is right; which is a proof that a work of art may be markedly open to objection and at the same time be rare in its kind, and that when it is perfect to this point nothing else particularly matters. "Madame Bovary" has a perfection that not only stamps it, but that makes it stand almost alone; it holds itself with such a supreme unapproachable assurance as both excites and defies judgment. For it deals not in the least, as to unapproachability, with things exalted or refined; it only confers on its sufficiently vulgar elements of exhibition a final unsurpassable form. The form is in *itself* as interesting, as active, as much of the essence of the subject as the idea, and yet so close is its fit and so inseparable its life that we catch it at no moment on any errand of its own. That verily is to *be* interesting—all round; that is to be genuine and whole. The work is a classic because the thing, such as it is, is ideally *done*, and because it shows that in such doing eternal beauty may dwell. A pretty young woman who lives, socially and morally speaking, in a hole, and who is ignorant, foolish, flimsy, unhappy, takes a pair of lovers by whom she is successively deserted; in the midst of the bewilderment of which, giving up her husband and her child, letting everything go, she sinks deeper into duplicity, debt, despair, and arrives on the spot, on the small scene itself of her poor depravities, at a pitiful tragic end. In especial she does these things while remaining absorbed in romantic intention and vision, and she remains absorbed in romantic intention and vision while fairly rolling in the dust. That is the triumph of the book as the triumph stands, that Emma interests us by the nature of her consciousness and the play of her mind, thanks to the reality and beauty with which those sources are invested. It is not only that they represent *her* state; they are so true, so observed and felt, and especially so shown, that they represent the state, actual or potential, of all persons like her, persons romantically determined. Then her setting, the medium in which she struggles, becomes in its way as important, becomes eminent with the eminence of art; the tiny world in which she revolves, the contracted cage in which she flutters, is hung out in space for her, and her companions in captivity there are as true as herself.

I have said enough to show what I mean by Flaubert's having in this picture expressed something of his intimate self, given his heroine something of his own imagination: a point precisely that brings me back to the restriction at which I just now hinted, in which M. Faguet fails to indulge and yet which is immediate for the alien reader. Our complaint is that Emma Bovary, in spite of the nature of her consciousness and in spite of her reflecting so much that of her creator, is really too small an affair. This, critically speaking, is in view both of the value and the fortune of her history, a wonderful circumstance. She associates herself with Frédéric Moreau in "L'Éducation" to suggest for us a question that can be answered, I hold, only to Flaubert's detriment. Emma taken alone would possibly not so directly press it, but in her company the hero of our author's second study of the "real" drives it home. Why did Flaubert choose, as special conduits of the life he proposed to depict, such inferior and in the case of Frédéric such abject human specimens? I insist only in respect to the latter, the perfection of Madame Bovary scarce leaving one much warrant for wishing anything other. Even here,

however, the general scale and size of Emma, who is
small even of her sort, should be a warning to hyperbole.
If I say that in the matter of Frédéric at all events the
answer is inevitably detrimental I mean that it weighs
heavily on our author's general credit. He wished in
each case to make a picture of experience—middling
experience, it is true—and of the world close to him;
but if he imagined nothing better for his purpose than
such a heroine and such a hero, both such limited re-
flectors and registers, we are forced to believe it to
have been by a defect of his mind. And that sign of
weakness remains even if it be objected that the images
in question were addressed to his purpose better than
others would have been: the purpose itself then shows
as inferior. "L'Éducation Sentimentale" is a strange,
an indescribable work, about which there would be
many more things to say than I have space for, and
all of them of the deepest interest. It is moreover, to
simplify my statement, very much less satisfying a
thing, less pleasing whether in its unity or its variety,
than its specific predecessor. But take it as we will,
for a success or a failure—M. Faguet indeed ranks it,
by the measure of its quantity of intention, a failure,
and I on the whole agree with him—the personage
offered us as bearing the weight of the drama, and in
whom we are invited to that extent to interest ourselves,
leaves us mainly wondering what our entertainer could
have been thinking of. He takes Frédéric Moreau on
the threshold of life and conducts him to the extreme
of maturity without apparently suspecting for a moment either our wonder or our protest—"Why, why
him?" Frédéric is positively too poor for his part,
too scant for his charge; and we feel with a kind of
embarrassment, certainly with a kind of compassion,

that it is somehow the business of a protagonist to
prevent in his designer an excessive waste of faith.
When I speak of the faith in Emma Bovary as proportionately wasted I reflect on M. Faguet's judgment
that she is from the point of view of deep interest
richly or at least roundedly representative.   Representative of what? he makes us ask even while granting all the grounds of misery and tragedy involved.
The plea for her is the plea made for all the figures
that live without evaporation under the painter's hand
—that they are not only particular persons but types
of their kind, and as valid in one light as in the other.
It is Emma's "kind" that I question for this responsibility, even if it be inquired of me why I then fail to
question that of Charles Bovary, in its perfection, or
that of the inimitable, the immortal Homais.   If we
express Emma's deficiency as the poverty of her consciousness for the typical function, it is certainly not,
one must admit, that she is surpassed in this respect
either by her platitudinous husband or by his friend
the pretentious apothecary.   The difference is none
the less somehow in the fact that they are respectively
studies but of their character and office, which function
in each expresses adequately *all* they are.   It may be,
I concede, because Emma is the only woman in the
book that she is taken by M. Faguet as *femininely*
typical, typical in the larger illustrative way, whereas
the others pass with him for images specifically conditioned.   Emma is this same for myself, I plead; she
is conditioned to such an excess of the specific, and the
specific in her case leaves out so many even of the
commoner elements of conceivable life in a woman
when we are invited to see that life as pathetic, as
dramatic agitation, that we challenge both the author's

and the critic's scale of importances. The book is a
picture of the middling as much as they like, but does
Emma attain even to *that*? Hers is a narrow middling
even for a little imaginative person whose "social"
significance is small. It is greater on the whole than
her capacity of consciousness, taking this all round;
and so, in a word, we feel her less illustrational than she
might have been not only if the world had offered her
more points of contact, but if she had had more of
these to give it.

We meet Frédéric first, we remain with him long, as
a *moyen*, a provincial bourgeois of the mid-century,
educated and not without fortune, thereby with freedom, in whom the life of his day reflects itself. Yet
the life of his day, on Flaubert's showing, hangs together with the poverty of Frédéric's own inward or
for that matter outward life; so that, the whole thing
being, for scale, intention and extension, a sort of epic
of the usual (with the Revolution of 1848 introduced
indeed as an episode,) it affects us as an epic without
air, without wings to lift it; reminds us in fact more
than anything else of a huge balloon, all of silk pieces
strongly sewn together and patiently blown up, but
that absolutely refuses to leave the ground. The discrimination I here make as against our author is, however, the only one inevitable in a series of remarks so
brief. What it really represents—and nothing could
be more curious—is that Frédéric enjoys his position
not only without the aid of a single "sympathetic"
character of consequence, but even without the aid of
one with whom we can directly communicate. Can we
communicate with the central personage? or would we
really if we could? A hundred times no, and if he him-

self can communicate with the people shown us as surrounding him this only proves him of their kind. Flaubert on his "real" side was in truth an ironic painter, and ironic to a tune that makes his final accepted state, his present literary dignity and "classic" peace, superficially anomalous. There is an explanation to which I shall immediately come; but I find myself feeling for a moment longer in presence of "L'Éducation" how much more interesting a writer may be on occasion by the given failure than by the given success. Successes pure and simple disconnect and dismiss him; failures—though I admit they must be a bit qualified—keep him in touch and in relation. Thus it is that as the work of a "grand écrivain" "L'Éducation," large, laboured, immensely "written," with beautiful passages and a general emptiness, with a kind of leak in its stored sadness, moreover, by which its moral dignity escapes—thus it is that Flaubert's ill-starred novel is a curiosity for a literary museum. Thus it is also that it suggests a hundred reflections, and suggests perhaps most of them directly to the intending labourer in the same field. If in short, as I have said, Flaubert is the novelist's novelist, this performance does more than any other toward making him so.

I have to add in the same connection that I had not lost sight of Madame Arnoux, the main ornament of "L'Éducation," in pronouncing just above on its deficiency in the sympathetic. Madame Arnoux is exactly the author's one marked attempt, here or elsewhere, to represent beauty otherwise than for the senses, beauty of character and life; and what becomes of the attempt is a matter highly significant. M.

Faguet praises with justice his conception of the figure
and of the relation, the relation that never bears fruit,
that keeps Frédéric adoring her, through hindrance and
change, from the beginning of life to the end; that
keeps her, by the same constraint, forever immacu-
lately "good," from youth to age, though deeply
moved and cruelly tempted and sorely tried. Her
contacts with her adorer are not even frequent, in proportion to the field of time; her conditions of fortune,
of association and occupation are almost sordid, and
we see them with the march of the drama, such as it
is, become more and more so; besides which—I again
remember that M. Faguet excellently notes it—nothing
in the nature of "parts" is attributed to her; not only
is she not presented as clever, she is scarce invested
with a character at all. Almost nothing that she says
is repeated, almost nothing that she does is shown.
She is an image none the less beautiful and vague, an
image of passion cherished and abjured, renouncing
all sustenance and yet persisting in life. Only she has
for real distinction the extreme drawback that she is
offered us quite preponderantly through Frédéric's
vision of her, that we see her practically in no other
light. Now Flaubert unfortunately has not been able
not so to discredit Frédéric's vision in general, his
vision of everyone and everything, and in particular of
his own life, that it makes a medium good enough to
convey adequately a noble impression. Madame Arnoux is of course ever so much the best thing in his
life—which is saying little; but his life is made up of
such queer material that we find ourselves displeased
at her being "in" it on whatever terms; all the more
that she seems scarcely to affect, improve or determine it. Her creator in short never had a more awk-

ward idea than this attempt to give us the benefit of such a conception in such a way; and even though I have still something else to say about that I may as well speak of it at once as a mistake that gravely counts against him. It is but one of three, no doubt, in all his work; but I shall not, I trust, pass for extravagant if I call it the most indicative. What makes it so is its being the least superficial; the two others are, so to speak, intellectual, while this is somehow moral. It was a mistake, as I have already hinted, to propose to register in so mean a consciousness as that of such a hero so large and so mixed a quantity of life as "L'Éducation" clearly intends; and it was a mistake of the tragic sort that is a theme mainly for silence to have embarked on "Bouvard et Pécuchet" at all, not to have given it up sooner than be given up by it. But these were at the worst not wholly compromising blunders. What *was* compromising—and the great point is that it remained so, that nothing has an equal weight against it—is the unconsciousness of error in respect to the opportunity that would have counted as his finest. We feel not so much that Flaubert misses it, for that we could bear; but that he doesn't *know* he misses it is what stamps the blunder. We do not pretend to say how he might have shown us Madame Arnoux better—that was his own affair. What is ours is that he really thought he was showing her as well as he could, or as she might be shown; at which we veil our face. For once that he had a conception quite apart, apart I mean from the array of his other conceptions and more delicate than any, he "went," as we say, and spoiled it. Let me add in all tenderness, and to make up for possibly too much insistence, that it is the only stain on his shield; let me even con-

fess that I should not wonder if, when all is said, it is
a blemish no one has ever noticed.

Perhaps no one has ever noticed either what was
present to me just above as the partial makeweight
there glanced at, the fact that in the midst of this
general awkwardness, as I have called it, there is at
the same time a danger so escaped as to entitle our
author to full credit. I scarce know how to put it
with little enough of the ungracious, but I think that
even the true Flaubertist finds himself wondering a
little that some flaw of taste, some small but unfortunate lapse by the way, *should* as a matter of fact
not somehow or somewhere have waited on the demonstration of the platonic purity prevailing between
this heroine and her hero—so far as we do find that
image projected. It is alike difficult to indicate without offence or to ignore without unkindness a fond
reader's apprehension here of a possibility of the wrong
touch, the just perceptibly false note. I would not
have staked my life on Flaubert's security of instinct
in such a connection—as an absolutely fine and predetermined security; and yet in the event that felicity
has settled, there is not so much as the lightest wrong
breath (speaking of the matter in this light of tact and
taste) or the shade of a crooked stroke. One exclaims
at the end of the question "Dear old Flaubert after
all—!" and perhaps so risks seeming to patronise for
fear of not making a point. The point made for what
it is worth, at any rate, I am the more free to recover
the benefit of what I mean by critical "tenderness" in
our general connection—expressing in it as I do our
general respect, and my own particular, for our author's method and process and history, and my sense

of the luxury of such a sentiment at such a vulgar literary time. It is a respect positive and settled and the thing that has most to do with consecrating for us that loyalty to him as the novelist of the novelist— unlike as it is even the best feeling inspired by any other member of the craft. He may stand for our operative conscience or our vicarious sacrifice; animated by a sense of literary honour, attached to an ideal of perfection, incapable of lapsing in fine from a self-respect, that enable us to sit at ease, to surrender to the age, to indulge in whatever comparative meannesses (and no meanness in art is so mean as the sneaking economic,) we may find most comfortable or profitable. May it not in truth be said that we practise our industry, so many of us, at relatively little cost just *because* poor Flaubert, producing the most expensive fictions ever written, so handsomely paid for it ? It is as if this put it in our power to produce cheap and thereby sell dear; as if, so expressing it, literary honour being by his example effectively secure for the firm at large and the general concern, on its whole esthetic side, floated once for all, we find our individual attention free for literary and esthetic indifference. All the while we thus lavish our indifference the spirit of the author of "Madame Bovary," in the cross-light of the old room above the Seine, is trying to the last admiration for the thing itself. That production puts the matter into a nutshell: "Madame Bovary," subject to whatever qualification, is absolutely the most literary of novels, so literary that it covers us with its mantle. It shows us once for all that there is no *intrinsic* call for a debasement of the type. The mantle I speak of is wrought with surpassing fineness, and we may always, under stress of whatever charge of illiteracy, frivolity, vulgarity, flaunt it as the flag of the guild. Let us therefore frankly concede that to surround Flaubert with our consideration is the least return we can make for such a privilege. The consideration moreover is idle unless it be real, unless it be intelligent enough to measure his effort and his success. Of the effort as mere effort I have already spoken, of the desperate difficulty involved for him in making his form square with his conception; and I by no means attach general importance to these secrets of the workshop, which are but as the contortions of the fastidious muse who is the servant of the oracle. They are really rather secrets of the kitchen and contortions of the priestess of *that* tripod—they are not an upstairs matter. It is of their specially distinctive importance I am now speaking, of the light shed on them by the results before us.

They all represent the pursuit of a style, of the ideally right one for its relations, and would still be interesting if the style had not been achieved. "Madame Bovary," "Salammbô," "Saint-Antoine," "L'Éducation" are so written and so composed (though the last-named in a minor degree) that the more we look at them the more we find in them, under this head, a beauty of intention and of effect; the more they figure in the too often dreary desert of fictional prose a class by themselves and a little living oasis. So far as that desert is of the complexion of our own English speech it supplies with remarkable rarity this particular source of refreshment. So strikingly is that the case, so scant for the most part any dream of a scheme of beauty in these connections, that a critic betrayed at artless moments into a plea for composition may find himself as blankly met as if his plea were for trigonometry. He makes inevitably his reflections, which are numerous enough; one of them being that if we turn our back so squarely, so universally to this order of considerations it is because the novel is so preponderantly cultivated among us by women, in other words by a sex ever gracefully, comfortably, enviably unconscious (it would be too much to call them even suspicious,) of the requirements of form. The case is at any rate sharply enough made for us, or against us, by the circumstance that women are held to have achieved on all our ground, in spite of this weakness and others, as great results as any. The judgment is undoubtedly founded: Jane Austen was instinctive and charming, and the other recognitions—even over the heads of the ladies, some of them, from Fielding to Pater—are obvious; without, however, in the least touching my contention. For signal examples of what composition, distribution, arrangement can do, of how they intensify the life of a work of art, we have to go elsewhere; and the value of Flaubert for us is that he admirably points the moral. This is the explanation of the "classic" fortune of "Madame Bovary" in especial, though I may add that also of Hérodias and Saint-Julien l'Hospitalier in the "Trois Contes," as well as an aspect of these works endlessly suggestive. I spoke just now of the small field of the picture in the longest of them, the small capacity, as I called it, of the vessel; yet the way the thing is done not only triumphs over the question of value but in respect to it fairly misleads and confounds us. Where else shall we find in anything proportionately so small such an air of dignity of size? Flaubert *made* things big—it was his way, his ambition and his necessity; and I say this while remembering that in "L'Éducation" (in proportion I mean again,) the effect has not been produced. The subject of "L'Éducation" is in spite of Frédéric large, but an indefinable shrinkage has overtaken it in the execution. The exception so marked, however, is single; "Salammbô" and "Saint-Antoine" are both at once very "heavy" conceptions and very consistently and splendidly high applications of a manner.

It is in this assured manner that the lesson sits aloft, that the spell for the critical reader resides; and if the conviction under which Flaubert labours is more and more grossly discredited among us his compact mass is but the greater. He regarded the work of art as *existing* but by its expression, and defied us to name any other measure of its life that is not a stultification. He held style to be accordingly an indefeasible part of it, and found beauty, interest and distinction as dependent on it for emergence as a letter committed to the post-office is dependent on an addressed envelope. Strange enough it may well appear to us to have to apologise for such notions as eccentric. There are persons who consider that style comes of itself—we see and hear at present, I think, enough of them; and to whom he would doubtless have remarked that it goes, of itself, still faster. The thing naturally differs in fact with the nature of the imagination; the question is one of proprieties and affinities, sympathy and proportion. The sympathy of the author of "Salammbô" was all with the magnificent, his imagination for the phrase as variously noble or ignoble in itself, contributive or destructive, adapted and harmonious or casual and common. The worse among such possibilities have been multiplied by the infection of bad writing, and he

denied that the better ever do anything so obliging as
to come of themselves. They scarcely indeed for
Flaubert "came" at all; their arrival was determined
only by fasting and prayer or by patience of pursuit,
the arts of the chase, long waits and watches, figura-
tively speaking, among the peaks or by the waters.
The production of a book was of course made inordinately slow by the fatigue of these measures; in illustration of which his letters often record that it has
taken him three days[1] to arrive at one right sentence,
tested by the pitch of his ideal of the right for the suggestion aimed at. His difficulties drew from the author,
as I have mentioned, much resounding complaint;
but those voices have ceased to trouble us and the
final voice remains. No feature of the whole business
is more edifying than the fact that he in the first place
never misses style and in the second never appears
to have beaten about for it. That betrayal is of course
the worst betrayal of all, and I think the way he has
escaped it the happiest form of the peace that has
finally visited him. It was truly a wonderful success
to be so the devotee of the phrase and yet never its
victim. Fine as he inveterately desired it should be
he still never lost sight of the question Fine for what?
It is always so related and associated, so properly part
of something else that is in turn part of something
other, part of a reference, a tone, a passage, a page,

---

[1] It was true, delightfully true, that, extravagance in this province of his
life, though apparently in no other, being Flaubert's necessity and law, he
deliberated and hung fire, wrestled, retreated and returned, indulged generally in a tragi-comedy of waste; which I recall a charming expression of
on the lips of Edmond de Goncourt, who quite recognised the heroic legend,
but prettily qualified it: "Il faut vous dire qu'il y avait là-dedans beaucoup
de coucheries et d'école buissonière." And he related how on the occasion of a stay with his friend under the roof of the Princess Mathilde, the
friend, missed during the middle hours of a fine afternoon, was found to
have undressed himself and gone to bed to think!

that the simple may enjoy it for its least bearing and the initiated for its greatest. That surely is to be a writer of the first order, to resemble when in the hand and however closely viewed a shapely crystal box, and yet to be seen when placed on the table and opened to contain innumerable compartments, springs and tricks. One is ornamental either way, but one is in the second way precious too.

The crystal box then figures the style of "Salammbô" and "Saint-Antoine" in a greater degree than that of "Bovary," because, as the two former express the writer's romantic side, he had in them, while equally covering his tracks, still further to fare and still more to hunt. Beyond this allusion to their completing his duality I shall not attempt closely to characterise them; though I admit that in not insisting on them I press most lightly on the scale into which he had in his own view cast his greatest pressure. He lamented the doom that drove him so oddly, so ruefully, to choose his subjects, but he lamented it least when these subjects were most pompous and most exotic, feeling as he did that they had then after all most affinity with his special eloquence. In dealing with the near, the directly perceived, he had to keep down his tone, to make the eloquence small; though with the consequence, as we have seen, that in spite of such precautions the whole thing mostly insists on being ample. The familiar, that is, under his touch, took on character, importance, extension, one scarce knows what to call it, in order to carry the style or perhaps rather, as we may say, sit with proper ease in the vehicle, and there was accordingly a limit to its smallness; whereas in the romantic books, the preferred world of Flaubert's imagination, there was practically no need of compromise. The compromise gave him throughout endless trouble, and nothing would be more to the point than to show, had I space, why in particular it distressed him. It was obviously his strange predicament that the only spectacle open to him by experience and direct knowledge was the bourgeois, which on that ground imposed on him successively his three so intensely bourgeois themes. He was obliged to treat these themes, which he hated, because his experience left him no alternative; his only alternative was given by history, geography, philosophy, fancy, the world of erudition and of imagination, the world especially of this last. In the bourgeois sphere his ideal of expression laboured under protest; in the other, the imagined, the projected, his need for facts, for matter, and his pursuit of them, sat no less heavily. But as his style all the while required a certain exercise of pride he was on the whole more at home in the exotic than in the familiar; he escaped above all in the former connection the associations, the disparities he detested. He could be frankly noble in "Salammbô" and "Saint-Antoine," whereas in "Bovary" and "L'Éducation" he could be but circuitously and insidiously so. He could in the one case cut his coat according to his cloth—if we mean by his cloth his predetermined tone, while in the other he had to take it already cut. Singular enough in his life the situation so constituted: the comparatively meagre human consciousness—for we must come back to that in him—struggling with the absolutely large artistic; and the large artistic half wreaking itself on the meagre human and half seeking a refuge from it, as well as a revenge against it, in something quite different.

Flaubert had in fact command of two refuges which he worked in turn. The first of these was the attitude of irony, so constant in him that "L'Éducation" bristles and hardens with it and "Bouvard et Pécuchet"—strangest of "poetic" justices—is made as dry as sand and as heavy as lead; the second only was, by processes, by journeys the most expensive, to get away altogether. And we inevitably ask ourselves whether, eschewing the policy of flight, he might not after all have fought out his case a little more on the spot. Might he not have addressed himself to the human still otherwise than in "L'Éducation" and in "Bouvard"? When one thinks of the view of the life of his country, of the vast French community and its constituent creatures, offered in these productions, one declines to believe it could make up the *whole* vision of a man of his quality. Or when all was said and done was he absolutely and exclusively condemned to irony? The second refuge I speak of, the getting away from the human, the congruously and measurably human, altogether, perhaps becomes in the light of this possibility but an irony the more. Carthage and the Thebaid, Salammbô, Spendius, Matho, Hannon, Saint Anthony, Hilarion, the Paternians, the Marcosians and the Carpocratians, what are all these, inviting because queer, but a confession of supreme impatience with the actual and the near, often queer enough too, no doubt, but not consolingly, not transcendently? Last remains the question whether, even if our author's immediate as distinguished from his remote view had had more reach, the particular gift we claim for him, the perfection of arrangement and form, would have had in certain directions the acquired flexibility. States of mind, states of soul, of the simpler kind, the kinds supposable in the Emma Bovarys, the Frédérics, the Bouvards and the Pécuchets, to say nothing of the Carthaginians and the Eremites—for Flaubert's eremites are eminently artless—these conditions represent, I think, his proved psychological range. And that throws us back remarkably, almost confoundingly, upon another face of the general anomaly. The "gift" was of the greatest; a force in itself, in virtue of which he is a consummate writer; and yet there are whole sides of life to which it was never addressed and which it apparently quite failed to suspect as a field of exercise. If he never approached the complicated character in man or woman—Emma Bovary is not the least little bit complicated—or the really furnished, the finely civilised, was this because, surprisingly, he could not? *L'âme française* at all events shows in him but ill.

This undoubtedly marks a limit, but limits are for the critic familiar country, and he may mostly well feel the prospect wide enough when he finds something positively well enough done. By disposition or by obligation Flaubert selected, and though his selection was in some respects narrow he stops not too short to have left us three really "cast" works and a fourth of several perfect parts, to say nothing of the element of perfection, of the superlative for the size, in his three *nouvelles*. What he attempted he attempted in a spirit that gives an extension to the idea of the achievable and the achieved in a literary thing, and it is by this that we contentedly gauge the matter. As success goes in this world of the approximate it may pass for success of the greatest. If I am unable to pursue the proof of my remark in "Salammbô" and "Saint-Antoine" it is because I have also had to

select and have found the questions connected with
their two companions more interesting. There are
numerous judges, I hasten to mention, who, showing
the opposite preference, lose themselves with rapture
in the strange bristling archæological picture—yet all
amazingly vivified and co-ordinated—of the Cartha-
ginian mercenaries in revolt and the sacred veil of the
great goddess profaned and stolen; as well in the still
more peopled panorama of the ancient sects, superstitions and mythologies that swim in the desert before
the fevered eyes of the Saint. One may be able, however, at once to breathe more freely in "Bovary"
than in "Salammbô" and yet to hope that there is no
intention of the latter that one has missed. The
great intention certainly, and little as we may be
sweetly beguiled, holds us fast; which is simply the
author's indomitable purpose of fully pervading his
field. There are countries beyond the sea in which
tracts are allowed to settlers on condition that they
will really, not nominally, cultivate them. Flaubert
is on his romantic ground like one of these settlers; he
makes good with all his might his title to his tract, and
in a way that shows how it is not only for him a question of safety but a question of honour. Honour demands that he shall set up his home and his faith there
in such a way that every inch of the surface be planted
or paved. He would have been ashamed merely to
encamp and, after the fashion of most other adventurers, knock up a log hut among charred stumps.
This was not what would have been for him taking
artistic possession, it was not what would have been
for him even personal honour, let alone literary; and
yet the general lapse from integrity was a thing that,
wherever he looked, he saw not only condoned but ac-

claimed and rewarded. He lived, as he felt, in an age of mean production and cheap criticism, the practical upshot of which took on for him a name that was often on his lips. He called it the hatred of literature, a hatred in the midst of which, the most literary of men, he found himself appointed to suffer. I may not, however, follow him in that direction—which would take us far; and the less that he was for himself after all, in spite of groans and imprecations, a man of resources and remedies, and that there was always his possibility of building himself in.

This he did equally in all his books—built himself into literature by means of a material put together with extraordinary art; but it leads me again to the question of what such a stiff ideal imposed on him for the element of exactitude. This element, in the romantic, was his merciless law; it was perhaps even in the romantic that—if there could indeed be degrees for him in such matters—he most despised the loose and the more-or-less. To be intensely definite and perfectly positive, to know so well what he meant that he could at every point strikingly and conclusively verify it, was the first of his needs; and if in addition to being thus synthetically final he could be strange and sad and terrible, and leave the cause of these effects inscrutable, success then had for him its highest savour. We feel the inscrutability in those memorable few words that put before us Frédéric Moreau's start upon his vain course of travel, "Il connût alors la mélancholie des paquebots;" an image to the last degree comprehensive and embracing, but which haunts us, in its droll pathos, without our quite knowing why. But he was really never so pleased as when he could be both rare and precise about the dreadful. His own sense of all this, as I have already indicated, was that beauty comes with expression, that expression is creation, that it *makes* the reality, and only in the degree in which it *is*, exquisitely, expression; and that we move in literature through a world of different values and relations, a blest world in which we know nothing except by style, but in which also everything is saved by it, and in which the image is thus always superior to the thing itself. This quest and multiplication of the image, the image tested and warranted and consecrated for the occasion, was accordingly his high elegance, to which he too much sacrificed and to which "Salammbô" and partly "Saint-Antoine" are monstrous monuments. Old cruelties and perversities, old wonders and errors and terrors, endlessly appealed to him; they constitute the unhuman side of his work, and if we have not the bribe of curiosity, of a lively interest in method, or rather in evocation just *as* evocation, we tread our way among them, especially in "Salammbô," with a reserve too dry for our pleasure. To my own view the curiosity and the literary interest are equal in dealing with the non-romantic books, and the world presented, the aspects and agents, are less deterrent and more amenable both to our own social and expressional terms. Style itself moreover, with all respect to Flaubert, never *totally* beguiles; since even when we are so queerly constituted as to be ninety-nine parts literary we are still a hundredth part something else. This hundredth part may, once we possess the book—or the book possesses us—make us imperfect as readers, and yet without it should we want or get the book at all? The curiosity at any rate, to repeat, is even greatest for me in "Ma-

dame Bovary," say, for here I can measure, can more
directly appreciate, the terms. The aspects and impressions being of an experience conceivable to me I
am more touched by the beauty; my interest gets
more of the benefit of the beauty even though this be
not intrinsically greater. Which brings back our appreciation inevitably at last to the question of our
author's lucidity.

I have sufficiently remarked that I speak from the
point of view of his interest to a reader of his own craft,
the point of view of his extraordinary technical wealth
—though indeed when I think of the general power of
"Madame Bovary" I find myself desiring not to narrow the ground of the lesson, not to connect the lesson,
to its prejudice, with that idea of the "technical,"
that question of the way a thing is done, so abhorrent,
as a call upon attention, in whatever art, to the wondrous Anglo-Saxon mind. Without proposing Flaubert as the type of the newspaper novelist, or as an
easy alternative to golf or the bicycle, we should do
him less than justice in failing to insist that a masterpiece like "Madame Bovary" may benefit even with
the simple-minded by the way it has been done. It
derives from its firm roundness that sign of all rare
works that there is something in it for every one. It
may be read ever so attentively, ever so freely, without a suspicion of how it is written, to say nothing of
put together; it may equally be read under the excitement of these perceptions alone, one of the greatest
known to the reader who is fully open to them. Both
readers will have been transported, which is all any
can ask. Leaving the first of them, however that may
be, to state the case for himself, I state it yet again for

the second, if only on this final ground. The book and
its companions represent for us a practical solution,
Flaubert's own troubled but settled one, of the eternal
dilemma of the painter of life. From the moment
this rash adventurer deals with his mysterious matter
at all directly his desire is not to deal with it stintedly.
It at the same time remains true that from the moment
he desires to produce forms in which it shall be preserved, he desires that these forms, things of *his* creation, shall not be, as testifying to his way with them,
weak or ignoble. He must make them complete and
beautiful, of satisfactory production, intrinsically interesting, under peril of disgrace with those who know.
Those who don't know of course don't count for him,
and it neither helps nor hinders him to say that every
one knows about life. Every one does not—it is distinctly the case of the few; and if it were in fact the
case of the many the knowledge still might exist, on
the evidence around us, even in an age of unprecedented
printing, without attesting itself by a multiplication of
masterpieces. The question for the artist can only be
of doing the artistic utmost, and thereby of *seeing* the
general task. When it is seen with the intensity with
which it presented itself to Flaubert a lifetime is none
too much for fairly tackling it. It must either be left
alone or be dealt with, and to leave it alone is a comparatively simple matter.

To deal with it is on the other hand to produce a
certain number of finished works; there being no other
known method; and the quantity of life depicted will
depend on this array. What will this array, however,
depend on, and what will condition the number of pieces
of which it is composed? The "finish," evidently,

that the formula so glibly postulates and for which the novelist is thus so handsomely responsible. He has on the one side to feel his subject and on the other side to render it, and there are undoubtedly two ways in which his situation may be expressed, especially perhaps by himself. The more he feels his subject the more he *can* render it—that is the first way. The more he renders it the more he *can* feel it—that is the second way. This second way was unmistakeably Flaubert's, and if the result of it for him was a bar to abundant production he could only accept such an incident as part of the game. He probably for that matter would have challenged any easy definition of "abundance," contested the application of it to the repetition, however frequent, of the thing not "done." What but the "doing" makes the thing, he would have asked, and how can a positive result from a mere iteration of negatives, or wealth proceed from the simple addition of so many instances of penury? We should here, in closer communion with him, have got into his highly characteristic and suggestive view of the fertilisation of subject by form, penetration of the sense, ever, by the expression—the latter reacting creatively on the former; a conviction in the light of which he appears to have wrought with real consistency and which borrows from him thus its high measure of credit. It would undoubtedly have suffered if his books had been things of a loose logic, whereas we refer to it not only without shame but with an encouraged confidence by their showing of a logic so close. Let the phrase, the form that the whole is at the given moment staked on, be beautiful and related, and the rest will take care of itself—such is a rough indication of Flaubert's faith; which has the importance that it was a faith sincere, active and inspiring. I hasten to add indeed that we must most of all remember how in these matters everything hangs on definitions. The "beautiful," with our author, covered for the phrase a great deal of ground, and when every sort of propriety had been gathered in under it and every relation, in a complexity of such, protected, the idea itself, the presiding thought, ended surely by being pretty well provided for.

These, however, are subordinate notes, and the plain question, in the connection I have touched upon, is of whether we would really wish him to have written more books, say either of the type of "Bovary" or of the type of "Salammbô," and not have written them so well. When the production of a great artist who has lived a length of years has been small there is always the regret; but there is seldom, any more than here, the conceivable remedy. For the case is doubtless predetermined by the particular kind of great artist a writer happens to be, and this even if when we come to the conflict, to the historic case, deliberation and delay may not all have been imposed by temperament. The admirable George Sand, Flaubert's beneficent friend and correspondent, is exactly the happiest example we could find of the genius constitutionally incapable of worry, the genius for whom style "came," for whom the sought effect was ever quickly and easily struck off, the book freely and swiftly written, and who consequently is represented for us by upwards of ninety volumes. If the comparison were with this lady's great contemporary the elder Dumas the disparity would be quadrupled, but that ambiguous genius, somehow never really caught by us in the *fact* of composition, is out of our concern here: the issue is of those

developments of expression which involve a style,
and as Dumas never so much as once grazed one in
all his long career, there was not even enough of that
grace in him for a fillip of the finger-nail. Flaubert is
at any rate represented by six books, so that he may on
that estimate figure as poor, while Madame Sand,
falling so little short of a hundred, figures as rich;
and yet the fact remains that I can refer the congenial
mind to him with confidence and can do nothing of
the sort for it in respect to Madame Sand. She is
loose and liquid and iridescent, as iridescent as we may
undertake to find her; but I can imagine compositions
quite without virtue—the virtue I mean, of sticking
together—begotten by the impulse to emulate her.
She had undoubtedly herself the benefit of her facility,
but are we not left wondering to what extent *we* have
it? There is too little in her, by the literary connection,
for the critical mind, weary of much wandering, to
rest upon. Flaubert himself wandered, wandered far,
went much roundabout and sometimes lost himself
by the way, but how handsomely he provided for our
present repose! He found the French language incon-
ceivably difficult to write with elegance and was confronted with the equal truths that elegance is the last
thing that languages, even as they most mature, seem
to concern themselves with, and that at the same time
taste, asserting rights, insists on it, to the effect of
showing us in a boundless circumjacent waste of effort
what the absence of it may mean. He saw the less of
this desert of death come back to that—that everything at all saved from it for us since the beginning
had been saved by a soul of elegance within, or in
other words by the last refinement of selection, by the
indifference on the part of the very idiom, huge quite

other than "composing" agent, to the individual pretension. Recognising thus that to carry through the
individual pretension is at the best a battle, he adored
a hard surface and detested a soft one—much more a
muddled; regarded a style without rhythm and harmony as in a work of pretended beauty no style at all.
He considered that the failure of complete expression
so registered made of the work of pretended beauty a
work of achieved barbarity. It would take us far to
glance even at his fewest discriminations; but rhythm
and harmony were for example most menaced in his
scheme by repetition—when repetition had not a
positive grace; and were above all most at the mercy
of the bristling particles of which our modern tongues
are mainly composed and which make of the desired
surface a texture pricked through, from beneath, even
to destruction, as by innumerable thorns.

On these lines production was of course slow work for
him—especially as he met the difficulty, met it with
an inveteracy which shows how it *can* be met; and full
of interest for readers of English speech is the reflection he causes us to make as to the possibility of success at all comparable among ourselves. I have spoken
of his groans and imprecations, his interminable waits
and deep despairs; but what would these things have
been, what would have become of him and what of his
wrought residuum, had he been condemned to deal
with a form of speech consisting, like ours, as to one
part, of "that" and "which"; as to a second part, of
the blest "it," which an English sentence may repeat
in three or four opposed references without in the least
losing caste; as to a third face of all the "tos" of the
infinitive and the preposition; as to a fourth of our pre-

cious auxiliaries "be" and "do"; and as to a fifth, of whatever survives in the language for the precious art of pleasing? Whether or no the fact that the painter of "life" among us has to contend with a medium intrinsically indocile, on certain sides, like our own, whether this drawback accounts for his having failed, in our time, to treat us, arrested and charmed, to a single case of crowned classicism, there is at any rate no doubt that we in some degree owe Flaubert's counterweight for that deficiency to *his* having, on his own ground, more happily triumphed. By which I do not mean that "Madame Bovary" is a classic because the "thats," the "its" and the "tos" are made to march as Orpheus and his lute made the beasts, but because the element of order and harmony works as a symbol of everything else that is preserved for us by the history of the book. The history of the book remains the lesson and the important, the delightful thing, remains above all the drama that moves slowly to its climax. It is what we come back to for the sake of what it shows us. We see—from the present to the past indeed, never alas from the present to the future—how a classic almost inveterately grows. Unimportant, unnoticed, or, so far as noticed, contested, unrelated, alien, it has a cradle round which the fairies but scantly flock and is waited on in general by scarce a hint of significance. The significance comes by a process slow and small, the fact only that one perceptive private reader after another discovers at his convenience that the book is rare. The addition of the perceptive private readers is no quick affair, and would doubtless be a vain one did they not—while plenty of other much more remarkable books come and go—accumulate and count. They count by their quality and continuity of

attention; so they have gathered for "Madame Bovary," and so they are held. That is really once more
the great circumstance. It is always in order for us
to feel yet again what it is we are held by. Such is
my reason, definitely, for speaking of Flaubert as the
novelist's novelist. Are we not moreover—and let it
pass this time as a happy hope!—pretty well all novelists now?

HONORÉ DE BALZAC

1902

I

STRONGER than ever, even than under the spell of first acquaintance and of the early time, is the sense—thanks to a renewal of intimacy and, I am tempted to say, of loyalty—that Balzac stands signally apart, that he is the first and foremost member of his craft, and that above all the Balzac-lover is in no position till he has cleared the ground by saying so. The Balzac-lover alone, for that matter, is worthy to have his word on so happy an occasion as this[1] about the author of "La Comédie Humaine," and it is indeed not easy to see how the amount of attention so inevitably induced could at the worst have failed to find itself turning to an act of homage. I have been deeply affected, to be frank, by the mere refreshment of memory, which has brought in its train moreover consequences critical and sentimental too numerous to figure here in their completeness. The authors and the books that have, as we say, done something for us, become part of the answer to our curiosity when our curiosity had the freshness of youth, these particular agents exist for us, with the lapse of time, as the substance itself of knowledge: they have been intellectually so swallowed, digested and assimilated that we take their general

[1] The appearance of a translation of the "Deux Jeunes Mariées" in A Century of French Romance.

use and suggestion for granted, cease to be aware of them because they have passed out of sight. But they have passed out of sight simply by having passed into our lives. They have become a part of our personal history, a part of ourselves, very often, so far as we may have succeeded in best expressing ourselves. Endless, however, are the uses of great persons and great things, and it may easily happen in these cases that the connection, even as an "excitement"—the form mainly of the connections of youth —is never really broken. We have largely been living on our benefactor—which is the highest acknowledgment one can make; only, thanks to a blest law that operates in the long run to rekindle excitement, we are accessible to the sense of having neglected him. Even when we may not constantly have read him over the neglect is quite an illusion, but the illusion perhaps prepares us for the finest emotion we are to have owed to the acquaintance. Without having abandoned or denied our author we yet come expressly back to him, and if not quite in tatters and in penitence like the Prodigal Son, with something at all events of the tenderness with which we revert to the parental threshold and hearthstone, if not, more fortunately, to the parental presence. The beauty of this adventure, that of seeing the dust blown off a relation that had been put away as on a shelf, almost out of reach, at the back of one's mind, consists in finding the precious object not only fresh and intact, but with its firm lacquer still further figured, gilded and enriched. It is all overscored with traces and impressions—vivid, definite, almost as valuable as itself—of the recognitions and agitations it originally produced in us. Our old—that is our young—feelings are very nearly what page after page most gives us. The case has become a case of authority *plus* association. If Balzac in himself is indubitably wanting in the sufficiently common felicity we know as charm, it is this association that may on occasion contribute the grace.

The impression then, confirmed and brightened, is of the mass and weight of the figure and of the extent of ground it occupies; a tract on which we might all of us together quite pitch our little tents, open our little booths, deal in our little wares, and not materially either diminish the area or impede the circulation of the occupant. I seem to see him in such an image moving about as Gulliver among the pigmies, and not less good-natured than Gulliver for the exercise of any function, without exception, that can illustrate his larger life. The first and the last word about the author of "Les Contes Drolatiques" is that of all novelists he is the most serious—by which I am far from meaning that in the human comedy as he shows it the comic is an absent quantity. His sense of the comic was on the scale of his extraordinary senses in general, though his expression of it suffers perhaps exceptionally from that odd want of elbow-room—the penalty somehow of his close-packed, pressed-down contents—which reminds us of some designedly beautiful thing but half-disengaged from the clay or the marble. It is the scheme and the scope that are supreme in him, applying this moreover not to mere great intention, but to the concrete form, the proved case, in which we possess them. We most of us aspire to achieve at the best but a patch here and there, to pluck a sprig or a single branch, to break ground in a corner of the great garden of life. Balzac's plan was

simply to do everything that could be done. He
proposed to himself to "turn over" the great garden
from north to south and from east to west; a task—
immense, heroic, to this day immeasurable—that he
bequeathed us the partial performance of, a prodigious ragged clod, in the twenty monstrous years representing his productive career, years of concentration
and sacrifice the vision of which still makes us ache.
He had indeed a striking good fortune, the only one
he was to enjoy as an harassed and exasperated worker:
the great garden of life presented itself to him absolutely and exactly in the guise of the great garden of
France, a subject vast and comprehensive enough, yet
with definite edges and corners. This identity of his
universal with his local and national vision is the
particular thing we should doubtless call his greatest
strength were we preparing agreeably to speak of it
also as his visible weakness. Of Balzac's weaknesses,
however, it takes some assurance to talk; there is
always plenty of time for them; they are the last
signs we know him by—such things truly as in other
painters of manners often come under the head of
mere exuberance of energy. So little in short do they
earn the invidious name even when we feel them as
defects.

What he did above all was to read the universe, as
hard and as loud as he could, *into* the France of his
time; his own eyes regarding his work as at once the
drama of man and a mirror of the mass of social phenomena the most rounded and registered, most organised and administered, and thereby most exposed
to systematic observation and portrayal, that the
world had seen. There are happily other interesting

societies, but these are for schemes of such an order comparatively loose and incoherent, with more extent and perhaps more variety, but with less of the great enclosed and exhibited quality, less neatness and sharpness of arrangement, fewer categories, sub-divisions, juxtapositions. Balzac's France was both inspiring enough for an immense prose epic and re-ducible enough for a report or a chart. To allow his achievement all its dignity we should doubtless say also treatable enough for a history, since it was as a patient historian, a Benedictine of the actual, the living painter of his living time, that he regarded him-self and handled his material. All painters of manners and fashions, if we will, are historians, even when they least don the uniform: Fielding, Dickens, Thackeray, George Eliot, Hawthorne among ourselves. But the great difference between the great Frenchman and the eminent others is that, with an imagination of the highest power, an unequalled intensity of vision, he saw his subject in the light of science as well, in the light of the bearing of all its parts on each other, and under pressure of a passion for exactitude, an appetite, the appetite of an ogre, for *all* the kinds of facts. We find I think in the union here suggested something like the truth about his genius, the nearest approach to a final account of him. Of imagination on one side all compact, he was on the other an insatiable reporter of the immediate, the material, the current combina-tion, and perpetually moved by the historian's impulse to fix, preserve and explain them. One asks one's self as one reads him what concern the poet has with so much arithmetic and so much criticism, so many statistics and documents, what concern the critic and the economist have with so many passions, characters and adventures. The contradiction is always before us; it springs from the inordinate scale of the author's two faces; it explains more than anything else his eccentricities and difficulties. It accounts for his want of grace, his want of the lightness associated with an amusing literary form, his bristling surface, his closeness of texture, so rough with richness, yet so productive of the effect we have in mind when we speak of not being able to see the wood for the trees.

A thorough-paced votary, for that matter, can easily afford to declare at once that this confounding duality of character does more things still, or does at least the most important of all—introduces us without mercy (mercy for ourselves I mean) to the oddest truth we could have dreamed of meeting in such a connection. It was certainly *a priori* not to be expected we should feel it of him, but our hero is after all not in his magnificence totally an artist: which would be the strangest thing possible, one must hasten to add, were not the smallness of the practical difference so made even stranger. His endowment and his effect are each so great that the anomaly makes at the most a difference only by adding to his interest for the critic. The critic worth his salt is indiscreetly curious and wants ever to know how and why—whereby Balzac is thus a still rarer case for him, suggesting that exceptional curiosity may have exceptional rewards. The question of what makes the artist on a great scale is interesting enough; but we feel it in Balzac's company to be nothing to the question of what on an equal scale frustrates him. The scattered pieces, the *disjecta membra* of the character are here so numerous and so splendid that they prove misleading; we pile

them together, and the heap assuredly is monumental;
it forms an overtopping figure. The genius this figure
stands for, none the less, is really such a lesson to the
artist as perfection itself would be powerless to give;
it carries him so much further into the special mystery. Where it carries him, at the same time, I must
not in this scant space attempt to say—which would
be a loss of the fine thread of my argument. I stick
to our point in putting it, more concisely, that the
artist of the Comédie Humaine is half smothered by
the historian. Yet it belongs as well to the matter
also to meet the question of whether the historian
himself may not be an artist—in which case Balzac's
catastrophe would seem to lose its excuse. The answer
of course is that the reporter, however philosophic, has
one law, and the originator, however substantially fed,
has another; so that the two laws can with no sort of
harmony or congruity make, for the finer sense, a
common household. Balzac's catastrophe—so to name
it once again—was in this perpetual conflict and final
impossibility, an impossibility that explains his defeat
on the classic side and extends so far at times as to
make us think of his work as, from the point of view of
beauty, a tragic waste of effort.

What it would come to, we judge, is that the irreconcilability of the two kinds of law is, more simply
expressed, but the irreconcilability of two different
ways of composing one's effect. The principle of
composition that his free imagination would have, or
certainly might have, handsomely imposed on him is
perpetually dislocated by the quite opposite principle
of the earnest seeker, the inquirer to a useful end, in
whom nothing is free but a born antipathy to his yoke-

fellow. Such a production as "Le Curé de Village," the wonderful story of Madame Graslin, so nearly a masterpiece yet so ultimately not one, would be, in this connection, could I take due space for it, a perfect illustration. If, as I say, Madame Graslin's creator was confined by his doom to patches and pieces, no piece is finer than the first half of the book in question, the half in which the picture is determined by his unequalled power of putting people on their feet, planting them before us in their habit as they lived—a faculty nourished by observation as much as one will, but with the inner vision all the while wide-awake, the vision for which ideas are as living as facts and assume an equal intensity. This intensity, greatest indeed in the facts, has in Balzac a force all its own, to which none other in any novelist I know can be likened. His touch communicates on the spot to the object, the creature evoked, the hardness and permanence that certain substances, some sorts of stone, acquire by exposure to the air. The hardening medium, for the image soaked in it, is the air of his mind. It would take but little more to make the peopled world of fiction as we know it elsewhere affect us by contrast as a world of rather gray pulp. This mixture of the solid and the vivid is Balzac at his best, and it prevails without a break, without a note not admirably true, in "Le Curé de Village"—since I have named that instance—up to the point at which Madame Graslin moves out from Limoges to Montégnac in her ardent passion of penitence, her determination to expiate her strange and undiscovered association with a dark misdeed by living and working for others. Her drama is a particularly inward one, interesting, and in the highest degree, so long as she herself, her nature,

her behaviour, her personal history and the relations
in which they place her, control the picture and feed
our illusion.   The firmness with which the author
makes them play this part, the whole constitution of
the scene and of its developments from the moment
we cross the threshold of her dusky stuffy old-time
birth-house, is a rare delight, producing in the reader
that sense of local and material immersion which is
one of Balzac's supreme secrets.   What characteristically befalls, however, is that the spell accompanies
us but part of the way—only until, at a given moment,
his attention ruthlessly transfers itself from inside to
outside, from the centre of his subject to its circumference.

This is Balzac caught in the very fact of his monstrous duality, caught in his most complete self-ex-
pression.   He is clearly quite unwitting that in hand-
ing over his *data* to his twin-brother the impassioned
economist and surveyor, the insatiate general inquirer
and reporter, he is in any sort betraying our confidence,
for his good conscience at such times, the spirit of
edification in him, is a lesson even to the best of us,
his rich robust temperament nowhere more striking,
no more marked anywhere the great push of the
shoulder with which he makes his theme move, over-
charged though it may be like a carrier's van.   It is
not therefore assuredly that he loses either sincerity or
power in putting before us to the last detail such a matter as, in this case, his heroine's management of her
property, her tenantry, her economic opportunities and
visions, for these are cases in which he never shrinks
nor relents, in which positively he stiffens and terribly
towers—to remind us again of M. Taine's simplifying

word about his being an artist doubled with a man of
business. Balzac was indeed doubled if ever a writer
was, and to that extent that we almost as often, while
we read, feel ourselves thinking of him as a man of
business doubled with an artist. Whichever way we
turn it the oddity never fails, nor the wonder of the
ease with which either character bears the burden of
the other. I use the word burden because, as the fusion
is never complete—witness in the book before us the
fatal break of "tone," the one unpardonable sin for
the novelist—we are beset by the conviction that but
for this strangest of dooms one or other of the two
partners might, to our relief and to his own, have been
disembarrassed. The disembarrassment, for each, by
a more insidious fusion, would probably have conduced
to the mastership of interest proceeding from form, or
at all events to the search for it, that Balzac fails to
embody. Perhaps the possibility of an artist constructed on such strong lines is one of those fine things
that are not of this world, a mere dream of the fond
critical spirit. Let these speculations and condona-
tions at least pass as the amusement, as a result of the
high spirits—if high spirits be the word—of the reader
feeling himself again in touch. It was not of our
author's difficulties—that is of his difficulty, the great
one—that I proposed to speak, but of his immense
clear action. Even that is not truly an impression of
ease, and it is strange and striking that we are in fact
so attached by his want of the unity that keeps surfaces smooth and dangers down as scarce to feel sure
at any moment that we shall not come back to it
with most curiosity. We are never so curious about
successes as about interesting failures. The more
reason therefore to speak promptly, and once for all,

of the scale on which, in its own quarter of his genius, success worked itself out for him.

It is to that I *should* come back—to the infinite reach in him of the painter and the poet. We can never know what might have become of him with less importunity in his consciousness of the machinery of life, of its furniture and fittings, of all that, right and left, he causes to assail us, sometimes almost to suffocation, under the general rubric of *things*. Things, in this sense with him, are at once our delight and our despair; we pass from being inordinately beguiled and convinced by them to feeling that his universe fairly smells too much of them, that the larger ether, the diviner air, is in peril of finding among them scarce room to circulate. His landscapes, his "local colour" —thick in his pages at a time when it was to be found in his pages almost alone—his towns, his streets, his houses, his Saumurs, Angoulêmes, Guérandes, his great prose Turner-views of the land of the Loire, his rooms, shops, interiors, details of domesticity and traffic, are a short list of the terms into which he saw the real as clamouring to be rendered and into which he rendered it with unequalled authority. It would be doubtless more to the point to make our profit of this consummation than to try to reconstruct a Balzac planted more in the open. We hardly, as the case stands, know most whether to admire in such an example as the short tale of "La Grenadière" the exquisite feeling for "natural objects" with which it overflows like a brimming wine-cup, the energy of perception and description which so multiplies them for beauty's sake and for the love of their beauty, or the general wealth of genius that can calculate, or at

least count, so little and spend so joyously. The tale
practically exists for the sake of the enchanting aspects involved—those of the embowered white house
that nestles on its terraced hill above the great French
river, and we can think, frankly, of no one else with
an equal amount of business on his hands who would
either have so put himself out for aspects or made them
almost by themselves a living subject. A born son of
Touraine, it must be said, he pictures his province,
on every pretext and occasion, with filial passion and
extraordinary breadth. The prime aspect in his
scene all the while, it must be added, is the money
aspect. The general money question so loads him up
and weighs him down that he moves through the human
comedy, from beginning to end, very much in the
fashion of a camel, the ship of the desert, surmounted
with a cargo. "Things" for him are francs and cen-
times more than any others, and I give up as inscrutable, unfathomable, the nature, the peculiar avidity
of his interest in them. It makes us wonder again
and again what then is the use on Balzac's scale of
the divine faculty. The imagination, as we all know,
may be employed up to a certain point in inventing
uses for money; but its office beyond that point is
surely to make us forget that anything so odious exists.
This is what Balzac never forgot; his universe goes on
expressing itself for him, to its furthest reaches, on
its finest sides, in the terms of the market. To say
these things, however, is after all to come out where
we want, to suggest his extraordinary scale and his
terrible completeness. I am not sure that he does not
see character too, see passion, motive, personality, as
quite in the order of the "things" we have spoken of.
He makes them no less concrete and palpable, handles

them no less directly and freely. It is the whole business in fine—that grand total to which he proposed to himself to do high justice—that gives him his place apart, makes him, among the novelists, the largest weightiest presence. There are some of his obsessions —that of the material, that of the financial, that of the "social," that of the technical, political, civil— for which I feel myself unable to judge him, judgment losing itself unexpectedly in a particular shade of pity. The way to judge him is to try to walk all round him— on which we see how remarkably far we have to go. He is the only member of his order really monumental, the sturdiest-seated mass that rises in our path.

II

We recognise none the less that the finest consequence of these re-established relations is linked with just that appearance in him, that obsession of the actual under so many heads, that makes us look at him, as we would at some rare animal in captivity, between the bars of a cage. It amounts to a sort of suffered doom, since to be solicited by the world from all quarters at once, what is that for the spirit but a denial of escape? We feel his doom to be his want of a private door, and that he felt it, though more obscurely, himself. When we speak of his want of charm therefore we perhaps so surrender the question as but to show our own poverty. If charm, to cut it short, is what he lacks, how comes it that he so touches and holds us that—above all if we be actual or possible fellow-workers—we are uncomfortably conscious of the disloyalty of almost any shade of surrender? We are lodged perhaps by our excited sensibility in a di-

lemma of which one of the horns is a compassion that
savours of patronage; but we must resign ourselves
to that by reflecting that our partiality at least takes
nothing away from him. It leaves him solidly where
he is and only brings us near, brings us to a view of *all*
his formidable parts and properties. The conception
of the Comédie Humaine represents them all, and represents them mostly in their felicity and their triumph
—or at least the execution does: in spite of which we
irresistibly find ourselves thinking of him, in reperusals,
as most essentially the victim of a cruel joke. The
joke is one of the jokes of fate, the fate that rode him
for twenty years at so terrible a pace and with the whip
so constantly applied. To have wanted to do so much,
to have thought it possible, to have faced and in a manner resisted the effort, to have felt life poisoned and
consumed by such a bravery of self-committal—these
things form for us in him a face of trouble that, oddly
enough, is not appreciably lighted by the fact of his
success. It was the having wanted to do so much that
was the trap, whatever possibilities of glory might
accompany the good faith with which he fell into it.
What accompanies *us* as we frequent him is a sense of
the deepening ache of that good faith with the increase
of his working consciousness, the merciless development of his huge subject and of the rigour of all the
conditions. We see the whole thing quite as if Destiny had said to him: "You want to 'do' France, presumptuous, magnificent, miserable man—the France
of revolutions, revivals, restorations, of Bonapartes,
Bourbons, republics, of war and peace, of blood and
romanticism, of violent change and intimate continuity,
the France of the first half of your century? Very
well; you most distinctly *shall*, and you shall partic-

ularly let me hear, even if the great groan of your labour do fill at moments the temple of letters, how you like the job." We must of course not appear to deny the existence of a robust joy in him, the joy of power and creation, the joy of the observer and the dreamer who finds a use for his observations and his dreams as fast as they come. The "Contes Drolatiques" would by themselves sufficiently contradict us, and the savour of the "Contes Drolatiques" is not confined to these productions. His work at large tastes of the same kind of humour, and we feel him again and again, like any other great healthy producer of these matters, beguiled and carried along. He would have been, I dare say, the last not to insist that the artist has pleasures forever indescribable; he lived in short in his human comedy with the largest life we can attribute to the largest capacity. There are particular parts of his subject from which, with our sense of his enjoyment of them, we have to check the impulse to call him away—frequently as I confess in this relation that impulse arises.

The relation is with the special element of his spectacle from which he never fully detaches himself, the element, to express it succinctly, of the "old families" and the great ladies. Balzac frankly revelled in his conception of an aristocracy—a conception that never succeeded in becoming his happiest; whether, objectively, thanks to the facts supplied him by the society he studied, or through one of the strangest deviations of taste that the literary critic is in an important connection likely to encounter. Nothing would in fact be more interesting than to attempt a general measure of the part played in the total comedy, to his imagina-

tion, by the old families; and one or two contributions
to such an attempt I must not fail presently to make.
I glance at them here, however, the delectable class,
but as most representing on the author's part free and
amused creation; by which too I am far from hinting
that the amusement is at all at their expense. It is in
their great ladies that the old families most shine out
for him, images of strange colour and form, but "felt"
as we say, to their finger-tips, and extraordinarily interesting as a mark of the high predominance—predominance of character, of cleverness, of will, of general "personality"—that almost every scene of the
Comedy attributes to women. It attributes to them
in fact a recognised, an uncontested supremacy; it
is through them that the hierarchy of old families most
expresses itself; and it is as surrounded by them even
as some magnificent indulgent pasha by his overflowing seraglio that Balzac sits most at his ease. All of
which reaffirms—if it be needed—that his inspiration,
and the sense of it, were even greater than his task.
And yet such betrayals of spontaneity in him make
for an old friend at the end of the chapter no great difference in respect to the pathos—since it amounts to
that—of his genius-ridden aspect. It comes to us as
we go back to him that his spirit had fairly made of
itself a cage in which he was to turn round and round,
always unwinding his reel, much in the manner of
a criminal condemned to hard labour for life. The
cage is simply the complicated but dreadfully definite
French world that built itself so solidly in and roofed
itself so impenetrably over him.

It is not that, caught there with him though we be,
we ourselves prematurely seek an issue: we throw our-

selves back, on the contrary, for the particular sense of it, into his ancient superseded comparatively *rococo* and quite patriarchal France—patriarchal in spite of social and political convulsions; into his old-time ante-diluvian Paris, all picturesque and all workable, full, to the fancy, of an amenity that has passed away; into his intensely differentiated sphere of *la province*, evoked in each sharpest or faintest note of its difference, described systematically as narrow and flat, and yet attaching us if only by the contagion of the author's overflowing sensibility. He feels in his vast exhibition many things, but there is nothing he feels with the communicable shocks and vibrations, the sustained fury of perception—not always a fierceness of judgment, which is another matter—that *la province* excites in him. Half our interest in him springs still from our own sense that, for all the convulsions, the revolutions and experiments that have come and gone, the order he describes is the old order that our sense of the past perversely recurs to as to something happy we have irretrievably missed. His pages bristle with the revelation of the lingering earlier world, the world in which places and people still had their queerness, their strong marks, their sharp type, and in which, as before the platitude that was to come, the observer with an appetite for the salient could by way of precaution fill his lungs. Balzac's appetite for the salient was voracious, yet he came, as it were, in time, in spite of his so often speaking as if what he sees about him is but the last desolation of the modern. His conservatism, the most entire, consistent and convinced that ever was—yet even at that much inclined to whistling in the dark as if to the tune of "Oh how mediæval I *am!*"—was doubtless the best point of view from which he could rake his

field. But if what he sniffed from afar in that position
was the extremity of change, we in turn feel both
subject and painter drenched with the smell of the past.
It is preserved in his work as nowhere else—not vague
nor faint nor delicate, but as strong to-day as when
first distilled.

It may seem odd to find a conscious melancholy in
the fact that a great worker succeeded in clasping his
opportunity in such an embrace, this being exactly
our usual measure of the felicity of great workers. I
speak, I hasten to reassert, all in the name of sympathy—without which it would have been detestable to
speak at all; and the sentiment puts its hand instinctively on the thing that makes it least futile. This
particular thing then is not in the least Balzac's own
hold of his terrible mass of matter; it is absolutely the
convolutions of the serpent he had with a magnificent
courage invited to wind itself round him. We must
use the common image—he had created his Franken-
stein monster. It is the fellow-craftsman who can
most feel for him—it being apparently possible to read
him from another point of view without getting really
into his presence. We undergo with him from book
to book, from picture to picture, the convolutions of
the serpent, we especially whose refined performances
are given, as we know, but with the small common or
garden snake. I stick to this to justify my image
just above of his having been "caged" by the intensity
with which he saw his general matter as a whole. To
see it always as a whole is our wise, our virtuous effort,
the very condition, as we keep in mind, of superior
art. Balzac was in this connection then wise and virtuous to the most exemplary degree; so that he doubt-

less ought logically but to prompt to complacent reflections. No painter ever saw his general matter nearly so much as a whole. Why is it then that we hover about him, if we are real Balzacians, not with cheerful chatter, but with a consideration deeper in its reach than any mere moralising? The reason is largely that if you wish with absolute immaculate virtue to look at your matter as a whole and yet remain a theme for cheerful chatter, you must be careful to take some quantity that will not hug you to death. Balzac's active intention was, to vary our simile, a beast with a hundred claws, and the spectacle is in the hugging process of which, as energy against energy, the beast was capable. Its victim died of the process at fifty, and if what we see in the long gallery in which it is mirrored is not the defeat, but the admirable resistance, we none the less never lose the sense that the fighter is shut up with his fate. He has locked himself in—it is doubtless his own fault—and thrown the key away. Most of all perhaps the impression comes—the impression of the adventurer committed and anxious, but with no retreat—from the so formidably concrete nature of his plastic stuff. When we work in the open, as it were, our material is not classed and catalogued, so that we have at hand a hundred ways of being loose, superficial, disingenuous, and yet passing, to our no small profit, for remarkable. Balzac had no "open"; he held that the great central normal fruitful country of his birth and race, overarched with its infinite social complexity, yielded a sufficiency of earth and sea and sky. We seem to see as his catastrophe that the sky, all the same, came down on him. He couldn't keep it up—in more senses than one. These are perhaps fine fancies for a critic to weave about a literary figure of whom he has undertaken to give a plain account; but I leave them so on the plea that there are relations in which, for the Balzacian, criticism simply drops out. That is not a liberty, I admit, ever to be much encouraged; critics in fact are the only people who have a right occasionally to take it. There is no such plain account of the Comédie Humaine as that it makes us fold up our yard-measure and put away our note-book quite as we do with some extraordinary character, some mysterious and various stranger, who brings with him his own standards and his own air. There is a kind of eminent presence that abashes even the interviewer, moves him to respect and wonder, makes him, for consideration itself, not insist. This takes of course a personage sole of his kind. But such a personage precisely is Balzac.

III

By all of which have I none the less felt it but too clear that I must not pretend in this place to take apart the pieces of his immense complicated work, to number them or group them or dispose them about. The most we can do is to pick one up here and there and wonder, as we weigh it in our hand, at its close compact substance. That is all even M. Taine could do in the longest and most penetrating study of which our author has been the subject. Every piece we handle is so full of stuff, condensed like the edibles provided for campaigns and explorations, positively so charged with distilled life, that we find ourselves dropping it, in certain states of sensibility, as we drop an object unguardedly touched that startles us by being animate. We seem really scarce to want anything to *be* so animate. It would verily take Balzac to detail Balzac, and he has had in fact Balzacians nearly enough affiliated to affront the task with courage. The "Répertoire de la Comédie Humaine" of MM. Anatole Cerfberr and Jules Christophe is a closely-printed octavo of 550 pages which constitutes in relation to his characters great and small an impeccable biographical dictionary. His votaries and expositors are so numerous that the Balzac library of comment and research must be, of its type, one of the most copious. M. de Lovenjoul has laboured all round the subject; his "Histoire des Œuvres" alone is another crowded octavo of 400 pages; in connection with which I must mention Miss Wormeley, the devoted American translator, interpreter, worshipper, who in the course of her own studies has so often found occasion to differ from M. de Lovenjoul on matters of fact and questions of date and of appreciation. Miss Wormeley, M. Paul Bourget and many others are examples of the passionate piety that our author can inspire. As I turn over the encyclopedia of his characters I note that whereas such works usually commemorate but the ostensibly eminent of a race and time, every creature so much as named in the fictive swarm is in this case preserved to fame: so close is the implication that to have *been* named by such a dispenser of life and privilege is to be, as we say it of baronets and peers, created. He infinitely divided moreover, as we know, he subdivided, altered and multiplied his heads and categories—his "Vie Parisienne," his "Vie de Province," his "Vie Politique," his "Parents Pauvres," his "Études Philosophiques," his "Splendeurs et Misères des Courtisanes," his "Envers de l'Histoire Contemporaine" and all the rest; so that nominal reference to them becomes the more difficult. Yet without prejudice either to the energy of conception with which he mapped out his theme as with chalk on a huge blackboard, or to the prodigious patience with which he executed his plan, practically filling in with a wealth of illustration, from sources that to this day we fail to make out, every compartment of his table, M. de Lovenjoul draws up the list, year by year, from 1822 to 1848, of his mass of work, giving us thus the measure of the tension represented for him by almost any twelvemonth. It is wholly unequalled, considering the quality of Balzac's show, by any other eminent abundance.

I must be pardoned for coming back to it, for seeming unable to leave it; it enshrouds so interesting a mystery. How was so solidly systematic a literary attack on life to be conjoined with whatever workable minimum of needful intermission, of free observation, of personal experience? Some small possibility of personal experience and disinterested life must, at the worst, from deep within or far without, feed and fortify the strained productive machine. These things were luxuries that Balzac appears really never to have tasted on any appreciable scale. His published letters—the driest and most starved of those of any man of equal distinction—are with the exception of those to Madame de Hanska, whom he married shortly before his death, almost exclusively the audible wail of a galley-slave chained to the oar. M. Zola, in our time, among the novelists, has sacrificed to the huge plan in something of the same manner, yet with goodly modern differences that leave him a comparatively simple instance. His work assuredly has been more nearly dried up by the

sacrifice than ever Balzac's was—so miraculously,
given the conditions, was Balzac's to escape the anti-
climax.   Method and system, in the chronicle of the
tribe of Rougon-Macquart, an economy in itself certainly of the rarest and most interesting, have spread
so from centre to circumference that they have ended
by being almost the only thing we feel.   And then
M. Zola has survived and triumphed in his lifetime,
has continued and lasted, has piled up and, if the
remark be not frivolous, enjoyed in all its *agréments*
the reward for which Balzac toiled and sweated in
vain.   On top of which he will have had also his
literary great-grandfather's heroic example to start
from and profit by, the positive heritage of a *fils de
famille* to enjoy, spend, save, waste.   Balzac had
frankly no heritage at all but his stiff subject, and by
way of model not even in any direct or immediate
manner that of the inner light and kindly admonition
of his genius.   Nothing adds more to the strangeness
of his general performance than his having failed so
long to find his inner light, groped for it almost ten
years, missed it again and again, moved straight away
from it, turned his back on it, lived in fine round about
it, in a darkness still scarce penetrable, a darkness into
which we peep only half to make out the dreary little
waste of his numerous *œuvres de jeunesse*.   To M. Zola
was vouchsafed the good fortune of settling down to the
Rougon-Macquart with the happiest promptitude; it
was as if time for one look about him—and I say it
without disparagement to the reach of his look—had
sufficiently served his purpose.   Balzac moreover might
have written five hundred novels without our feeling
in him the faintest hint of the breath of doom, if he
had only been comfortably capable of conceiving the

short cut of the fashion practised by others under his
eyes.   As Alexandre Dumas and George Sand, illustrious contemporaries, cultivated a personal life and
a disinterested consciousness by the bushel, having, for
their easier duration, not too consistently known, as
the true painter knows it, the obsession of the thing to
be done, so Balzac was condemned by his constitution
itself, by his inveterately seeing this "thing to be done"
as part and parcel, as of the very essence, of his enterprise.   The latter existed for him, as the process worked
and hallucination settled, in the form, and the form
only, of the thing done, and not in any hocus-pocus
about doing.   There was no kindly convenient escape
for him by the little swinging back-door of the thing
not done.   He desired—no man more—to get out of
his obsession, but only at the other end, that is by
boring through it.   "How then, thus deprived of the
outer air almost as much as if he were gouging a passage for a railway through an Alp, *did* he live ?" is the
question that haunts us—with the consequence for
the most part of promptly meeting its fairly tragic
answer.   He did *not* live—save in his imagination, or
by other aid than he could find there; his imagination
was all his experience; he had provably no time for
the real thing.   This brings us to the rich if simple
truth that his imagination alone did the business, carried through both the conception and the execution—
as large an effort and as proportionate a success, in all
but the vulgar sense, as the faculty when equally
handicapped was ever concerned in.   Handicapped I
say because this interesting fact about him, with the
claim it makes, rests on the ground, the high distinction, that more than all the rest of us put together he
went in, as we say, for detail, circumstance and spec-

ification, proposed to himself *all* the connections of every part of his matter and the full total of the parts. The whole thing, it is impossible not to keep repeating, was what he deemed treatable. One really knows in all imaginative literature no undertaking to compare with it for courage, good faith and sublimity. There, once more, was the necessity that rode him and that places him apart in our homage. It is no light thing to have been condemned to become provably sublime. And looking through, or trying to, at what is beneath and behind, we are left benevolently uncertain if the predominant quantity be audacity or innocence.

It is of course inevitable at this point to seem to hear the colder critic promptly take us up. He undertook the whole thing—oh exactly, the ponderous person! But *did* he "do" the whole thing, if you please, any more than sundry others of fewer pretensions? The retort to this it can only be a positive joy to make, so high a note instantly sounds as an effect of the inquiry. Nothing is more interesting and amusing than to find one's self recognising both that Balzac's pretensions were immense, portentous, and that yet, taking him —and taking *them*—altogether, they but minister in the long run to our fondness. They affect us not only as the endearing eccentricities of a person we greatly admire, but fairly as the very condition of his having become such a person. We take them thus in the first place for the very terms of his plan, and in the second for a part of that high robustness and that general richness of nature which made him in face of such a project believe in himself. One would really scarce have liked to see such a job as La Comédie Humaine tackled without swagger. To think of the thing

really as practicable *was* swagger, and of the very
rarest order. So to think assuredly implied pretensions,
pretensions that risked showing as monstrous should
the enterprise fail to succeed. It is for the colder
critic to take the trouble to make out that of the two
parties to it the body of pretension remains greater
than the success. One may put it moreover at the
worst for him, may recognise that it is in the matter
of opinion still more than in the matter of knowledge
that Balzac offers himself as universally competent.
He has flights of judgment—on subjects the most
special as well as the most general—that are vertig-
inous and on his alighting from which we greet him
with a special indulgence. We can easily imagine
him to respond, confessing humorously—if he had only
time—to such a benevolent understanding smile as
would fain hold our own eyes a moment. Then it is
that he would most show us his scheme and his necessities and how in operation they all hang together.
Naturally everything about everything, though how
he had time to learn it is the last thing he has time to
tell us; which matters the less, moreover, as it is not
over the question of his knowledge that we sociably
invite him, as it were (and remembering the two augurs
behind the altar) to wink at us for a sign. His convictions it is that are his great pardonable "swagger";
to them in particular I refer as his general operative
condition, the constituted terms of his experiment,
and not less as his consolation, his support, his amusement by the way. They embrace everything in the
world—that is in his world of the so parti-coloured
France of his age: religion, morals, politics, economics,
physics, esthetics, letters, art, science, sociology, every
question of faith, every branch of research. They

represent thus his equipment of ideas, those ideas of which it will never do for a man who aspires to constitute a State to be deprived. He must take them with him as an ambassador extraordinary takes with him secretaries, uniforms, stars and garters, a gilded coach and a high assurance. Balzac's opinions are his gilded coach, in which he is more amused than anything else to feel himself riding, but which is indispensably concerned in getting him over the ground. What more inevitable than that they should be intensely Catholic, intensely monarchical, intensely saturated with the real genius—as between 1830 and 1848 he believed it to be—of the French character and French institutions?

Nothing is happier for us than that he should have enjoyed his outlook before the first half of the century closed. He could then still treat his subject as comparatively homogeneous. Any country could have a Revolution—every country *had* had one. A Restoration was merely what a revolution involved, and the Empire had been for the French but a revolutionary incident, in addition to being by good luck for the novelist an immensely pictorial one. He was free therefore to arrange the background of the comedy in the manner that seemed to him best to suit anything so great; in the manner at the same time prescribed according to his contention by the noblest traditions. The church, the throne, the noblesse, the bourgeoisie, the people, the peasantry, all in their order and each solidly kept in it, these were precious things, things his superabundant insistence on the price of which is what I refer to as his exuberance of opinion. It was a luxury for more reasons than one, though one, presently to be mentioned, handsomely predominates. The meaning of that exchange of intelligences in the rear of the oracle which I have figured for him with the perceptive friend bears simply on his pleading guilty to the purport of the friend's discrimination. The point the latter makes with him—a beautiful cordial critical point—is that he truly cares for nothing in the world, thank goodness, so much as for the passions and embroilments of men and women, the free play of character and the sharp revelation of type, all the real stuff of drama and the natural food of novelists. Religion, morals, politics, economics, esthetics would be thus, as systematic matter, very well in their place, but quite secondary and subservient. Balzac's attitude is again and again that he cares for the adventures and emotions because, as his last word, he cares for the good and the greatness of the State— which is where his swagger, with a whole society on his hands, comes in. What we on our side in a thousand places gratefully feel is that he cares for his monarchical and hierarchical and ecclesiastical society because it rounds itself for his mind into the most congruous and capacious theatre for the repertory of his innumerable comedians. It has above all, for a painter abhorrent of the superficial, the inestimable benefit of the accumulated, of strong marks and fine shades, contrasts and complications. There had certainly been since 1789 dispersals and confusions enough, but the thick tradition, no more at the most than half smothered, lay under them all. So the whole of his faith and no small part of his working omniscience were neither more nor less than that historic sense which I have spoken of as the spur of his invention and which he possessed as no other novelist has done.

We immediately feel that to name it in connection with him is to answer every question he suggests and to account for each of his idiosyncrasies in turn. The novel, the tale, however brief, the passage, the sentence by itself, the situation, the person, the place, the motive exposed, the speech reported—these things were in his view history, with the absoluteness and the dignity of history. This is the source both of his weight and of his wealth. What is the historic sense after all but animated, but impassioned knowledge seeking to enlarge itself? I have said that his imagination did the whole thing, no other explanation—no reckoning of the possibilities of personal saturation— meeting the mysteries of the case. Therefore his imagination achieved the miracle of absolutely resolving itself into multifarious knowledge. Since history proceeds by documents he constructed, as he needed them, the documents too—fictive sources that imitated the actual to the life. It was of course a terrible business, but at least in the light of it his claims to creatorship are justified—which is what was to be shown.

IV

It is very well even in the sketchiest attempt at a portrait of his genius to try to take particulars in their order: one peeps over the shoulder of another at the moment we get a feature into focus. The loud appeal not to be left out prevails among them all, and certainly with the excuse that each as we fix it seems to fall most into the picture. I have so indulged myself as to his general air that I find a whole list of vivid contributive marks almost left on my hands. Such a list, in any study of Balzac, is delightful for intimate

edification as well as for the fine humour of the thing;
we proceed from one of the items of his breathing
physiognomy to the other with quite the same sense
of life, the same active curiosity, with which we push
our way through the thick undergrowth of one of the
novels. The difficulty is really that the special point
for which we at the moment observe him melts into
all the other points, is swallowed up before our eyes in
the formidable mass. The French apply the happiest
term to certain characters when they speak of them
as *entiers*, and if the word had been invented for Balzac
it could scarce better have expressed him. He is
"entire" as was never a man of his craft; he moves
always in his mass; wherever we find him we find him
in force; whatever touch he applies he applies it with
his whole apparatus. He is like an army gathered to
besiege a cottage equally with a city, and living vo-
raciously in either case on all the country about. It
may well be, at any rate, that his infatuation with the
idea of the social, the practical primacy of "the sex"
is the article at the top of one's list; there could certainly be no better occasion than this of a rich reissue
of the "Deux Jeunes Mariées" for placing it there at
a venture. Here indeed precisely we get a sharp example of the way in which, as I have just said, a capital
illustration of one of his sides becomes, just as we take
it up, a capital illustration of another. The correspondence of Louise de Chaulieu and Renée de Mau-
combe is in fact one of those cases that light up with
a great golden glow all his parts at once. We needn't
mean by this that such parts are themselves absolutely
all golden—given the amount of tinsel for instance in
his view, supereminent, transcendent here, of the old
families and the great ladies. What we do convey,

however, is that his creative temperament finds in such *data* as these one of its best occasions for shining out. Again we fondly recognise his splendid, his attaching swagger—that of a "bounder" of genius and of feeling; again we see how, with opportunity, its elements may vibrate into a perfect ecstasy of creation.

Why shouldn't·a man swagger, he treats us to the diversion of asking ourselves, who has created from top to toe the most brilliant, the most historic, the most insolent, above all the most detailed and discriminated of aristocracies? Balzac carried the uppermost class of his comedy, from the princes, dukes, and unspeakable duchesses down to his poor barons *de province*, about in his pocket as he might have carried a tolerably befingered pack of cards, to deal them about with a flourish of the highest authority whenever there was the chance of a game. He knew them up and down and in and out, their arms, infallibly supplied, their quarterings, pedigrees, services, intermarriages, relationships, ramifications and other enthralling attributes. This indeed is comparatively simple learning; the real wonder is rather when we linger on the ground of the patrician consciousness itself, the innermost, the esoteric, the spirit, temper, tone—tone above all—of the titled and the proud. The questions multiply for every scene of the comedy; there is no one who makes us walk in such a cloud of them. The clouds elsewhere, in comparison, are at best of questions not worth asking. *Was* the patrician consciousness that figured as our author's model so splendidly fatuous as he—almost without irony, often in fact with a certain poetic sympathy—everywhere represents it? His imagination lives in it, breathes its scented air, swallows

this element with the smack of the lips of the con-
noisseur; but I feel that we never know, even to the
end, whether he be here directly historic or only quite
misguidedly romantic. The romantic side of him has
the extent of all the others; it represents in the oddest
manner his escape from the walled and roofed structure into which he had built himself—his longing for
the vaguely-felt outside and as much as might be of the
rest of the globe. But it is characteristic of him that
the most he could do for this relief was to bring the
fantastic into the circle and fit it somehow to his conditions. Was his tone for the duchess, the marquise
but the imported fantastic, one of those smashes of
the window-pane of the real that reactions sometimes
produce even in the stubborn? or are we to take it as
observed, as really reported, as, for all its difference
from our notion of the natural—and, quite as much,
of the artificial—in another and happier strain of manners, substantially true? The whole episode, in "Les
Illusions Perdues," of Madame de Bargeton's "chuck-
ing" Lucien de Rubempré, on reaching Paris with
him, under pressure of Madame d'Espard's shock-
ability as to his coat and trousers and other such matters, is either a magnificent lurid document or the
baseless fabric of a vision. The great wonder is that,
as I rejoice to put it, we can never really discover
which, and that we feel as we read that we can't, and
that we suffer at the hands of no other author this particular helplessness of immersion. It is *done*—we are
always thrown back on that; we can't get out of it;
all we can do is to say that the true itself can't be more
than done and that if the false in this way equals it
we must give up looking for the difference. Alone
among novelists Balzac has the secret of an insistence
that somehow makes the difference nought. He

warms his facts into life—as witness the certainty that the episode I just cited has absolutely as much of that property as if perfect matching had been achieved. If the great ladies in question *didn't* behave, wouldn't, couldn't have behaved, like a pair of nervous snobs, why so much the worse, we say to ourselves, for the great ladies in question. We *know* them so—they owe their being to our so seeing them; whereas we never can tell ourselves how we should otherwise have known them or what quantity of being they would on a different footing have been able to put forth.

The case is the same with Louise de Chaulieu, who besides coming out of her convent school, as a quite young thing, with an amount of sophistication that would have chilled the heart of a horse-dealer, exhales —and to her familiar friend, a young person of a supposedly equal breeding—an extravagance of complacency in her "social position" that makes us rub our eyes. Whereupon after a little the same phenomenon occurs; we swallow her bragging, against our better reason, or at any rate against our startled sense, under coercion of the total intensity. We do more than this, we cease to care for the question, which loses itself in the hot fusion of the whole picture. He has "gone for" his subject, in the vulgar phrase, with an avidity that makes the attack of his most eminent rivals affect us as the intercourse between introduced indifferences at a dull evening party. He squeezes it till it cries out, we hardly know whether for pleasure or pain. In the case before us for example—without wandering from book to book, impossible here, I make the most of the ground already broken—he has seen at once that the state of marriage itself, sounded to its depths, is, in the connection, his real theme. He sees it of course in the conditions that exist for him, but he weighs it to the last ounce, feels it in all its dimensions, as well as in all his own, and would scorn to take refuge in any engaging side-issue. He gets, for further intensity, into the very skin of his *jeunes mariées*—into each alternately, as they are different enough; so that, to repeat again, any other mode of representing women, or of representing anybody, becomes, in juxtaposition, a thing so void of the active contortions of truth as to be comparatively wooden. He bears children with Madame de l'Estorade, knows intimately how she suffers for them, and not less intimately how her correspondent suffers, as well as enjoys, without them. Big as he is he makes himself small to be handled by her with young maternal passion and positively to handle her in turn with infantile innocence. These things are the very flourishes, the little technical amusements of his penetrating power. But it is doubtless in his hand for such a matter as the jealous passion of Louise de Chaulieu, the free play of her intelligence and the almost beautiful good faith of her egotism, that he is most individual. It is one of the neatest examples of his extraordinary leading gift, his art—which is really moreover not an art—of working the exhibition of a given character up to intensity. I say it is not an art because it acts for us rather as a hunger on the part of his nature to take on in all freedom another nature—take it by a direct process of the senses. Art is for the mass of us who have only the process of art, comparatively so stiff. The thing amounts with him to a kind of shameless personal, physical, not merely intellectual, duality—the very spirit and secret of transmigration.

HONORÉ DE BALZAC

1913

It is a pleasure to meet M. Émile Faguet[1] on the same ground of mastered critical method and in the same air of cool deliberation and conclusion that so favoured his excellent study of Flaubert in the rich series to which the present volume belongs. It was worth while waiting these many years for a Balzac to get it at last from a hand of so firm a grip, if not quite of the very finest manipulative instinct. It can scarce ever be said of M. Faguet that he tends to play with a subject, at least a literary one; but nobody is better for circling his theme in sound and easy pedestrian fashion, for taking up each of its aspects in order, for a sense, above all, of the order in which they *should* be taken, and for then, after doing them successively justice, reaching the point from which they appear to melt together. He thus gives us one of those literary portraits the tradition of which, so far at least as they are the fruit of method, has continued scantily to flourish among ourselves. We cannot help thinking indeed that an ideally authoritative portrait of Balzac would be the work of some pondering painter able to measure the great man's bequest a little more from within or by a coincidence of special faculty, or that in other words the particular initiation and fellow-

[1] Balzac. Par Émile Faguet, de l'Académie Française. Les Grands Ecrivains Français. Paris, Hachette, 1913.

feeling of some like—that is not too unlike—imaginative projector as well are rather wanted here to warm
and colour the critical truth to the right glow of appreciation. Which comes to saying, we quite acknowledge,
that a "tribute" to Balzac, of however embracing an
intention, may still strike us as partly unachieved if
we fail to catch yearning and shining through it, like
a motive in a musical mixture or a thread of gold in a
piece of close weaving, the all but overriding sympathy
of novelist with novelist. M. Faguet's intelligence at
any rate sweeps his ground clear of the anecdotal,
the question-begging reference to odds and ends of
the personal and superficial, in a single short chapter,
and, having got so promptly over this second line of
defence, attacks at once the issue of his author's general ideas—matters apt to be, in any group of con-
tributors to a "series" of our own, exactly what the
contributor most shirks considering.

It is true that few writers, and especially few novelists, bring up that question with anything like the
gross assurance and systematic confidence of Balzac,
who clearly took for involved in his plan of a complete
picture of the manners and aspects of his country
and his period that he should have his confident "say"
about as many things as possible, and who, throughout his immense work, appears never for an instant or
in any connection to flinch from that complacency.
Here it is easy to await him, waylay him and catch
him in the act, with the consequence, for the most
part, of our having to recognise almost with compassion the disparity between the author of "La Cousine
Bette" exercising his genius, as Matthew Arnold said
of Ruskin, in making a like distinction, and the same

writer taking on a character not in the least really rooted in that soil. The fact none the less than his generalising remains throughout so markedly inferior to his particularising—which latter element and very essence of the novelist's art it was his greatness to carry further and apply more consistently than any member of the craft, without exception, has felt the impulse, to say nothing of finding the way, to do—by no means wholly destroys the interest of the habit itself or relieves us of a due attention to it; so characteristic and significant, so suggestive even of his special force, though in a manner indirect, are the very folds and redundancies of this philosopher's robe that flaps about his feet and drags along the ground like an assumed official train. The interest here—where it is exactly that a whole face of his undertaking would be most illumined for the fellow-artist we imagine trying to exhibit him—depends much less on what his reflection and opinion, his irrepressible *obiter dicta* and monstrous *suffisances* of judgment may be, than on the part played in his scheme by his holding himself ready at every turn and at such short notice to judge. For this latter fact probably lights up more than any other his conception of the range of the novel, the fashion after which, in his hands, it had been felt as an all-inclusive form, a form without rift or leak, a tight mould, literally, into which everything relevant to a consideration of the society surrounding him—and the less relevant unfortunately, as well as the more —might be poured in a stream of increasing consistency, the underlapping subject stretched, all so formidably, to its own constituted edge and the compound appointed to reproduce, as in finest and subtlest relief, its every minutest feature, overlying and corresponding with it all round to the loss of no fraction of an inch.

It is thus the painter's aspiring and rejoicing consciousness of the great square swarming picture, the picture of France from side to side and from top to bottom, which he proposes to copy—unless we see the collective quantity rather as the vast primary model or sitter that he is unprecedentedly to portray, it is this that, rendering him enviable in proportion to his audacity and his presumption, gives a dignity to everything that makes the consciousness whole. The result is a state of possession of his material unlike that of any other teller of tales whatever about a circumjacent world, and the process of his gain of which opens up well-nigh the first of those more or less baffling questions, parts indeed of the great question of the economic rule, the practical secret, of his activity, that beset us as soon as we study him. To fit what he was and what he did, that is the measure of how he used himself and how he used every one and everything else, into his after all so brief career (for twenty years cover the really productive term of it) is for ourselves, we confess, to renounce any other solution than that of his having proceeded by a sense for facts, the multitudinous facts of the scene about him, that somehow involved a preliminary, a pre-experiential inspiration, a straightness of intuition truly impossible to give an account of and the like of which had never before been shown. He had not to learn things in order to know them; and even though he multiplied himself in more ways than we can reckon up, going hither and thither geographically, leading his life with violence, as it were, though always with intention, and

wasting almost nothing that had ever touched him,
the natural man, the baptised and registered Honoré,
let loose with harsh promptitude upon a world formed
from the first moment to excite his voracity, can only
have been *all* the exploiting agent, the pushing inquirer,
the infallible appraiser, the subject of an *arrière-pensée*
as merciless, in spite of being otherwise genial, as the
black care riding behind the horseman. There was
thus left over for him less of mere human looseness,
of mere emotion, of mere naturalness, or of any curiosity whatever, that didn't "pay"—and the extent
to which he liked things to pay, to see them, think of
them, and describe them as prodigiously paying, is
not to be expressed—than probably marks any recorded relation between author and subject as we
know each of these terms.

So it comes that his mastership of whatever given
identity might be in question, and much more of the
general identity of his rounded (for the artistic vision),
his compact and containing France, the fixed, felt
frame to him of the vividest items and richest char-
acteristics of human life, can really not be thought of
as a matter of degrees of confidence, as acquired or
built up or cumbered with verifying fears. He *was*
the given identity and, on the faintest shade of a hint
about it caught up, became one with it and lived it—
this in the only way in which he could live, anywhere
or at any time: which was by losing himself in its
relation to his need or to what we call his voracity.
Just so his mind, his power of apprehension, worked
naturally in the interest of a society disclosed to that
appetite; on the mere approach to the display he in-
haled information, he recognised himself as what he

might best be known for, an historian unprecedented, an historian documented as none had not only ever been, but had ever dreamed of being—and even if the method of his documentation can leave us for the most part but wondering. The method of his use of it, or of a portion of it, we more or less analyse and measure; but the wealth of his provision or outfit itself, the crammed store of his categories and *cadres*, leaves us the more stupefied as we feel it to have been honestly come by. All this is what it is impossible not to regard as in itself a fundamental felicity such as no *confrère* had known; so far, indeed, as Balzac suffered *confrères* or as the very nature of his faculty could be thought of for them. M. Brunetière's monograph of some years ago, which is but a couple of degrees less weighty, to our sense, than this of M. Faguet before us, justly notes that, whatever other felicity may have graced the exercise of such a genius, for instance, as that rare contemporary George Sand, she was reduced well-nigh altogether to drawing upon resources and enjoying advantages comparatively vague and unassured. She had of course in a manner her special resource and particular advantage, which consisted, so to speak, in a finer feeling about what she did possess and could treat of with authority, and particularly in a finer command of the terms of expression, than any involved in Balzac's "happier" example. But her almost fatal weakness as a novelist—an exponent of the art who has waned exactly as, for our general long-drawn appreciation, Balzac has waxed—comes from her having had to throw herself upon ground that no order governed, no frame, as we have said, enclosed, and no safety attended; safety of the sort, we mean, the safety of the constitutive, illustrative

fact among facts, which we find in her rival as a warm
socialised air, an element supremely assimilable.

It may freely be pronounced interesting that
whereas, in her instinct for her highest security, she
threw herself upon the consideration of love as the
type attraction or most representable thing in the
human scene, so, assuredly, no student of that field
has, in proportion to the thoroughness of his study,
felt he could afford to subordinate or almost even to
neglect it to anything like the tune in which we see it
put and kept in its place through the parts of the
Comédie Humaine that most count. If this passion
but too often exhales a tepid breath in much other
fiction—much other of ours at least—that is apt to
come decidedly less from the writer's sense of proportion than from his failure of art, or in other words
of intensity. It is rarely absent by intention or by
intelligence, it is pretty well always there as the theo-
retic principal thing—any difference from writer to
writer being mostly in the power to put the principal
thing effectively forward. It figures as a pressing, an
indispensable even if a perfunctory motive, for example,
in every situation devised by Walter Scott; the case
being simply that if it doesn't in fact attractively
occupy the foreground this is because his hand has had
so native, so much greater, an ease for other parts of
the picture. What makes Balzac so pre-eminent and
exemplary that he was to leave the novel a far other and
a vastly more capacious and significant affair than he
found it, is his having felt his fellow-creatures (almost
altogether for him his contemporaries) as quite failing
of reality, as swimming in the vague and the void and
the abstract, unless their social conditions, to the last

particular, their generative and contributive circumstances, of every discernible sort, enter for all these
are "worth" into his representative attempt. This
great compound of the total looked into and starting
up in its element, as it always does, to meet the eye
of genius and patience half way, bristled for him with
all its branching connections, those thanks to which
any figure could *be* a figure but by showing for endlessly
entangled in them.

So it was then that his huge felicity, to re-empha-
sise our term, was in his state of circulating where
recognitions and identifications didn't so much await
as rejoicingly assault him, having never yet in all the
world, grudged or at the best suspected feeders as they
were at the board where sentiment occupied the head,
felt themselves so finely important or subject to such a
worried intention. They hung over a scene as to which
it was one of the forces of his inspiration that history had lately been there at work, with incomparable
energy and inimitable art, to pile one upon another,
not to say squeeze and dovetail violently into each
other, after such a fashion as might defy competition
anywhere, her successive deposits and layers of form
and order, her restless determinations of appearance
—so like those of the different "states" of an engraver's
impression; all to an effect which *should* have constituted, as by a miracle of coincidence it did, the
paradise of an extraordinary observer. Balzac lived
accordingly, extraordinary since he was, in an earthly
heaven so near perfect for his kind of vision that he
could have come at no moment more conceivably blest
to him. The later part of the eighteenth century,
with the Revolution, the Empire and the Restoration,

had inimitably conspired together to scatter abroad their separate marks and stigmas, their separate trails of character and physiognomic hits—for which advantage he might have arrived too late, as his hapless successors, even his more or less direct imitators, visibly have done. The fatal fusions and uniformities inflicted on our newer generations, the running together of all the differences of form and tone, the ruinous liquefying wash of the great industrial brush over the old conditions of contrast and colour, doubtless still have left the painter of manners much to do, but have ground him down to the sad fact that his ideals of differentiation, those inherent oppositions from type to type, in which drama most naturally resides, have well-nigh perished. They pant for life in a hostile air; and we may surely say that their last successful struggle, their last bright resistance to eclipse among ourselves, was in their feverish dance to the great fiddling of Dickens. Dickens made them dance, we seem to see, caper and kick their heels, wave their arms, and above all agitate their features, for the simple reason that he couldn't make them stand or sit *at once* quietly and expressively, couldn't make them look straight out as for themselves—quite in fact as through his not daring to, not feeling he could afford to, in a changing hour when ambiguities and the wavering line, droll and "dodgy" dazzlements and the possibly undetected factitious alone, might be trusted to keep him right with an incredibly uncritical public, a public blind to the difference between a shade and a patch.

Balzac on the other hand, born as we have seen to confidence, the tonic air of his paradise, might make character, in the sense in which we use it, that of the

element exposable to the closest verification, sit or
stand for its "likeness" as still as ever it would. It is
true that he could, as he often did, resort to fond extravagance, since he was apt at his worst to plunge
into agitation for mere agitation's sake—which is a
course that, by any turn, may cast the plunger on the
barrenest strand. But he is at his best when the conditions, the whole complex of subdivisible form and
pressure, are virtually themselves the situation, the
action and the interest, or in other words when these
things exhaust themselves, as it were, in expressing
the persons we are concerned with, agents and victims
alike, and when by such vivified figures, whether victims or agents, they are themselves completely expressed. The three distinguished critics who have
best studied him, Taine, Brunetière and now (as well
as before this) M. Faguet—the first the most eloquent
but the loosest, and the last the closest even if the
dryest—are in agreement indeed as to the vast quantity
of waste in him, inevitably judging the romanticist as
whom he so frequently, speculatively, desperately
paraded altogether inferior to the realist whose function he could still repeatedly and richly and for his
greater glory exercise. This estimate of his particularly greater glory is of a truth not wholly shared by
M. Taine; but the three are virtually at one, where
we of course join them, or rather go further than they,
as to the enviability, so again to call it (and by which we
mean the matchless freedom of play), of his harvest-
ing sense when he gave himself up in fullest measure
to his apprehension of the dense wholeness of reality.
It was this that led him on and kept him true to that
happily largest side of his labour by which he must
massively live; just as it is this, the breath of his real

geniality, when every abatement is made, that stirs
to loyalty those who under his example also take his
direction and find their joy in watching him thoroughly
at work. We see then how, when social character
and evolved type are the prize to be grasped, the facts
of observation and certification, unrestingly social and
historic too, that form and fondle and retouch it,
never relaxing their action, are so easily and blessedly
absolute to him that this is what we mean by their
virtue.

When there were enough of these quantities and
qualities flowering into the definite and the absolute
for him to feed on, feed if not to satiety at least to the
largest loosening of his intellectual belt, there were
so many that we may even fall in with most of M.
Faguet's discriminations and reserves about him and
yet find his edifice rest on proportioned foundations.
For it is his assimilation of things and things, of his
store of them and of the right ones, the right for representation, that leaves his general image, even with
great chunks of surface surgically, that is critically,
removed, still coherent and erect. There are moments when M. Faguet—most surgical he!—seems to
threaten to remove so much that we ask ourselves in
wonder what may be left; but no removal matters
while the principle of observation animating the mass
is left unattacked. Our present critic for instance is
"down"—very understandingly down as seems to us
—on some of the sides of his author's rich temperamental vulgarity; which is accompanied on those
sides by want of taste, want of wit, want of style, want
of knowledge of ever so many parts of the general subject, too precipitately proposed, and want of fineness

of feeling about ever so many others. We agree with him freely enough, subject always to this reserve already glanced at, that a novelist of a high esthetic sensibility must always find more in any other novelist worth considering seriously at all than he can perhaps hope to impart even to the most intelligent of critics pure and simple his subtle reasons for. This said, we lose ourselves, to admiration, in such a matter for example as the tight hug of the mere material, the supremely important if such ever was, represented by the appeal to us on behalf of the money-matters of César Birotteau.

This illustration gains logically, much more than loses, from the rank predominance of the money-question, the money-vision, throughout all Balzac. There are lights in which it can scarce not appear to us that his own interest is greater, his possibilities of attention truer, in these pressing particulars than in all other questions put together; there could be no better sign of the appreciation of "things," exactly, than so never relaxed a grasp of the part played in the world by just these. Things for things, the franc, the shilling, the dollar, are the very most underlying and conditioning, even dramatically, even poetically, that call upon him; and we have everywhere to recognise how little he feels himself to be telling us of this, that and the other person unless he has first given us full information, with every detail, either as to their private means, their income, investments, savings, losses, the state in fine of their pockets, or as to their immediate place of habitation, their home, their outermost shell, with its windows and doors, its outside appearance and inside plan, its rooms and furniture and arrangements,

its altogether intimate facts, down to its very smell.
This prompt and earnest evocation of the shell and
its lining is but another way of testifying with due
emphasis to economic conditions. The most personal
shell of all, the significant dress of the individual,
whether man or woman, is subject to as sharp and as
deep a notation—it being no small part of his wealth
of luck that the age of dress differentiated and spe-
cialised from class to class and character to character,
not least moreover among men, could still give him
opportunities of choice, still help him to define and
intensify, or peculiarly to *place* his apparitions. The
old world in which costume had, to the last refinement
of variety, a social meaning happily lingered on for
him; and nothing is more interesting, nothing goes
further in this sense of the way the social concrete
could minister to him, than the fact that "César
Birotteau," to instance that masterpiece again, besides
being a money-drama of the closest texture, the very
epic of retail bankruptcy, is at the same time the all-
vividest exhibition of the habited and figured, the
representatively stamped and countenanced, buttoned
and buckled state of the persons moving through it.
No livelier example therefore can we name of the
triumphant way in which any given, or as we should
rather say taken, total of conditions works out under
our author's hand for accentuation of type. The
story of poor Birotteau is just in this supreme degree
a hard total, even if every one's money-relation does
loom larger, for his or her case, than anything else.

The main thing doubtless to agree with M. Faguet
about, however, is the wonder of the rate at which
this genius for an infatuated grasp of the environment

could multiply the creatures swarming, and swarming at their best to perfection, in that jungle of elements. A jungle certainly the environment, the rank many-coloured picture of France, would have been had it not really created in our observer the joy, thanks to his need of a clear and marked order, of its becoming so arrangeable. Nothing could interest us more than to note with our critic that such multiplications—taken after all at such a rush—have to be paid for by a sort of limitation of quality in each, the quality that, beyond a certain point and after a certain allowance, ever looks askance at any approach to what it may be figured as taking for *insolence* of quantity. Some inquiry into the general mystery of such laws of payment would beckon us on had we the space—whereby we might glance a little at the wondrous why and wherefore of the sacrifice foredoomed, the loss, greater or less, of those ideals now compromised by the tarnished names of refinement and distinction, yet which we are none the less, at our decentest, still ashamed too entirely to turn our backs on, in the presence of energies that, shaking the air by their embrace of the common, tend to dispossess the rare of a certified place in it. Delightful to the critical mind to estimate the point at which, in the picture of life, a sense for the element of the rare ceases to consort with a sense, necessarily large and lusty, for the varieties of the real that super-abound. Reducible perhaps to some exquisite measure is this point of fatal divergence. It declared itself, the divergence, in the heart of Balzac's genius; for nothing about him is less to be gainsaid than that on the other or further side of a certain line of rareness drawn his authority, so splendid on the hither or familiar side, is sadly liable to lapse. It fails to take in whatever fine truth experience may have vouchsafed to us about the highest kinds of temper, the inward life of the mind, the *cultivated* consciousness. His truest and vividest people are those whom the conditions in which they are so palpably embedded have simplified not less than emphasised; simplified mostly to singleness of motive and passion and interest, to quite measurably finite existence; whereas his ostensibly higher spirits, types necessarily least observed and most independently thought out, in the interest of their humanity, as we would fain ourselves think them, are his falsest and weakest and show most where his imagination and his efficient sympathy break down.

To say so much as this is doubtless to provoke the question of where and how then, under so many other restrictions, he is so great—which question is answered simply by our claim for his unsurpassed mastery of the "middling" sort, so much the most numerous in the world, the middling sort pressed upon by the vast variety of their dangers. These it is in their multitude whom he makes individually living, each with a clustered bunch of concomitants, as no one, to our mind, has equalled him in doing—above all with the amount of repetition of the feat considered. Finer images than the middling, but so much fewer, other creative talents have thrown off; swarms of the common, on the other hand, have obeyed with an even greater air of multitude perhaps than in Balzac's pages the big brandished enumerative wand—only with a signal forfeiture in this case of that gift of the sharply separate, the really rounded, personality which he untiringly conferred. Émile Zola, by so far the

strongest example of his influence, mustered groups
and crowds beyond even the master's own compass;
but as throughout Zola we live and move for the most
part but in crowds (he thinking his best but in terms
of crowdedness), so in Balzac, where he rises highest,
we deal, whether or no more for our sense of ugliness
than of beauty, but with memorable person after person. He thought, on his side—when he thought at
least to good purpose—in terms the most expressively
personal, in such as could even eventuate in monsters
and forms of evil the most finished we know; so that
if he too has left us a multitude of which we may say
that it stands alone for solidity, it nevertheless exists
by addition and extension, not by a chemical shaking-
together, a cheapening or diminishing fusion.

It is not that the series of the Rougon-Macquart
has not several distinct men and women to show—
though they occur, as a fact, almost in "L'Assommoir"
alone; it is not either that Zola did not on occasion
try for the cultivated consciousness, a thing of course,
so far as ever achieved anywhere, necessarily separate
and distinguished; it is that he tried, on such ground,
with a futility only a shade less marked than Balzac's,
and perhaps would have tried with equal disaster had
he happened to try oftener. If we find in his pages no
such spreading waste as Balzac's general picture of
the classes "enjoying every advantage," that is of the
socially highest—to the elder writer's success in depicting particularly the female members of which
Sainte-Beuve, and Brunetière in his footsteps, have
rendered such strange and stupefying homage—the
reason may very well be that such groups could not
in the nature of the case figure to him after the fashion

in which he liked groups to figure, as merely herded
and compressed. To Balzac they were groups in
which individualisation might be raised to its very
finest; and it is by this possibility in them that we
watch him and his fertile vulgarity, his peccant taste,
so fallible for delicacies, so unerring for simplicities,
above all doubtless the homeliest, strongest and grim-
mest, wofully led astray. But it is fairly almost a
pleasure to our admiration, before him, to see what
we have permitted ourselves to call the "chunks" of
excision carted off to the disengagement of the values
that still live. The wondrous thing is that they live
best where his grand vulgarity—since we are not
afraid of the word—serves him rather than betrays;
which it *has* to do, we make out, over the greater part
of the field of any observer for whom man is on the
whole cruelly, crushingly, deformedly conditioned. We
grant *that* as to Balzac's view, and yet feel the view to
have been at the same time incomparably active and
productively genial; which are by themselves somehow qualities and reactions that redress the tragedy
and the doom. The vulgarity was at any rate a force
that simply got nearer than any other could have done
to the whole detail, the whole intimate and evidenced
story, of submission and perversion, and as such it
could but prove itself immensely human. It is on all
this considered ground that he has for so many years
stood firm and that we feel him by reason of it and in
spite of them, in spite of all that has come and gone,
not to have yielded, have "given," an inch.

GEORGE SAND

1897

I HAVE been reading in the Revue de Paris for November 1st, 1896, some fifty pages, of an extraordinary interest, which have had in respect to an old admiration a remarkable effect. Undoubtedly for other admirers too who have come to fifty year—admirers, I mean, once eager, of the distinguished woman involved —the perusal of the letters addressed by George Sand to Alfred de Musset in the course of a famous friendship will have stirred in an odd fashion the ashes of an early ardour. I speak of ashes because early ardours for the most part burn themselves out, while the place they hold in our lives varies, I think, mainly according to the degree of tenderness with which we gather up and preserve their dust; and I speak of oddity because in the present case it is difficult to say whether the agitation of the embers results at last in a returning glow or in a yet more sensible chill. That indeed is perhaps a small question compared with the simple pleasure of the reviving emotion. One reads and wonders and enjoys again, just for the sake of the renewal. The small fry of the hour submit to further shrinkage, and we revert with a sigh of relief to the free genius and large life of one of the greatest of all masters of expression. Do people still handle the works of this master—people other than young ladies studying French with "La Mare au Diable" and a dictionary? Are there persons who still read "Valentine"? Are there others capable of losing themselves in "Mauprat"? Has "André," the exquisite, dropped out of knowledge, and is any one left who remembers "Teverino"? I ask these questions for the mere sweet sound of them, without the least expectation of an answer. I remember asking them twenty years ago, after Madame Sand's death, and not then being hopeful of the answer of the future. But the only response that matters to us perhaps is our own, even if it be after all somewhat ambiguous. "André" and "Valentine" then are rather on our shelves than in our hands, but in the light of what is given us in the "Revue de Paris" who shall say that we do not, and with avidity, "read" George Sand? She died in 1876, but she lives again intensely in these singular pages, both as to what in her spirit was most attaching and what most disconcerting. We are vague as to what they may represent for the generation that has come to the front since her death; nothing, I dare say, very imposing or even very pleasing. But they give out a great deal to a reader for whom thirty years ago—the best time to have taken her as a whole—she was a high clear figure, a great familiar magician. This impression is a strange mixture, but perhaps not quite incommunicable; and we are steeped as we receive it in one of the most curious episodes in the annals of the literary race.

I

It is the great interest of such an episode that, apart from its proportionate place in the unfolding of a personal life it has a wonderful deal to say on the relation between experience and art at large. It con-

stitutes an eminent special case, in which the workings
of that relation are more or less uncovered; a case too
of which one of the most striking notes is that we are
in possession of it almost exclusively by the act of one
of the persons concerned. Madame Sand at least,
as we see to-day, was eager to leave nothing undone
that could make us further acquainted than we were
before with one of the liveliest chapters of her personal history. We cannot, doubtless, ·be sure that
her conscious purpose in the production of "Elle et
Lui" was to show us the process by which private
ecstasies and pains find themselves transmuted in the
artist's workshop into promising literary material—
any more than we can be certain of her motive for
making toward the end of her life earnest and complete arrangements for the ultimate publication of the
letters in which the passion is recorded and in which
we can remount to the origin of the volume. If "Elle
et Lui" had been the inevitable picture, postponed
and retouched, of the great adventure of her youth, so
the letters show us the crude primary stuff from which
the moral detachment of the book was distilled. Were
they to be given to the world for the encouragement
of the artist-nature—as a contribution to the view
that no suffering is great enough, no emotion tragic
enough to exclude the hope that such pangs may sooner
or later be esthetically assimilated? Was the whole
proceeding, in intention, a frank plea for the intellectual
and in some degree even the commercial profit, to a
robust organism, of a store of erotic reminiscence?
Whatever the reasons behind the matter, that is to a
certain extent the moral of the strange story.

It may be objected that this moral is qualified to
come home to us only when the relation between art

and experience really proves a happier one than it may be held to have proved in the combination before us. The element in danger of being most absent from the process is the element of dignity, and its presence, so far as that may ever at all be hoped for in an appeal from a personal quarrel, is assured only in proportion as the esthetic event, standing on its own feet, represents a noble gift. It was vain, the objector may say, for our author to pretend to justify by so slight a performance as "Elle et Lui" that sacrifice of all delicacy which has culminated in this supreme surrender. "If you sacrifice all delicacy," I hear such a critic contend, "show at least that you were right by giving us a masterpiece. The novel in question is no more a masterpiece," I even hear him proceed, "than any other of the loose liquid lucid works of its author. By your supposition of a great intention you give much too fine an account on the one hand of a personal habit of incontinence and on the other of a literary habit of egotism. Madame Sand, in writing her tale and in publishing her love-letters, obeyed no prompting more exalted than that of exhibiting her personal (in which I include her verbal) facility, and of doing so at the cost of whatever other persons might be concerned; and you are therefore—and you might as well immediately confess it—thrown back for the element of interest on the attraction of her general eloquence, the plausibility of her general manner and the great number of her particular confidences. You are thrown back on your mere curiosity or sympathy—thrown back from any question of service rendered to 'art.'" One might be thrown back doubtless still further even than such remarks would represent if one were not quite prepared with the confession they propose. It is only because

such a figure is interesting—in every manifestation—
that its course is marked for us by vivid footprints
and possible lessons. And to enable us to find these
it scarcely need have aimed after all so extravagantly
high. George Sand lived her remarkable life and drove
her perpetual pen, but the illustration that I began by
speaking of is for ourselves to gather—if we can.

I remember hearing many years ago in Paris an
anecdote for the truth of which I am far from vouching,
though it professed to come direct—an anecdote that
has recurred to me more than once in turning over the
revelations of the Revue de Paris, and without the
need of the special reminder (in the shape of an allusion
to her intimacy with the hero of the story) contained
in those letters to Sainte-Beuve which are published
in the number of November 15th. Prosper Mérimée
was said to have related—in a reprehensible spirit—
that during a term of association with the author of
"Lélia" he once opened his eyes, in the raw winter
dawn, to see his companion, in a dressing-gown, on
her knees before the domestic hearth, a candlestick
beside her and a red *madras* round her head, making
bravely, with her own hands, the fire that was to
enable her to sit down betimes to urgent pen and
paper. The story represents him as having felt that
the spectacle chilled his ardour and tried his taste;
her appearance was unfortunate, her occupation an
inconsequence and her industry a reproof—the result
of all of which was a lively irritation and an early
rupture. To the firm admirer of Madame Sand's
prose the little sketch has a very different value, for
it presents her in an attitude which is the very key
to the enigma, the answer to most of the questions

with which her character confronts us. She rose early because she was pressed to write, and she was pressed to write because she had the greatest instinct of expression ever conferred on a woman; a faculty that put a premium on all passion, on all pain, on all experience and all exposure, on the greatest variety of ties and the smallest reserve about them. The really interesting thing in these posthumous *laideurs* is the way the gift, the voice, carries its possessor through them and lifts her on the whole above them. It gave her, it may be confessed at the outset and in spite of all magnanimities in the use of it, an unfair advantage in every connection. So at least we must continue to feel till—for our appreciation of this particular one —we have Alfred de Musset's share of the correspondence. For we shall have it at last, in whatever faded fury or beauty it may still possess—to that we may make up our minds. Let the galled jade wince, it is only a question of time. The greatest of literary quarrels will in short, on the general ground, once more come up—the quarrel beside which all others are mild and arrangeable, the eternal dispute between the public and the private, between curiosity and delicacy.

This discussion is precisely all the sharper because it takes place for each of us within as well as without. When we wish to know at all we wish to know everything; yet there happen to be certain things of which no better description can be given than that they are simply none of our business. "What *is* then forsooth of our business?" the genuine analyst may always ask; and he may easily challenge us to produce any rule of general application by which we shall know when to push in and when to back out. "In the first place," he may continue, "half the 'interesting' people in the world have at one time or another set themselves to drag us in with all their might; and what in the world in such a relation is the observer that he should absurdly pretend to be in more of a flutter than the object observed? The mannikin, in all schools, is at an early stage of study of the human form inexorably superseded by the man. Say that we are to give up the attempt to understand: it might certainly be better so, and there would be a delightful side to the new arrangement. But in the name of common-sense don't say that the continuity of life is not to have some equivalent in the continuity of pursuit, the renewal of phenomena in the renewal of notation. There is not a door you can lock here against the critic or the painter, not a cry you can raise or a long face you can pull at him, that are not quite arbitrary things. The only thing that makes the observer competent is that he is neither afraid nor ashamed; the only thing that makes him decent—just think!—is that he is not superficial." All this is very well, but somehow we all equally feel that there is clean linen and soiled and that life would be intolerable without some acknowledgment even by the pushing of such a thing as forbidden ground. M. Émile Zola, at the moment I write, gives to the world his reasons for rejoicing in the publication of the physiological *enquête* of Dr. Toulouse—a marvellous catalogue or handbook of M. Zola's outward and inward parts, which leaves him not an inch of privacy, so to speak, to stand on, leaves him nothing about himself that is *for* himself, for his friends, his relatives, his intimates, his lovers, for discovery, for emulation, for fond conjecture or flattering deluded envy. It is enough for M. Zola that everything is for the public and no sacrifice worth thinking of when it is a question of presenting to the open mouth of that apparently gorged but still gaping monster the smallest spoonful of truth. The truth, to his view, is never either ridiculous or unclean, and the way to a better life lies through telling it, so far as possible, about everything and about every one.

There would probably be no difficulty in agreeing to this if it didn't seem on the part of the speaker the result of a rare confusion between give and take, between "truth" and information. The true thing that most matters to us is the true thing we have most use for, and there are surely many occasions on which the truest thing of all is the necessity of the mind, its simple necessity of feeling. Whether it feels in order to learn or learns in order to feel, the event is the same: the side on which it shall most feel will be the side to which it will most incline. If it feels more about a Zola functionally undeciphered it will be governed more by that particular truth than by the truth about his digestive idiosyncrasies, or even about his "olfactive perceptions" and his "arithmomania or impulse to count." An affirmation of our "mere taste" may very supposedly be our individual contribution to the general clearing up. Nothing often is less superficial than to ignore and overlook, or more constructive (for living and feeling at all) than to want impatiently to choose. If we are aware that in the same way as about a Zola undeciphered we should have felt more about a George Sand unexposed, the true thing we have gained becomes a poor substitute for the one we have lost; and I scarce see what difference it makes that the view of the elder novelist appears in this mat-

ter quite to march with that of the younger. I hasten
to add that as to being of course asked why in the
world with such a leaning we have given time either
to M. Zola's physician or to Musset's correspondent,
this is only another illustration of the bewildering
state of the subject.

When we meet on the broad highway the rueful
denuded figure we need some presence of mind to
decide whether to cut it dead or to lead it gently home,
and meanwhile the fatal complication easily occurs.
We have *seen*, in a flash of our own wit, and mystery
has fled with a shriek. These encounters are indeed
accidents which may at any time take place, and the
general guarantee in a noisy world lies, I judge, not so
much in any hope of really averting them as in a regular organisation of the struggle. The reporter and
the reported have duly and equally to understand that
they carry their life in their hands. There are secrets
for privacy and silence; let them only be cultivated
on the part of the hunted creature with even half the
method with which the love of sport—or call it the
historic sense—is cultivated on the part of the inves-
tigator. They have been left too much to the natural,
the instinctive man; but they will be twice as effective
after it begins to be observed that they may take their
place among the triumphs of civilisation. Then at
last the game will be fair and the two forces face to
face; it will be "pull devil, pull tailor," and the hard-
est pull will doubtless provide the happiest result.
Then the cunning of the inquirer, envenomed with
resistance, will exceed in subtlety and ferocity anything
we to-day conceive, and the pale forewarned victim,
with every track covered, every paper burnt and

every letter unanswered, will, in the tower of art, the invulnerable granite, stand, without a sally, the siege of all the years.

II

It was not in the tower of art that George Sand ever shut herself up; but I come back to a point already made in saying that it is in the citadel of style that, notwithstanding rash *sorties*, she continues to hold out. The outline of the complicated story that was to cause so much ink to flow gives, even with the omission of a hundred features, a direct measure of the strain to which her astonishing faculty was exposed. In the summer of 1833, as a woman of nearly thirty, she encountered Alfred de Musset, who was six years her junior. In spite of their youth they were already somewhat bowed by the weight of a troubled past. Musset, at twenty-three, had that of his confirmed libertinism—so Madame Arvède Barine, who has had access to materials, tells us in the admirable short biography of the poet contributed to the rather markedly unequal but very interesting series of Hachette's Grands Ecrivains Français. Madame Sand had a husband, a son and a daughter, and the impress of that succession of lovers—Jules Sandeau had been one, Prosper Mérimée another—to which she so freely alludes in the letters to Sainte-Beuve, a friend more disinterested than these and qualified to give much counsel in exchange for much confidence. It cannot be said that the situation of either of our young persons was of good omen for a happy relation, but they appear to have burnt their ships with much promptitude and a great blaze, and in the December of that year they started together for Italy. The following month saw them settled, on a frail basis, in Venice, where the elder companion remained till late in the summer of 1834 and where she wrote, in part, "Jacques" and the "Lettres d'un Voyageur," as well as "André" and "Léone-Léoni," and gathered the impressions to be embodied later in half-a-dozen stories with Italian titles—notably in the delightful "Consuelo." The journey, the Italian climate, the Venetian winter at first agreed with neither of the friends; they were both taken ill—the young man very gravely —and after a stay of three months Musset returned, alone and much ravaged, to Paris.

In the meantime a great deal had happened, for their union had been stormy and their security small. Madame Sand had nursed her companion in illness (a matter-of-course office, it must be owned) and her companion had railed at his nurse in health. A young physician, called in, had become a close friend of both parties, but more particularly a close friend of the lady, and it was to his tender care that on quitting the scene Musset solemnly committed her. She took up life with Pietro Pagello—the transition is startling—for the rest of her stay, and on her journey back to France he was no inconsiderable part of her luggage. He was simple, robust and kind—not a man of genius. He remained, however, but a short time in Paris; in the autumn of 1834 he returned to Italy, to live on till our own day but never again, so far as we know, to meet his illustrious mistress. Her intercourse with her poet was, in all its intensity, one may almost say its ferocity, promptly renewed, and was sustained in that key for several months more. The effect of this strange and tormented passion on the mere student of its records is simply to make him ask himself what on earth is the matter with the subjects of it. Nothing is more easy than to say, as I have intimated, that it has no need of records and no need of students; but this leaves out of account the thick medium of genius in which it was foredoomed to disport itself. It was self-registering, as the phrase is, for the genius on both sides happened to be the genius of eloquence. It is all rapture and all rage and all literature. The "Lettres d'un Voyageur" spring from the thick of the fight; "La Confession d'un Enfant du Siècle" and "Les Nuits" are immediate echoes of the concert. The lovers are naked in the market-place and perform for the benefit of society. The matter with them, to the perception of the stupefied spectator, is that they entertained for each other every feeling in life but the feeling of respect. What the absence of that article may do for the passion of hate is apparently nothing to what it may do for the passion of love.

By our unhappy pair at any rate the luxury in question—the little luxury of plainer folk—was not to be purchased, and in the comedy of their despair and the tragedy of their recovery nothing is more striking than their convulsive effort either to reach up to it or to do without it. They would have given for it all else they possessed, but they only meet in their struggle the inexorable *never*. They strain and pant and gasp, they beat the air in vain for the cup of cold water of their hell. They missed it in a way for which none of their superiorities could make up. Their great affliction was that each found in the life of the

other an armoury of weapons to wound. Young as
they were, young as Musset was in particular, they
appeared to have afforded each other in that direction
the most extraordinary facilities; and nothing in the
matter of the mutual consideration that failed them is
more sad and strange than that even in later years,
when their rage, very quickly, had cooled, they never
arrived at simple silence. For Madame Sand, in her
so much longer life, there was no hush, no letting
alone; though it would be difficult indeed to exag-
gerate the depth of relative indifference from which,
a few years after Musset's death, such a production
as "Elle et Lui" could spring. Of course there had
been floods of tenderness, of forgiveness; but those,
for all their beauty of expression, are quite another
matter. It is just the fact of our sense of the ugliness
of so much of the episode that makes a wonder and a
force of the fine style, all round, in which it is offered
us. That force is in its turn a sort of clue to guide,
or perhaps rather a sign to stay, our feet in paths after
all not the most edifying. It gives a degree of importance to the somewhat squalid and the somewhat
ridiculous story, and, for the old George-Sandist at
least, lends a positive spell to the smeared and yel-
lowed paper, the blotted and faded ink. In this twi-
light of association we seem to find a reply to our own
challenge and to be able to tell ourselves why we med-
dle with such old dead squabbles and waste our time
with such grimacing ghosts. If we were superior to
the weakness, moreover, how should we make our
point (which we must really make at any cost) as to
the so valuable vivid proof that a great talent is the
best guarantee—that it may really carry off almost
anything?

The rather sorry ghost that beckons us on furthest is the rare personality of Madame Sand. Under its influence—or that of old memories from which it is indistinguishable—we pick our steps among the *laideurs* aforesaid: the misery, the levity, the brevity of it all, the greatest ugliness in particular that this life shows us, the way the devotions and passions that we see heaven and earth called to witness are over before we can turn round. It may be said that, for what it was, the intercourse of these unfortunates surely lasted long enough; but the answer to that is that if it had only lasted longer it wouldn't have been what it was. It was not only preceded and followed by intimacies, on one side and the other, as unadorned by the stouter sincerity, but was mixed up with them in a manner that would seem to us dreadful if it didn't still more seem to us droll, or rather perhaps if it didn't refuse altogether to come home to us with the crudity of contemporary things. It is antediluvian history, a queer vanished world—another Venice from the actually, the deplorably familiarised, a Paris of greater bonhomie, an inconceivable impossible Nohant. This relegates it to an order agreeable somehow to the imagination of the fond quinquegenarian, the reader with a fund of reminiscence. The vanished world, the Venice unrestored, the Paris unextended, is a bribe to his judgment; he has even a glance of complacency for the lady's liberal *foyer*. Liszt, one lovely year at Nohant, "jouait du piano au rez-de-chaussée, et les rossignols, ivres de musique et de soleil, s'égosillaient avec rage sur les lilas environnants." The beautiful manner confounds itself with the conditions in which it was exercised, the large liberty and variety overflow into admirable prose, and the whole thing makes a charming faded medium in which Chopin gives a hand to Consuelo and the small Fadette has her elbows on the table of Flaubert.

There is a terrible letter of the autumn of 1834 in which our heroine has recourse to Alfred Tattet on a dispute with the bewildered Pagello—a disagreeable matter that involved a question of money. "À Venise il comprenait," she somewhere says, "à Paris il ne comprend plus." It was a proof of remarkable intelligence that he did understand in Venice, where he had become a lover in the presence and with the exalted approval of an immediate predecessor—an alternate representative of the part, whose turn had now, on the removal to Paris, come round again and in whose resumption of office it was looked to him to concur. This attachment—to Pagello—had lasted but a few months; yet already it was the prey of complication and change, and its sun appears to have set in no very graceful fashion. We are not here in truth among very graceful things, in spite of superhuman attitudes and great romantic flights. As to these forced notes Madame Arvède Barine judiciously says that the picture of them contained in the letters to which she had had access, and some of which are before us, "presents an example extraordinary and unmatched of what the romantic spirit could do with beings who had become its prey." She adds that she regards the records in question, "in which we follow step by step the ravages of the monster," as "one of the most precious psychological documents of the first half of the century." That puts the story on its true footing, though we may regret that it should not divide these documentary honours more equally with

some other story in which the monster has not quite
so much the best of it.   But it is the misfortune of the
comparatively short and simple annals of conduct and
character that they should ever seem to us somehow
to cut less deep.   Scarce—to quote again his best
biographer — had Musset, at Venice, begun to recover from his illness than the two lovers were seized
afresh by *le vertige du sublime et de l'impossible*.   "Ils
imaginèrent les déviations de sentiment les plus bi-
zarres, et leur intérieur fut le théâtre de scènes qui
égalaient en étrangeté les fantaisies les plus audacieuses
de la littérature contemporaine;" that is of the literature of their own day.   The register of virtue contains no such lively items—save indeed in so far as
these contortions and convulsions were a conscious
tribute to virtue.

Ten weeks after Musset has left her in Venice his
relinquished but not dissevered mistress writes to him
in Paris: "God keep you, my friend, in your present
disposition of heart and mind.   Love is a temple built
by the lover to an object more or less worthy of his
worship, and what is grand in the thing is not so much
the god as the altar.   Why should you be afraid of
the risk?"—of a new mistress she means.   There
would seem to be reasons enough why he should have
been afraid, but nothing is more characteristic than her
eagerness to push him into the arms of another woman
—more characteristic either of her whole philosophy
in these matters or of their tremendous, though somewhat conflicting, effort to be good.   She is to be good
by showing herself so superior to jealousy as to stir up
in him a new appetite for a new object, and he is to
be so by satisfying it to the full.   It appears not to

occur to either one that in such an arrangement his
own honesty is rather sacrificed. Or is it indeed because he has scruples—or even a sense of humour—
that she insists with such ingenuity and such eloquence?
"Let the idol stand long or let it soon break, you will
in either case have built a beautiful shrine. Your soul
will have lived in it, have filled it with divine incense,
and a soul like yours must produce great works. The
god will change perhaps, the temple will ·last as long
as yourself." "Perhaps," under the circumstances,
was charming. The letter goes on with the ample
flow that was always at the author's command—an
ease of suggestion and generosity, of beautiful melancholy acceptance, in which we foresee, on her own
horizon, the dawn of new suns. Her simplifications
are delightful — they remained so to the end; her
touch is a wondrous sleight-of-hand. The whole of
this letter in short is a splendid utterance and a masterpiece of the shade of sympathy, not perhaps the
clearest, which consists of wishing another to feel as
you feel yourself. To feel as George Sand felt, however, one had to be, like George Sand, of the true male
inwardness; which poor Musset was far from being.
This, we surmise, was the case with most of her lovers,
and the truth that makes the idea of her *liaison* with
Mérimée, who *was* of a consistent virility, sound almost
like a union against nature. She repeats to her correspondent, on grounds admirably stated, the injunc-
tion that he is to give himself up, to let himself go, to
take his chance. That he took it we all know—he followed her advice only too well. It is indeed not long
before his manner of doing so draws from her a cry of
distress. "Ta conduite est déplorable, impossible.
Mon Dieu, à quelle vie vais-je te laisser? l'ivresse, le

vin, les filles, et encore et toujours!" But appre-
hensions were now too late; they would have been too
late at the very earliest stage of this celebrated connection.

III

The great difficulty was that, though they were sublime, the couple were really not serious. But on the
other hand if on a lady's part in such a relation the
want of sincerity or of constancy is a grave reproach
the matter is a good deal modified when the lady, as I
have mentioned, happens to be—I may not go so far
as to say a gentleman. That George Sand just fell
short of this character was the greatest difficulty of
all; because if a woman, in a love affair, may be—for
all she is to gain or to lose—what she likes, there is
only one thing that, to carry it off with any degree of
credit, a man may be. Madame Sand forgot this on
the day she published "Elle et Lui"; she forgot it
again more gravely when she bequeathed to the great
snickering public these present shreds and relics of
unutterably personal things. The aberration refers
itself to the strange lapses of still other occasions—
notably to the extraordinary absence of scruples with
which she in the delightful "Histoire de ma Vie"
gives away, as we say, the character of her remarkable
mother. The picture is admirable for vividness, for
breadth of touch; it would be perfect from any hand
not a daughter's, and we ask ourselves wonderingly
how through all the years, to make her capable of it, a
long perversion must have worked and the filial fibre
—or rather the general flower of sensibility—have been
battered. Not this particular anomaly, however, but

many another, yields to the reflection that as just after her death a very perceptive person who had known her well put it to the author of these remarks, she was a woman quite by accident. Her immense plausibility was almost the only sign of her sex. She needed always to prove that she had been in the right; as how indeed could a person fail to who, thanks to the special equipment I have named, might prove it so brilliantly ? It is not too much to say of her gift of expression—and I have already in effect said so—that from beginning to end it floated her over the real as a high tide floats a ship over the bar. She was never left awkwardly straddling on the sandbank of fact.

For the rest, in any case, with her free experience and her free use of it, her literary style, her love of ideas and questions, of science and philosophy, her comradeship, her boundless tolerance, her intellectual patience, her personal good-humour and perpetual tobacco (she smoked long before women at large felt the cruel obligation), with all these things and many I don't mention she had more of the inward and outward of the other sex than of her own. She had above all the mark that, to speak at this time of day with a freedom for which her action in the matter of publicity gives us warrant, the history of her personal passions reads singularly like a chronicle of the ravages of some male celebrity. Her relations with men closely resembled those relations with women that, from the age of Pericles or that of Petrarch, have been complacently commemorated as stages in the unfolding of the great statesman and the great poet. It is very much the same large list, the same story of free appropriation and consumption. She appeared in short to have lived through a succession of such ties exactly in the manner of a Goethe, a Byron or a Napoleon; and if millions of women, of course, of every condition, had had more lovers, it was probable that no woman independently so occupied and so diligent had had, as might be said, more unions. Her fashion was quite her own of extracting from this sort of experience all that it had to give her and being withal only the more just and bright and true, the more sane and superior, improved and improving. She strikes us as in the benignity of such an intercourse even more than maternal: not so much the mere fond mother as the supersensuous grandmother of the wonderful affair. Is not that practically the character in which Thérèse Jacques studies to present herself to Laurent de Fauvel? the light in which "Lucrezia Floriani" (a memento of a friendship for Chopin, for Liszt) shows the heroine as affected toward Prince Karol and his friend? George Sand is too inveterately moral, too preoccupied with that need to do good which is in art often the enemy of doing well; but in all her work the story-part, as children call it, has the freshness and good faith of a monastic legend. It is just possible indeed that the moral idea was the real mainspring of her course—I mean a sense of the duty of avenging on the unscrupulous race of men their immemorial selfish success with the plastic race of women. Did she wish above all to turn the tables—to show how the sex that had always ground the other in the volitional mill was on occasion capable of being ground?

However this may be, nothing is more striking than the inward impunity with which she gave herself to conditions that are usually held to denote or to involve a state of demoralisation. This impunity (to speak only of consequences or features that concern us) was not, I admit, complete, but it was sufficiently so to warrant us in saying that no one was ever less demoralised. She presents a case prodigiously discouraging to the usual view—the view that there is no surrender to "unconsecrated" passion that we escape paying for in one way or another. It is frankly difficult to see where this eminent woman conspicuously paid. She positively got off from paying—and in a cloud of fluency and dignity, benevolence, competence, intelligence. She sacrificed, it is true, a handful of minor coin—suffered by failing wholly to grasp in her picture of life certain shades and certain delicacies. What she paid was this irrecoverable loss of her touch for them. That is undoubtedly one of the reasons why to-day the picture in question has perceptibly faded, why there are persons who would perhaps even go so far as to say that it has really a comic side. She doesn't know, according to such persons, her right hand from her left, the crooked from the straight and the clean from the unclean: it was a sense she lacked or a tact she had rubbed off, and her great work is by the fatal twist quite as lopsided a monument as the leaning tower of Pisa. Some readers may charge her with a graver confusion still—the incapacity to distinguish between fiction and fact, the truth straight from the well and the truth curling in steam from the kettle and preparing the comfortable tea. There is no word oftener on her pen, they will remind us, than the verb to "arrange." She arranged constantly, she arranged beautifully; but from this point of view, that of a general suspicion of arrangements, she always proved too much. Turned over in the light of it the story of

"Elle et Lui" for instance is an attempt to prove that
the mistress of Laurent de Fauvel was little less than
a prodigy of virtue. What is there not, the intem-
perate admirer may be challenged to tell us, an attempt
to prove in "L'Histoire de ma Vie"?—a work from
which we gather every delightful impression but the
impression of an impeccable veracity.

These reservations may, however, all be sufficiently
just without affecting our author's peculiar air of having eaten her cake and had it, been equally initiated
in directions the most opposed. Of how much cake
she partook the letters to Musset and Sainte-Beuve
well show us, and yet they fall in at the same time, on
other sides, with all that was noble in her mind, all
that is beautiful in the books just mentioned and in
the six volumes of the general "Correspondance: 1812–
1876," out of which Madame Sand comes so immensely
to her advantage. She had, as liberty, all the adventures of which the dots are so put on the i's by the
documents lately published, and then she had, as law,
as honour and serenity, all her fine reflections on them
and all her splendid busy literary use of them. Nothing perhaps gives more relief to her masculine stamp
than the rare art and success with which she cultivated
an equilibrium. She made from beginning to end a
masterly study of composure, absolutely refusing to be
upset, closing her door at last against the very approach of irritation and surprise. She had arrived at
her quiet elastic synthesis—a good-humour, an indulgence that were an armour of proof. The great felicity
of all this was that it was neither indifference nor renunciation, but on the contrary an intense partaking;
imagination, affection, sympathy and life, the way she

had found for herself of living most and living longest.
However well it all agreed with her happiness and her
manners, it agrees still better with her style, as to
which we come back with her to the sense that this
was really her *point d'appui* or sustaining force.   Most
people have to say, especially about themselves, only
what they can; but she said—and we nowhere see it
better than in the letters to Musset—everything in
life that she wanted.   We can well imagine the effect
of that consciousness on the nerves of this particular
correspondent, his own poor gift of occasional song
(to be so early spent) reduced to nothing by so unequalled a command of the last word.   We feel it, I
hasten to add, this last word, in all her letters: the
occasion, no matter which, gathers it from her as the
breeze gathers the scent from the garden.   It is always
the last word of sympathy and sense, and we meet it
on every page of the voluminous "Correspondance."
These pages are not so "clever" as those, in the same
order, of some other famous hands—the writer always
denied, justly enough, that she had either wit or
presence of mind—and they are not a product of high
spirits or of a marked avidity for gossip.   But they
have admirable ease, breadth and generosity; they
are the clear quiet overflow of a very full cup.   They
speak above all for the author's great gift, her eye for
the inward drama.   Her hand is always on the fiddle-
string, her ear is always at the heart.   It was in the
soul, in a word, that she saw the drama begin, and to
the soul that, after whatever outward flourishes, she
saw it confidently come back.   She herself lived with
all her perceptions and in all her chambers—not
merely in the showroom of the shop.   This brings us
once more to the question of the instrument and the

tone, and to our idea that the tone, when you are so lucky as to possess it, may be of itself a solution.

By a solution I mean a secret for saving not only your reputation but your life—that of your soul; an antidote to dangers which the unendowed can hope to escape by no process less uncomfortable or less inglorious than that of prudence and precautions. The unendowed must go round about, the others may go straight through the wood. Their weaknesses, those of the others, shall be as well redeemed as their books shall be well preserved; it may almost indeed be said that they are made wise in spite of themselves. If you have never in all your days *had* a weakness worth mentioning, you can be after all no more, at the very most, than large and cheerful and imperturbable. All these things Madamē Sand managed to be on just the terms she had found, as we see, most convenient. So much, I repeat, does there appear to be in a tone. But if the perfect possession of one made her, as it well might, an optimist, the action of it is perhaps more consistently happy in her letters and her personal records than in her "creative" work. Her novels to-day have turned rather pale and faint, as if the image projected—not intense, not absolutely concrete —failed to reach completely the mind's eye. And the odd point is that the wonderful charm of expression is not really a remedy for this lack of intensity, but rather an aggravation of it through a sort of suffusion of the whole thing by the voice and speech of the author. These things set the subject, whatever it be, afloat in the upper air, where it takes a happy bath of brightness and vagueness or swims like a soap-bubble kept up by blowing. This is no drawback when she is on the ground of her own life, to which she is tied by a certain number of tangible threads; but to embark on one of her confessed fictions is to have—after all that has come and gone, in our time, in the trick of persuasion—a little too much the feeling of going up in a balloon. We are borne by a fresh cool current and the car delightfully dangles; but as we peep over the sides we see things—as we usually know them—at a dreadful drop beneath. Or perhaps a better way to express the sensation is to say what I have just been struck with in the re-perusal of "Elle et Lui"; namely that this book, like others by the same hand, affects the reader—and the impression is of the oddest—not as a first but as a second echo or edition of the immediate real, or in other words of the subject. The tale may in this particular be taken as typical of the author's manner; beautifully told, but told, as if on a last remove from the facts, by some one repeating what he has read or what he has had from another and thereby inevitably becoming more general and superficial, missing or forgetting the "hard" parts and slurring them over and making them up. Of everything but feelings the presentation is dim. We recognise that we shall never know the original narrator and that the actual introducer is the only one we can deal with. But we sigh perhaps as we reflect that we may never confront her with her own informant.

To that, however, we must resign ourselves; for I remember in time that the volume from which I take occasion to speak with this levity is the work that I began by pronouncing a precious illustration. With the aid of the disclosures of the Revue de Paris it was, as I hinted, to show us that no mistakes and no pains are too great to be, in the air of art, triumphantly convertible. Has it really performed this function? I thumb again my copy of the limp little novel and wonder what, alas, I shall reply. The case is extreme, for it was the case of a suggestive experience particularly dire, and the literary flower that has bloomed upon it is not quite the full-blown rose. "Oeuvre de rancune" Arvède Barine pronounces it, and if we take it as that we admit that the artist's distinctness from her material was not ideally complete. Shall I not better the question by saying that it strikes me less as a work of rancour than—in a peculiar degree—as a work of egotism? It becomes in that light at any rate a sufficiently happy affirmation of the author's infallible form. This form was never a more successful vehicle for the conveyance of sweet reasonableness. It is all superlatively calm and clear; there never was a kinder, balmier last word. Whatever the measure of justice of the particular representation, moreover, the picture has only to be put beside the recent documents, the "study," as I may call them, to illustrate the general phenomenon. Even if "Elle et Lui" is not the full-blown rose we have enough here to place in due relief an irrepressible tendency to bloom. In fact I seem already to discern that tendency in the very midst of the storm; the "tone" in the letters too has its own way and performs on its own account— which is but another manner of saying that the literary instinct, in the worst shipwreck, is never out of its depth. The worker observed at the fire by Mérimée could be drowned but in an ocean of ink. Is that a sufficient account of what I have called the laying bare of the relation between experience and art? With the two elements, the life and the genius, face to face

—the smutches and quarrels at one end of the chain and the high luminosity at the other—does some essential link still appear to be missing? How do the graceless facts after all confound themselves with the beautiful spirit? They do so, incontestably, before our eyes, and the mystification remains. We try to trace the process, but before we break down we had better perhaps hasten to grant that—so far at least as George Sand is concerned—some of its steps are impenetrable secrets of the grand manner.

GEORGE SAND

1899

THOSE among us comfortably conscious of our different usage—aware, some would say, of our better conscience —may well have remarked the general absence from French practice of biographic commemoration of extinct worthies. The Life as we understand it, the prompt pious spacious record and mirror of the eminent career, rarely follows the death. The ghost of the great man, when he happens to have been a Frenchman, "sits" for such portraiture, we gather, with a confidence much less assured than among ourselves, and with fewer relatives and friends to surround the chair. The manner in which even for persons of highest mark among our neighbours biography either almost endlessly hangs back or altogether fails, suggests that the approach is even when authorised too often difficult. This general attitude toward the question, it would thus appear, implies for such retrospects the predominance of doors bolted and barred. Hesitation is therefore fairly logical, for it rests on the assumption that men and women of great gifts will have lived with commensurate intensity, and that as regards some of the forms of this intensity the discretion of the inquirer may well be the better part of his enthusiasm. The critic can therefore only note with regret so much absent opportunity for the play of perception and the art of composition. The race that produced Balzac—to say nothing of Sainte-Beuve

—would surely have produced a Boswell, a Lockhart and a Trevelyan if the fashion had not set so strongly against it. We have lately had a capital example of the encounter of an admirable English portraitist and an admirable English subject. It is not irrelevant to cite such a book as Mr. Mackail's "Life of William Morris" as our high-water mark—a reminder of how we may be blessed on both faces of the question. Each term of the combination appears supposable in France, but only as distinct from the other term. The artist, we gather, would there have lost his chance and the sitter his ease.

It completes in an interesting way these observations, which would bear much expansion, to perceive that when we at last have a Life of George Sand—a celebrity living with the imputed intensity, if ever a celebrity did—we are indebted for it to the hand of a stranger. No fact could more exactly point the moral of my few remarks. Madame Sand's genius and renown would have long ago made her a subject at home if alacrity in such a connection had been to be dreamed of. There is no more significant sign of the general ban under which alacrity rests. Everything about this extraordinary woman is interesting, and we can easily imagine the posthumous honours we ourselves would have hastened to assure to a part taken, in literature and life, with such brilliancy and sincerity. These demonstrations, where we should most look for them, have been none the less as naught—save indeed, to be exact, for the publication of a number of volumes of letters. It is just Madame Sand's letters, however— letters interesting and admirable, peculiarly qualified to dispose the reader in her favour—that in En-

gland or in America would have quickened the need
for the rest of the evidence.   But now that, as befalls,
we do at last have the rest of the evidence as we never
have had it before, we are of course sufficiently enlightened as to the reasons for a special application
of the law of reserves and delays.   It is not in fact easy
to see how a full study of our heroine could have been
produced earlier; and even at present there is a sensible
comfort in its being produced at such a distance as
practically assigns the act to a detached posterity.
Contemporaneously it was wise to forbear; but to-
day, and in Russia, by good luck, it is permitted to
plunge.

Mme. Wladimir Karénine's extraordinarily diffuse,
but scarcely less valuable, biography, of which the
first instalment,[1] in two large volumes, brings the story
but to the year 1838, reaches us in a French version,
apparently from the author's own hand, of chapters
patiently contributed to Russian periodicals.   Were it
not superficially ungrateful to begin with reserves
about a book so rich and full, there might be some complaint to make of this wonderful tribute on grounds
of form and taste.   Ponderous and prolix, the author
moves in a mass, escorted by all the penalties of her
indifference to selection and compression.   She insists and repeats, she wanders wide; her subject spreads
about her, in places, as rather a pathless waste.   Above
all she has produced a book which manages to be at
once remarkably expert and singularly provincial.
Our innocence is perhaps at fault, but we are moved
to take the mixture for characteristically Russian.
Would indeed any but that admirable "Slav" supe-

[1] "George Sand, sa Vie et ses Œuvres, 1804-1876."   Paris, 1899.

riority to prejudice of which we have lately heard so much have availed to handle the particular facts in this large free way? Nothing is at all events more curious than the union, on the part of our biographer, of psychological intelligence and a lame esthetic. The writer's literary appreciations lag in other words half a century behind her human and social. She treats us to endless disquisitions on pages of her author to which we are no longer in any manageable relation at all—disquisitions pathetic, almost grotesque, in their misplaced good faith. But her attitude to her subject is admirable, her thoroughness exemplary, the spirit of service in her of the sort that builds the monument stone by stone. When we see it reared to the summit, as we are clearly to do, we shall feel the structure to be solid if not shapely. Nothing is more possible meanwhile than that a culture more homogeneous—a French hand or a German—could not have engaged in the work with anything like the same sincerity. An English hand—and the fact, for *our* culture, means much—would have been incapable of touching it. The present scale of it at all events is certainly an exotic misconception. But we can take of it what concerns us.

The whole thing of course, we promptly reflect, concerns at the best only those of us who can remount a little the stream of time. The author of "L'Histoire de ma Vie" died in 1876, and the light of actuality rests to-day on very different heads. It may seem to belittle her to say that to care for her at all one must have cared for her from far back, for such is not in general the proviso we need to make on behalf of the greatest figures. It describes Madame Sand with

breadth, but not with extravagance, to speak of her
as a sister to Goethe, and we feel that for Goethe it
can never be too late to care. But the case exempli-
fies perhaps precisely the difference even in the most
brilliant families between sisters and brothers. She
was to have the family spirit, but she was to receive
from the fairies who attended at her cradle the silver
cup, not the gold. She was to write a hundred books
but she was not to write "Faust." She was to have
all the distinction but not all the perfection; and there
could be no better instance of the degree in which a
woman may achieve the one and still fail of the other.
When it is a question of the rare originals who have
either she confirms us, masculine as she is, in believing
that it takes a still greater masculinity to have both.
What she had, however, she had in profusion; she
was one of the deepest voices of that great mid-century
concert against the last fine strains of which we are
more and more banging the doors. Her work, beautiful, plentiful and fluid, has floated itself out to sea
even as the melting snows of the high places are floated.
To feel how she has passed away as a "creator" is to
feel anew the immense waste involved in the general
ferment of an age, and how much genius and beauty,
let alone the baser parts of the mixture, it takes to
produce a moderate quantity of literature. Smaller
people have conceivably ceased to count; but it is
strange for a member of the generation immediately
succeeding her own that she should have had the
same fate as smaller people: all the more that such
a mourner may be ruefully conscious of contributing
not a little himself to the mishap. Does he still read,
re-read, can he to-day at all deal with, this wonderful
lady's novels? It only half cheers him up that on the

occasion of such a publication as I here speak of he finds himself as much interested as ever.

The grounds of the interest are difficult to give—they presuppose so much of the old impression. If the old impression therefore requires some art to sustain and justify itself we must be content, so far as we are still under the charm, to pass, though only at the worst, for eccentric. The work, whether we still hold fast to it or not, has twenty qualities and would still have an immense one if it had only its style; but what I suppose it has paid for in the long-run is its want of plastic intensity. Does any work of representation, of imitation, live long that is predominantly loose? It may live in spite of looseness; but that, we make out, is only because closeness has somewhere, where it has most mattered, played a part. It is hard to say of George Sand's productions, I think, that they show closeness anywhere; the sense of that fluidity which is more than fluency is what, in speaking of them, constantly comes back to us, and the sense of fluidity is fundamentally fatal to the sense of particular truth. The thing presented by intention is never the stream of the artist's inspiration; it is the deposit of the stream. For the things presented by George Sand, for the general picture, we must look elsewhere, look at her life and her nature, and find them in the copious documents in which these matters and many others are now reflected. All *this* mass of evidence it is that constitutes the "intensity" we demand. The mass has little by little become large, and our obligation to Madame Karénine is that she makes it still larger. She sets our face, and without intending to, more and more in the right direction. Her injudicious analyses of forgotten fictions only confirm our discrimination. We feel ourselves in the presence of the extraordinary author of the hundred tales, and yet also feel it to be not by reason of them that she now presents herself as one of the most remarkable of human creatures. By reason then of what? Of everything that determined, accompanied, surrounded their appearance. They formed all together a great feature in a career and a character, but the career and the character are the real thing.

Such is far from usually the case, I hasten to recognise, with the complete and consistent artist. Poor is the art, a thing positively to be ashamed of, that, generally speaking, is not far more pressing for this servant of the altar than anything else, anything outside the church, can possibly be. To have been the tempered and directed hammer that makes the metal hard: if that be not good enough for such a ministrant, we may know him by whatever he has found better —we shall not know him by the great name. The immense anomaly in Madame Sand was that she freely took the form of being, with most zest, quite another sort of hammer. It testifies sufficiently to her large endowment that, given the wide range of the rest of her appetite, she should seem to us to-day to have sacrificed even superficially to *any* form of objective expression. She had in spite of herself an imagination almost of the first order, which overflowed and irrigated, turning by its mere swift current, without effort, almost without direction, every mill it encountered, and launching as it went alike the lightest skiff and the stateliest ship. She had in especial the gift of speech, speech supreme and inspired, to which we particularly owe the high value of the "case" she presents. For the case was definitely a bold and direct experiment, not at all in "art," not at all in literature, but conspicuously and repeatedly in the business of living; so that our profit of it is before anything else that it was conscious, articulate, vivid—recorded, reflected, imaged. The subject of the experiment became also at first hand the journalist—much of her work being simply splendid journalism—commissioned to bring it up to date. She interviewed nobody else, but she admirably interviewed herself, and this is exactly our good fortune. Her autobiography, her letters, her innumerable prefaces, all her expansive parentheses and excursions, make up the generous report. We have in this form accordingly a literary title for her far superseding any derived from her creative work. But that is the result of a mere betrayal, not the result of an intention. Her masterpiece, by a perversity of fate, is the thing she least sat down to. It consists—since she is a case—in the mere notation of her symptoms, in help given to the study of them. To this has the author of "Consuelo" come.

But how in the world indeed was the point so indicated *not* to be the particular cross-road at which the critic should lie in wait for a poor child of the age whom preceding ages and generations had almost infernally conspired to trap for him, to give up, candidly astray, to his hands? If the element of romance for which our heroine's name stands is best represented by her personal sequences and solutions, it is sufficiently visible that her heredity left her a scant alternative. Space fails me for the story of this heredity, queer and complicated, the very stuff that stories are made of—

a chain of generations succeeding each other in confidence and joy and with no aid asked of legal or other
artificial sanctions. The facts are, moreover, sufficiently familiar, though here as elsewhere Madame
Karénine adds to our knowledge. Presented, foreshortened, stretching back from the quiet Nohant
funeral of 1876 to the steps of the throne of King
Augustus the Strong of Poland, father of Maurice de
Saxe, great-great-grandfather of Aurore Dupin, it all
hangs together as a cluster of components more provoc-
ative than any the great novelist herself ever handled.
Her pre-natal past was so peopled with *dramatis
personæ* that her future was really called on to supply
them in such numbers as would preserve the balance.
The tide of illegitimacy sets straight through the
series. No one to speak of—Aurore's father is an exception—seems to have had a "regular" paternity.
Aurore herself squared with regularity but by a month
or two; the marriage of her parents gave her a bare
escape. She was brought up by her paternal grandmother between a son of her father and a daughter of
her mother born out of wedlock. It all moves before
us as a vivid younger world, a world on the whole more
amused and more amusing than ours. The period
from the Restoration to the events of 1848 is the
stretch of time in which, for more reasons than we can
now go into, French life gives out to those to whom
its appeal never fails most of its charm—most, at all
events, of its ancient sociability. Happy is our sense
of the picturesque Paris unconscious of a future all
"avenues" and exhibitions; happy our sense of these
middle years of a great generation, easy and lusty
despite the ensanguined spring that had gone before.
They live again, piecing themselves ever so pleasantly

and strangely together, in Madame Sand's records and references; almost as much as the conscious close of the old régime so vaunted by Talleyrand they strike us as a season it would have been indispensable to know for the measure of what intercourse could richly be.

The time was at any rate unable to withhold from the wonderful young person growing up at Nohant the conditions she was so freely to use as measures of her own. Though the motto of her autobiography is *Wahrheit und Dichtung* quite as much as it had been that of Goethe's, there is a truth beyond any projected by her more regular compositions in her evocation of the influences of her youth. Upon these influences Madame Karénine, who has enjoyed access through her heroine's actual representatives to much evidence hitherto unpublished, throws a hundred interesting lights. Madame Dupin de Francueil and Madame Dupin the younger survive and perform for us, "convince" us as we say, better than any Lélia or any Consuelo. Our author's whole treatment of her remarkable mother's figure and history conveniently gives the critic the pitch of the great fact about her—the formation apparently at a given moment, yet in very truth, we may be sure, from far back, of the capacity and the determination to live with high consistency for herself. What she made of this resolve to allow her nature all its chances and how she carried on the process—these things are, thanks to the immense illustration her genius enabled her to lend them, the essence of her story; of which the full adumbration is in the detached pictorial way she causes her mother to live for us. Motherhood, daugh-

terhood, childhood, embarrassed maturity, were phenomena she early encountered in her great adventure,
and nothing is more typical of her energy and sincerity
than the short work we can scarce help feeling she
makes of them. It is not that she for a moment
blinks or dodges them; she weaves them straight in
—embarks with them indeed as her principal baggage.
We know to-day from the pages before us everything
we need to know about her marriage and the troubled
years that followed; about M. Casimir Dudevant
and his possible points of view, about her separation,
her sharp secession, rather, as it first presents itself,
and her discovery, at a turn of the road as it can only
be called, of her genius.

She stumbled on this principle, we see, quite by
accident and as a consequence of the attempt to do the
very humblest labour, to support herself from day to
day. It would be difficult to put one's finger more
exactly upon a case of genius unaided and unprompted.
She embarked, as I have called it, on her great voyage
with no grounds of confidence whatever; she had
obscurely, unwittingly the spirit of Columbus, but not
so much even as his exiguous outfit. She found her
gift of improvisation, found her tropic wealth, by leap-
ing—a surprised *conquistador* of "style"—straight upon
the coral strand. No awakened instinct, probably, was
ever such a blessing to a writer so much in need. This
instinct was for a long time all her initiation, practically all her equipment. The curious thing is that
she never really arrived at the fruit of it as the result
of a process, but that she started with the whole thing
as a Patti or a Mario starts with a voice which *is* a
method, which *is* music, and that it was simply the

train in which she travelled. It was to render her
as great a service as any supreme faculty ever rendered its possessor, quite the same service as the stra-
tegic eye renders a commander in the field or instant
courage the attacking soldier: it was to carry her
through life still more inimitably than through the
career of authorship. Her books are all rich and
resonant with it, but they profit by it meagrely compared with her character. She walks from first to
last in music, that is in literary harmonies, of her own
making, and it is in truth sometimes only, with her
present biographer to elbow us a little the way, that
these triumphant sounds permit us a near enough
approach to the procession to make out quite exactly
its course.

No part of her career is to my sense so curious as
this particular sudden bound into the arena. Nothing but the indescribable heredity I have spoken of
appears traceably to have prepared it. We have on
one side the mere poverty and provinciality of her
marriage and her early contacts, the crudity of her
youth and her ignorance (which included so small a
view of herself that she had begun by looking for a
future in the bedaubing, for fancy-shops, of little
boxes and fans); and on the other, at a stride, the full-
blown distinction of "Valentine" and "Jacques,"
which had had nothing to lead up to it, we seem to
make out, but the very rough sketch of a love-affair
with M. Jules Sandeau. I spoke just now of the possible points of view of poor M. Dudevant; at which,
had we space, it might be of no small amusement to
glance—of an amusement indeed large and suggestive.
We see him, surely, in the light of these records, as the

most "sold" husband in literature, and not at all, one
feels, by his wife's assertion of her freedom, but simply by her assertion of her mind. He appears to
have married her for a nobody approved and guaranteed, and he found her, on his hands, a sister, as we
have seen, of Goethe—unless it be but a figure to say
that he ever "found" her anything. He appears to
have lived to an advanced age without having really
—in spite of the lawsuits he lost—comprehended his
case; not the least singular feature of which had in
fact positively been the deceptive delay of his fate.
It was not till after several years of false calm that it
presented itself in its special form. We see him and his
so ruthlessly superseded name, never to be gilded by
the brilliant event, we see him reduced, like a leaf in a
whirlwind, to a mere vanishing-point.

We deal here, I think, with something very different from the usual tittle-tattle about "private" relations, for the simple reason that we deal with relations
foredoomed to publicity by the strange economy involved in the play of genius itself. Nothing was ever
less wasted, from beginning to end, than all this amorous experience and all this luxury of woe. The parties
to it were to make an inveterate use of it, the principal
party most of all; and what therefore on that marked
ground concerns the critic is to see what they were appreciably to get out of it. The principal party, the
constant one through all mutations, was alone qualified to produce the extract that affects us as final.
It was by the publication four years since of her letters
to Alfred de Musset and to Sainte-Beuve, by the appearance also of Madame Arvède Barine's clear compact biography of Musset, that we began to find her

personal history brought nearer to us than her own communications had in her lifetime already brought it. The story of her relations with Musset is accordingly so known that I need only glance at the fact of her having—shortly after the highest degree of intimacy between them had, in the summer of 1833, established itself in Paris—travelled with him to Italy, settled with him briefly in Venice, and there passionately quarrelled and parted with him—only, however, several months later, on their return to France, to renew again, to quarrel and to part again, all more passionately, if possible, even than before. Madame Karénine, besides supplying us with all added light on this episode, keeps us abreast of others that were to follow, leaves us no more in the dark about Michel de Bourges, Félicien Mallefille and Chopin than we had already been left about their several predecessors. She is commendably lucid on the subject of Franz Liszt, impartially examines the case and authoritatively dismisses it. Her second volume brings her heroine to the eve of the historic departure with Chopin for Majorca. We have thus in a convenient form enough for one mouthful of entertainment, as well as for superabundant reflection.

We have indeed the whole essence of what most touches us, for this consists not at all of the quantity of the facts, nor even of their oddity: they are practically all there from the moment the heroine's general attitude defines itself. That is the solid element—the details to-day are smoke. Yet I hasten to add that it was in particular by taking her place of an autumn evening in the southward-moving diligence with Alfred de Musset, it was on this special occasion that

she gave most the measure of her choice of the consistent, even though it so little meant the consequent,
life. She had reached toward such a life obviously
in quitting the conjugal roof in 1831—had attacked
the experiment clumsily, but according to her light,
by throwing herself on such material support as faculties yet untested might furnish, and on such moral
as several months of the *intimité* of Jules Sandeau and
a briefer taste of that of Prosper Mérimée might further contribute. She had done, in other words, what
she could; subsequent lights show it as not her fault
that she had not done better. With Musset her
future took a long stride; emotionally speaking it
"looked up." Nothing was wanting in this case—
independently of what might then have appeared her
friend's equal genius—quite ideally to qualify it. He
was several years her junior, and as she had her husband and her children, he had, in the high degree of
most young Frenchmen of sensibility, his mother. It
is recorded that with this lady on the eve of the celebrated step she quite had the situation, as the phrase
is, out; which is a note the more in the general, the
intellectual lucidity. The only other note in fact to
be added is that of the absence of funds for the undertaking. Neither partner had a penny to spare; the
plan was wholly to "make money," on a scale, as they
went. A great deal was in the event, exactly speaking, to be made—but the event was at the time far from
clear to them. The enterprise was in consequence
purely and simply, with a rounded perfection that
gives it its value for the critic, an affair of the heart.
That the heart, taking it as a fully representative
organ, should fail of no good occasion completely and
consistently to engage itself was the definite and, as

appeared, the promising assumption on which everything rested. The heart was real life, frank, fearless,
intelligent and even, so far as might be, intelligible
life; everything else was stupid as well as poor, mud-
dle as well as misery. The heart of course might be
misery, for nothing was more possible than that life
predominantly was; but it was at all events the misery
that is least ignoble.

This was the basis of Madame Sand's personal
evolution, of her immense moral energy, for many a
year; it was a practical system, applied and reapplied,
and no "inquiry" concerning her has much point save
as settling what, for our enlightenment and our es-
teem, she made of it. The answer meets us, I think,
after we have taken in the facts, promptly enough and
with great clearness, so long as we consider that it is
not, that it cannot be in the conditions, a simple one.
She made of it then intellectually a splendid living,
but she was able to do this only because she was an
altogether exceptional example of our human stuff.
It is here that her famous heredity comes in: we see
what a race-accumulation of "toughness" had been
required to build her up. Monstrous monarchs and
bastards of kings, great generals and bastards of
bastards, courtesans, dancers supple and hard, accomplished men and women of the old dead great world,
seasoned young soldiers of the Imperial epic, grisettes
of the *pavé de Paris*, Parisian to the core; the mixture
was not quite the blood of people in general, and obviously such a final flower of such a stem might well
fix the attention and appeal to the vigilance of those
qualified to watch its development. These persons
would, doubtless, however, as a result of their obser-

vation, have acquired betimes a sense of the high vitality of their young friend. Formed essentially for independence and constructed for resistance and survival she was to be trusted, as I have hinted, to take care of herself: this was always the residuary fact when a passion was spent. She took care of Musset, she took care of Chopin, took care, in short, through her career, of a whole series of nurslings, but never failed, under the worst ingratitude, to be by her own elasticity still better taken care of. This is why we call her anomalous and deprecate any view of her success that loses sight of the anomaly. The success was so great that but *for* the remainder she would be too encouraging. She was one in a myriad, and the cluster of circumstances is too unlikely to recur.

It is by her success, none the less, we must also remember, that we know her; it is this that makes her interesting and calls for study. She had all the illumination that sensibility, that curiosity, can give, and that so ingeniously induces surrender to it; but the too numerous weaknesses, vulgarities and penalties of adventure and surrender she had only in sufficient degree to complete the experience before they shaped themselves into the eloquence into which she could always reascend. Her eloquence—it is the simplest way to explain her—fairly *made* her success; and eloquence is superlatively rare. When passion can always depend upon it to vibrate passion becomes to that extent action, and success is nothing but action repeated and confirmed. In Madame Sand's particular case the constant recurrence of the malady of passion promoted in the most extraordinary way the superior appearance, the general expression, of health. It is of course not to be denied that there are in her work infirmities and disfigurements, odd smutches even, or unwitting drolleries, which show a sense on some sides enfeebled. The sense of her characters themselves for instance is constantly a confused one; they are too often at sea as to what is possible and what impossible for what we roughly call decent people. Her own categories, loose and liberal, are yet ever positive enough; when they err it is by excess of indulgence and by absence of the humorous vision, a nose for the ridiculous—the fatal want, this last almost always, we are reminded, the heel of Achilles, in the sentimental, the romantic estimate. The general validity of her novels, at any rate, I leave impugned, and the feature I have just noted in them is but one of the points at which they fail of reality. I stick to the history of her personal experiment, as the now so numerous documents show it; for it is here, and here only, that her felicity is amusing and confounding; amusing by the quaintness of some of the facts exposed, and yet confounding by reason of the beauty mixed with them.

The "affair" with Musset for example has come to figure, thanks to the talent of both parties, as one of the great affairs in the history of letters; and yet on the near view of it now enjoyed we learn that it dragged out scarce more than a year. Even this measure indeed is excessive, so far as any measure serves amid so much that is incoherent. It supposed itself to have dropped for upwards of six months, during which another connection, another imperious heart-history, reigned in its stead. The enumeration of these trifles is not, I insist, futile; so that while we are about it we shall find an interest in being clear.

The events of Venice, with those that immediately preceded and followed them, distinctly repay inspection
as an epitome, taken together, of the usual process.
They appear to contain, as well as an intensity all
their own, the essence of all that of other occasions.
The young poet and the young novelist met then,
appear to have met for the first time, toward the end
of June 1833, and to have become finally intimate in
the month of August of that year.   They started together for Italy at the beginning of the winter and
were settled—if settled be not too odd a word to use—
by the end of January in Venice.   I neglect the question of Musset's serious illness there, though it is not
the least salient part of the adventure, and observe
simply that by the end of March he had started to
return to Paris, while his friend, remaining behind,
had yielded to a new affection.   This new affection,
the connection with Pietro Pagello, dates unmistakably from before Musset's departure; and, with the
completion of "Jacques" and the composition of the
beautiful "André," the wonderful "Léone-Léoni" and
some of the most interesting of the "Lettres d'un
Voyageur," constituted the main support of our heroine during the spring and early summer.   By midsum-
mer she had left Italy with Pagello, and they arrive in
Paris on August 14th.   This arrival marks immediately the term of their relations, which had by that
time lasted some six or seven months.   Pagello returned
to Italy, and if they ever met again it was the merest
of meetings and after long years.

   In October, meanwhile, the connection with Musset
was renewed, and renewed—this is the great point—
because the sentiments still entertained by each (in

spite of Pagello, in spite of everything) are stronger even than any awkwardness of which either might have been conscious. The whole business really is one in which we lose our measure alike of awkwardness and of grace. The situation is in the hands of comedy—or *would* be, I should rather say, were it not so distinctly predestined to fall, as I have noted, into those of the nobler form. It is prolonged till the following February, we make out, at furthest, and only after having been more than once in the interval threatened with violent extinction. It bequeaths us thus in a handful of dates a picture than which probably none other in the annals of "passion" was ever more suggestive. The passion is of the kind that is called "immortal"—and so called, wonderful to say, with infinite reason and justice. The poems, the letters, the diaries, the novels, the unextinguished accents and lingering echoes that commemorate it are among the treasures of the human imagination. The literature of the world is appreciably the richer for it. The noblest forms, in a word, on both sides, marked it for their own; it was born, according to the adage, with a silver spoon in its mouth. It was an affection in short transcendent and sublime, and yet the critic sees it come and go before he can positively turn round. The brief period of some seventeen or eighteen months not only affords it all its opportunity, but places comfortably in its lap a relation founded on the same elements and yet wholly distinct from it. Musset occupied in fact but two-thirds of his mistress's time. Pagello overlapped him because Pagello also appealed to the heart; but Pagello's appeal to the heart was disposed of as expeditiously. Musset, in the same way, succeeded Pagello at the voice of a similar appeal, and this claim, in its turn, was polished off in yet livelier fashion.

Liveliness is of course the tune of the "gay" career; it has always been supposed to relegate to comedy the things to which it puts its mark—so that as a series of sequences amenable mainly to satire the approximations I have made would fall neatly into place. The anomaly here, as on other occasions of the same sort depicted in Madame Karénine's volumes, is that the facts, as we are brought near to them, strike us as so out of relation to the beautiful tone. The effect and the achieved dignity are those of tragedy—tragedy rearranging, begetting afresh, in its own interest, all the elements of ecstasy and despair. How can it not be tragedy when this interest is just the interest, which I have touched on, of exemplary eloquence? There are lights in which the material, with its want of nobleness, want of temper, want even of manners, seems scarcely life at all, as the civilised conscience understands life; and yet it is as the most magnanimous of surrenders to life that the whole business is triumphantly reflected in the documents. It is not only that "La Nuit d'Octobre" is divine, that Madame Sand's letters are superb and that nothing can exceed, in particular, the high style of the passage that we now perceive Musset to have borrowed from one of them for insertion in "On ne Badine pas avec l'Amour"—to the extreme profit of the generation which was, for many years thereafter, to hear Delaunay exquisitely declaim it at the Théâtre Français; it is that, strange to say, almost the finest flower of the bouquet is the now-famous written "declaration" addressed to Pagello one evening by the lady. Musset was ill in bed; he was the

attendant doctor; and while, watching and ignorant
of French, he twirled his thumbs or dipped into a book,
his patient's companion, on the other side of the table
and with the lamp between them, dashed off (it took
time) a specimen of her finest prose, which she then
folded and handed to him, and which, for perusal more
at leisure, he carried off in his pocket. It proved
neither more nor less than one of the pontoon bridges
which a force engaged in an active campaign holds
itself ready at any time to throw across a river, and
was in fact of its kind a stout and beautiful structure.
It happily spanned at all events the gulf of a short
acquaintance.

The incident bears a family resemblance to another
which our biographer finds in her path in the year 1837.
Having to chronicle the close of the relation with
Michel de Bourges, from which again her heroine had
so much to suffer, she has also to mention that this
catastrophe was precipitated, to all appearance, by
the contemporaneous dawn of an affection "plus
douce, moins enthousiaste, moins âpre aussi, et j'es-
père plus durable." The object of this affection was
none other than the young man then installed at
Nohant as preceptor to Madame Sand's children—
but as to whom in the event we ask ourselves what by
this time her notion of measure or durability can have
become. It is just this element that has positively
least to do, we seem to make out, with "affection" as
so practised. Affection in any sense worth speaking
of *is* durability; and it is the repeated impermanence
of those manifestations of it on behalf of which the
high horse of "passion" is ridden so hard that makes us
wonder whether such loves and such licences, in spite

of the quality of free experience they represent, had really anything to do with it. It was surely the last thing they contained. Félicien Mallefille may be, to his heart's content, of 1837 and even of a portion of 1838; it is Chopin who is of the rest of the year and—let us hope our biographer will have occasion to show us—of at least the whole of the following. It is here that, as I have mentioned, she pauses.

One of the most interesting contributions to her subject is the long letter from Balzac to his future wife, Madame Hanska, now reproduced in the most substantial of the few volumes of his correspondence ("Lettres à l'Étrangère, 1833–1842," published 1899) and printed by Madame Karénine. The author, finding himself near Nohant in the spring of 1838, went over to pay his illustrious colleague a visit and spent more than a day in sustained conversation with her. He had the good fortune to find her alone, so that they could endlessly talk and smoke by the fire, and nothing can be all at once more vivid, more curious and more judicious than his immediate report of the occasion. It lets into the whole question of his hostess's character and relations—inevitably more or less misrepresented by the party most involved—air and light and truth; it fixes points and re-establishes proportions. It shows appearances confronted, in a word, with Balzac's strong sense of the real and offers the grateful critic still another chance to testify for that precious gift. This same critic's mind, it must be added, rests with complacency on the vision thus evoked, the way that for three days, from five o'clock in the afternoon till five in the morning, the wonderful friends must have had things out. For once, we feel sure, fundamental

questions were not shirked. As regards his comrade
at any rate Balzac puts his finger again and again on
the truth and the idiosyncrasy. "She is not *aimable*
and in consequence will always find it difficult to be
loved." He adds—and it is here that he comes nearest
straightening the question—that she has in character
all the leading marks of the man and as few as possible
those of his counterpart. He implies that, though
judged as a woman she may be puzzling enough, she
hangs together perfectly if judged as a man. She *is*
a man, he repeats, "and all the more that she wants
to be, that she has sunk the woman, that she isn't
one. Women attract, and she repels; and, as I am
much of a man, if this is the effect she produces on me
she must produce it on men who are like me—so that
she will always be unhappy." He qualifies as justly,
I may parenthesise, her artistic side, the limits of which,
he moreover intimates, she had herself expressed to
him. "She has neither intensity of conception, nor
the constructive gift, nor the faculty of reaching the
truth"—Balzac's own deep dye of the truth—"nor
the art of the pathetic. But she holds that, without
knowing the French language, she has *style*. And
it's true."

The light of mere evidence, the light of such re-
searches as Madame Karénine's, added to her so
copious correspondence and autobiography, makes
Madame Sand so much of a riddle that we grasp at
Balzac's authoritative word as at an approach to a
solution. It is, strange to say, by reading another
complexity into her image that we finally simplify it.
The riddle consists in the irreconcilability of her distinction and her vulgarity. Vulgar somehow in spite

of everything is the record of so much taking and tasting and leaving, so much publicity and palpability of "heart," so much experience reduced only to the terms of so many more or less greasy males. And not only vulgar but in a manner grotesque—from the moment, that is, that the experience is presented to us with any emphasis in the name of terror and pity. It was not a passive but an active situation, that of a nature robust and not too fastidious, full at all times of resistance and recovery. No history gives us really more ground to protest against the new fashion, rife in France, of transporting "love," as there mainly represented, to the air of morals and of melancholy. The fashion betrays only the need to rejuvenate, at a considerable cost of falsity, an element in connection with which levity is felt either to have exhausted itself or to look thin as a motive. It is in the light of levity that many of the facts presented by Madame Karénine are most intelligible, and that is the circumstance awkward for sensibility and for all the graces it is invited to show.

The scene quite changes when we cease to expect these graces. As a man Madame Sand was admirable —especially as a man of the dressing-gown and slippers order, easy of approach and of *tutoiement*, rubbing shoulders with queer company and not superstitiously haunted by the conception of the gentleman. There have been many men of genius, delightful, prodigal and even immortal, who squared but scantly with that conception, and it is a company to which our heroine is simply one of the most interesting of recruits. She has in it all her value and loses none of her charm. Above all she becomes in a manner comprehensible, as any frank Bohemian is comprehensible. We have only to imagine the Bohemian really endowed, the Bohemian, that is, both industrious and wise, to get almost all her formula. She keeps here and there a feminine streak—has at moments an excess of volubility and too great an insistence on having been in the right; but for the rest, as Balzac says, the character, confronted with the position, is an explanation. "Son mâle," he tells Madame Hanska, "était rare"— than which nothing could have been more natural. Yet for this masculine counterpart—so difficult to find —she ingenuously spent much of her early life in looking. That the search was a mistake is what constitutes, in all the business of which the Musset episode is the type, the only, the real melancholy, the real moral tragedy.

For all such mistakes, none the less, the whole lesson of the picture is precisely in the disconcerting success of her system. Everything was at the start against that presumption; but everything at the end was to indicate that she was not to have been defeated. Others might well have been, and the banks of the stream of her career are marked, not invisibly, with mouldering traces of the less lucky or the less buoyant; but her attitude as life went on was more and more that of showing how she profited of all things for wisdom and sympathy, for a general expertness and nobleness. These forces, all clarified to an admirable judgment, kept her to the last day serene and superior, and they are one of the reasons why the monument before us is felt not to be misplaced. There should always be a monument to those who have achieved a prodigy. What greater prodigy than to have bequeathed in such mixed elements, to have principally made up of them, the affirmation of an unprecedented intensity of life? For though this intensity was one that broke down in each proposed exhibition the general example remains, incongruously, almost the best we can cite. And all we can say is that this brings us back once more to the large manner, the exceptional energy and well-nigh monstrous vitality, of the individual concerned. Nothing is so absurd as a half-disguise, and Madame Sand's abiding value will probably be in her having given her sex, for its new evolution and transformation, the real standard and measure of change. This evolution and this transformation are all round us unmistakable; the change is in the air; women are turned more and more to looking at life as men look at it and to getting from it what men get. In this direction their aim has been as yet comparatively modest and their emulation low; the challenge they have hitherto picked up is but the challenge of the "average" male. The approximation of the extraordinary woman has been practically, in other words, to the ordinary man. George Sand's service is that she planted the flag much higher—her own approximation at least was to the extraordinary. She reached him, she surpassed him, and she showed how, with native dispositions, the thing could be done. So far as we have come these new records will live as the precious text-book of the business.

GEORGE SAND

1914

IT has much occurred to us, touching those further liberations of the subordinate sex which fill our ears just now with their multitudinous sound, that the promoters of the great cause make a good deal less than they might of one of their very first contentious "assets," if it may not indeed be looked at as quite the first; and thereby fail to pass about, to the general elation, a great vessel of truth. Is this because the life and example of George Sand are things unknown or obscure to the talkers and fighters of to-day —present and vivid as they were to those of the last mid-century, or because of some fear that to invoke victory in her name might, for particular, for even rueful reasons, not be altogether a safe course? It is difficult to account otherwise for the fact that so ample and embossed a shield, and one that shines too at last with a strong and settled lustre, is rather left hanging on the wall than seen to cover advances or ward off attacks in the fray. Certain it is that if a lapse of tradition appeared at one time to have left a little in the lurch the figure of the greatest of all women of letters, of Letters in truth most exactly, as we hold her surely to have been, that explanation should have begun to fail, some fourteen years ago, with the publication of the first volume of Madame Wladimir Karénine's biography, and even in spite of the fact that this singularly interesting work was not till a twelvemonth ago to arrive at the dignity of a third,[1] which leaves it, for all its amplitude, still incomplete. The latest instalment, now before us, follows its predecessors after an interval that had alarmed us not a little for the proper consummation; and the story is even now carried but to the eve of the Revolution of 1848, after which its heroine (that of the Revolution, we may almost say, as well as of the narrative) was to have some twenty-seven years to live. Madame Karénine appears to be a Russian critic writing under a pseudonym; portions of her overbrimming study have appeared dispersedly, we gather, in Russian periodicals, but the harmonious French idiom, of which she is all-sufficient mistress, welds them effectively together, and the result may already be pronounced a commemorative monument of all but the first order. The first order in such attempts has for its sign a faculty of selection and synthesis, not to say a sense of composition and proportion, which neither the chronicler nor the critic in these too multiplied pages is able consistently to exhibit; though on the other hand they represent quite the high-water mark of patience and persistence, of the ideal biographic curiosity. They enjoy further the advantage of the documented state in a degree that was scarce to have been hoped for, every source of information that had remained in reserve—and these proved admirably numerous—having been opened to our inquirer by the confidence of the illustrious lady's two great-granddaughters, both alive at the time the work was begun. Add to this that there has grown up in France a copious George Sand literature, a vast body of illustrative odds and ends,

[1] George Sand, sa Vie et ses Œuvres, vol. iii. (1838–1848). Par Wladimir Karénine. Paris, Plon, 1912.

relics and revelations, on which the would-be prop-
agator of the last word is now free to draw—always
with discrimination. Ideally, well-nigh overwhelmingly informed we may at present therefore hold ourselves; and were that state all that is in question for
us nothing could exceed our advantage.

I

Just the beauty and the interest of the case are,
however, that such a condition by no means exhausts
our opportunity, since in no like connection could it
be less said that to know most is most easily or most
complacently to conclude. May we not decidedly feel
the sense and the "lesson," the suggestive spread, of
a career as a thing scarce really to be measured when
the effect of more and more acquaintance with it is
simply to make the bounds of appreciation recede?
This is why the figure now shown us, blazed upon to
the last intensity by the lamplight of investigation,
and with the rank oil consumed in the process fairly
filling the air, declines to let us off from an hour of
that contemplation which yet involves discomfiture
for us so long as certain lucidities on our own part,
certain serenities of assurance, fail correspondingly to
play up. We feel ourselves so outfaced, as it were;
we somehow want in any such case to meet and match
the assurances with which the subject himself or herself immitigably bristles, and are nevertheless by no
means certain that our bringing up premature forces
or trying to reply with lights of our own may not check
the current of communication, practically without
sense for us unless flowing at its fullest. At our biographer's rate of progress we shall still have much to

wait for; but it can meanwhile not be said that we
have not plenty to go on with. To this may be added
that the stretch of "life," apart from the more concrete exhibition, already accounted for by our three
volumes (if one may discriminate between "production" and life to a degree that is in this connection
exceptionally questionable), represents to all appearance the most violently and variously agitated face
of the career. The establishment of the Second
Empire ushered in for Madame Sand, we seem in
course of preparation to make out, the long period
already more or less known to fame, that is to criticism, as the period of her great placidity, her more
or less notorious appeasement; a string of afternoon
hours as hazily golden as so many reigns of Antonines,
when her genius had mastered the high art of acting
without waste, when a happy play of inspiration had
all the air, so far as our spectatorship went, of filling
her large capacity and her beautiful form to the brim,
and when the gathered fruit of what she had daunt-
lessly done and been heaped itself upon her table as
a rich feast for memory and philosophy. So she came
in for the enjoyment of all the *sagesse* her contemporaries (with only such exceptions as M. Paul de Musset and Madame Louise Colet and the few discordant
pleaders for poor Chopin) finally rejoiced on their side
to acclaim; the sum of her aspects "composing," ar-
ranging themselves in relation to each other, with a
felicity that nothing could exceed and that swept with
great glosses and justifications every aspect of the
past. To few has it been given to "pay" so little,
according to *our* superstition of payment, in proportion
to such enormities of ostensibly buying or borrowing
—which fact, we have to recognise, left an existence

as far removed either from moral, or intellectual, or even social bankruptcy as if it had proceeded from the first but on the most saving lines.

That is what remains on the whole most inimitable in the picture—the impression it conveys of an art of life by which the rough sense of the homely adage that we may not both eat our cake and have it was to be signally falsified; this wondrous mistress of the matter strikes us so as having consumed *her* refreshment, her vital supply, to the last crumb, so far as the provision meant at least freedom and ease, and yet having ever found on the shelf the luxury in question undiminished. Superlatively interesting the idea of how this result was, how it *could* be, achieved—given the world as we on our side of the water mainly know it; and it is as meeting the mystery that the monument before us has doubtless most significance. We shall presently see, in the light of our renewed occasion, how the question is solved; yet we may as well at once say that this will have had for its conclusion to present our heroine— mainly figuring as a novelist of the romantic or sentimental order once pre-eminent but now of shrunken credit—simply as a supreme case of the successful practice of life itself. We have to distinguish for this induction after a fashion in which neither Madame Sand nor her historian has seemed at all positively concerned to distinguish; the indifference on the historian's part sufficiently indicated, we feel, by the complacency with which, to be thorough, she explores even the most thankless tracts of her author's fictional activity, telling the tales over as she comes to them on much the same scale on which she unfolds the situations otherwise documented. The writer of "Con-

suelo" and "Claudie" and a hundred other things is
to this view a literary genius whose output, as our
current term so gracefully has it, the exercise of an
inordinate personal energy happens to mark; whereas
the exercise of personal energy is for ourselves what
most reflects the genius—recorded though this again
chances here to be through the inestimable fact of the
possession of style. Of the action of that perfect, that
only real preservative in face of other perils George
Sand is a wondrous example; but her letters alone
suffice to show it, and the style of her letters is no more
than the breath of her nature, her so remarkable one,
in which expression and aspiration were much the same
function. That is what it is really to *have* style—
when you set about performing the act of life. The
forms taken by this latter impulse then cover everything; they serve for your adventures not less than
they may serve at their most refined pitch for your
Lélias and your Mauprats.

This means accordingly, we submit, that those of us
who at the present hour "feel the change," as the
phrase is, in the computation of the feminine range,
with the fullest sense of what it may portend, shirk
at once our opportunity and our obligation in not
squeezing for its last drop of testimony such an exceptional body of illustration as we here possess. It has
so much to say to any view—whether, in the light of
old conventions, the brightest or the darkest—of what
may either glitter or gloom in a conquest of every
license by our contemporaries of the contending sex,
that we scarce strain a point in judging it a provision
of the watchful fates for this particular purpose and
profit: its answers are so full to most of our uncer-

tainties. It is to be noted of course that the creator
of Lélia and of Mauprat was on the one hand a woman
of an extraordinary gift and on the other a woman
resignedly and triumphantly voteless—doing without
that boon so beautifully, for free development and the
acquisition and application of "rights," that we seem
to see her sardonically smile, before our present tu-
mults, as at a rumpus about nothing; as if women
need set such preposterous machinery in motion for
obtaining things which she had found it of the first
facility, right and left, to stretch forth her hand and
take. There it is that her precedent stands out—apparently to a blind generation; so that some little
insistence on the method of her appropriations would
seem to be peculiarly in place. It was a method that
may be summed up indeed in a fairly simple, if comprehensive, statement: it consisted in her dealing with
life exactly as if she had been a man—exactly not
being too much to say. Nature certainly had contributed on her behalf to this success; it had given her
a constitution and a temperament, the kind of health,
the kind of mind, the kind of courage, that might most
directly help—so that she had but to convert these
strong matters into the kind of experience. The
writer of these lines remembers how a distinguished
and intimate friend of her later years, who was a very
great admirer, said of her to him just after her death
that her not having been born a man seemed, when
one knew her, but an awkward accident: she had been
to all intents and purposes so fine and frank a specimen
of the sex. This anomalous native turn, it may be
urged, can have no general application—women cannot be men by the mere trying or by calling themselves
"as good"; they must have been provided with what

we have just noted as the outfit. The force of George
Sand's exhibition consorts, we contend, none the less
perfectly with the logic of the consummation awaiting
us, if a multitude of signs are to be trusted, in a more
or less near future: that effective repudiation of the
distinctive, as to function and opportunity, as to working and playing activity, for which the definite removal of immemorial disabilities is but another name.
We are in presence already of a practical shrinkage of
the distinctive, at the rapidest rate, and that it must
shrink till nothing of it worth mentioning be left,
what is this but a war-cry (presenting itself also indeed
as a plea for peace) with which our ears are familiar?
Unless the suppression of the distinctive, however, is
to work to the prejudice, as we may fairly call it, of
men, drawing them over to the feminine type rather
than drawing women over to theirs—which is not
what seems most probable—the course of the business
will be a virtual undertaking on the part of the half of
humanity acting ostensibly for the first time in freedom to annex the male identity, that of the other half,
so far as may be at all contrivable, to its own cluster
of elements. Individuals are in great world and race
movements negligible, and if that undertaking must
inevitably appeal to different recruits with a differing
cogency, its really enlisting its army or becoming reflected, to a perfectly conceivable vividness, in the
mass, is all our demonstration requires. At that
point begins the revolution, the shift of the emphasis
from the idea of woman's weakness to the idea of her
strength—which is where the emphasis has lain, from
far back, by his every tradition, on behalf of man;
and George Sand's great value, as we say, is that she
gives us the vision, gives us the particular case, of the

shift achieved, displayed with every assurance and
working with every success.

The answer of her life to the question of what an
effective annexation of the male identity may amount
to, amount to in favouring conditions certainly, but
in conditions susceptible to the highest degree of encouragement and cultivation, leaves nothing to be
desired for completeness. This is the moral of her
tale, the beauty of what she does for us—that at no
point whatever of her history or her character do their
power thus to give satisfaction break down; so that
what we in fact on the whole most recognise is not the
extension she gives to the feminine nature, but the
richness that she adds to the masculine. It is not
simply that she could don a disguise that gaped at
the seams, that she could figure as a man of the mere
carnival or pantomime variety, but that she made so
virile, so efficient and homogeneous a one. Admirable child of the old order as we find her, she was far
from our late-coming theories and fevers—by the
reason simply of her not being reduced to them; as
to which nothing about her is more eloquent than her
living at such ease with a conception of the main rel-
evance of women that is viewed among ourselves as
antiquated to "quaintness." She could afford the
traditional and sentimental, the old romantic and historic theory of the function most natural to them,
since she entertained it exactly as a man would. It is
not that she fails again and again to represent her
heroines as doing the most unconventional things—
upon these they freely embark; but they never in the
least do them for themselves, themselves as the "sex,"
they do them altogether for men. Nothing could well

be more interesting thus than the extraordinary union
of the pair of opposites in her philosophy of the relation of the sexes—than the manner in which her immense imagination, the imagination of a man for range
and abundance, intervened in the whole matter for
the benefit, absolutely, of the so-called stronger party,
or to liberate her sisters up to the point at which men
may most gain and least lose by the liberation. She
read the relation essentially in the plural term—the
relations, and her last word about these was as far as
possible from being that they are of minor importance
to women. Nothing in her view could exceed their
importance to women—it left every other far behind it;
and nothing that could make for authority in her, no
pitch of tone, no range of personal inquiry nor wealth
of experience, no acquaintance with the question that
might derive light from free and repeated adventure,
but belonged to the business of driving this argument
home.

II

Madame Karénine's third volume is copiously devoted to the period of her heroine's intimacy with
Chopin and to the events surrounding this agitated
friendship, which largely fill the ten years precedent
to '48. Our author is on all this ground overwhelmingly
documented, and enlisted though she is in the service
of the more successful party to the association—in the
sense of Madame Sand's having heartily outlived and
survived, not to say professionally and brilliantly
"used," it—the great composer's side of the story
receives her conscientious attention. Curious and
interesting in many ways, these reflections of George
Sand's middle life afford above all the most pointed

illustration of the turn of her personal genius, her aptitude for dealing with men, in the intimate relation, exactly after the fashion in which numberless celebrated men have contributed to their reputation, not to say crowned their claim to superiority, by dealing with women. This being above all the note of her career, with its vivid show of what such dealing could mean for play of mind, for quickening of gift, for general experience and, as we say, intellectual development, for determination of philosophic bent and education of character and fertilisation of fancy, we seem to catch the whole process in the fact, under the light here supplied us, as we catch it nowhere else. It gives us in this application endlessly much to consider—it is in itself so replete and rounded a show; we at once recognise moreover how comparatively little it matters that such works as "Lucrezia Floriani" and "Un Hiver à Majorque" should have proceeded from it, cast into the shade as these are, on our biographer's evidence, by a picture of concomitant energies still more attaching. It is not here by the force of her gift for rich improvisation, beautiful as this was, that the extraordinary woman holds us, but by the force of her ability to act herself out, given the astounding quantities concerned in this self. That energy too, we feel, was in a manner an improvisation—so closely allied somehow are both the currents, the flow of literary composition admirably instinctive and free, and the handling power, as we are constantly moved to call it, the flow of a splendid intelligence all the while at its fullest expressional ease, for the *actual* situations created by her, for whatever it might be that vitally confronted her. Of how to bring about, or at the least find one's self "in for," an

inordinate number of situations, most of them of the
last difficulty, and then deal with them on the spot,
in the narrowest quarters as it were, with an eloquence
and a plausibility that does them and one's own nature at once a sort of ideal justice, the demonstration
here is the fullest—as of what it was further to have her
unfailing verbal as well as her unfailing moral inspiration. What predicament could have been more of
an hourly strain for instance, as we cannot but suppose, than her finding herself inevitably accompanied
by her two children during the stay at Majorca made
by Chopin in '38 under her protection? The victory
of assurance and of the handling power strikes us as
none the less never an instant in doubt, that being
essentially but over the general *kind* of inconvenience
or embarrassment involved for a mother and a friend
in any real consistency of attempt to carry things off
male fashion. We do not, it is true, see a man as a
mother, any more than we easily see a woman as a
gentleman—and least of all perhaps in either case as
an awkwardly placed one; but we see Madame Sand
as a sufficiently bustling, though rather a rough and
ready, father, a father accepting his charge and doing
the best possible under the circumstances; the truth
being of course that the circumstances never *can* be,
even at the worst, or still at the best, the best for
parental fondness, so awkward for him as for a mother.

What call, again, upon every sort of presence of
mind could have been livelier than the one made by
the conditions attending and following the marriage
of young Solange Dudevant to the sculptor Clésinger
in 1846, when our heroine, summoned by the stress of
events both to take responsible action and to rise to

synthetic expression, in a situation, that is in presence
of a series of demonstrations on her daughter's part,
that we seem to find imaginable for a perfect dramatic
adequacy only in that particular home circle, fairly
surpassed herself by her capacity to "meet" everything, meet it much incommoded, yet undismayed,
unabashed and unconfuted, and have on it all, to her
great advantage, the always prodigious last word?
The elements of this especial crisis claim the more
attention through its having been, as a test of her
powers, decidedly the most acute that she was in her
whole course of life to have traversed, more acute
even, because more complicated, than the great occasion of her rupture with Alfred de Musset, at Venice
in '35, on which such a wealth of contemplation and
of ink has been expended. Dramatic enough in their
relation to each other certainly those immortal circumstances, immortal so far as immortalised on either
side by genius and passion: Musset's return, ravaged
and alone, to Paris; his companion's transfer of her
favour to Pietro Pagello, whom she had called in to
attend her friend medically in illness and whose intervention, so far from simplifying the juncture, complicated it in a fashion probably scarce paralleled in
the history of the erotic relation; her retention of
Pagello under her protection for the rest of her period
in Venice; her marvellously domesticated state, in
view of the literary baggage, the collection of social
standards, even taking these but at what they were,
and the general amplitude of personality, that she
brought into residence with her; the conveyance of
Pagello to Paris, on her own return, and the apparent
signification to him at the very gate that her countenance was then and there withdrawn. This was a

brilliant case for her—of coming off with flying colours;
but it strikes us as a mere preliminary flourish of the
bow or rough practice of scales compared to the high
virtuosity which Madame Karénine's new material in
respect to the latter imbroglio now enables us ever so
gratefully to estimate. The protagonist's young children were in the Venetian crisis quite off the scene, and
on occasions subsequent to the one we now glance at
were old enough and, as we seem free to call it, initiated
enough not to solicit our particular concern for them;
whereas at the climax of the connection with Chopin
they were of the perfect age (which was the fresh
marriageable in the case of Solange) to engage our best
anxiety, let alone their being of a salience of sensibility
and temper to leave no one of their aspects negligible.
That their parent should not have found herself conclusively "upset," sickened beyond repair, or otherwise morally bankrupt, on her having to recognise in
her daughter's hideous perversity and depravity, as
we learn these things to have been, certain inevita-
bilities of consequence from the social air of the maternal circle, is really a monumental fact in respect to
our great woman's elasticity, her instinct for never
abdicating by mere discouragement. Here in especial
we get the broad male note—it being so exactly the
manly part, and so very questionably the womanly,
not to have to draw from such imputations of responsibility too crushing a self-consciousness. Of the
extent and variety of danger to which the enjoyment
of a moral tone could be exposed and yet superbly survive Madame Karénine's pages give us the measure;
they offer us in action the very ideal of an exemplary
triumph of character and mind over one of the very
highest tides of private embarrassment that it is well

possible to conceive. And it is no case of that *passive* acceptance of deplorable matters which has abounded in the history of women, even distinguished ones, whether to the pathetic or to the merely scandalous effect; the acceptance is active, constructive, almost exhilarated by the resources of affirmation and argument that it has at its command. The whole instance is sublime in its sort, thanks to the acuteness of *all* its illustrative sides, the intense interest of which loses nothing in the hands of our chronicler; who perhaps, however, reaches off into the vast vague of Chopin's native affiliations and references with an energy with which we find it a little difficult to keep step.

In speaking as we have done of George Sand's "use" of each twist of her road as it came—a use which we now recognise as the very thriftiest—we touch on that principle of vital health in her which made nothing that might by the common measure have been called one of the graver dilemmas, that is one of the checks to the continuity of life, really matter. What this felicity most comes to in fact is that doing at any cost the work that lies to one's hand shines out again and yet again as the saving secret of the soul. She affirmed her freedom right and left, but her most characteristic assertion of it throughout was just in the luxury of labour. The exhaustive account we at any rate now enjoy of the family life surrounding her during the years here treated of and as she had constituted it, the picture of all the queer conflicting sensibilities engaged, and of the endless ramifications and reflections provided for these, leaves us nothing to learn on that congested air, that obstructive medium for the range of the higher tone, which the lady of

Nohant was so at her "objective" happiest, even if
at her superficially, that is her nervously, most flurried
and depressed, in bravely breasting. It is as if the
conditions there and in Paris during these several years
had been consistently appointed by fate to throw into
relief the applications of a huge facility, a sort of
universal readiness, with a rare intelligence to back it.
Absolutely nothing was absent, or with all the data
could have been, that might have bewildered a weaker
genius into some lapse of eloquence or of industry;
everything that might have overwhelmed, or at least
have disconcerted, the worker who could throw off the
splendid "Lucrezia Floriani" in the thick of battle
came upon her at once, inspiring her to show that on
her system of health and cheer, of experiential economy,
as we may call it, to be disconcerted was to be lost.
To be lacerated and calumniated was in comparison
a trifle; with a certain sanity of reaction these things
became as naught, for the sanity of reaction was but
the line of consistency, the theory and attitude of
sincerity kept at the highest point. The artist in
general, we need scarcely remind ourselves, is in a
high degree liable to arrive at the sense of what he may
have seen or felt, or said or suffered, by working it out
as a subject, casting it into some form prescribed by his
art; but even here he in general knows limits—unless
perchance he be loose as Byron was loose, or possess
such a power of disconnection, such a clear stand-off of
the intelligence, as accompanied the experiments of
Goethe. Our own experiments, we commonly feel, are
comparatively timid, just as we can scarce be said, in
the homely phrase, to serve our esthetic results of them
hot and hot; we are too conscious of a restrictive instinct about the conditions we may, in like familiar

language let ourselves in for, there being always the
question of what we should be able "intellectually" to
show for them. The life of the author of "Lucrezia
Floriani" at its most active may fairly be described
as an immunity from restrictive instincts more ably
cultivated than any we know. Again and yet again
we note the positive premium so put upon the surrender to sensibility, and how, since the latter was
certain to spread to its maximum and to be admired
in proportion to its spread, some surrender was always
to have been worth while. "Lucrezia Floriani" ought
to have been rather measurably bad—lucidity, harmony, maturity, definiteness of sense, being so likely
to fail it in the troubled air in which it was born.
Yet how can we do less than applaud a composition
throwing off as it goes such a passage as the splendid
group of pages cited by Madame Karénine from the
incident of the heroine's causing herself to be rowed
over to the island in her Italian lake on that summer
afternoon when the sense of her situation had become
sharp for her to anguish, in order to take stock of the
same without interruption and see, as we should say
to-day, where she is? The whole thing has the grand
manner and the noblest eloquence, reaching out as
it does on the spot to the lesson and the moral of the
convulsions that have been prepared in the first instance with such complacency, and illustrating in perfection the author's faculty for the clear re-emergence
and the prompt or, as we may call it, the paying reaction. The case is put for her here as into its final
nutshell: you may "live" exactly as you like, that is
live in perfect security and fertility, when such breadth
of rendering awaits your simply sitting down to it. Is
it not true, we say, that without her breadth our won-

derful woman would have been "nowhere"?—whereas
with it she is effectively and indestructibly at any
point of her field where she may care to pretend to
stand.

This biographer, I must of course note, discriminates
with delicacy among her heroine's felicities and mistakes, recognising that some of the former, as a latent
awkwardness in them developed, inevitably parted
with the signs that distinguished them from the latter;
but I think we feel, as the instances multiply, that no
regret could have equalled for us that of our not having
the display vivid and complete. Once all the elements
of the scarce in advance imaginable were there it
would have been a pity that they should not offer us
the show of their full fruition. What more striking
show, for example, than that, as recorded by Madame
Karénine in a footnote, the afflicted parent of Solange
should have lived to reproduce, or rather, as she would
herself have said, to "arrange" the girlish character
and conduct of that young person, so humiliating at the
time to any near relation, let alone a mother, in the
novel of "Mademoiselle Merquem," where the truth
to the original facts and the emulation of the graceless prime "effects" are such as our author can vouch
for? The fiction we name followed indeed after long
years, but during the lifetime of the displeasing daughter and with an ease of reference to the past that may
fairly strike us as the last word of superiority to blight-
ing association. It is quite as if the close and amused
matching of the character and its play in the novel
with the wretched old realities, those that had broken
in their day upon the scared maternal vision, had been
a work of ingenuity attended with no pang. The

example is interesting as a measure of the possible victory of time in a case where we might have supposed the one escape to have been by forgetting. Madame Sand remembers to the point of gratefully— gratefully as an artist—reconstituting; we in fact feel her, as the irrepressible, the "healthy" artist, positively to enjoy so doing. Thus it clearly defined itself for her in the fulness of time that, humiliating, to use our expression, as the dreadful Solange might have been and have incessantly remained, she herself had never in the least consented to the stupidity or sterility of humiliation. So it could be that the free mind and the free hand were ever at her service. A beautiful indifferent agility, a power to cast out that was at least proportioned to the power to take in, hangs about all this and meets us in twenty connections. Who of her readers has forgotten the harmonious dedication— her inveterate dedications have always, like her clear light prefaces, the last grace—of "Jeanne," so anciently, so romantically readable, to her faithful Berrichon servant who sits spinning by the fire? "Vous ne savez pas lire, ma paisible amie," but that was not to prevent the association of her name with the book, since both her own daughter and the author's are in happy possession of the art and will be able to pass the entertainment on to her. This in itself is no more than a sign of the writer's fine democratic ease, which she carried at all times to all lengths, and of her charming habit of speech; but it somehow becomes further illustrational, testifying for the manner in which genius, if it be but great enough, lives its life at small cost, when we learn that after all, by a turn of the hand, the "paisible amie" was, under provocation, bundled out of the house as if the beautiful relation had not meant half of what appeared. Françoise and her presence were dispensed with, but the exquisite lines remain, which we would not be without for the world.

III

The various situations determined for the more eminent of George Sand's intimate associates would always be independently interesting, thanks to the intrinsic appeal of these characters and even without the light reflected withal on the great agent herself; which is why poor Chopin's figuration in the events of the year 1847, as Madame Karénine so fully reconstitutes them, is all that is wanted to point their almost nightmare quality. Without something of a close view of them we fail of a grasp of our heroine's genius—her genius for keeping her head in deep seas morally and reflectively above water, though but a glance at them must suffice us for averting this loss. The old-world quality of drama, which throughout so thickens and tones the air around her, finds remarkable expression in the whole picture of the moment. Every connection involved bristles like a conscious consequence, tells for all it is worth, as we say, and the sinister complexity of reference—for all the golden clearings-up that awaited it on the ideal plane—leaves nothing to be desired. The great and odd sign of the complications and convulsions, the alarms and excursions recorded, is that these are all the more or less direct fruits of sensibility, which had primarily been indulged in, under the doom of a preparation of them which no preparation of anything else was to emulate, with a good faith fairly touching in presence of the eventual ugliness. Madame Sand's wonderful mother, commemorated for us in "L'Histoire de ma Vie" with the truth surely attaching in a like degree to no mother in all the literature of so-called confession, had had for cousin a "fille entretenue" who had married a mechanic. This Adèle Brault had had in the course of her adventures a daughter in whom, as an unfortunate young relative, Madame Dupin had taken an interest, introducing her to the heiress of Nohant, who viewed her with favour—she appears to have been amiable and commendable—and eventually associated her with her own children. She was thus the third member of that illegitimate progeny with which the Nohant scene was to have become familiar, George Sand's natural brother on her father's side and her natural sister on her mother's representing this element from the earlier time on. The young Augustine, fugitive from a circle still less edifying, was thus made a companion of the son and the daughter of the house, and was especially held to compare with the latter to her great advantage in the matter of character, docility and temper. These young persons formed, as it were, with his more distinguished friend, the virtual family of Chopin during those years of specifically qualified domestication which affect us as only less of a mystification to taste than that phase of the unrestricted which had immediately preceded them. Hence a tangled tissue of relations within the circle that became, as it strikes us, indescribable for difficulty and "delicacy," not to say for the perfection of their impracticability, and as to which the great point is that Madame Sand's having taken them so robustly for granted throws upon her temperamental genius a more direct light than any other. The whole case belongs doubtless even more to the hapless history of Chopin himself than to that

of his terrible friend—terrible for her power to flourish
in conditions sooner or later fatal to weaker vessels;
but is in addition to this one of the most striking illustrations possible of that view or theory of social life
handed over to the reactions of sensibility almost alone
which, while ever so little the ideal of the Anglo-Saxon
world, has largely governed the manners of its sister
societies. It has been our view, very emphatically,
in general, that the sane and active social body—or,
for that matter, the sane and active individual, addressed to the natural business of life—goes wrongly
about it to *encourage* sensibility, or to do anything on
the whole but treat it as of no prime importance; the
traps it may lay for us, however, being really of the
fewest in a race to which the very imagination of it
may be said, I think, to have been comparatively
denied. The imagination of it sat irremovably, on the
other hand, and as a matter of course, at the Nohant
fireside; where indeed we find the play and the
ravage chiefly interesting through our thus seeing the
delicate Chopin, whose semi-smothered appeal remains
peculiarly pathetic, all helpless and foredoomed at the
centre of the whirl. Nothing again strikes us more
in the connection than the familiar truth that interesting persons make everything that concerns them interesting, or seldom fail to redeem from what might in
another air seem but meanness and vanity even their
most compromised states and their greatest wastes of
value. Every one in the particular Nohant drama
here exposed loses by the exposure—so far as loss could
be predicated of amounts which, in general, excepting
the said sensibility, were so scant among them; every
one, that is, save the ruling spirit of all, with the extraordinary mark in her of the practical defiance of

waste and of her inevitable enrichment, for our measure, as by reflection from the surrounding shrinkage.
One of the oddest aspects of the scene is also one of
the wretchedest, but the oddity makes it interesting,
by the law I just glanced at, in spite of its vulgar side.
How could it not be interesting, we ask as we read,
to feel that Chopin, though far from the one man, was
the one gentleman of the association, the finest set of
nerves and scruples, and yet to see how little that
availed him, in exasperated reactions, against mistakes
of perverted sympathy?   It is relevant in a high degree
to our view of his great protectress as reducible at her
best to male terms that she herself in this very light
fell short, missed the ideal safeguard which for her
friend had been preinvolved—as of course may be the
peril, ever, with the creature so transmuted, and as is
so strikingly exemplified, in the pages before us, when
Madame Karénine ingenuously gives us chapter and
verse for her heroine's so unqualified demolition of
the person of Madame d'Agoult, devotee of Liszt,
mother to be, by that token, of Richard Wagner's
second wife, and sometime intimate of the author
of "Isidora," in which fiction we are shown the parody
perpetrated. If women rend each other on occasion
with sharper talons than seem to belong on the whole
to the male hand, however intendingly applied, we
find ourselves reflect parenthetically that the loss of
this advantage may well be a matter for them to consider when the new approximation is the issue.

The great sign of the Nohant circle on all this showing, at any rate, is the intense personalism, as we may
call it, reigning there, or in other words the vivacity,
the acuity and irritability of the personal relations—

which flourished so largely, we at the same time feel,
by reason of the general gift for expression, that gift
to which we owe the general superiority of every letter,
from it scarce matters whom, laid under contribution
by our author. How could people not feel with acuity
when they could, when they had to, write with such
point and such specific intelligence?—just indeed as
one asks how letters could fail to remain at such a level
among them when they incessantly generated choice
matter for expression. Madame Sand herself is of
course on this ground easily the most admirable, as
we have seen; but every one "knows how" to write,
and does it well in proportion as the matter in hand
most demands and most rewards proper saying. Much
of all this stuff of history seems indeed to have been
susceptible of any amount of force of statement; yet
we note all the while how in the case of the great
mistress of the pen at least some shade of intrinsic
beauty attends even the presentation of quite abominable facts. We can only see it as abominable, at least,
so long as we have Madame Sand's words—which are
somehow a different thing from her word—for it, that
Chopin had from the first "sided" with the atrocious
Solange in that play of her genius which is characterised by our chronicler as wickedness for the sake of
wickedness, as art for the sake of art, without other
logic or other cause. "Once married," says Madame
Karénine, "she made a double use of this wickedness.
She had always hated Augustine; she wished, one
doesn't know why, to break off her marriage, and by
calumnies and insinuations she succeeded. Then
angry with her mother she avenged herself on her as
well by further calumnies. Thereupon took place at
Nohant such events that"—that in fine we stop before

them with this preliminary shudder. The cross-
currents of violence among them would take more
keeping apart than we have time for, the more that
everything comes back, for interest, to the intrinsic
weight of the tone of the principal sufferer from them—
as we see her, as we wouldn't for the world not see her,
in spite of the fact that Chopin was to succumb scarce
more than a year later to multiplied lacerations, and
that she was to override and reproduce and pre-ap-
pointedly flourish for long years after. If it is interesting, as I have pronounced it, that Chopin, again,
should have consented to be of the opinion of Solange
that the relations between her brother Maurice and
the hapless Augustine were of the last impropriety, I
fear I can account no better for this than by our sense
that the more the *genius loci* has to feed her full tone
the more our faith in it, as such a fine thing in itself,
is justified. Almost immediately after the precipitated marriage of the daughter of the house has taken
place, the Clésinger couple, avid and insolent, of a
breadth of old time impudence in fact of which our
paler day has lost the pattern, are back on the mother's
hands, to the effect of a vividest picture of Maurice
well-nigh in a death-grapple with his apparently quite
monstrous "bounder" of a brother-in-law, a picture
that further gives us Madame Sand herself smiting
Clésinger in the face and receiving from him a blow
in the breast, while Solange "coldly," with an iciness
indeed peculiarly her own, fans the rage and approves
her husband's assault, and while the divine composer,
though for that moment much in the background, approves the wondrous approval. He still approves, to
all appearance, the daughter's interpretation of the
mother's wish to "get rid" of him as the result of an

amorous design on the latter's part in respect of a
young man lately introduced to the circle as Maurice's
friend and for the intimate relation with whom it is
thus desirable that the coast shall be made clear.
How else than through no fewer consistencies of the
unedifying on the part of these provokers of the expressional reaction should we have come by innumerable fine epistolary passages, passages constituting in
themselves verily such adornments of the tale, such
notes in the scale of all the damaged dignity redressed,
that we should be morally the poorer without them?
One of the vividest glimpses indeed is not in a letter
but in a few lines from "L'Histoire de ma Vie," the
composition of which was begun toward the end of
this period and while its shadow still hung about—
early in life for a projected autobiography, inasmuch
as the author had not then reached her forty-fifth
year. Chopin at work, improvising and composing,
was apt to become a prey to doubts and depressions,
so that there were times when to break in upon these
was to render him a service.

But it was not always possible to induce him to leave the piano,
often so much more his torment than his joy, and he began gradually to resent my proposing he should do so. I never ventured
on these occasions to insist. Chopin in displeasure was appalling,
and as with me he always controlled himself it was as if he might
die of suffocation.

It is a vision of the possibilities of vibration in such
organisms that does in fact appal, and with the clash
of vibrations, those both of genius and of the general
less sanctioned sensibility, the air must have more than
sufficiently resounded. Some eight years after the beginning of their friendship and the year after the final

complete break in it she writes to Madame Pauline Viardot:

Do you see Chopin? Tell me about his health. I have been unable to repay his fury and his hatred by hatred and fury. I think of him as of a sick, embittered, bewildered child. I saw much of Solange in Paris, the letter goes on, and made her my constant occupation, but without finding anything but a stone in the place of her heart. I have taken up my work again while waiting for the tide to carry me elsewhere.

All the author's "authority" is in these few words, and in none more than in the glance at the work and the tide. The work and the tide rose ever as high as she would to float her, and wherever we look there is always the authority. "I find Chopin *magnificent*," she had already written from the thick of the fray, "to keep seeing, frequenting and approving Clésinger, who struck me because I snatched from his hands the hammer he had raised upon Maurice—Chopin whom every one talks of as my most faithful and devoted friend." Well indeed may our biographer have put it that from a certain date in May 1847 "the two *Leitmotive* which might have been called in the terms of Wagner the *Leitmotif* of soreness and the *Leitmotif* of despair—Chopin, Solange—sound together now in fusion, now in a mutual grip, now simply side by side, in all Madame Sand's unpublished letters and in the few (of the moment) that have been published. A little later a third joins in—Augustine Brault, a motive narrowly and tragically linked to the *basso obligato* of Solange." To meet such a passage as the following under our heroine's hand again is to feel the whole temper of intercourse implied slip straight out of our analytic grasp. The allusion is to Chopin and to the "defection" of which he had been guilty, to her view, at the time when it had been most important that she might count on him. What we have first, as outsiders, to swallow down, as it were, is the state of things, the hysteric pitch of family life, in which any ideal of reticence, any principle, as we know it, of minding one's business, for mere dignity's sake if for none other, had undergone such collapse.

I grant you I am not sorry that he has withdrawn from me the government of his life, for which both he and his friends wanted to make me responsible in so much too absolute a fashion. His temper kept growing in asperity, so that it had come to his constantly blowing me up, from spite, ill-humour and jealousy, in presence of my friends and my children. Solange made use of it with the astuteness that belongs to her, while Maurice began to give way to indignation. Knowing and seeing *la chasteté de nos rapports*, he saw also that the poor sick soul took up, without *wanting to* and perhaps without being able to help it, the attitude of the lover, the husband, the proprietor of my thoughts and actions. He was on the point of breaking out and telling him to his face that he was making me play, at forty-three years of age, a ridiculous part, and that it was an abuse of my kindness, my patience, and my pity for his nervous morbid state. A few months more, a few days perhaps, of this situation, and an impossible frightful struggle would have broken out between them. Foreseeing the storm, I took advantage of Chopin's predilection for Solange and left him to sulk, without an effort to bring him round. We have not for three months exchanged a word in writing, and I don't know how such a cooling-off will end.

She develops the picture of the extravagance of his sick irritability; she accepts with indifference the certainty that his friends will accuse her of having cast him out to take a lover; the one thing she "minds" is the force of evil in her daughter, who is the centre of all the treachery. "She will come back to me when she needs me, that I know. But her return will be neither tender nor consoling." Therefore it is when at the beginning of the winter of this same dreadful year she throws off the free rich summary of what she has been through in the letter to M. Charles Poncy already published in her Correspondence we are swept into the current of sympathy and admiration. The preceding months had been the heaviest and most painful of her life.

I all but broke down under them utterly, though I had for long seen them coming. But you know how one is not always overhung by the evil portent, however clear one may read it—there are days, weeks, even whole months, when one lives on illusion and fondly hopes to divert the blow that threatens. It is always at last the most probable ill that surprises us unarmed and unprepared. To this explosion of unhappy underground germs joined themselves sundry contributive matters, bitter things too and quite unexpected; so that I am broken by grief in body and soul. I believe my grief incurable, for I never succeed in throwing it off for a few hours without its coming upon me again during the next in greater force and gloom. I nevertheless struggle against it without respite, and if I don't hope for a victory which would have to consist of not feeling at all, at least I have reached that of still bearing with life, of even scarcely feeling ill, of having recovered my taste for work and of not showing my distress. I have got back outside calm and cheer, which are so necessary for others, and everything in my life seems to go on well.

We had already become aware, through commemorations previous to the present, of that first or innermost line of defence residing in George Sand's splendid mastery of the letter, the gift that was always so to assure her, on every issue, the enjoyment of the first chance with posterity. The mere cerebral and manual activity represented by the quantity no less than the quality of her outflow through the post at a season when her engagements were most pressing and her anxieties of every sort most cruel is justly qualified by

Madame Karénine as astounding; the new letters here given to the world heaping up the exhibition and testifying even beyond the finest of those gathered in after the writer's death—the mutilations, suppressions and other freedoms then used, for that matter, being now exposed. If no plot of her most bustling fiction ever thickened at the rate at which those agitations of her inner circle at which we have glanced multiplied upon her hands through the later 'forties, so we are tempted to find her rather less in possession of her great *moyens* when handling the artificial presentation than when handling what we may call the natural. It is not too much to say that the long letter addressed to the cynical Solange in April '52, and which these pages give us *in extenso*, would have made the fortune of any mere interesting "story" in which one of the characters might have been presented as writing it. It is a document of the highest psychological value and a practical summary of all the elements of the writer's genius, of all her indefeasible advantages; it is verily the gem of her biographer's collection. Taken in connection with a copious communication to her son, of the previous year, on the subject of his sister's character and vices, and of their common experience of these, it offers, in its ease of movement, its extraordinary frankness and lucidity, its splendid apprehension and interpretation of realities, its state, as it were, of saturation with these, exactly the kind of interest for which her novels were held remarkable, but in a degree even above their maximum. Such a letter is an effusion of the highest price; none of a weight so baffling to estimation was probably ever inspired in a mother by solicitude for a clever daughter's possibilities. Never surely had an accomplished daughter laid under such contribution a mother of high culture; never had such remarkable and pertinent things had to flow from such a source; never in fine was so urgent an occasion so admirably, so inimitably risen to. Marvellous through it all is the way in which, while a common recognition of the "facts of life," as between two perfectly intelligent men of the world, gives the whole diapason, the abdication of moral authority and of the rights of wisdom never takes place. The tone is a high implication of the moral advantages that Solange had inveterately enjoyed and had decided none the less to avail herself of so little; which advantages we absolutely believe in as we read—*there* is the prodigious part: such an education of the soul, and in fact of every faculty, such a claim for the irreproachable, it would fairly seem, do we feel any association with the great fluent artist, in whatever conditions taking place, inevitably, necessarily to have been. If we put ourselves questions we yet wave away doubts, and with whatever remnants of prejudice the writer's last word may often have to clash, our own is that there is nothing for grand final rightness like a sufficiently *general* humanity—when a particularly beautiful voice happens to serve it.

GABRIELE D'ANNUNZIO

1902

THE great feast-days of all, for the restless critic, are those much interspaced occasions of his really meeting a "case," as he soon enough learns to call, for his convenience and assistance, any supremely contributive or determinant party to the critical question. These are recognitions that make up for many dull hours and dry contacts, many a thankless, a disconcerted gaze into faces that have proved expressionless. Always looking, always hoping for his happiest chance, the inquirer into the reasons of things—by which I mean especially into the reasons of books—so often misses it, so often wastes his steps and withdraws his confidence, that he inevitably works out for himself, sooner or later, some handy principle of recognition. It may be a rough thing, a mere home-made tool of his trade, but it serves his purpose if it keeps him from beginning with mistakes. He becomes able to note in its light the signs and marks of the possible precious identity, able to weigh with some exactitude the appearances that make for its reality. He ends, through much expenditure of patience, by seeing when, how, why, the "case" announces and presents itself, and he perhaps even feels that failure and felicity have worked together to produce in him a sense for it that may at last be trusted as an instinct. He thus arrives at a view of all the candidates, frequently interesting enough, who fall short of the effective title, because he has at need, perhaps even from afar, scented along the wind the strongest member of the herd. He may perhaps not always be able to give us the grounds of his certainty, but he is at least never without knowing it in presence of one of the full-blown products that are the joy of the analyst. He recognises as well how the state of being full-blown comes above all from the achievement of consistency, of that last consistency which springs from the unrestricted enjoyment of freedom.

Many of us will doubtless not have forgotten how we were witnesses a certain number of years since to a season and a society that had found themselves of a sudden roused, as from some deep drugged sleep, to the conception of the "esthetic" law of life; in consequence of which this happy thought had begun to receive the honours of a lively appetite and an eager curiosity, but was at the same time surrounded and manipulated by as many different kinds of inexpertness as probably ever huddled together on a single pretext. The spectacle was strange and finally was wearisome, for the simple reason that the principle in question, once it was proclaimed—a principle not easily formulated, but which we may conveniently speak of as that of beauty at any price, beauty appealing alike to the senses and to the mind—was never felt to fall into its place as really adopted and efficient. It remained for us a queer high-flavoured fruit from overseas, grown under another sun than ours, passed round and solemnly partaken of at banquets organised to try it, but not found on the whole really to agree with us, not proving thoroughly digestible. It brought with it

no repose, brought with it only agitation. We were
not really, not fully convinced, for the state of conviction is quiet. This was to have been the state itself
—that is the state of mind achieved and established—
in which we were to know ugliness no more, to make
the esthetic consciousness feel at home with us, or
learn ourselves at any rate to feel at home with *it*.
That would have been the reign of peace, the supreme
beatitude; but stability continued to elude us. We
had mustered a hundred good reasons for it, yet the
reasons but lighted up our desert. They failed to
flower into a single concrete esthetic "type." One
authentic, one masterful specimen would have done
wonders for us, would at least have assuaged our curiosity. But we were to be left till lately with our curiosity on our hands.

This is a yearning, however, that Signor D'Annunzio
may at last strike us as supremely formed to gratify;
so promptly we find in him as a literary figure the highest expression of the reality that our own conditions
were to fail of making possible. He has immediately
the value of giving us by his mere logical unfolding
the measure of our shortcomings in the same direction,
that of our timidities and penuries and failures. He
throws a straighter and more inevitable light on the
esthetic consciousness than has, to my sense, in our
time, reached it from any other quarter; and there is
many a mystery that properly interrogated he may
help to clear up for us, many an explanation of our
misadventure that—as I have glanced at it—he may
give. He starts with the immense advantage of enjoying the invoked boon by grace and not by effort, of
claiming it under another title than the sweat of his

brow and the aspiration of his culture. He testifies to the influence of things that have had time to get themselves taken for granted. Beauty at any price is an old story to him; art and form and style as the aim of the superior life are a matter of course; and it may be said of him, I think, that, thanks to these transmitted and implanted instincts and aptitudes, his individual development begins where the struggle of the mere earnest questioner ends. Signor D'Annunzio is earnest in his way, quite extraordinarily—which is a feature of his physiognomy that we shall presently come to and about which there will be something to say; but we feel him all the while in such secure possession of his heritage of favouring circumstance that his sense of intellectual responsibility is almost out of proportion. This is one of his interesting special marks, the manner in which the play of the esthetic instinct in him takes on, for positive extravagance and as a last refinement of freedom, the crown of solicitude and anxiety. Such things but make with him for ornament and parade; they are his tribute to civility; the essence of the matter is meanwhile in his blood and his bones. No mistake was possible from the first as to his being of the inner literary camp—a new form altogether of perceptive and expressive energy; the question was settled by the intensity and variety, to say nothing of the precocity, of his early poetic production.

Born at Pescara, in the Regno, the old kingdom of Naples, "toward" 1863, as I find noted by a cautious biographer, he had while scarce out of his teens allowed his lyric genius full opportunity of scandalising even the moderately austere. He defined himself betimes very much as he was to remain, a rare imagination, a poetic, an artistic intelligence of extraordinary range and fineness concentrated almost wholly on the life of the senses. For the critic who simplifies a little to state clearly, the only ideas he urges upon us are the erotic and the plastic, which have for him about an equal intensity, or of which it would be doubtless more correct to say that he makes them interchangeable faces of the same figure. He began his career by playing with them together in verse, to innumerable light tunes and with an extraordinary general effect of curiosity and brilliancy. He has continued still more strikingly to play with them in prose; they have remained the substance of his intellectual furniture. It is of his prose only, however, that, leaving aside the Intermezzo, L'Isottèo, La Chimera, Odi Navali and other such matters, I propose to speak, the subject being of itself ample for one occasion. His five novels and his four plays have extended his fame; they suggest by themselves as many observations as we shall have space for. The group of productions, as the literary industry proceeds among us to-day, is not large, but we may doubt if a talent and a temperament, if indeed a whole "view of life," ever built themselves up as vividly for the reader out of so few blocks. The writer is even yet enviably young; but this solidity of his literary image, as of something already seated on time and accumulation, makes him a rare example. Precocity is somehow an inadequate name for it, as precocity seldom gets away from the element of promise, and it is not exactly promise that blooms in the hard maturity of such a performance as "The Triumph of Death." There are certain expressions of experience, of the experience of the whole man, that are like final milestones, milestones for his possible

fertility if not for his possible dexterity; a truth that
has not indeed prevented "Il Fuoco," with its doubtless
still ampler finality, from following the work just mentioned. And we have had particularly before us, in
verse, I must add, "Francesca da Rimini," with the
great impression a great actress has enabled this drama
to make.

Only I must immediately in this connection also add
that Signor D'Annunzio's plays are, beside his novels,
of decidedly minor weight; testifying abundantly to
his style, his romantic sense and his command of images,
but standing in spite of their eloquence only for half
of his talent, largely as he yet appears in "Il Fuoco" to
announce himself by implication as an intending, indeed as a pre-eminent dramatist. The example is
interesting when we catch in the fact the opportunity
for comparing with the last closeness the capacity of
the two rival canvases, as they become for the occasion,
on which the picture of life may be painted. The
closeness is never so great, the comparison never so
pertinent, as when the separate efforts are but different
phases of the same talent. It is not at any rate under
this juxtaposition that the infinitely greater amplitude
of portrayal resident in the novel strikes us least. It
in fact strikes us the more, in this quarter, for Signor
D'Annunzio, that his plays have been with one exception successes. We must none the less take "Francesca" but for a success of curiosity; on the part of
the author I mean even more than on the part of the
public. It is primarily a pictorial and ingenious thing
and, as a picture of passion, takes, in the total collection, despite its felicities of surface and arrangement,
distinctly a "back seat." Scarcely less than its com-

panions it overflows with the writer's plenitude of verbal expression, thanks to which, largely, the series will always prompt a curiosity and even a tenderness in any reader interested precisely in this momentous question of "style in a play"—interested in particular to learn by what esthetic chemistry a play would as a work of art propose to eschew it. It is in any such connection so inexpugnable that we have only to be cheated of it in one place to feel the subject cry aloud for it, like a sick man forsaken, in another.

I may mention at all events the slightly perverse fact that, thanks, on this side, to the highest watermark of translation, Signor D'Annunzio makes his best appeal to the English public as a dramatist. Of each of the three English versions of other examples of his work whose titles are inscribed at the beginning of these remarks it may be said that they are adequate and respectable considering the great difficulty encountered. The author's highest good fortune has nevertheless been at the hands of his French interpreter, who has managed to keep constantly close to him—allowing for an occasional inconsequent failure of courage when the directness of the original *brave l'honnêteté*—and yet to achieve a tone not less idiomatic, and above all not less marked by "authority," than his own. Mr. Arthur Symons, among ourselves, however, has rendered the somewhat insistent eloquence of "La Gioconda" and the intricate and difficult verse of "Francesca" with all due sympathy, and in the latter case especially—a highly arduous task—with remarkably patient skill. It is not his fault, doubtless, if the feet of his English text strike us as moving with less freedom than those of his original; such being the hard

price paid always by the translator who tries for correspondence from step to step, tries for an identical
order. Even less is he responsible for its coming still
more home to us in a translation that the meagre anecdote here furnishing the subject, and on which the
large superstructure rests, does not really lend itself
to those developments that make a full or an interesting tragic complexity. Behind the glamour of its immense literary association the subject of "Francesca"
is for purposes of essential, of enlarged exhibition delusive and "short."

These, however, are for the moment side-issues;
what is more relevant is the stride taken by our author's
early progress in his first novel and his second, "Il
Piacere" and "L'Innocente"; a pair from the freshness, the direct young energy of which he was, for some
of his admirers, too promptly and to markedly to decline. We may take it as characteristic of the intensity
of the literary life in him that his brief career falls
already thus into periods and supplies a quantity of
history sufficient for those differences among students
by which the dignity of history appears mainly to be
preserved. The nature of his prime inspiration I have
already glanced at; and we are helped to a characterisation if I say that the famous enthroned "beauty"
which operates here, so straight, as the great obsession, is not in any perceptible degree moral beauty. It
would be difficult perhaps to find elsewhere in the
same compass so much expression of the personal life
resting so little on any picture of the personal character and the personal will. It is not that Signor
D'Annunzio has not more than once pushed his fur-
row in this latter direction; but nothing is exactly more

interesting, as we shall see, than the seemingly inevitable way in which the attempt falls short.

"Il Piacere," the first in date of the five tales, has, though with imperfections, the merit of giving us strongly at the outset the author's scale and range of view, and of so constituting a sort of prophetic summary of his elements. All that is done in the later things is more or less done here, and nothing is absent here that we are not afterwards also to miss. I propose, however, that it shall not be prematurely a question with us of what we miss; no intelligible statement of which, for that matter, in such considerations as these, is ever possible till there has been some adequate statement of what we find. Count Andrea Sperelli is a young man who pays, pays heavily, as we take it that we are to understand, for an unbridled surrender to the life of the senses; whereby it is primarily a picture of that life that the story gives us. He is represented as inordinately, as quite monstrously, endowed for the career that from the first absorbs and that finally is to be held, we suppose, to engulf him; and it is a tribute to the truth with which his endowment is presented that we should scarce know where else to look for so complete and convincing an account of such adventures. Casanova de Seingalt is of course infinitely more copious, but his autobiography is cheap loose journalism compared with the directed, finely-condensed iridescent epic of Count Andrea.

This young man's years have run but half their course from twenty to thirty when he meets and becomes entangled with a woman more infernally expert even than himself in the matters in which he is most expert—and he is given us as a miracle of social and intellectual accomplishment—the effect of whom is fatally to pervert and poison his imagination. As his imagination is applied exclusively to the employments of "love," this means, for him, a frustration of all happiness, all comfortable consistency, in subsequent relations of the same order. The author's view—this is fundamental—is all of a world in which relations of any other order whatever mainly fail to offer themselves in any attractive form. Andrea Sperelli, loving, accordingly—in the manner in which D'Annunzio's young men love and to which we must specifically return—a woman of good faith, a woman as different as possible from the creature of evil communications, finds the vessel of his spirit itself so infected and disqualified that it falsifies and dries up everything that passes through it. The idea that has virtually determined the situation appears in fact to be that the hero *would* have loved in another manner, or would at least have wished to, but that he had too promptly put any such fortune, so far as his capacity is concerned, out of court. We have our reasons, presently manifest, for doubting the possibility itself; but the theory has nevertheless given its direction to the fable.

For the rest the author's three sharpest signs are already unmistakable: first his rare notation of states of excited sensibility; second his splendid visual sense, the quick generosity of his response to the message, as we nowadays say, of aspects and appearances, to the beauty of places and things; third his ample and exquisite style, his curious, various, inquisitive, always active employment of language as a means of communication and representation. So close is the marriage between his power of "rendering," in the light of the imagination, and whatever he sees and feels, that we should much mislead in speaking of his manner as a thing distinct from the matter submitted to it. The fusion is complete and admirable, so that, though his work is nothing if not "literary," we see at no point of it where literature or where life begins or ends: we swallow our successive morsels with as little question as we swallow food that has by proper preparation been reduced to singleness of savour. It is brought home to us afresh that there is no complete creation without style any more than there is complete music without sound; also that when language becomes as closely applied and impressed a thing as for the most part in the volumes before us the fact of artistic creation is registered at a stroke. It is never more present than in the thick-sown illustrative images and figures that fairly bloom under D'Annunzio's hand. I find examples in "Il Piacere," as elsewhere, by simply turning the pages. "His will"—of the hero's weakness —"useless as a sword of base temper hung at the side of a drunkard or a dullard." Or of his own southern land in September: "I scarce know why, looking at the country in this season, I always think of some beautiful woman after childbirth, who lies back in her white bed, smiling with a pale astonished inextinguishable smile." Or the incision of this: "Where for him now were those unclean short-lived loves that left in the mouth the strange acidity of fruit cut with a steel knife?" Or the felicity of the following, of a southern night seen and felt from the terrace of a villa. "Clear meteors at intervals streaked the motionless air, running over it as lightly and silently as drops of water on a crystal pane." "The sails on the sea," he says of the same look-out by day, "were as pious and number-less as the wings of cherubim on the gold grounds of old Giottesque panels."

But it is above all here for two things that his faculty is admirable; one of them his making us feel through the windows of his situation, or the gaps, as it were, of his flowering wood, the golden presence of Rome, the charm that appeals to him as if he were one of the pilgrims from afar, save that he reproduces it with an authority in which, as we have seen, the pilgrims from afar have mainly been deficient. The other is the whole category of the phenomena of "passion," as passion prevails between his men and his women—and scarcely anything else prevails; the states of feeling, of ecstasy and suffering engendered, the play of sensibility from end to end of the scale. In this direction he has left no dropped stitches for any worker of like tapestries to pick up. We shall here have made out that many of his "values" are much to be contested, but that where they are true they are as fresh as discoveries; witness the passage where Sperelli, driving back to Rome after a steeplechase in which he has been at the supreme moment worsted, meets nothing that does not play with significance into his vision and act with force on his nerves. He has before the race had "words," almost blows, on the subject of one of the ladies present, with one of the other riders, of which the result is that they are to send each other their seconds; but the omens are not for his adversary, in spite of the latter's success on the course.

From the mail-coach, on the return, he overtook the flight toward Rome of Giannetto Rutolo, seated in a small two-wheeled trap, behind the quick trot of a great roan, over whom he bent with tight reins, holding his head down and his cigar in his teeth, heedless of the attempts of policemen to keep him in line. Rome, in the distance, stood up dark against a zone of light as yellow as sulphur; and the statues crowning St. John Lateran looked huge, above the zone, in their violet sky. *Then it was that Andrea fully knew the pain he was making another soul suffer.*

Nothing could be more characteristic of the writer than the way what has preceded flowers into that last reality; and equally in his best manner, doubtless, is such a passage as the following from the same volume, which treats of the hero's first visit to the sinister great lady whose influence on his soul and his senses is to become as the trail of a serpent. She receives him, after their first accidental meeting, with extraordinary promptitude and the last intimacy, receives him in the depths of a great Roman palace which the author, with a failure of taste that is, unfortunately for him, on ground of this sort, systematic, makes a point of naming. "Then they ceased to speak. Each felt the presence of the other flow and mingle with his own, with her own, very blood; till it was *her* blood at last that seemed to have become his life, and his that seemed to have become hers. The room grew larger in the deep silence; the crucifix of Guido Reni made the shade of the canopy and curtains religious; the rumour of the city came to them like the murmur of some far-away flood." Or take for an instance of the writer's way of showing the consciousness as a full, mixed cup, of touching us ourselves with the mystery at work in his characters, the description of the young man's leaving the princely apartments in question after the initiation vouchsafed to him. He has found the great lady ill in bed, with remedies and medicine-bottles at her side, but not too ill, as we have seen, to make him

welcome.   "Farewell," she has said.   "Love me!
Remember!"

It seemed to him, crossing the threshold again, that he heard
behind him a burst of sobs.   But he went on, a little uncertain,
wavering like a man who sees imperfectly.   The odour of the
chloroform clung to his sense like some fume of intoxication; but
at each step something intimate passed away from him, wasting
itself in the air, so that, impulsively, instinctively, he would have
kept himself as he was, have closed himself in, have wrapped himself up to prevent the dispersion.   The rooms in front of him were
deserted and dumb.   At one of the doors "Mademoiselle" appeared,
with no sound of steps, with no rustle of skirts, standing there like
a ghost.   "This way, signor conte.   You won't find it."   She had
an ambiguous, irritating smile, and her curiosity made her grey
eyes more piercing.   Andrea said nothing.   The woman's presence again disconcerted and troubled him, affected him with a
vague repugnance, stirred indeed his wrath.

Even the best things suffer by detachment from
their context; but so it is that we are in *possession* of
the young man's exit, so it is that the act interests us.
Fully announced from the first, among these things,
was D'Annunzio's signal gift of never approaching the
thing particularly to be done, the thing that so presents
itself to the painter, without consummately doing it.
Each of his volumes offers thus its little gallery of
episodes that stand out like the larger pearls occurring
at intervals on a string of beads.   The steeplechase in
"Il Piacere," the auction sale of precious trinkets in
Via Sistina on the wet afternoon, the morning in the
garden at Schifanoia, by the southern sea, when Donna
Maria, the new revelation, first comes down to Andrea,
who awaits her there in the languor of convalescence
from the almost fatal wound received in the duel of
which the altercation on the race-course has been the
issue: the manner of such things as these has an ex-

traordinary completeness of beauty. But they are, like similar pages in "Il Trionfo" and "Il Fuoco," not things for adequate citation, not things that lend themselves as some of the briefer felicities. Donna Maria, on the September night at Schifanoia, has been playing for Andrea and their hostess certain old quaint gavottes and toccatas.

It lived again wondrously beneath her fingers, the eighteenth-century music, so melancholy in its dance-tunes—tunes that might have been composed to be danced, on languid afternoons of some St. Martin's summer, in a deserted park, among hushed fountains and pedestals without their statues, over carpets of dead roses, by pairs of lovers soon to love no more.

Autobiographic in form, "L'Innocente" sticks closely to its theme, and though the form is on the whole a disadvantage to it the texture is admirably close. The question is of nothing less than a young husband's relation to the illegitimate child of his wife, born confessedly as such, and so born, marvellous to say, in spite of the circumstance that the wife adores him, and of the fact that, though long grossly, brutally false to her, he also adores his wife. To state these data is sufficiently to express the demand truly made by them for superiority of treatment; they require certainly two or three almost impossible postulates. But we of course never play the fair critical game with an author, never get into relation with him at all, unless we grant him his postulates. His subject is what is given him— given him by influences, by a process, with which we have nothing to do; since what art, what revelation, can ever really make such a mystery, such a passage in the private life of the intellect, adequately traceable for us? His treatment of it, on the other hand, is what he actively gives; and it is with what he gives that we are critically concerned. If there is nothing in him that effectually induces us to make the postulate, he is then empty for us altogether, and the sooner we have done with him the better; little as the truly curious critic enjoys, as a general thing, having publicly to throw up the sponge.

Tullio Hermil, who finally compasses ·the death of the little "innocent," the small intruder whose presence in the family life has become too intolerable, retraces with a master's hand each step of the process by which he has arrived at this sole issue. Save that his wife dumbly divines and accepts it his perpetration of the deed is not suspected, and we take the secret confession of which the book consists as made for the relief and justification of his conscience. The action all goes forward in that sphere of exasperated sensibility which Signor D'Annunzio has made his own so triumphantly that other story-tellers strike us in comparison as remaining at the door of the inner precinct, as listening there but to catch an occasional faint sound, while he alone is well within and moving through the place as its master. The sensibility has again in itself to be qualified; the exasperation of feeling is ever the essence of the intercourse of some man with some woman who has reduced him, as in "L'Innocente" and in "Il Trionfo," to homicidal madness, or of some woman with some man who, as in "Il Fuoco," and also again by a strange duplication of its office in "L'Innocente," causes her atrociously to suffer. The plane of the situation is thus visibly a singularly special plane; that, always, of the more or less insanely demoralised pair of lovers, for neither of whom is any other personal relation indicated either as actual or as conceivably possible.   Here, it may be said on such a showing, is material rather alarmingly cut down as to range, as to interest and, not least, as to charm; but here precisely it is that, by a wonderful chance, the author's magic comes effectively into play.

Little in fact as the relation of the erotically exasperated *with* the erotically exasperated, when pushed on either side to frenzy, would appear to lend itself to luminous developments, the difficulty is surmounted each time in a fashion that, for consistency no less than for brilliancy, is all the author's own.   Though surmounted triumphantly as to interest, that is, the trick is played without the least falsification of the luckless subjects of his study.   They remain the abject victims of sensibility that his plan has originally made them;   they remain exasperated, erotic, hysterical, either homicidally or suicidally determined, cut off from any personal source of life that does not poison them;   notwithstanding all of which they neither starve dramatically nor suffer us to starve with them.   How then is this seemingly inevitable catastrophe prevented ?   We ask it but to find on reflection that the answer opens the door to their historian's whole secret. The unfortunates are deprived of any enlarging or saving personal relation, that is of any beneficent reciprocity;   but they make up for it by their relation both to the *idea* in general and to the whole world of the senses, which is the completest that the author can conceive for them.   He may be described as thus executing on their behalf an artistic *volte-face* of the most effective kind, with results wonderful to note. The world of the senses, with which he surrounds them

—a world too of the idea, that is of a few ideas admirably expressed—yields them such a crop of impressions that the need of other occasions to vibrate and respond, to act or to aspire, is superseded by their immense factitious agitation. This agitation runs its course in strangely brief periods—a singular note, the brevity, of every situation; but the period is while it lasts, for all its human and social poverty, quite inordinately peopled and furnished. The innumerable different ways in which his concentrated couples are able to feel about each other and about their enclosing cage of golden wire, the nature and the art of Italy—these things crowd into the picture and pervade it, lighting it scarcely less, strange to say, because they are things of bitterness and woe.

It is one of the miracles of the imagination; the great shining element in which the characters flounder and suffer becomes rich and beautiful for them, as well as in so many ways for us, by the action of the writer's mind. They not only live in his imagination, but they borrow it from him in quantities; indeed without this charitable advance they would be poor creatures enough, for they have in each case almost nothing of their own. On the aid thus received they start, they get into motion; it makes their common basis of "passion," desire, enchantment, aversion. The essence of the situation is the same in "Il Trionfo" and "Il Fuoco" as in "L'Innocente": the temporarily united pair devour each other, tear and rend each other, wear each other out through a series of erotic convulsions and nervous reactions that are made interesting—interesting to *us*—almost exclusively by the special wealth of their consciousness. The medium in which they move is admirably reflected in it; the autumn light of Venice, the afterglow of her past, in the drama of the elderly actress and the young rhetorician of "Il Fuoco"; the splendour of the summer by the edge of the lower Adriatic in that of the two isolated erotomaniacs of "Il Trionfo," indissolubly linked at last in the fury of physical destruction into which the man drags the woman by way of retribution for the fury of physical surrender into which she has beguiled him.

As for "L'Innocente" again, briefly, there is perhaps nothing in it to match the Roman passages of "Il Piacere"; but the harmony of the general, the outer conditions pervades the picture; the sweetness of the villeggiatura life, the happiness of place and air, the lovability of the enclosing scene, all at variance with the sharpness of the inner tragedy. The inner tragedy of "L'Innocente" has a concentration that is like the carrying, through turns and twists, upstairs and down, of some cup filled to the brim, of which no drop is yet spilled; such cumulative truth rules the scene after we have once accepted the postulate. It is true that the situation as exhibited involves for Giuliana, the young wife, the vulgarest of adventures; yet she becomes, as it unfolds, the figure of the whole gallery in whom the pathetic has at once most of immediate truth and of investing poetry. I much prefer her for beauty and interest to Donna Maria in "Il Piacere," the principal other image of faith and patience sacrificed. We see these virtues as still supreme in her even while she faces, in advance, her ordeal, in respect to which it has been her hope, in fact her calculation, that her husband will have been deceived about the

paternity of her child; and she is so truthfully touching when this possibility breaks down that even though
we rub our eyes at the kind of dignity claimed for her
we participate without reserve in her predicament.
The origin of the infant is frankly ignoble, whereas it
is on the nobleness of Giuliana that the story essentially hinges; but the contradiction is wonderfully kept
from disconcerting us altogether. What the author
has needed for his strangest truth is that the mother
shall feel exactly as the husband does, and that the
husband shall after the first shock of his horror
feel intimately and explicitly with the mother. They
take in this way the same view of their woeful ex-
crescence; and the drama of the child's advent and of
the first months of his existence, his insistent and
hated survival, becomes for them in respect to the rest
of the world a drama of silence and dissimulation, in
every step of which we feel a terror.

The effect, I may add, gains more than one kind of
intensity from that almost complete absence of *other*
contacts to which D'Annunzio systematically condemns his creatures; introducing here, however, just
the two or three that more completely mark the
isolation. It may doubtless be conceded that our
English-speaking failure of insistence, of inquiry and
penetration, in certain directions, springs partly from
our deep-rooted habit of dealing with man, dramatically, on his social and gregarious side, as a being the
variety of whose intercourse with his fellows, whatever
forms his fellows may take, is positively half his interesting motion. We fear to isolate him, for we remember
that as we see and know him he scarce understands
himself save in action, action which inevitably mixes

him with his kind. To see and know him, like Signor D'Annunzio, almost only in passion is another matter, for passion spends itself quickly in the open and burns hot mainly in nooks and corners. Nothing, too, in the picture is more striking than the manner in which the merely sentimental abyss—that of the couple brought together by the thing that might utterly have severed them—is consistently and successfully avoided. We should have been certain to feel it in many other hands yawning but a few steps off. We see the dreadful facts in themselves, are brought close to them with no interposing vaguenesses or other beggings of the question, and are forcibly reminded how much more this "crudity" makes for the communication of tenderness—what is aimed at—than an attitude conventionally more reticent. We feel what the tenderness can be when it rests on *all* the items of a constituted misery, not one of which is illogically blinked.

For the pangs and pities of the flesh in especial D'Annunzio has in all his work the finest hand—those of the spirit exist with him indeed only as proceeding from these; so that Giuliana for instance affects us, beyond any figure in fiction we are likely to remember, as living and breathing under our touch and before our eyes, as a creature of organs, functions and processes, palpable, audible, pitiful physical conditions. These are facts, many of them, of an order in pursuit of which many a spectator of the "picture of life" will instinctively desire to stop short, however great in general his professed desire to enjoy the borrowed consciousness that the picture of life gives us; and nothing, it may well be said, is more certain than that we have a right in such matters to our preference, a right to choose the kind of adventure of the imagination we like best. No obligation whatever rests on us in respect to a given kind—much light as our choice may often throw for the critic on the nature of our own intelligence. *There* at any rate, we are disposed to say of such a piece of penetration as "L'Innocente," there is a particular dreadful adventure, as large as life, for those who can bear it. The conditions are all present; it is only the reader himself who may break down. When in general, it may be added, we see readers do so, this is truly more often because they are shocked at really finding the last consistency than because they are shocked at missing it.

"Il Trionfo della Morte" and "Il Fuoco" stand together as the amplest and richest of our author's histories, and the earlier, and more rounded and faultless thing of the two, is not unlikely to serve, I should judge, as an unsurpassable example of his talent. His accomplishment here reaches its maximum; all his powers fight for him; the wealth of his expression drapes the situation represented in a mantle of voluminous folds, stiff with elaborate embroidery. The "story" may be told in three words: how Giorgio Aurispa meets in Rome the young and extremely pretty wife of a vulgar man of business, her unhappiness with whom is complete, and, falling in love with her on the spot, eventually persuades her—after many troubled passages—to come and pass a series of weeks with him in a "hermitage" by the summer sea, where, in a delirium of free possession, he grows so to hate her, and to hate himself for his subjection to her, and for the prostration of all honour and decency proceeding from it, that his desire to destroy her even at the cost of perishing with her at last takes uncontrollable form and he drags her, under a pretext, to the edge of a sea-cliff and hurls her, interlocked with him in appalled resistance, into space. We get at an early stage the note of that aridity of agitation in which the narrator has expended treasures of art in trying to interest us. "Fits of indescribable fury made them try which could torture each other best, which most lacerate the other's heart and keep it in martyrdom." But they understand, at least the hero does; and he formulates for his companion the essence of their *impasse*. It is not her fault when she tears and rends.

Each human soul carries in it for love but a determinate quantity of sensitive force. It is inevitable that this quantity should use itself up with time, as everything else does; so that when it *is* used up no effort has power to prevent love from ceasing. Now it's a long time that you have been loving me; nearly two years!

The young man's intelligence is of the clearest; the woman's here is inferior, though in "Il Fuoco" the two opposed faculties are almost equal; but the pair are alike far from living in their intelligence, which only serves to bestrew with lurid gleams the black darkness of their sensual life. So far as the intelligence is one with the will our author fundamentally treats it as cut off from all communication with any other quarter—that is with the senses arrayed and encamped. The most his unfortunates arrive at is to carry their extremely embellished minds with them through these dusky passages as a kind of gilded glimmering lantern, the effect of which is merely fantastic and ironic—a thing to make the play of their shadows over the walls of their catacomb more monstrous and sinister. Again in the first pages of "Il Trionfo" the glimmer is given.

He recognised the injustice of any resentment against her, because he recognised the fatal necessities that controlled them alike.
No, his misery came from no other human creature; it came from
the very essence of life. The lover had not the lover to complain
of, but simply love itself. Love, toward which his whole being
reached out, from within, with a rush not to be checked, love was
of all the sad things of this earth the most lamentably sad. And
to this supreme sadness he was perhaps condemned till death.

That, in a nutshell, is D'Annunzio's subject-matter;
not simply that his characters see in advance what
love is worth for them, but that they nevertheless need
to make it the totality of their consciousness. In
"Il Trionfo" and "Il Fuoco" the law just expressed
is put into play at the expense of the woman, with
the difference, however, that in the latter tale the
woman perceives and judges, suffers in mind, so to
speak, as well as in nerves and in temper. But it
would be hard to say in which of these two productions the inexhaustible magic of Italy most helps the
effect, most hangs over the story in such a way as to
be one with it and to make the ugliness and the beauty
melt together. The ugliness, it is to be noted, is continually *presumed* absent; the pursuit and cultivation
of beauty—that fruitful preoccupation which above all,
I have said, gives the author his value as our "case"—
being the very ground on which the whole thing rests.
The ugliness is an accident, a treachery of fate, the
intrusion of a foreign substance—having for the most
part in the scheme itself no admitted inevitability.
Against it every provision is made that the most developed taste in the world can suggest; for, ostensibly,
transcendently, Signor D'Annunzio's *is* the most developed taste in the world—his and that of the ferocious yet so contracted *conoscenti* his heroes, whose

virtual identity with himself, affirmed with a strangely misplaced complacency by some of his critics, one would surely hesitate to take for granted. It is the wondrous physical and other endowments of the two heroines of "Il Piacere," it is the joy and splendour of the hero's intercourse with them, to say nothing of the lustre of his own person, descent, talents, possessions, and of the great general setting in which everything is offered us—it is all this that makes up the picture, with the constant suggestion that nothing of a baser quality for the esthetic sense, or at the worst for a pampered curiosity, might hope so much as to live in it. The case is the same in "L'Innocente," a scene all primarily smothered in flowers and fruits and fragrances and soft Italian airs, in every implication of flattered embowered constantly-renewed desire, which happens to be a blighted felicity only for the very reason that the cultivation of delight—in the form of the wife's luckless experiment—has so awkwardly overleaped itself. Whatever furthermore we may reflectively think either of the Ippolita of "Il Trionfo" or of her companion's scheme of existence with her, it is enchanting grace, strange, original, irresistible in kind and degree, that she is given us as representing; just as her material situation with her young man during the greater part of the tale is a constant communion, for both of them, with the poetry and the nobleness of classic landscape, of nature consecrated by association.

The mixture reaches its maximum, however, in "Il Fuoco," if not perhaps in "The Virgins of the Rocks"; the mixture I mean of every exhibited element of personal charm, distinction and interest, with every insidious local influence, every glamour of place, season and surrounding object. The heroine of the first-named is a great tragic actress, exquisite of aspect, intelligence and magnanimity, exquisite for everything but for being unfortunately middle-aged, battered, marked, as we are constantly reminded, by all the after-sense of a career of promiscuous carnal connections. The hero is a man of letters, a poet, a dramatist of infinite reputation and resource, and their union is steeped to the eyes in the gorgeous medium of Venice, the moods of whose melancholy and the voices of whose past are an active part of the perpetual concert. But we see *all* the persons introduced to us yearn and strain to exercise their perceptions and taste their impressions as deeply as possible, conspiring together to interweave them with the pleasures of passion. They "go in" as the phrase is, for beauty at any cost—for each other's own to begin with; their creator, in the inspiring quest, presses them hard, and the whole effect becomes for us that of an organised general sacrifice to it and an organised general repudiation of everything else. It is not idle to repeat that the value of the Italian background has to this end been inestimable, and that every spark of poetry it had to contribute has been struck from it—with what supreme felicity we perhaps most admiringly learn in "The Virgins of the Rocks." To measure the assistance thus rendered, and especially the immense literary lift given, we have only to ask ourselves what appearance any one of the situations presented would have made in almost any Cisalpine or "northern" frame of circumstance whatever. Supported but by such associations of local or of literary elegance as *our* comparatively thin resources are able to furnish, the latent weakness in them all, the rock, as to final effect, on which they split and of which I shall presently speak, would be immeasurably less dissimulated. All this is the lesson of style, by which we here catch a writer in the very act of profiting after a curious double fashion. D'Annunzio arrives at it both by expression and by material—that is, by a whole side of the latter; so that with such energy at once and such good fortune it would be odd indeed if he had not come far. It is verily in the very name and interest of beauty, of the lovely impression, that Giorgio Aurispa becomes homicidal in thought and finally in act.

> She would in death become for me matter of thought, pure ideality. From a precarious and imperfect existence she would enter into an existence complete and definitive, forsaking forever the infirmity of her weak luxurious flesh. Destroy to possess— there is no other way for him who seeks the absolute in love.

To these reflections he has been brought by the long, dangerous past which, as the author says, his connection with his mistress has behind it—a past of recriminations of which the ghosts still walk. "It dragged behind it, through time, an immense dark net, all full of dead things." To quote here at all is always to desire to continue, and "Il Trionfo" abounds in the illustrative episodes that are ever made so masterfully concrete. Offering in strictness, incidentally, the only exhibition in all the five volumes of a human relation other than the acutely sexual, it deals admirably enough with this opportunity when the hero pays his visit to his provincial parents before settling with his mistress at their hermitage. His people are of ancient race and have been much at their ease; but the home in the old Apulian town, overdarkened by the misdeeds of a demoralised father, is on the verge of ruin, and the dull mean despair of it all, lighted by outbreaks of helpless rage on the part of the injured mother, is more than the visitor can bear, absorbed as he is in impatiences and concupiscences which make everything else cease to exist for him. His terror of the place and its troubles but exposes of course the abjection of his weakness, and the sordid squabbles, the general misery and mediocrity of life that he has to face, constitute precisely, for his personal design, the abhorred challenge of ugliness, the interference of a call other than erotic. He flees before it, leaving it to make shift as it can; but nothing could be more "rendered" in detail than his overwhelmed vision of it.

So with the other finest passages of the story, notably the summer day spent by the lovers in a long dusty dreadful pilgrimage to a famous local miracle-working shrine, where they mingle with the multitude of the stricken, the deformed, the hideous, the barely human, and from which they return, disgusted and appalled, to plunge deeper into consoling but too temporary transports; notably also the incident, masterly in every touch, of the little drowned contadino, the whole scene of the small starved dead child on the beach, in all the beauty of light and air and view, with the effusions and vociferations and grimnesses round him, the sights and sounds of the quasi-barbaric life that have the relief of antique rites portrayed on old tombs and urns, that quality and dignity of looming larger which a great feeling on the painter's part ever gives to small things. With this ampler truth the last page of the book is above all invested, the description of the supreme moment—for some time previous creeping nearer and nearer—at which the delirious protagonist beguiles his vaguely but not fully suspicious companion into coming out with him toward the edge of a dizzy place over the sea, where he suddenly grasps her for her doom and the sense of his awful intention, flashing a light back as into their monstrous past, makes her shriek for her life. She dodges him at the first betrayal, panting and trembling.

"Are you crazy?" she cried with wrath in her throat. "Are you crazy?" But as she saw him make for her afresh in silence, as she felt herself seized with still harsher violence and dragged afresh toward her danger, she understood it all in a great sinister flash which blasted her soul with terror. "No, no, Giorgio! Let me go! Let me go! Another minute—listen, listen! Just a minute! I want to say——!" She supplicated, mad with terror, getting herself free and hoping to make him wait, to put him off with pity. "A minute! Listen! I love you! Forgive me! Forgive me!" She stammered incoherent words, desperate, feeling herself overcome, losing her ground, seeing death close. "Murder!" she then yelled in her fury. And she defended herself with her nails, with her teeth, biting like a wild beast. "Murder!" she yelled, feeling herself seized by the hair, felled to the ground on the edge of the precipice, lost. The dog meanwhile barked out at the scuffle. The struggle was short and ferocious, as between implacable enemies who had been nursing to this hour in the depths of their souls an intensity of hate. And they plunged into death locked together.

The wonder-working shrine of the Abruzzi, to which they have previously made their way, is a local Lourdes, the resort from far and wide of the physically afflicted, the evocation of whose multitudinous presence, the description of whose unimaginable miseries and ecstasies, grovelling struggles and supplications, has the mark of a pictorial energy for such matters not inferior to that of Émile Zola—to the degree even that the originality of the pages in question was, if I remember rightly, rather sharply impugned in Paris. D'Annunzio's defence, however, was easy, residing as it does in the fact that to handle any subject successfully handled by Zola (his failures are another matter) is quite inevitably to walk more or less in his footsteps, in prints so wide and deep as to leave little margin for passing round them. To which I may add that, though the judgment may appear odd, the truth and force of the young man's few abject days at Guardiagrele, his *casa paterna*, are such as to make us wish that other such corners of life were more frequent in the author's pages. He has the supremely interesting quality in the novelist that he *fixes*, as it were, the tone of every cluster of objects he approaches, fixes it by the consistency and intensity of his reproduction. In "The Virgins of the Rocks" we have also a *casa paterna*, and a thing, as I have indicated, of exquisite and wonderful tone; but the tone here is of poetry, the truth and the force are less measurable and less familiar, and the whole question, after all, in its refined and attenuated form, is still that of sexual pursuit, which keeps it within the writer's too frequent limits. Giorgio Aurispa, in "Il Trionfo," lives in communion with the spirit of an amiable and melancholy uncle who had committed suicide and made him the heir of his fortune, and one of the nephew's most frequent and faithful loyalties is to hark back, in thought, to the horror of his first knowledge of the dead man's act, put before us always with its accompaniment of loud southern resonance and confusion. He is in the place again, he is in the room, at Guardiagrele, of the original appalled vision.

He heard, in the stillness of the air and of his arrested soul, the small shrill of an insect in the wainscot. And the little fact sufficed to dissipate for the moment the extreme violence of his nervous tension, as the puncture of a needle suffices to empty a swollen bladder. Every particular of the terrible day came back to his memory: the news abruptly brought to Torretta di Sarsa, toward three in the afternoon, by a panting messenger who stammered and whimpered; the ride on horseback, at lightning speed, under the canicular sky and up the torrid slopes, and, during the rush, the sudden faintnesses that turned him dizzy in his saddle; then the house at home, filled with sobs, filled with a noise of doors slamming in the general scare, filled with the strumming of his own arteries; and at last his irruption into the room, the sight of the corpse, the curtains inflated and rustling, the tinkle on the wall of the little font for holy water.

This young man's great mistake, we are told, had been his insistence on regarding love as a form of enjoyment. He would have been in a possible relation to it only if he had learned to deal with it as a form of suffering. This is the lesson brought home to the heroine of "Il Fuoco," who suffers indeed, as it seems to us, so much more than is involved in the occasion. We ask ourselves continually why; that is we do so at first; we do so before the special force of the book takes us captive and reduces us to mere charmed absorption of its successive parts and indifference to its moral sense. Its defect is verily that it has no moral sense proportionate to the truth, the constant high style of the general picture; and this fact makes the whole thing appear given us simply because it has happened, because it was material that the author had become possessed of, and not because, in its almost journalistic "actuality," it has any large meaning. We get the impression of a direct transfer, a "lift," bodily, of something seen and known, something not really produced by the chemical process of art, the crucible or retort from which things emerge for a new function. Their meaning here at any rate, extracted with difficulty, would seem to be that there is an inevitable leak of ease and peace when a mistress happens to be considerably older than her lover; but even this interesting yet not unfamiliar truth loses itself in the great poetic, pathetic, psychologic ceremonial.

That matters little indeed, as I say, while we read; the two sensibilities concerned bloom, in all the Venetian glow, like wondrous water-plants, throwing out branches and flowers of which we admire the fantastic growth even while we remain, botanically speaking, bewildered. They are other sensibilities than those with which we ourselves have community—one of the main reasons of their appearing so I shall presently explain; and, besides, they are isolated, sequestrated, according to D'Annunzio's constant view of such cases, for an exclusive, an intensified and arid development. The mistress has, abnormally, none of the protection, the alternative life, the saving sanity of other interests, ties, employments; while the hero, a young poet and dramatist with an immense consciousness of genius and fame, has for the time at least only those poor contacts with existence that the last intimacies of his contact with his friend's person, her poor *corpo non più giovane*, as he so frequently repeats, represent for him. It is not for us, however, to contest the relation; it is in the penetrating way again in which the relation is rendered that the writer has his triumph; the way above all in which the world-weary interesting sensitive woman, with her infinite intelligence, yet with her longing for some happiness still among all her experiments untasted, and her genius at the same time for familiar misery, is marked, featured, individualised for us, and, with the strangest art in the world—one of those mysteries of which great talents alone have the trick—at once ennobled with beauty and desecrated by a process that we somehow feel to be that of exposure, to spring from some violation of a privilege. " 'Do with me,' " says the Foscarina on a certain occasion, " 'whatever you will'; and she smiled in her offered abjection. She belonged to him like the thing one holds in one's fist, like the ring on one's finger, like a glove, like a garment, like a word that may be spoken or not, like a draught that may be drunk or poured on the ground." There are some lines describing an hour in which she has made him feel as never before "the incalculable capacity of the heart of man. And it seemed to him as he heard the beating of his own heart and divined the violence of the other beside him that he had in his ears the loud repercussion of the hammer on the hard anvil where human destiny is forged." More than ever here the pitch of the personal drama is taken up by everything else in the scene—everything else being in fact but the immediate presence of Venice, her old faded colour and old vague harmonies, played with constantly as we might play with some rosy fretted faintly-sounding sea-shell.

It would take time to say what we play with in the silver-toned "Virgins of the Rocks," the history of a visit paid by a transcendent young man—always pretty much the same young man—to an illustrious family whose fortunes have tragically shrunken with the expulsion of the Bourbons from the kingdom of Naples, and the three last lovely daughters of whose house are beginning to wither on the stem, undiscovered, unsought, in a dilapidated old palace, an old garden of neglected pomp, a place of fountains and colonnades, marble steps and statues, all circled with hard bright sun-scorched volcanic scenery. They are tacitly candidates for the honour of the hero's hand, and the subject of the little tale, which deals with scarce more than a few summer days, is the manner of their presenting themselves for his admiration and his choice. I decidedly name this exquisite composition as my preferred of the series; for if its tone is thoroughly romantic the romance is yet of the happiest kind, the kind that consists in the imaginative development of observable things, things present, significant, related to us, and not in a weak false fumble for the remote and the disconnected.

It is indeed the romantic mind itself that makes the picture, and there could be no better case of the absolute artistic vision. The mere facts are soon said; the main fact, above all, of the feeble remnant of an exhausted race waiting in impotence to see itself cease to be. The father has nothing personal left but the ruins of his fine presence and of his old superstitions, a handful of silver dust; the mother, mad and under supervision, stalks about with the delusion of imperial greatness (there is a wonderful page on her parading through the gardens in her rococo palanquin, like a Byzantine empress, attended by sordid keepers, while the others are hushed into pity and awe); the two sons, hereditarily tainted, are virtually imbecile; the three daughters, candidly considered, are what we should regard in our Anglo-Saxon world as but the stuff of rather particularly dreary and shabby, quite unutterably idle old maids. Nothing, within the picture, occurs; nothing is done or, more acutely than usual,

than everywhere, suffered; it is all a mere affair of
the rich impression, the complexity of images projected
upon the quintessential spirit of the hero, whose own
report is what we have—an affair of the quality of
observation, sentiment and eloquence brought to bear.
It is not too much to say even that the whole thing
is in the largest sense but a theme for style, style of
substance as well as of form. Within this compass it
blooms and quivers and shimmers with light, becomes
a wonderful little walled garden of romance. The
young man has a passage of extreme but respectful
tenderness with each of the sisters in turn, and the
general cumulative effect is scarcely impaired by the
fact that "nothing comes" of any of these relations.
Too little comes of anything, I think, for any very
marked human analogy, inasmuch as if it is interesting
to be puzzled to a certain extent by what an action,
placed before us, is designed to show or to signify, so
we require for this refined amusement at least the sense
that some general idea *is* represented. We must feel
it present.

Therefore if making out nothing very distinct in "Le
Vergini" but the pictorial idea, and yet cleaving to
the preference I have expressed, I let the anomaly pass
as a tribute extorted by literary art, I may seem to
imply that a book may have a great interest without
showing a perfect sense. The truth is undoubtedly
that I am in some degree beguiled and bribed by the
particularly intense expression given in these pages to
the author's esthetic faith. If he is so supremely a
"case" it is because this production has so much to
say for it, and says it with such a pride of confidence,
with an assurance and an elegance that fairly make it

the last conceivable word of such a profession. The
observations recorded have their origin in the narrator's passionate reaction against the vulgarity of the
day. All the writer's young men react; but Cantelmo,
in the volume before us, reacts with the finest contempt. He is, like his brothers, a *raffiné* conservative,
believing really, so far as we understand it, only in
the virtue of "race" and in the grand manner. The
blighted Virgins, with all that surrounds them, are an
affirmation of the grand manner—that is of the shame
and scandal of what in an odious age it has been reduced to. It consists indeed of a number of different
things which I may not pretend to have completely
fitted together, but which are, with other elements, the
sense of the supremacy of beauty, the supremacy of
style and, last not least, of the personal will, manifested for the most part as a cold insolence of attitude
—not manifested as anything much more edifying.
What it really appears to come to is that the will is
a sort of romantic ornament, the application of which,
for life in the present and the future, remains awkwardly vague, though we are always to remember that
it has been splendidly forged in the past. The will in
short *is* beauty, is style, is elegance, is art—especially
in members of great families and possessors of large
fortunes. That of the hero of "Le Vergini" has been
handed down to him direct, as by a series of testamen-
tary provisions, from a splendid young ancestor for
whose memory and whose portrait he has a worship,
a warrior and virtuoso of the Renaissance, the model
of his spirit.

He represents for me the mysterious meaning of the power of
style, not violable by any one, and least of all ever by myself in
my own person.

And elsewhere:—

The sublime hands of Violante [the beauty and interest of hands play a great part, in general, in the picture], pressing out in drops the essence of the tender flowers and letting them fall bruised to the ground, performed an act which, as a symbol, corresponded perfectly to the character of my style; this being ever to extract from a thing its very last scent of life, to take from it all it could give and leave it exhausted. Was not this one of the most important offices of my art of life?

The book is a singularly rich exhibition of an inward state, the state of private poetic intercourse with things, the kind of current that in a given personal experience flows to and fro between the imagination and the world. It represents the esthetic consciousness, proud of its conquests and discoveries, and yet trying, after all, as with the vexed sense of a want, to look through other windows and eyes. It goes all lengths, as is of course indispensable on behalf of a personage constituting a case. "I firmly believe that the greatest sum of future dominion will be precisely that which shall have its base and its apex in Rome"—such being in our personage the confidence of the "Latin" spirit. Does it not really all come back to style? It was to the Latin spirit that the Renaissance was primarily vouchsafed; and was not, for a simplified statement, the last word of the Renaissance the question of taste? That is the esthetic question; and when the Latin spirit after many misadventures again clears itself we shall see how all the while this treasure has been in its keeping. Let us as frankly as possible add that there is a whole side on which the clearance may appear to have made quite a splendid advance with Signor D'Annunzio himself.

But there is another side, which I have been too long in coming to, yet which I confess is for me much the more interesting. No account of our author is complete unless we really make out what becomes of that esthetic consistency in him which, as I have said, our own collective and cultivated effort is so earnestly attempting and yet so pathetically, if not so grotesquely, missing. We are struck, unmistakably, early in our acquaintance with these productions, by the fact that their total beauty somehow extraordinarily fails to march with their beauty of parts, and that something is all the while at work undermining that bulwark against ugliness which it is their obvious theory of their own office to throw up. The disparity troubles and haunts us just in proportion as we admire; and our uneasy wonderment over the source of the weakness fails to spoil our pleasure only because such questions have so lively an interest for the critic. We feel ourselves somehow in presence of a singular incessant *leak* in the effect of distinction so artfully and copiously produced, and we apply our test up and down in the manner of the inquiring person who, with a tin implement and a small flame, searches our premises for an escape of gas. The bad smell has, as it were, to be accounted for; and yet where, amid the roses and lilies and pomegranates, the thousand essences and fragrances, can such a thing possibly be? Quite abruptly, I think, at last (if we have been much under the spell) our test gives us the news, not unaccompanied with the shock with which we see our escape of gas spring into flame. There is no mistaking it; the leak of distinction is produced by a positive element of the vulgar; and that the vulgar should flourish in an air so charged, intellectually speaking, with the "aristocratic" element, becomes for us straightway the greatest of oddities and at the same time, critically speaking, one of the most interesting things conceivable.

The interest then springs from its being involved for us in the "case." We recognise so many suggested consequences if the case is really to prove responsible for it. We ask ourselves if there be not a connection, we almost tremble lest there shouldn't be; since what is more obvious than that, if a high example of exclusive æstheticism—as high a one as we are likely ever to meet—is bound sooner or later to spring a leak, the general question receives much light? We recognise here the value of our author's complete consistency: he would have kept his bottom sound, so to speak, had he not remained so long at sea. If those imperfect exponents of his faith whom we have noted among ourselves fail to flower, for a climax, in any proportionate way, we make out that they are embarrassed not so much by any force they possess as by a force—a force of temperament—that they lack. The anomaly I speak of presents itself thus as the dilemma in which Signor D'Annunzio's consistency has inexorably landed him; and the disfigurement breaks out, strikingly enough, in the very forefront of his picture, at the point where he has most lavished his colour. It is where he has most trusted and depended that he is most betrayed, the traitor sharing certainly his tent and his confidence. What is it that in the interest of beauty he most elaborately builds on if not on the love-affairs of his heroes and heroines, if not on his exhibition of the free play, the sincere play, the play closely studied and frankly represented, of the sexual relation? It is round this exercise, for him, that expressible, demonstrable, communicable beauty prevailingly clusters; a view indeed as to which we all generously go with him, subject to the reserve for each of us of our own expression and demonstration. It is these things on his part that break down, it is his discrimination that falls short, and thereby the very kind of intellectual authority most implied by his pretension. There is according to him an immense amenity that can be saved—saved by style—from the general wreck and welter of what is most precious, from the bankruptcy determined more and more by our basely democratic conditions. As we watch the actual process, however, it is only to see the lifeboat itself founder. The vulgarity into which he so incongruously drops is, I will not say the space he allots to love-affairs, but the weakness of his sense of "values" in depicting them.

We begin to ask ourselves at an early stage what this queer passion may be in the representation of which the sense of beauty ostensibly finds its richest expression and which is yet attended by nothing else at all—neither duration, nor propagation, nor common kindness, nor common consistency with other relations, common congruity with the rest of life—to make its importance good. If beauty is the supreme need so let it be; nothing is more certain than that we can never get too much of it if only we get it of the right sort. It is therefore on this very ground—the ground of its own sufficiency—that Signor D'Annunzio's invocation of it collapses at our challenge. The vulgarity comes from the disorder really introduced into values, as I have called them; from the vitiation suffered—that we should have to record so mean an accident—by taste, impeccable taste, itself. The truth of this would come out fully in copious examples, now impossible; but it is not too much to say, I think, that in every principal situation presented the fundamental weakness causes the particular interest to be inordinately compromised.

I must not, I know, make too much of "Il Piacere" —one of those works of promising youth with which criticism is always easy—and I should indeed say nothing of it if it were also a work of less ability. It really, however, to my mind, quite gives us the key, all in the morning early, to our author's general misadventure. Andrea Sperelli is the key; Donna Maria is another key of a slightly different shape. They have neither of them the esthetic importance, any more than the moral, that their narrator claims for them and in his elaborate insistence on which he has so hopelessly lost his way. If they *were* important—by which I mean if they showed in any other light than that of their particular erotic exercise—they would justify the claim made for them with such superior art. They have no general history, since their history is only, and immediately and extravagantly, that of their too cheap and too easy romance. Why should the career of the young man be offered as a sample of pathetic, of tragic, of edifying corruption?—in which case it might indeed be matter for earnest exhibition. The march of corruption, the insidious influence of propinquity, opportunity, example, the ravage of false estimates and the drama of sterilising passion—all this is a thinkable theme, thinkable especially in the light of a great talent. But for Andrea Sperelli there is not only no march, no drama, there is not even a weakness to give him the semblance of dramatic, of plastic material; he is solidly, invariably, vulgarly strong, and not a bit more corrupt at the end of his disorders than at the beginning. His erudition, his intellectual ac-

complishments and elevation, are too easily spoken for;
no view of him is given in which we can feel or taste
them. Donna Maria is scarcely less signal an instance
of the apparent desire on the author's part to impute
a "value" defeated by his apparently not knowing
what a value is. She is apparently an immense value
for the occasions on which the couple secretly meet,
but how is she otherwise one? and what becomes
therefore of the beauty, the interest, the pathos, the
struggle, or whatever else, of her relation—relation of
character, of judgment, even of mere taste—to her
own collapse? The immediate physical sensibility that
surrenders in her is, as throughout, exquisitely painted;
but since nothing operates for her, one way or the
other, *but* that familiar faculty, we are left casting
about us almost as much for what else she has to give
as for what, in any case, she may wish to keep.

The author's view of the whole matter of durations
and dates, in these connections, gives the scale of
"distinction" by itself a marked downward tilt; it
confounds all differences between the trivial and the
grave. Giuliana, in "L'Innocente," is interesting because she has had a misadventure, and she is exquisite
in her delineator's view because she has repented of
it. But the misadventure, it appears, was a matter
but of a minute; so that we oddly see this particular
romance attenuated on the ground of its brevity.
Given the claims of the exquisite, the attenuation
should surely be sought in the very opposite quarter;
since, where these remarkable affections are concerned,
how otherwise than by the element of comparative
duration do we obtain the element of comparative
good faith, on which we depend for the element, in

turn, of comparative dignity? Andrea Sperelli becomes in the course of a few weeks in Rome the lover of some twenty or thirty women of fashion—the number scarce matters; but to make this possible his connection with each has but to last a day or two; and the effect of that in its order is to reduce to nothing, by vulgarity, by frank grotesqueness of association, the romantic capacity in him on which his chronicler's whole appeal to us is based. The association rising before us more nearly than any other is that of the manners observable in the most mimetic department of any great menagerie.

The most serious relation depicted—in the sense of being in some degree the least suggestive of mere zoological sociability—is that of the lovers in "Il Fuoco," as we also take this pair for their creator's sanest and most responsible spirits. It is a question between them of an heroic affection, and yet the affection appears to make good for itself no place worth speaking of in their lives. It holds but for a scant few weeks; the autumn already reigns when the connection begins, and the connection is played out (or if it be not the ado is about nothing) with the first flush of the early Italian spring. It suddenly, on our hands, becomes trivial, with all our own estimate of reasons and realities and congruities falsified. The Foscarina has, on professional business, to "go away," and the young poet has to do the same; but such a separation, so easily bridged over by such great people, makes a beggarly climax for an intercourse on behalf of which all the forces of poetry and tragedy have been set in motion. Where then we ask ourselves is the weakness? —as we ask it, very much in the same way, in respect

to the vulgarised aspect of the tragedy of Giorgio Aurispa.   The pang of pity, the pang that springs from
a conceivable community in doom, is in this latter case
altogether wanting.   Directly we lift a little the em-
broidered mantle of that gift for appearances which
plays, on Signor D'Annunzio's part, such tricks upon
us, we find ourselves put off, as the phrase is, with an
inferior article.   The inferior article is the hero's poverty of life, which cuts him down for pathetic interest
just as the same limitation in "Il Piacere" cuts down
Donna Maria.   Presented each as victims of another
rapacious person who has got the better of them, there
is no process, no complexity, no suspense in their
story; and thereby, we submit, there is no esthetic
beauty.   Why *shouldn't* Giorgio Aurispa go mad?
Why shouldn't Stelio Effrena go away?   We make the
inquiry as disconcerted spectators, not feeling in the
former case that we have had any communication with
the wretched youth's sanity, and not seeing in the latter why the tie of all the passion that has been made
so admirably vivid for us should not be able to weather
change.

Nothing is so singular with D'Annunzio as that the
very basis and subject of his work should repeatedly
go aground on such shallows as these.   He takes for
treatment a situation that is substantially none—the
most fundamental this of his values, and all the more
compromising that his immense art of producing illusions still leaves it exposed.   The idea in each case is
superficially specious, but *where* it breaks down is what
makes all the difference.   "Il Piacere" would have
meant what it seems to try to mean only if a provision had been made in it for some adequate "inward-

ness" on the part either of the nature disintegrated or
of the other nature to which this poisoned contact
proves fatal. "L'Innocente," of the group, comes
nearest to justifying its idea; and I leave it unchal-
lenged, though its meaning surely would have been
written larger if the attitude of the wife toward her
misbegotten child had been, in face of the husband's,
a little less that of the dumb detached animal suffering
in her simplicity. As a picture of such suffering, the
pain of the mere dumb animal, the work is indeed
magnificent; only its connections are poor with the
higher dramatic, the higher poetic, complexity of
things.

I can only repeat that to make "The Triumph of
Death" a fruitful thing we should have been able to
measure the triumph by its frustration of some conceivable opportunity at least for life. There is a moment at which we hope for something of this kind,
the moment at which the young man pays his visit to
his family, who have grievous need of him and toward
whom we look to see some one side or other of his
fine sensibility turn. But nothing comes of that for
the simple reason that the personage is already dead
—that nothing exists in him but the established *fear*
of life. He turns his back on everything but a special
sensation, and so completely shuts the door on the
elements of contrast and curiosity. Death really triumphs, in the matter, but over the physical terror of
the inordinate woman; a pang perfectly communicated to us, but too small a surface to bear the weight
laid on it, which accordingly affects us as that of a
pyramid turned over on its point. It is throughout
one of D'Annunzio's strongest marks that he treats

"love" as a matter not to be mixed with life, in the larger sense of the word, at all—as a matter all of whose other connections are dropped; a sort of secret game that can go on only if each of the parties has nothing to do, even on any *other* terms, with any one else.

I have dwelt on the fact that the sentimental intention in "Il Fuoco" quite bewilderingly fails, in spite of the splendid accumulation of material. We wait to the end to see it declare itself, and then are left, as I have already indicated, with a mere meaningless anecdote on our hands. Brilliant and free, each freighted with a talent that is given us as incomparable, the parties to the combination depicted have, for their affection, the whole world before them—and not the simple terraqueous globe, but that still vaster sphere of the imagination in which, by an exceptionally happy chance, they are able to move together on very nearly equal terms. A tragedy is a tragedy, a comedy is a comedy, when the effect, in either sense, is *determined* for us, determined by the interference of some element that starts a complication or precipitates an action. As in "Il Fuoco" nothing whatever interferes—or nothing certainly that need weigh with the high spirits represented—we ask why such precious revelations are made us for nothing. Admirably made in themselves they yet strike us as, esthetically speaking, almost cruelly wasted.

This general remark would hold good, as well, of "Le Vergini," if I might still linger, though its application has already been virtually made. Anatolia, in

this tale, the most robust of the three sisters, declines
marriage in order to devote herself to a family who
have, it would certainly appear, signal need of her
nursing. But this, though it sufficiently represents *her*
situation, covers as little as possible the ground of the
hero's own, since he, quivering intensely with the
treasure of his "will," inherited in a straight line from
the *cinque-cento*, only asks to affirm his sublimated
energy. The temptation to affirm it erotically, at
least, has been great for him in relation to each of the
young women in turn; but it is for Anatolia that his
admiration and affection most increase in volume, and
it is accordingly for her sake that, with the wonderful
moral force behind him (kept as in a Florentine casket,)
we most look to see him justified. He has a fine image
—and when has the author not fine images?—to illustrate the constant readiness of this possession. The
young woman says something that inspires him, whereupon, "as a sudden light playing over the dusky wall
of a room causes the motionless sword in a trophy to
shine, so her word drew a great flash from my suspended *volontà*. There was a virtue in her," the narrator adds, "which could have produced portentous
fruit. Her substance might have nourished a superhuman germ." In spite of which it never succeeds in
becoming so much as a question that his affection for
her shall *act*, that this grand imagination in him shall
operate, that he himself is, in virtue of such things,
exactly the person to come to her aid and to combine
with her in devotion. The talk about the *volontà* is
amusing much in the same way as the complacency of
a primitive man, unacquainted with the uses of things,
who becomes possessed by some accident of one of the
toys of civilisation, a watch or a motor-car. And yet

artistically and for our author the will *has* an application, since without it he could have done no rare
vivid work.

Here at all events we put our finger, I think, on the
very point at which his esthetic plenitude meets the
misadventure that discredits it. We see just where it
"joins on" with vulgarity. That sexual passion from
which he extracts such admirable detached pictures insists on remaining for him *only* the act of a moment,
beginning and ending in itself and disowning any representative character. From the moment it depends
on itself alone for its beauty it endangers extremely
its distinction, so precarious at the best. For what it
represents, precisely, is it poetically interesting; it
finds its extension and consummation only in the rest
of life. Shut out from the rest of life, shut out from
all fruition and assimilation, it has no more dignity
than—to use a homely image—the boots and shoes
that we see, in the corridors of promiscuous hotels,
standing, often in double pairs, at the doors of rooms.
Detached and unassociated these clusters of objects
present, however obtruded, no importance. What the
participants do with their agitation, in short, or even
what it does with them, *that* is the stuff of poetry, and
it is never really interesting save when something
finely contributive in themselves makes it so. It is
this absence of anything finely contributive in themselves, on the part of the various couples here concerned, that is the open door to the trivial. I have
said, with all appreciation, that they present the great
"relation," for intimacy, as we shall nowhere else find
it presented; but to see it related, in its own turn, to
nothing in the heaven above or the earth beneath,

this undermines, we definitely learn, the charm of that achievement.

And so it is, strangely, that our esthetic "case" enlightens us. The only question is whether it be the only case of the kind conceivable. May we not suppose another with the elements differently mixed? May we not in imagination alter the proportions within or the influences without, and look with cheerfulness for a different issue? *Need* the esthetic adventure, in a word, organised for real discovery, give us no more comforting news of success? Are there not, so to speak, finer possible combinations? are there not safeguards against futility that in the example before us were but too presumably absent? To which the sole answer probably is that no man can say. It is Signor D'Annunzio alone who has really sailed the sea and brought back the booty. The actual case is so good that all the potential fade beside it. It has for it that it exists, and that, whether for the strength of the original outfit or for the weight of the final testimony, it could scarce thinkably be bettered.

MATILDE SERAO

FEW attentive readers, I take it, would deny that the English novelist—from whom, in this case, there happens to be even less occasion than usual for distinguishing the American—testifies in his art much more than his foreign comrade, from whatever quarter, to the rigour of convention. There are whole sides of life about which he has as little to say as possible, about which he observes indeed in general a silence that has visibly ended by becoming for the foreign comrade his great characteristic. He strikes the spectator as having with a misplaced humility consented once for all to be admonished as to what he shall or shall not "mention"—and to be admonished in especial by an authority altogether indefinite. He subscribes, when his turn comes round, to an agreement in the drawing-up of which he has had no hand; he sits down to his task with a certain received canon of the "proper" before his eyes. The critic I am supposing reproaches him, naturally, in this critic's way, with a marked failure ever to challenge, much less to analyse, that conception; with having never, as would appear, so much as put to himself in regard to most of the matters of which he makes his mystery the simple question "Proper to what?" How can any authority, even the most embodied, asks the exponent of other views, decide for us in advance what shall in any case be proper—with the consequent implication of impropriety—to our given subject?

The English novelist would, I imagine, even sometimes be led on to finding that he has practically had
to meet such an overhauling by a further admission,
though an admission still tacit and showing him not
a little shy of the whole discussion—principles and for-
mulas being in general, as we know, but little his
affair. Would he not, if off his guard, have been in
peril of lapsing into the doctrine—suicidal when reflected upon—that there may be also an *a priori* rule,
a "Thou shalt not," if not a "Thou shalt," as to treatable subjects themselves? Then it would be that his
alien foe might fairly revel in the sense of having him
in a corner, laughing an evil laugh to hear him plead
in explanation that it is exactly *most* as to the subject to be treated that he feels the need laid upon him
to conform. What is he to do when he has an idea to
embody, we might suspect him rashly to inquire, unless, frankly to ask himself in the first place of *all* if
it be proper? Not indeed—we catch the reservation—
that he is consciously often accessible to ideas for
which that virtue may not be claimed. Naturally,
however, still, such a plea only brings forth for his
interlocutor a repetition of the original appeal: "Proper
to what?" There is only one propriety the painter of
life can ask of his morsel of material: Is it, or is it
not, of the stuff of life? So, in simplified terms at
any rate, I seem to hear the interchange; to which I
need listen no longer than thus to have derived from
it a word of support for my position. The question of
our possible rejoinder to the scorn of societies otherwise affected I must leave for some other connection.
The point is—if point I may expect to obtain any
countenance to its being called—that, in spite of our
great Dickens and, in a minor degree, of our great

George Eliot, the limitations of our practice are elsewhere than among ourselves pretty well held to have
put us out of court.   The thing least conceded to us
moreover is that we handle at all frankly—if we put
forward such a claim—even our own subject-matter or
in other words our own life.   "Your own is all we
want of you, all we should like to see.   But that your
system really touches your own is exactly what we
deny.   Never, never!"   For what it really comes to
is that practically we, of all people in the world, are
accused of a system.   Call this system a conspiracy of
silence, and the whole charge is upon us.

The fact of the silence, whether or no of the system,
is fortunately all that at present concerns us.   Did this
not happen to be the case nothing could be more interesting, I think, than to follow somewhat further
several of the bearings of the matter, which would
bring us face to face with some wonderful and, I
hasten to add, by no means doubtless merely disconcerting truths about ourselves.   It has been given us
to read a good deal, in these latter days, about *l'âme
Française* and *l'âme Russe*—and with the result, in all
probability, of our being rather less than more penetrated with the desire, in emulation of these opportunities, to deliver ourselves upon the English or the
American soul.   There would appear to be nothing
we are totally conscious of that we are less eager to
reduce to the mere expressible, to hand over to publicity, current journalistic prose aiding, than either of
these fine essences;   and yet incontestably there are
neighbourhoods in which we feel ourselves within scent
and reach of them by something of the same sense
that in thick forests serves the hunter of great game.

He may not quite touch the precious presence, but he knows when it is near. So somehow we know that the "Anglo-Saxon" soul, the modern at least, is not far off when we frankly consider the practice of our race—comparatively recent though it be—in taking for granted the "innocence" of literature.

Our perhaps a trifle witless way of expressing our conception of this innocence and our desire for it is, characteristically enough, by taking refuge in another vagueness, by invoking the allowances that we understand works of imagination and of criticism to make to the "young." I know not whether it has ever officially been stated for us that, given the young, given literature, and given, under stress, the need of sacrificing one or the other party, it is not certainly by our sense of "style" that our choice would be determined: no great art in the reading of signs and symptoms is at all events required for a view of our probable instinct in such a case. That instinct, however, has too many deep things in it to be briefly or easily disposed of, and there would be no greater mistake than to attempt too simple an account of it. The account most likely to be given by a completely detached critic would be that we are as a race better equipped for action than for thought, and that to let the art of expression go by the board is through that very fact to point to the limits of what we mostly have to express. If we accept such a report we shall do so, I think, rather from a strong than from a weak sense of what may easily be made of it; but I glance at these things only as at objects almost too flooded with light, and come back after my parenthesis to what more immediately concerns me: the plain reflection that, if the element of compromise—compromise with fifty of the "facts of life"—be the common feature of the novel of English speech, so it is mainly indebted for this character to the sex comparatively without a feeling for logic.

Nothing is at any rate *a priori* more natural than to trace a connection between our general mildness, as it may conveniently be called, and the fact that we are likewise so generally feminine. Is the English novel "proper" because it is so much written by women, or is it only so much written by women because its propriety has been so firmly established? The intimate relation is on either determination all that is here pertinent—effect and cause may be left to themselves. What is further pertinent, as happens, is that on a near view the relation is not constant; by which I mean that, though the ladies are always productive, the fashion of mildness is not always the same. Convention in short has its ups and downs, and these votaries have of late years, I think, been as often seen weltering in the hollow of the wave as borne aloft on its crest. Some of them may even be held positively to have distinguished themselves most—whether or no in veils of anonymity—on the occasion of the downward movement; making us really wonder if their number might not fairly, under any steadier force of such a movement, be counted on to increase. All sorts of inquiries are suggested in truth by the sight. "Emancipations" are in the air, and may it not possibly be that we shall see two of the most striking coincide? If convention has, to the tune to which I just invited an ear, blighted our fiction, what shall we say of its admitted, its still more deprecated and in so

many quarters even deplored, effect upon the great
body under the special patronage of which the "output" has none the less insisted on becoming incomparably copious? Since the general inaptitude of
women appears by this time triumphantly to have
been proved an assumption particularly hollow, de-
spoiled more and more each day of the last tatters of
its credit, why should not the new force thus liberated really, in the connection I indicate, give something of its measure?

It is at any rate keeping within bounds to say that
the novel will surely not become less free in proportion as the condition of women becomes more easy.
It is more or less in deference to their constant concern with it that we have seen it, among ourselves,
pick its steps so carefully; but there are indications
that the future may reserve us the surprise of having
to thank the very class whose supposed sensibilities
have most oppressed us for teaching it not only a
longer stride, but a healthy indifference to an occasional splash. It is for instance only of quite recent
years that the type of fiction commonly identified as
the "sexual" has achieved—for purposes of reference,
so far as notices in newspapers may be held to constitute reference—a salience variously estimated. Now
therefore, though it is early to say that all "imaginative work" from the female hand is subject to this
description, there is assuredly none markedly so subject that is *not* from the female hand. The female
mind has in fact throughout the competition carried
off the prize in the familiar game, known to us all
from childhood's hour, of playing at "grown-up;"
finding thus its opportunity, with no small acuteness,

in the more and more marked tendency of the mind of the other gender to revert, alike in the grave and the gay, to those simplicities which there would appear to be some warrant for pronouncing puerile. It is the ladies in a word who have lately done most to remind us of man's relations with himself, that is with woman. His relations with the pistol, the pirate, the police, the wild and the tame beast—are not these prevailingly what the gentlemen have given us? And does not the difference sufficiently point my moral?

Let me, however, not seem to have gone too far afield to seek it; for my reflections—general perhaps to excess—closely connect themselves with a subject to which they are quite ready to yield in interest. I have lately been giving a happy extension to an old acquaintance, dating from early in the eighties, with the striking romantic work of Matilde Serao; a writer who, apart from other successes, has the excellent effect, the sign of the stronger few, that the end of her story is, for her reader, never the end of her work. On thus recently returning to her I have found in her something much more to my present purpose than the mere appearance of power and ease. If she is interesting largely because she is, in the light of her free, her extraordinary Neapolitan temperament, a vivid painter and a rich register of sensations and impressions, she is still more so as an exceptionally compact and suggestive *case*, a case exempt from interference and presenting itself with a beautiful unconsciousness. She has had the good fortune—if it be, after all, not the ill—to develop in an air in which convention, in our invidious sense, has had as little to say to her as possible; and she is accordingly a precious example of the possibilities of free exercise. The questions of the proper and the improper are comfortably far from her; and though more than in the line of her sisters of English speech she may have to reckon with pre-scriptions as to form—a burden at which in truth she snaps her fingers with an approach to impertinence—she moves in a circle practically void of all pre-judg-ment as to subject and matter. Conscious enough, doubtless, of a literary law to be offended, and caring little in fact, I repeat—for it is her weakness—what wrong it may suffer, she has not even the agreeable incentive of an ability to calculate the "moral" shocks she may administer.

Practically chartered then she is further happy—since they both minister to ease—in two substantial facts: she is a daughter of the veritable south and a product of the contemporary newspaper. A Neapol-itan by birth and a journalist by circumstance, by marriage and in some degree doubtless also by incli-nation, she strikes for us from the first the note of facility and spontaneity and the note of initiation and practice. Concerned, through her husband, in the conduct of a Neapolitan morning paper, of a large cir-culation and a radical colour, she has, as I infer, pro-duced her novels and tales mainly in such snatches of time and of inspiration as have been left her by ur-gent day-to-day journalism. They distinctly betray, throughout, the conditions of their birth—so little are they to the literary sense children of maturity and leisure. On the question of style in a foreign writer it takes many contributive lights to make us sure of our ground; but I feel myself on the safe side in con-ceiving that this lady, full of perception and vibration, can not only not figure as a purist, but must be supposed throughout, in spite of an explosive eloquence, to pretend but little to distinction of form: which for an Italian is a much graver predicament than for one of our shapeless selves. That, however, would perhaps pass for a small quarrel with a writer, or rather with a talker and—for it is what one must most insist on—a *feeler*, of Matilde Serao's remarkable spontaneity. Her Neapolitan nature is by itself a value, to whatever literary lapses it may minister. A torch kindled at that flame can be but freely waved, and our author's arm has a fine action. Loud, loquacious, abundant, natural, happy, with luxurious insistences on the handsome, the costly and the fleshly, the fine persons and fine clothes of her characters, their satin and velvet, their bracelets, rings, white waistcoats, general appointments and bedroom furniture, with almost as many repetitions and as free a tongue, in short, as Juliet's nurse, she reflects at every turn the wonderful mixture that surrounds her—the beauty, the misery, the history, the light and noise and dust, the prolonged paganism and the renewed reactions, the great style of the distant and the past and the generally compromised state of the immediate and the near. These things were all in the germ for the reader of her earlier novels—they have since only gathered volume and assurance—so that I well remember the impression made on me, when the book was new (my copy, apparently of the first edition, bears the date of 1885), by the rare energy, the immense *disinvoltura*, of "La Conquista di Roma." This was my introduction to the author, in consequence of which I immediately read "Fantasia" and the "Vita e Avventure di Riccardo Joanna," with some smaller pieces; after which, interrupted but not detached, I knew nothing more till, in the course of time, I renewed acquaintance on the ground of "Il Paese di Cuccagna," then, however, no longer in its first freshness. That work set me straightway to reading everything else I could lay hands on, and I think therefore that, save "Il Ventre di Napoli" and two or three quite recent productions that I have not met, there is nothing from our author that I have not mastered. Such as I find her in everything, she remains above all things the signal "case."

If, however, she appears, as I am bound to note, not to have kept the full promise of her early energy, this is because it has suited her to move less in the direction—where so much might have awaited her—of "Riccardo Joanna" and "La Conquista" than in that, on the whole less happily symptomatic, of "Fantasia." "Fantasia" is, before all else, a study of "passion," or rather of the intenser form of that mystery which the Italian *passione* better expresses; and I hasten to confess that had she not so marked herself an exponent of this specialty I should probably not now be writing of her. I conceive none the less that it would have been open to her to favour more that side of her great talent of which the so powerful "Paese di Cuccagna" is the strongest example. There is by good fortune in this large miscellaneous picture of Neapolitan life no *passione* save that of the observer curiously and pityingly intent upon it, that of the artist resolute at any cost to embrace and reproduce it. Admirably, easily, convincingly objective, the thing is a sustained panorama, a chronicle of manners finding its unity in one recurrent note, that of the consuming lottery-hun-

ger which constitutes the joy, the curse, the obsession
and the ruin, according to Matilde Serao, of her fellow-citizens. Her works are thus divided by a somewhat unequal line, those on one side of which the
critic is tempted to accuse her of having not altogether
happily sacrificed to those on the other. When she
for the most part invokes under the name of *passione*
the main explanation of the mortal lot it is to follow
the windings of this clue in the upper walks of life,
to haunt the aristocracy, to embrace the world of
fashion, to overflow with clothes, jewels and promiscuous intercourse, all to the proportionate eclipse of
her strong, full vision of the more usually vulgar.
"La Conquista" is the story of a young deputy who
comes up to the Chamber, from the Basilicata, with
a touching candour of ambition and a perilous ignorance of the pitfalls of capitals. His dream is to con-
quer Rome, but it is by Rome naturally that he is
conquered. He alights on his political twig with a
flutter of wings, but has reckoned in his innocence
without the strong taste in so many quarters for sport;
and it is with a charge of shot in his breast and a
drag of his pinions in the dust that he takes his way
back to mediocrity, obscurity and the parent nest.
It is from the ladies—as was indeed even from the
first to be expected with Serao—that he receives his
doom; *passione* is in these pages already at the door
and soon arrives; *passione* rapidly enough passes its
sponge over everything not itself.

In "Cuore Infermo," in "Addio Amore," in "Il
Castigo," in the two volumes of "Gli Amanti" and in
various other pieces this effacement is so complete that
we see the persons concerned but in the one relation,

with every other circumstance, those of concurrent
profession, possession, occupation, connection, interest, amusement, kinship, utterly superseded and ob-
scured. Save in the three or four books I have
named as exceptional the figures evoked are literally
professional lovers, "available," as the term is, for
passione alone: which is the striking sign, as I shall
presently indicate, of the extremity in which her enjoyment of the freedom we so often have to envy has
strangely landed our author. "Riccardo Joanna,"
which, like "La Conquista," has force, humour and
charm, sounding with freshness the note of the general life, is such a picture of certain of the sordid conditions of Italian journalism as, if I may trust my
memory without re-perusal, sharply and pathetically
imposes itself. I recall "Fantasia" on the other hand
as wholly *passione*—all concentration and erotics, the
latter practised in this instance, as in "Addio Amore,"
with extreme cruelty to the "good" heroine, the person innocent and sacrificed; yet this volume too contributes its part in the retrospect to that appearance
of marked discipleship which was one of the original
sources of my interest. Nothing could more have engaged one's attention in these matters at that moment
than the fresh phenomenon of a lady-novelist so confessedly flushed with the influence of Émile Zola.
Passing among ourselves as a lurid warning even to
workers of his own sex, he drew a new grace from the
candid homage—all implied and indirect, but, as I re-
figure my impression, not the less unmistakable—of
that half of humanity which, let alone attempting to
follow in his footsteps, was not supposed even to turn
his pages. There is an episode in "Fantasia"—a
scene in which the relations of the hero and the "bad"

heroine are strangely consolidated by a visit together
to a cattle-show—in which the courage of the pupil
has but little to envy the breadth of the master.   The
hot day and hot hour, the heavy air and the strong
smells, the great and small beasts, the action on the
sensibilities of the lady and the gentleman of the rich
animal life, the collapse indeed of the lady in the presence of the prize bull—all these are touches for which
luckily our author has the warrant of a greater name.
The general picture, in "Fantasia," of the agricultural
exhibition at Caserta is in fact not the worse at any
point for a noticeable echo of more than one French
model.   Would the author have found so full an occasion in it without a fond memory of the immortal
Comices of "Madame Bovary"?

These, however, are minor questions—pertinent only
as connecting themselves with the more serious side
of her talent.   We may rejoice in such a specimen of
it as is offered by the too brief series of episodes of
"The Romance of the Maiden."   These things, dealing mainly with the small miseries of small folk, have
a palpable truth, and it is striking that, to put the
matter simply, Madame Serao is at her best almost in
direct proportion as her characters are poor.   By poor
I mean literally the reverse of rich; for directly they
are rich and begin, as the phrase is, to keep their carriage, her taste totters and lapses, her style approxi-
mates at moments to that of the ladies who do the
fashions and the letters from the watering-places in
the society papers.   She has acutely and she renders
with excellent breadth the sense of benighted lives, of
small sordid troubles, of the general unhappy youthful (on the part of her own sex at least) and the gen-

eral more or less starved plebeian consciousness. The degree to which it testifies to all this is one of the great beauties of "Il Paese di Cuccagna," even if the moral of that dire picture be simply that in respect to the gaming-passion, the madness of "numbers," no walk of life at Naples is too high or too low to be ravaged. Beautiful, in "Il Romanzo della Fanciulla," are the exhibitions of grinding girl-life in the big tele-graph office and in the State normal school. The gem of "Gli Amanti" is the tiny tale of "Vicenzella," a masterpiece in twenty small pages—the vision of what three or four afternoon hours could contain for a slip of a creature of the Naples waterside, a poor girl who picks up a living by the cookery and sale, on the edge of a parapet, of various rank dismembered polyps of the southern sea, and who is from stage to stage de-spoiled of the pence she patiently pockets for them by the successive small emissaries of her artful, absent lover, constantly faithless, occupied, not too far off, in regaling a lady of his temporary preference, and proportionately clamorous for fresh remittances. The moment and the picture are but a scrap, yet they are as large as life.

"Canituccia," in "Piccole Anime," may happily pair with "Vicenzella," Canituccia being simply the hum-ble rustic guardian, in field and wood—scarce more than a child—of the still more tender Ciccotto; and Ciccotto being a fine young pink-and-white pig, an animal of endowments that lead, after he has had time to render infatuated his otherwise quite solitary and joyless friend, to his premature conversion into bacon. She assists, helplessly silent, staring, almost idiotic, from a corner of the cabin-yard, by night and lamplight, in the presence of gleaming knives and steaming pots and bloody tubs, at the sacrifice that deprives her of all company, and nothing can exceed the homely truth of the touch that finally rounds off the scene and for which I must refer my reader to the volume. Let me further not fail to register my admiration for the curious cluster of scenes that, in "Il Romanzo," bears the title of "Nella Lava." Here frankly, I take it, we have the real principle of "naturalism"—a consistent presentment of the famous "slice of life." The slices given us—slices of shabby hungry maidenhood in small cockney circles—are but sketchily related to the volcanic catastrophe we hear rumbling behind them, the undertone of all the noise of Naples; but they have the real artistic importance of showing us how little "story" is required to hold us when we get, before the object evoked and in the air created, the impression of the real thing. Whatever thing—interesting inference—has but effectively to *be* real to constitute in itself story enough. There is no story without it, none that is not rank humbug; whereas with it the very desert blooms.

This last-named phenomenon takes place, I fear, but in a minor degree in such of our author's productions as "Cuore Infermo," "Addio Amore," "Il Castigo" and the double series of "Gli Amanti"; and for a reason that I the more promptly indicate as it not only explains, I think, the comparative inanity of these pictures, but does more than anything else to reward our inquiry. The very first reflection suggested by Serao's novels of "passion" is that they perfectly meet our speculation as to what might with a little time become of our own fiction were our par-

ticular convention suspended. We see so what, on its
actual lines, does, what *has*, become of it, and are so
sated with the vision that a little consideration of the
latent other chance will surely but refresh us. The
effect then, we discover, of the undertaking to give
passione its whole place is that by the operation of a
singular law no place speedily appears to be left for
anything else; and the effect of that in turn is greatly
to modify, first, the truth of things, and second, with
small delay, what may be left them of their beauty.
We find ourselves wondering after a little whether
there may not really be more truth in the world misrepresented according to our own familiar fashion than
in such a world as that of Madame Serao's exuberant
victims of Venus. It is not only that if Venus herself
is notoriously beautiful her altar, as happens, is by no
means always proportionately august; it is also that
we draw, in the long run, small comfort from the virtual suppression, by any painter, of whatever skill—
and the skill of this particular one fails to rise to the
height—of every relation in life but that over which
Venus presides. In "Fior di Passione" and the several others of a like connection that I have named the
suppression is really complete; the common humanities and sociabilities are wholly absent from the picture.

The effect of this is extraordinarily to falsify the
total show and to present the particular affair—the
intimacy in hand for the moment, though the moment be but brief—as taking place in a strange false
perspective, a denuded desert which experience surely
fails ever to give us the like of and the action of which
on the faculty of observation in the painter is anything but favourable. It strikes at the root, in the

impression producible and produced, of discrimination and irony, of humour and pathos. Our present author would doubtless contend on behalf of the works I have mentioned that pathos at least does abound in them—the particular bitterness, the inevitable despair that she again and again shows to be the final savour of the cup of *passione*. It would be quite open to her to urge—and she would be sure to do so with eloquence —that if we pusillanimously pant for a moral, no moral really can have the force of her almost inveterate evocation of the absolute ravage of Venus, the dry desolation that in nine cases out of ten Venus may be perceived to leave behind her. That, however, but half meets our argument—which bears by no means merely on the desolation behind, but on the desolation before, beside and generally roundabout. It is not in short at all the moral but the fable itself that in the exclusively sexual light breaks down and fails us. Love, at Naples and in Rome, as Madame Serao exhibits it, is simply unaccompanied with any interplay of our usual conditions—with affection, with duration, with circumstances or consequences, with friends, enemies, husbands, wives, children, parents, interests, occupations, the manifestation of tastes. Who are these people, we presently ask ourselves, who love indeed with fury— though for the most part with astonishing brevity— but who are so without any suggested situation in life that they can only strike us as loving for nothing and in the void, to no gain of experience and no effect of a felt medium or a breathed air. We know them by nothing but their convulsions and spasms, and we feel once again that it is not the passion of hero and heroine that gives, that can ever give, the heroine and the hero interest, but that it is they themselves, with the ground they stand on and the objects enclosing them, who give interest to their passion. This element touches us just in proportion as we see it mixed with other things, with all the things with which it has to reckon and struggle. There is moreover another reflection with which the pathetic in this connection has to count, even though it undermine not a little the whole of the tragic effect of the agitations of *passione*. Is it, ruthlessly speaking, certain that the effect most consonant, for the spectator, with truth is half as tragic as it is something else? Should not the moral be sought in the very different quarter where the muse of comedy rather would have the last word? The ambiguity and the difficulty are, it strikes me, of a new growth, and spring from a perverse desire on the part of the erotic novelist to secure for the adventures he depicts a dignity that is not of the essence. To compass this dignity he has to cultivate the high pitch and beat the big drum, but when he has done so he has given everything the wrong accent and the whole the wrong extravagance. Why see it all, we ask him, as an extravagance of the solemn and the strained? Why make *such* an erotic a matter of tears and imprecations, and by so doing render so poor a service both to pleasure and to pain? Since by your own free showing it is pre-eminently a matter of folly, let us at least have folly with her bells, or when these must— since they must—sound knells and dirges, leave them only to the light hand of the lyric poet, who turns them at the worst to music. Matilde Serao is in this connection constantly lugubrious; even from the little so-called pastels of "Gli Amanti" she manages, with an ingenuity worthy of a better cause, to expunge the note of gaiety.

This dismal *parti pris* indeed will inevitably, it is be feared, when all the emancipations shall have said their last word, be that of the ladies. Yet perhaps too, whatever such a probability, the tone scarce signifies—in the presence, I mean, of the fundamental mistake from which the author before us warns us off. That mistake, we gather from her warning, would be to encourage, after all, any considerable lowering of the level of our precious fund of reserve. When we come to analyse we arrive at a final impression of what we pay, as lovers of the novel, for such a chartered state as we have here a glimpse of; and we find it to be an exposure, on the intervention at least of such a literary temperament as the one before us, to a new kind of vulgarity. We have surely as it is kinds enough. The absence of the convention throws the writer back on tact, taste, delicacy, discretion, subjecting these principles to a strain from which the happy office of its presence is, in a considerable degree and for performers of the mere usual endowment, to relieve him. When we have not a very fine sense the convention appears in a manner to have it on our behalf. And how frequent to-day, in the hurrying herd of brothers and sisters of the pen, *is* a fine sense—of *any* side of their affair? Do we not approach the truth in divining that only an eminent individual here and there may be trusted for it? Here—for the case is our very lesson—is this robust and wonderful Serao who is yet not to be trusted at all. Does not the dim religious light with which we surround its shrine do more, on the whole, for the poetry of *passione* than the flood of flaring gas with which, in her pages, and at her touch, it is drenched? Does it not shrink, as a subject under treatment, from such expert recognitions and easy discussions, from its so pitiless reduction to the category of the familiar? It issues from the ordeal with the aspect with which it might escape from a noisy family party or alight from a crowded omnibus. It is at the category of the familiar that vulgarity begins. There may be a cool virtue therefore even for "art," and an appreciable distinction even for truth, in the grace of hanging back and the choice of standing off, in that shade of the superficial which we best defend by simply practising it in season. A feeling revives at last, after a timed intermission, that we may not immediately be quite able, quite assured enough, to name, but which, gradually clearing up, soon defines itself almost as a yearning. We turn round in obedience to it—unmistakably we turn round again to the opposite pole, and there before we know it have positively laid a clinging hand on dear old Jane Austen.

THE NEW NOVEL

1914

WE feel it not to be the paradox it may at the first blush seem that the state of the novel in England at the present time is virtually very much the state of criticism itself; and this moreover, at the risk perhaps of some added appearance of perverse remark, by the very reason that we see criticism so much in abeyance. So far as we miss it altogether how and why does its "state" matter, and why and how can it or should it, as an absent force, enjoy a relation to that constant renewal of our supply of fiction which is a present one so far as a force at all? The relation is this, in the fewest words: that no equal outpouring of matter into the mould of literature, or what roughly passes for such, has been noted to live its life and maintain its flood, its level at least of quantity and mass, in such free and easy independence of critical attention. It constitutes a condition and a perversity on the part of this element to remain irresponsive before an appeal so vociferous at least and so incessant; therefore how can such a neglect of occasions, so careless a habit in spite of marked openings, be better described than as responsibility declined in the face of disorder? The disorder thus determines the relation, from the moment we feel that it might be less, that it might be different, that something in the way of an order even might be disengaged from it and replace it; from the moment in fact that the low critical pitch is logically *reflected* in

the poetic or, less pedantically speaking, the improv-
isational at large. The effect, if not the prime office,
of criticism is to make our absorption and our enjoyment of the things that feed the mind as aware of itself
as possible, since that awareness quickens the mental
demand, which thus in turn wanders further and further for pasture. This action on the part of the mind
practically amounts to a reaching out for the reasons
of its interest, as only by its so ascertaining them can
the interest grow more various. This is the very
education of our imaginative life; and thanks to it the
general question of how to refine, and of why certain
things refine more and most, on that happy consciousness, becomes for us of the last importance. Then
we cease to be only instinctive and at the mercy of
chance, feeling that we can ourselves take a hand in
our satisfaction and provide for it, making ourselves
safe against dearth, and through the door opened by
that perception criticism enters, if we but give it time,
as a flood, the great flood of awareness; so maintaining
its high tide unless through some lapse of our sense
for it, some flat reversion to instinct alone, we block up
the ingress and sit in stale and shrinking waters.
Stupidity may arrest any current and fatuity transcend
any privilege. The comfort of those who at such a
time consider the scene may be a little, with *their*
curiosity still insistent, to survey its platitude and
record the exhibited shrinkage; which amounts to the
attempt to understand how stupidity could so have
prevailed. We take it here that the answer to that
inquiry can but be ever the same. The flood of "production" has so inordinately exceeded the activity of
control that this latter anxious agent, first alarmed but
then indifferent, has been forced backward out of the

gate, leaving the contents of the reservoir to boil and
evaporate. It is verily on the wrong side of the gate
that we just now seem to see criticism stand, for never
was the reservoir so bubblingly and noisily full, at
least by the superficial measure of life. We have
caught the odd accident in the very fact of its occurrence; we have seen the torrent swell by extravagant
cheap contribution, the huge increase of affluents
turbid and unstrained. Beyond number are the ways
in which the democratic example, once gathering momentum, sets its mark on societies and seasons that
stand in its course. Nowhere is that example written
larger, to our perception, than in "the new novel";
though this, we hasten to add, not in the least because
prose fiction now occupies itself as never before with
the "condition of the people," a fact quite irrelevant
to the nature it has taken on, but because that nature
amounts exactly to the complacent declaration of a
common literary level, a repudiation the most operative even if the least reasoned of the idea of differences,
the virtual law, as we may call it, of sorts and kinds,
the values of individual quality and weight in the presence of undiscriminated quantity and rough-and-tum-
ble "output"—these attestations made, we naturally
mean, in the air of composition and on the esthetic
plane, if such terms have still an attenuated reference
to the case before us. With which, if we be asked, in
the light of that generalisation, whether we impute to
the novel, or in other words the novelist, *all* the stupidity against which the spirit of appreciation spends
itself in vain, we reply perforce that we stop short of
that, it being too obvious that of an exhibition so ster-
ilised, so void of all force and suggestion, there would
be nothing whatever to say. Our contention is exactly

that, in spite of all vain aspects, it does yet present an interest, and that here and there seem written on it likelihoods of its presenting still more—always on condition of its consenting to that more intimate education which is precisely what democratised movements look most askance at. It strikes us as not too much to say that our actual view of the practice of fiction gives as just a measure as could be desired of the general, the incurable democratic suspicion of the selective and comparative principles in almost any application, and the tendency therewith to regard, and above all to treat, one manner of book, like one manner of person, as, if not absolutely as good as another, yet good enough for any democratic use. Criticism reflects contentiously on that appearance, though it be an appearance in which comfort for the book and the manner much resides; so that the idea prompting these remarks of our own is that the comfort may be deeply fallacious.

I

Still not to let go of our imputation of interest to some part at least of what is happening in the world of production in this kind, we may say that non-selective and non-comparative practice appears bent on showing us all it can do and how far or to what appointed shores, what waiting havens and inviting inlets, the current that is mainly made a current by looseness, by want of observable direction, shall succeed in carrying it. We respond to any sign of an intelligent view or even of a lively instinct—which is why we give the appearance so noted the benefit of every presumption as to its life and health. It may be that the dim sense is livelier than the presentable

reason, but even that is no graceless fact for us, especially when the keenness of young curiosity and energy
is betrayed in its pace, and betrayed, for that matter,
in no small abundance and variety. The new or at
least the young novel is up and doing, clearly, with the
best faith and the highest spirits in the world; if we
but extend a little our measure of youth indeed, as we
are happily more and more disposed to, we may speak
of it as already chin-deep in trophies. The men who
are not so young as the youngest were but the other
day very little older than these: Mr. Joseph Conrad,
Mr. Maurice Hewlett and Mr. Galsworthy, Mr. H. G.
Wells and Mr. Arnold Bennett, have not quite perhaps
the early bloom of Mr. Hugh Walpole, Mr. Gilbert
Cannan, Mr. Compton Mackenzie and Mr. D. H.
Lawrence, but the spring unrelaxed is still, to our perception, in their step, and we see two or three of them
sufficiently related to the still newer generation in a
quasi-parental way to make our whole enumeration
as illustrational as we need it. Mr. Wells and Mr.
Arnold Bennett have their strongest mark, the aspect
by which we may most classify them, in common—
even if their three named contemporaries are doubtless
most interesting in one of the connections we are not
now seeking to make. The author of "Tono-Bungay"
and of "The New Machiavelli," and the author of
"The Old Wives' Tale" and of "Clayhanger," have
practically launched the boat in which we admire the
fresh play of oar of the author of "The Duchess of
Wrexe," and the documented aspect exhibited successively by "Round the Corner," by "Carnival" and
"Sinister Street," and even by "Sons and Lovers"
(however much we may find Mr. Lawrence, we confess, hang in the dusty rear). We shall explain in a

moment what we mean by this designation of the element that these best of the younger men strike us as
more particularly sharing, our point being provisionally that Mr. Wells and Mr. Arnold Bennett (speaking
now only of them) began some time back to show us,
and to show sundry emulous and generous young
spirits then in the act of more or less waking up, what
the state in question might amount to.   We confound
the author of "Tono-Bungay" and the author of
"Clayhanger" in this imputation for the simple reason
that with the sharpest differences of character and
range they yet come together under our so convenient
measure of value by *saturation*.   This is the greatest
value, to our sense, in either of them, their other
values, even when at the highest, not being quite in
proportion to it; and as to be saturated is to be documented, to be able even on occasion to prove quite
enviably and potently so, they are alike in the authority
that creates emulation.   It little signifies that Mr.
Wells's documented or saturated state in respect to a
particular matter in hand is but one of the faces of his
generally informed condition, of his extraordinary mass
of gathered and assimilated knowledge, a miscellaneous collection more remarkable surely than any teller
of "mere" tales, with the possible exception of Balzac,
has been able to draw upon, whereas Mr. Arnold
Bennett's corresponding provision affects us as, though
singularly copious, special, exclusive and artfully
economic.   This distinction avails nothing against
that happy fact of the handiest possession by Mr.
Wells of immeasurably more concrete material, amenable for straight and vivid reference, convertible into
apt illustration, than we should know where to look
for other examples of.   The author of "The New

Machiavelli" knows, somehow, to our mystified and dazzled apprehension, because he writes and because that act constitutes for him the need, on occasion a most desperate, of absorbing knowledge at the pores; the chronicler of the Five Towns writing so much more discernibly, on the other hand, because he knows, and conscious of no need more desperate than that particular circle of civilisation may satisfy.

Our argument is that each is ideally immersed in his own body of reference, and that immersion in any such degree and to the effect of any such variety, intensity and plausibility is really among us a new feature of the novelist's range of resource. We have seen him, we have even seen *her*, otherwise auspiciously endowed, seen him observant, impassioned, inspired, and in virtue of these things often very charming, very interesting, very triumphant, visibly qualified for the highest distinction before the fact and visibly crowned by the same after it—we have seen him with a great imagination and a great sense of life, we have seen him even with a great sense of expression and a considerable sense of art: so that we have only to reascend the stream of our comparatively recent literature to meet him serene and immortal, brow-bound with the bay and erect on his particular pedestal. We have only to do that, but have only also, while we do it, to recognise that meantime other things still than these various apotheoses have taken place, and that, to the increase of our recreation, and even if our limited space condemns us to put the matter a trifle clumsily, a change has come over our general receptive sensibility not less than over our productive tradition. In these connections, we admit, overstatement is easy and over-emphasis tempting; we confess furthermore to a frank desire to enrich the case, the historic, with all the meaning we can stuff into it. So viewed accordingly it gives us the "new," to repeat our expression, as an appetite for a closer notation, a sharper specification of the signs of life, of consciousness, of the human scene and the human subject in general, than the three or four generations before us had been at all moved to insist on. They had insisted indeed, these generations, we see as we look back to them, on almost nothing whatever; what was to come to them had come, in enormous affluence and freshness at its best, and to our continued appreciation as well as to the honour of their sweet susceptibility, because again and again the great miracle of genius took place, while they gaped, in their social and sentimental sky. For ourselves that miracle has not been markedly renewed, but it has none the less happened that by hook and by crook the case for appreciation remains interesting. The great thing that saves it, under the drawback we have named, is, no doubt, that we have simply—always for appreciation—learned a little to insist, and that we thus get back on one hand something of what we have lost on the other. We are unable of course, with whatever habit of presumption engendered, to insist upon genius; so that who shall describe the measure of success we still achieve as not virtually the search for freshness, and above all for closeness, in quite a different direction? To this nearer view of commoner things Mr. Wells, say, and Mr. Arnold Bennett, and in their degree, under the infection communicated, Mr. D. H. Lawrence and Mr. Gilbert Cannan and Mr. Compton Mackenzie and Mr. Hugh Walpole, strike us as having all gathered themselves up with a movement never yet undertaken on our literary scene, and, beyond anything else, with an instinctive divination of what had most waved their predecessors off it. What had this lion in the path been, we make them out as after a fashion asking themselves, what had it been from far back and straight down through all the Victorian time, but the fond superstition that the key of the situation, of each and every situation that could turn up for the novelist, was the sentimental key, which might fit into no door or window opening on closeness or on freshness at all? Was it not for all the world as if even the brightest practitioners of the past, those we now distinguish as saved for glory in spite of themselves, had been as sentimental as they could, or, to give the trick another name, as romantic and thereby as shamelessly "dodgy"?—just in order *not* to be close and fresh, not to be authentic, as that takes trouble, takes talent, and you can be sentimental, you can be romantic, you can be dodgy, alas, not a bit less on the footing of genius than on the footing of mediocrity or even of imbecility? Was it not as if the sentimental had been more and more noted as but another name for the romantic, if not indeed the romantic as but another name for the sentimental, and as if these things, whether separate or united, had been in the same degree recognised as unamenable, or at any rate unfavourable, to any consistent fineness of notation, once the tide of the copious as a condition of the thorough had fairly set in?

So, to express it briefly, the possibility of hugging the shore of the real as it had not, among us, been hugged, and of pushing inland, as far as a keel might float, wherever the least opening seemed to smile,

dawned upon a few votaries and gathered further confidence with exercise. Who could say, of course, that
Jane Austen had not been close, just as who could ask
if Anthony Trollope had not been copious?—just as
who could *not* say that it all depended on what was
meant by these terms? The demonstration of what
was meant, it presently appeared, could come but
little by little, quite as if each tentative adventurer
had rather anxiously to learn for himself what *might*
be meant—this failing at least the leap into the arena
of some great demonstrative, some sudden athletic
and epoch-making authority. Who could pretend that
Dickens was anything but romantic, and even more
romantic in his humour, if possible, than in pathos or
in queer perfunctory practice of the "plot"? Who
could pretend that Jane Austen didn't leave much
more untold than told about the aspects and manners
even of the confined circle in which her muse revolved?
Why shouldn't it be argued against her that where her
testimony complacently ends the pressure of appetite
within us presumes exactly to begin? Who could
pretend that the reality of Trollope didn't owe much
of its abundance to the diluted, the quite extravagantly watered strain, no less than to the heavy hand,
in which it continued to be ladled out? Who of the
younger persuasion would not have been ready to cite,
as one of the liveliest opportunities for the critic eager
to see representation searching, such a claim for the
close as Thackeray's sighing and protesting "look-in"
at the acquaintance between Arthur Pendennis and
Fanny Bolton, the daughter of the Temple laundress,
amid the purlieus of that settlement? The sentimental habit and the spirit of romance, it was unmistakably
chargeable, stood out to sea as far as possible the

moment the shore appeared to offer the least difficulty
to hugging, and the Victorian age bristled with perfect
occasions for our catching them in the act of this
showy retreat.　All revolutions have been prepared in
spite of their often striking us as sudden, and so it was
doubtless that when scarce longer ago than the other
day Mr. Arnold Bennett had the fortune to lay his
hand on a general scene and a cluster of agents deficient
to a peculiar degree in properties that might interfere
with a desirable density of illustration—deficient, that
is, in such connections as might carry the imagination
off to some sport on its own account—we recognised
at once a set of conditions auspicious to the newer kind
of appeal.　Let us confess that we were at the same
time doubtless to master no better way of describing
these conditions than by the remark that they were,
for some reason beautifully inherent in them, susceptible at once of being entirely known and of seeming
delectably thick.　Reduction to exploitable knowledge is apt to mean for many a case of the human complexity reduction to comparative thinness; and nothing was thereby at the first blush to interest us more
than the fact that the air and the very smell of packed
actuality in the subject-matter of such things as the
author's two longest works was clearly but another
name for his personal competence in that matter, the
fulness and firmness of his embrace of it.　This was a
fresh and beguiling impression—that the state of inordinate possession on the chronicler's part, the mere
state as such and as an energy directly displayed, *was*
the interest, neither more nor less, *was* the sense and the
meaning and the picture and the drama, all so sufficiently constituting them that it scarce mattered what
they were in themselves.　Of what they were in them-

selves their being in Mr. Bennett, as Mr. Bennett to
such a tune harboured them, represented their one
conceivable account—not to mention, as reinforcing
this, our own great comfort and relief when certain
high questions and wonderments about them, or about
our mystified relation to them, began one after another to come up.

Because such questions did come, we must at once
declare, and we are still in presence of them, for all
the world as if that case of the perfect harmony, the
harmony between subject and author, were just marked
with a flaw and didn't meet the whole assault of restless criticism. What we make out Mr. Bennett as
doing is simply recording his possession or, to put it
more completely, his saturation; and to see him as
virtually shut up to that process is a note of all the
more moment that we see our selected cluster of his
interesting juniors, and whether by his direct action
on their collective impulse or not, embroiled, as we
venture to call it, in the same predicament. The act
of squeezing out to the utmost the plump and more or
less juicy orange of a particular acquainted state and
letting this affirmation of energy, however directed or
undirected, constitute for them the "treatment" of a
theme—*that* is what we remark them as mainly engaged in, after remarking the example so strikingly, so
originally set, even if an undue subjection to it be here
and there repudiated. Nothing is further from our
thought than to undervalue saturation and possession,
the fact of the particular experience, the state and
degree of acquaintance incurred, however such a consciousness may have been determined; for these things
represent on the part of the novelist, as on the part of

any painter of things seen, felt or imagined, just one half of his authority—the other half being represented of course by the application he is inspired to make of them. Therefore that fine secured half is so much gained at the start, and the fact of its brightly being there may really by itself project upon the course so much colour and form as to make us on occasion, under the genial force, almost not miss the answer to the question of application. When the author of "Clayhanger" has put down upon the table, in dense unconfused array, every fact required, every fact in any way invocable, to make the life of the Five Towns press upon us, and to make our sense of it, so full-fed, content us, we may very well go on for the time in the captive condition, the beguiled and bemused condition, the acknowledgment of which is in general our highest tribute to the temporary master of our sensibility. Nothing at such moments—or rather at the end of them, when the end begins to threaten—may be of a more curious strain than the dawning unrest that suggests to us fairly our first critical comment: "Yes, yes—but is this *all?* These are the circumstances of the interest—we see, we see; but where is the interest itself, where and what is its centre, and how are we to measure it in relation to *that?*" Of course we may in the act of exhaling that plaint (which we have just expressed at its mildest) well remember how many people there are to tell us that to "measure" an interest is none of our affair; that we have but to take it on the cheapest and easiest terms and be thankful; and that if by our very confession we have been led the imaginative dance the music has done for us all it pretends to. Which words, however, have only to happen to be for us the most unintelligent conceivable not in the least to arrest our wonderment as to where our bedrenched consciousness may still not awkwardly leave us for the pleasure of appreciation. That appreciation is also a mistake and a priggishness, being reflective and thereby corrosive, is another of the fond dicta which we are here concerned but to brush aside—the more closely to embrace the welcome induction that appreciation, attentive and reflective, inquisitive and conclusive, is in this connection absolutely the golden *key* to our pleasure. The more it plays up, the more we recognise and are able to number the sources of our enjoyment, the greater the provision made for security in that attitude, which corresponds, by the same stroke, with the reduced danger of waste in the undertaking to amuse us. It all comes back to our amusement, and to the noblest surely, on the whole, we know; and it is in the very nature of clinging appreciation not to sacrifice consentingly a single shade of the art that makes for that blessing. From this solicitude spring our questions, and not least the one to which we give ourselves for the moment here—this moment of our being regaled as never yet with the fruits of the movement (if the name be not of too pompous an application where the flush and the heat of accident too seem so candidly to look forth), in favour of the "expression of life" in terms as loose as may pretend to an effect of expression at all. The relegation of terms to the limbo of delusions outlived so far as ever really cultivated becomes of necessity, it will be plain, the great mark of the faith that for the novelist to show he "knows all about" a certain congeries of aspects, the more numerous within their mixed circle the better, is thereby to set in motion, with due intensity, the pretension to interest. The state of knowing all about whatever it may be has thus only to become consistently and abundantly active to pass for his supreme function; and to its so becoming active few difficulties appear to be descried—so great may on occasion be the mere excitement of activity. To the fact that the exhilaration is, as we have hinted, often infectious, to this and to the charming young good faith and general acclamation under which each case appears to proceed —each case we of course mean really repaying attention—the critical reader owes his opportunity so considerably and so gratefully to generalise.

II

We should have only to remount the current with a certain energy to come straight up against Tolstoy as the great illustrative master-hand on all this ground of the disconnection of method from matter—which encounter, however, would take us much too far, so that we must for the present but hang off from it with the remark that of all great painters of the social picture it was given that epic genius most to serve admirably as a rash adventurer and a "caution," and execrably, pestilentially, as a model. In this strange union of relations he stands alone: from no other great projector of the human image and the human idea is so much truth to be extracted under an equal leakage of its value. All the proportions in him are so much the largest that the drop of attention to our nearer cases might by its violence leave little of that principle alive; which fact need not disguise from us, none the less, that as Mr. H. G. Wells and Mr. Arnold Bennett, to return to them briefly again, derive, by multiplied if

diluted transmissions, from the great Russian (from
whose all but equal companion Turgenieff we recognise no derivatives at all), so, observing the distances,
we may profitably detect an unexhausted influence in
our minor, our still considerably less rounded vessels.
Highly attaching as indeed the game might be, of inquiring as to the centre of the interest or the sense of
the whole in "The Passionate Friends," or in "The
Old Wives' Tale," after having sought those luxuries
in vain not only through the general length and breadth
of "War and Peace," but within the quite respectable
confines of any one of the units of effect there clustered:
this as preparing us to address a like friendly challenge
to Mr. Cannan's "Round the Corner," say, or to Mr.
Lawrence's "Sons and Lovers"—should we wish to be
very friendly to Mr. Lawrence—or to Mr. Hugh Walpole's "Duchess of Wrexe," or even to Mr. Compton
Mackenzie's "Sinister Street" and "Carnival," discernibly, we hasten to add, though certain betrayals
of a controlling idea and a pointed intention do comparatively gleam out of the two fictions last named.
"The Old Wives' Tale" is the history of two sisters,
daughters of a prosperous draper in a Staffordshire
town, who, separating early in life, through the flight
of one of them to Paris with an ill-chosen husband and
the confirmed and prolonged local pitch of the career
of the other, are reunited late in life by the return of
the fugitive after much Parisian experience and by her
pacified acceptance of the conditions of her birthplace.
The divided current flows together again, and the
chronicle closes with the simple drying up determined
by the death of the sisters.   That is all; the canvas is
covered, ever so closely and vividly covered, by the
exhibition of innumerable small facts and aspects, at

which we assist with the most comfortable sense of
their substantial truth. The sisters, and more particularly the less adventurous, are at home in their
author's mind, they sit and move at their ease in the
square chamber of his attention, to a degree beyond
which the production of that ideal harmony between
creature and creator could scarcely go, and all by an
art of demonstration so familiar and so "quiet" that
the truth and the poetry, to use Goethe's distinction,
melt utterly together and we see no difference between
the subject of the show and the showman's feeling,
let alone the showman's manner, about it. This felt
identity of the elements—because we at least consciously feel—becomes in the novel we refer to, and not
less in "Clayhanger," which our words equally describe, a source for us of abject confidence, confidence
truly *so* abject in the solidity of every appearance
that it may be said to represent our whole relation
to the work and completely to exhaust our reaction
upon it. "Clayhanger," of the two fictions even the
more densely loaded with all the evidence in what we
should call the case presented did we but learn meanwhile for what case, or for a case of what, to take it,
inscribes the annals, the private more particularly,
of a provincial printer in a considerable way of business, beginning with his early boyhood and going on
to the complications of his maturity—these not exhausted with our present possession of the record,
inasmuch as by the author's announcement there is
more of the catalogue to come. This most monumental of Mr. Arnold Bennett's recitals, taking it with its
supplement of "Hilda Lessways," already before us,
is so describable through its being a monument exactly
not to an idea, a pursued and captured meaning, or in

short *to* anything whatever, but just simply *of* the
quarried and gathered material it happens to contain,
the stones and bricks and rubble and cement and promiscuous constituents of every sort that have been
heaped in it and thanks to which it quite massively
piles itself up. Our perusal and our enjoyment are
our watching of the growth of the pile and of the
capacity, industry, energy with which the operation is
directed. A huge and in its way a varied aggregation,
without traceable lines, divinable direction, effect of
composition, the mere number of its pieces, the great
dump of its material, together with the fact that here
and there in the miscellany, as with the value of bits
of marble or porphyry, fine elements shine out, it
keeps us standing and waiting to the end—and largely
just because it keeps us wondering. We surely wonder
more what it may all propose to mean than any equal
appearance of preparation to relieve us of that strain,
any so founded and grounded a postponement of the
disclosure of a sense in store, has for a long time called
upon us to do in a like connection. A great thing it is
assuredly that *while* we wait and wonder we are amused
—were it not for that, truly, our situation would be
thankless enough; we may ask ourselves, as has
already been noted, why on such ambiguous terms we
should consent to be, and why the practice doesn't at
a given moment break down; and our answer brings
us back to that many-fingered grasp of the orange that
the author squeezes. This particular orange is of the
largest and most rotund, and his trust in the consequent
flow is of its nature communicative. Such is the case
always, and most naturally, with that air in a person
who has something, who at the very least has much to
tell us: we *like* so to be affected by it, we meet it half

way and lend ourselves, sinking in up to the chin. Up to the chin only indeed, beyond doubt; we even then feel our head emerge, for judgment and articulate question, and it is from that position that we remind ourselves how the real reward of our patience is still to come—the reward attending not at all the immediate sense of immersion, but reserved for the aftersense, which is a very different matter, whether in the form of a glow or of a chill.

If Mr. Bennett's tight rotundity then is of the handsomest size and his manipulation of it so firm, what are we to say of Mr. Wells's, who, a novelist very much as Lord Bacon was a philosopher, affects us as taking all knowledge for his province and as inspiring in us to the very highest degree the confidence enjoyed by himself—enjoyed, we feel, with a breadth with which it has been given no one of his fellow-craftsmen to enjoy anything. If confidence alone could lead utterly captive we should all be huddled in a bunch at Mr. Wells's heels—which is indeed where we *are* abjectly gathered so far as that force does operate. It is literally Mr. Wells's own mind, and the experience of his own mind, incessant and extraordinarily various, extraordinarily reflective, even with all sorts of conditions made, of whatever he may expose it to, that forms the reservoir tapped by him, that constitutes his provision of grounds of interest. It is, by our thinking, in his power to name to us, as a preliminary, more of these grounds than all his contemporaries put together, and even to exceed any competitor, without exception, in the way of suggesting that, thick as he may seem to lay them, they remain yet only contributive, are not in themselves full expression but are designed

strictly to subserve it, that this extraordinary writer's
spell resides. When full expression, the expression of
some particular truth, seemed to lapse in this or that
of his earlier novels (we speak not here of his shorter
things, for the most part delightfully wanton and exempt,) it was but by a hand's breadth, so that if we
didn't inveterately quite know what he intended we
yet always felt sufficiently that *he* knew. The particular intentions of such matters as "Kipps," as
"Tono-Bungay," as "Ann Veronica," so swarmed
about us, in their blinding, bluffing vivacity, that the
mere sum of them might have been taken for a sense
over and above which it was graceless to inquire. The
more this author learns and learns, or at any rate knows
and knows, however, the greater is this impression of
his holding it good enough for us, such as we are, that
he shall but turn out his mind and its contents upon us
by any free familiar gesture and as from a high window
forever open—an entertainment as copious surely as
any occasion should demand, at least till we have more
intelligibly expressed our title to a better. Such things
as "The New Machiavelli," "Marriage," "The Passionate Friends," are so very much more attestations
of the presence of material than attestations of an
interest in the use of it that we ask ourselves again
and again why so fondly neglected a state of leakage
comes not to be fatal to *any* provision of quantity,
or even to stores more specially selected for the ordeal
than Mr. Wells's always strike us as being. Is not
the pang of witnessed waste in fact great just in proportion as we are touched by our author's fine off-
handedness as to the value of the stores, about which
he can for the time make us believe what he will? so
that, to take an example susceptible of brief statement,

we wince at a certain quite peculiarly gratuitous sacrifice to the casual in "Marriage" very much as at seeing some fine and indispensable little part of a mechanism slip through profane fingers and lose itself. Who does not remember what ensues after a little upon the aviational descent of the hero of the fiction just named into the garden occupied, in company with her parents, by the young lady with whom he is to fall in love?—and this even though the whole opening scene so constituted, with all the comedy hares its function appears to be to start, remains with its back squarely turned, esthetically speaking, to the quarter in which the picture develops. The point for our mortification is that by one of the first steps in this development, the first impression on him having been made, the hero accidentally meets the heroine, of a summer eventide, in a leafy lane which supplies them with the happiest occasion to pursue their acquaintance —or in other words supplies the author with the liveliest consciousness (as we at least feel it should have been) that just so the relation between the pair, its seed already sown and the fact of that bringing about all that is still to come, pushes aside whatever veil and steps forth into life. To show it step forth and affirm itself as a relation, what is this but the interesting function of the whole passage, on the performance of which what follows is to hang?—and yet who can say that when the ostensible sequence *is* presented, and our young lady, encountered again by her stirred swain, under cover of night, in a favouring wood, is at once encompassed by his arms and pressed to his lips and heart (for celebration thus of their third meeting) we do not assist at a well-nigh heartbreaking miscarriage of "effect"? We see effect, invoked in vain, simply stand off unconcerned; effect not having been at all consulted in advance she is not to be secured on such terms. And her presence would so have redounded —perfectly punctual creature as she is on a made appointment and a clear understanding—to the advantage of all concerned. The bearing of the young man's act is all in our having begun to conceive it as possible, begun even to desire it, in the light of what has preceded; therefore if the participants have *not* been shown us as on the way to it, nor the question of it made beautifully to tremble for us in the air, its happiest connections fail and we but stare at it mystified. The instance is undoubtedly trifling, but in the infinite complex of such things resides for a work of art the shy virtue, shy at least till wooed forth, of the whole susceptibility. The case of Mr. Wells might take us much further—such remarks as there would be to make, say, on such a question as the due understanding, on the part of "The Passionate Friends" (not as associated persons but as a composed picture), of what that composition is specifically *about* and where, for treatment of this interest, it undertakes to find its centre: all of which, we are willing however to grant, falls away before the large assurance and incorrigible levity with which this adventurer carries his lapses—far more of an adventurer as he is than any other of the company. The composition, as we have called it, heaven saving the mark, is simply at any and every moment "about" Mr. Wells's general adventure; which is quite enough while it preserves, as we trust it will long continue to do, its present robust pitch.

We have already noted that "Round the Corner," Mr. Gilbert Cannan's liveliest appeal to our attention,

belongs to the order of *constatations* pure and simple;
to the degree that *as* a document of that nature and
of that rigour the book could perhaps not more completely affirm itself. When we have said that it puts
on record the "tone," the manners, the general domestic
proceedings and *train de vie* of an amiable clergyman's
family established in one of the more sordid quarters
of a big black northern city of the Liverpool or Man-
chester complexion we have advanced as far in the way
of descriptive statement as the interesting work seems
to warrant. For it *is* interesting, in spite of its leaving itself on our hands with a consistent indifference
to any question of the charmed application springing
from it all that places it in the forefront of its type.
Again as under the effect of Mr. Bennett's major productions our sole inference is that things, the things
disclosed, *go on and on, in any given case, in spite of
everything*—with Mr. Cannan's one discernible care
perhaps being for how extraordinarily much, in the
particular example here before him, they were able to
go on in spite of. The conception, the presentation
of this enormous inauspicious amount as bearing upon
the collective career of the Folyats is, we think, as
near as the author comes at any point to betraying
an awareness of a subject. Yet again, though so little
encouraged or "backed," a subject after a fashion makes
itself, even as it has made itself in "The Old Wives'
Tale" and in "Clayhanger," in "Sons and Lovers,"
where, as we have hinted, any assistance rendered us
for a view of one *most* comfortably enjoys its absence,
and in Mr. Hugh Walpole's newest novel, where we
wander scarcely less with our hand in no guiding
grasp, but where the author's good disposition, as we
feel it, to provide us with what we lack if he only knew

how, constitutes in itself such a pleading liberality.
We seem to see him in this spirit lay again and again a
flowered carpet for our steps. If we do not include
Mr. Compton Mackenzie to the same extent in our
generalisation it is really because we note a difference
in him, a difference in favour of his care for the application. Preoccupations seem at work in "Sinister
Street," and withal in "Carnival," the brush of which
we in other quarters scarce even suspect and at some of
which it will presently be of profit to glance. "I
answer for it, you know," we seem at any rate to
hear Mr. Gilbert Cannan say with an admirably
genuine young pessimism, "I answer for it that they
were really *like* that, odd or unpleasant or uncon-
tributive, and therefore tiresome, as it may strike
you;" and the charm of Mr. Cannan, so far as up or
down the rank we so disengage a charm, is that we
take him at his word. His guarantee, his straight
communication, of his general truth is a value, and
values are rare—the flood of fiction is apparently
capable of running hundreds of miles without a single
glint of one—and thus in default of satisfaction we
get stopgaps and are thankful often under a genial
touch to get even so much. The value indeed is crude,
it would be quadrupled were it only wrought and
shaped; yet it has still the rude dignity that it counts
to us for experience or at least for what we call under
our present pitch of sensibility force of impression.
The experience, we feel, is ever something to conclude
upon, while the impression is content to wait; to wait,
say, in the spirit in which we must accept this younger
bustle if we accept it at all, the spirit of its serving as
a rather presumptuous lesson to us in patience. While
we wait, again, we are amused—not in the least, also

to repeat, up to the notch of our conception of amusement, which draws upon still other forms and sources; but none the less for the wonder, the intensity, the actuality, the probity of the vision. This is much as in "Clayhanger" and in "Hilda Lessways," where, independently of the effect, so considerably rendered, of the long lapse of time, always in this type of recital a source of amusement in itself, and certainly of the noblest, we get such an admirably substantial thing as the collective image of the Orgreaves, the local family in whose ample lap the amenities and the humanities so easily sit, for Mr. Bennett's evocation and his protagonist's recognition, and the manner of the presentation of whom, with the function and relation of the picture at large, strikes such a note of felicity, achieves such a simulation of sense, as the author should never again be excused for treating, that is for neglecting, as beyond his range. Here figures signally the interesting case of a compositional function absolutely performed by mere multiplication, the flow of the facts: the Orgreaves, in "Clayhanger," are there, by what we make out, but for "life," for general life only, and yet, with their office under any general or inferential meaning entirely unmarked, come doubtless as near squaring esthetically with the famous formula of the "slice of life" as any example that could be adduced; happening moreover as they probably do to owe this distinction to their coincidence at once with reality and charm—a fact esthetically curious and delightful. For we attribute the bold stroke they represent much more to Mr. Arnold Bennett's esthetic instinct than to anything like a calculation of his bearings, and more to his thoroughly acquainted state, as we may again put it, than to all other causes together: which strikingly enough shows how much complexity of interest may be simulated by mere presentation of material, mere squeezing of the orange, when the material happens to be "handsome" or the orange to be sweet.

III

The orange of our persistent simile is in Mr. Hugh Walpole's hands very remarkably sweet—a quality we recognise in it even while reduced to observing that the squeeze pure and simple, the fond, the lingering, the reiterated squeeze, constitutes as yet his main perception of method. He enjoys in a high degree the consciousness of saturation, and is on such serene and happy terms with it as almost make of critical interference, in so bright an air, an assault on personal felicity. Full of material is thus the author of "The Duchess of Wrexe," and of a material which we should describe as the consciousness of youth were we not rather disposed to call it a peculiar strain of the extreme unconsciousness. Mr. Walpole offers us indeed a rare and interesting case—we see about the field none other like it; the case of a positive identity between the spirit, not to say the time of life or stage of experience, of the aspiring artist and the field itself of his vision. "The Duchess of Wrexe" reeks with youth and the love of youth and the confidence of youth—youth taking on with a charming exuberance the fondest costume or disguise, that of an adventurous and voracious felt interest, interest in life, in London, in society, in character, in Portland Place, in the Oxford Circus, in the afternoon tea-table, in the torrid weather, in fifty other immediate things as to which its passion and its curiosity are of the sincerest. The wonderful thing is that these latter forces operate, in their way, without yet being disengaged and hand-free—disengaged, that is, from their state of *being* young, with its billowy mufflings and other soft obstructions, the state of being present, being involved and aware, close "up against" the whole mass of possibilities, being in short intoxicated with the mixed liquors of suggestion. In the fumes of this acute situation Mr. Walpole's subject-matter is bathed; the situation being all the while so much more his own and that of a juvenility reacting, in the presence of everything, "for all it is worth," than the devised and imagined one, however he may circle about some such cluster, that every cupful of his excited flow tastes three times as much of his temperamental freshness as it tastes of this, that or the other character or substance, above all of this, that or the other group of antecedents and references, supposed to be reflected in it. All of which does not mean, we hasten to add, that the author of "The Duchess of Wrexe" has not the gift of life; but only that he strikes us as having received it, straight from nature, with such a concussion as to have kept the boon at the stage of violence—so that, fairly pinned down by it, he is still embarrassed for passing it on. On the day he shall have worked free of this primitive predicament, the crude fact of the convulsion itself, there need be no doubt of his exhibiting matter into which method may learn how to bite. The tract meanwhile affects us as more or less virgin snow, and we look with interest and suspense for the imprint of a process.

If those remarks represent all the while, further, that the performances we have glanced at, with others be-

sides, lead our attention on, we hear ourselves the more
naturally asked what it is then that we expect or want,
confessing as we do that we have been in a manner
interested, even though, from case to case, in a vary-
ing degree, and that Thackeray, Turgenieff, Balzac,
Dickens, Anatole France, no matter who, can not do
more than interest. Let us therefore concede to the
last point that small mercies are better than none,
that there are latent within the critic numberless lia-
bilities to being "squared" (the extent to which he may
on occasion betray his price!) and so great a preference
for being pleased over not being, that you may again
and again see him assist with avidity at the attempt
of the slice of life to butter itself thick. Its explanation that it *is* a slice of life and pretends to be nothing
else figures for us, say, while we watch, the jam super-
added to the butter. For since the jam, on this system, descends upon our desert, in its form of manna,
from quite another heaven than the heaven of method,
the mere demonstration of its agreeable presence is
alone sufficient to hint at our more than one chance
of being supernaturally fed. The happy-go-lucky fashion of it is indeed not then, we grant, an objection so
long as we do take in refreshment: the meal may be
of the last informality and yet produce in the event
no small sense of repletion. The slice of life devoured,
the butter and the jam duly appreciated, we are ready,
no doubt, on another day, to trust ourselves afresh to
the desert. We break camp, that is, and face toward
a further stretch of it, all in the faith that we shall be
once more provided for. We take the risk, we enjoy
more or less the assistance—more or less, we put it,
for the vision of a possible arrest of the miracle or
failure of our supply never wholly leaves us. The

phenomenon is too uncanny, the happy-go-lucky, as we know it in general, never *has* been trustable to the end; the absence of the last true touch in the preparation of its viands becomes with each renewal of the adventure a more sensible fact. By the last true touch we mean of course the touch of the hand of selection; the principle of selection having been involved at the worst or the least, one would suppose, in any approach whatever to the loaf of life with the *arrière-pensée* of a slice. There being no question of a slice upon which the further question of where and how to cut it does not wait, the office of method, the idea of choice and comparison, have occupied the ground from the first. This makes clear, to a moment's reflection, that there can be no such thing as an amorphous slice, and that any waving aside of inquiry as to the sense and value of a chunk of matter has to reckon with the simple truth of its having been *born* of naught else but measured excision. Reasons have been the fairies waiting on its cradle, the possible presence of a bad fairy in the form of a bad reason to the contrary notwithstanding. It has thus had connections at the very first stage of its detachment that are at no later stage logically to be repudiated; let it lie as lumpish as it will—for adoption, we mean, of the ideal of the lump—it has been tainted from too far back with the hard liability to form, and thus carries in its very breast the hapless contradiction of its sturdy claim to have none. This claim has the inevitable challenge at once to meet. How can a slice of life be anything but illustrational of the loaf, and how can illustration not immediately bristle with every sign of the extracted and related state? The relation is at once to what the thing comes from and to what it waits upon

—which last is our act of recognition. We accordingly appreciate it in proportion as it so accounts for itself; the quantity and the intensity of its reference are the measure of our knowledge of it. This is exactly why illustration breaks down when reference, otherwise application, runs short, and why before any assemblage of figures or aspects, otherwise of samples and specimens, the question of what these are, extensively, samples and specimens *of* declines not to beset us— why, otherwise again, we look ever for the supreme reference that shall avert the bankruptcy of sense.

Let us profess all readiness to repeat that we may still have had, on the merest "life" system, or that of the starkest crudity of the slice, all the entertainment that can come from watching a wayfarer engage with assurance in an alley that we know to have no issue —and from watching for the very sake of the face that he may show us on reappearing at its mouth. The recitals of Mr. Arnold Bennett, Mr. Gilbert Cannan, Mr. D. H. Lawrence, fairly smell of the real, just as the "Fortitude" and "The Duchess" of Mr. Hugh Walpole smell of the romantic; we have sufficiently noted then that, once on the scent, we are capable of pushing ahead. How far it is at the same time from being all a matter of smell the terms in which we just above glanced at the weakness of the spell of the happy-go-lucky may here serve to indicate. There faces us all the while the fact that the act of consideration as an incident of the esthetic pleasure, consideration confidently knowing us to *have* sooner or later to arrive at it, may be again and again postponed, but can never hope not some time to fall due. Consideration is susceptible of many forms, some one or other of which no conscious esthetic effort fails to cry out for; and the simplest description of the cry of the novel when sincere—for have we not heard such compositions bluff us, as it were, with false cries?—is as an appeal to us when we have read it once to read it yet again. *That* is the act of consideration; no other process of considering approaches this for directness, so that anything short of it is virtually not to consider at all. The word has sometimes another sense, that of the appeal to us *not*, for the world, to go back—this being of course consideration of a sort; the sort clearly that the truly flushed production should be the last to invoke. The effect of consideration, we need scarce remark, is to light for us in a work of art the hundred questions of how and why and whither, and the effect of these questions, once lighted, is enormously to thicken and complicate, even if toward final clarifications, what we have called the amused state produced in us by the work. The more our amusement multiplies its terms the more fond and the more rewarded consideration becomes; the fewer it leaves them, on the other hand, the less to be resisted for us is the impression of "bare ruined choirs where late the sweet birds sang." Birds that have appeared to sing, or whose silence we have not heeded, on a first perusal, prove on a second to have no note to contribute, and whether or no a second is enough to admonish us of those we miss, we mostly expect much from it in the way of emphasis of those we find. Then it is that notes of intention become more present or more absent; then it is that we take the measure of what we have already called our effective provision. The bravest providers and designers show at this point something still in store which only the second rummage was appointed to draw forth. To the variety of these ways of not letting our fondness fast is there not practically no limit ?—and of the arts, the devices, the graces, the subtle secrets applicable to such an end what presumptuous critic shall pretend to draw the list ? Let him for the moment content himself with saying that many of the most effective are mysteries, precisely, of method, or that even when they are not most essentially and directly so it takes method, blest method, to extract their soul and to determine their action.

It is odd and delightful perhaps that at the very moment of our urging this truth we should happen to be regaled with a really supreme specimen of the part playable in a novel by the source of interest, the principle of provision attended to, for which we claim importance. Mr. Joseph Conrad's "Chance" is none the less a signal instance of provision the most earnest and the most copious for its leaving ever so much to be said about the particular provision effected. It is none the less an extraordinary exhibition of method by the fact that the method is, we venture to say, without a precedent in any like work. It places Mr. Conrad absolutely alone as a votary of the way to do a thing that shall make it undergo most doing. The way to do it that shall make it undergo least is the line on which we are mostly now used to see prizes carried off; so that the author of "Chance" gathers up on this showing all sorts of comparative distinction. He gathers up at least two sorts—that of bravery in absolutely reversing the process most accredited, and that, quite separate, we make out, of performing the manœuvre under salvos of recognition. It is not in these days often given to a refinement of design to be recognised, but Mr. Conrad has made his achieve that miracle—save in so far indeed as the miracle has been one thing and the success another. The miracle is of the rarest, confounding all calculation and suggesting more reflections than we can begin to make place for here; but the sources of surprise surrounding it might be, were this possible, even greater and yet leave the fact itself in all independence, the fact that the whole undertaking was committed by its very first step either to be "art" exclusively or to be nothing. This is the prodigious rarity, since surely we have known for many a day no other such case of the whole clutch of eggs, and these withal of the freshest, in that one basket; to which it may be added that if we say for many a day this is not through our readiness positively to associate the sight with any very definite moment of the past. What concerns us is that the general effect of "Chance" is arrived at by a pursuance of means to the end in view contrasted with which every other current form of the chase can only affect us as cheap and futile; the carriage of the burden or amount of service required on these lines exceeding surely all other such displayed degrees of energy put together. Nothing could well interest us more than to see the exemplary value of attention, attention given by the author and asked of the reader, attested in a case in which it has had almost unspeakable difficulties to struggle with—since so we are moved to qualify the particular difficulty Mr. Conrad has "elected" to face: the claim for method in itself, method in this very sense of attention applied, would be somehow less lighted if the difficulties struck us as less consciously, or call it even less wantonly, invoked. What they consist of we should have to diverge here a little to say,

and should even then probably but lose ourselves in
the dim question of why so special, eccentric and desperate a course, so deliberate a plunge into threatened
frustration, should alone have seemed open. It has
been the course, so far as three words may here serve,
of his so multiplying his creators or, as we are now
fond of saying, producers, as to make them almost
more numerous and quite emphatically more material
than the creatures and the production itself in whom
and which we by the general law of fiction expect such
agents to lose themselves.   We take for granted by the
general law of fiction a primary author, take him so
much for granted that we forget him in proportion as
he works upon us, and that he works upon us most in
fact by making us forget him.

Mr. Conrad's first care on the other hand is expressly
to posit or set up a reciter, a definite responsible intervening first person singular, possessed of infinite
sources of reference, who immediately proceeds to set
up another, to the end that this other may conform
again to the practice, and that even at that point the
bridge over to the creature, or in other words to the
situation or the subject, the thing "produced," shall,
if the fancy takes it, once more and yet once more
glory in a gap.   It is easy to see how heroic the undertaking of an effective fusion becomes on these terms,
fusion between what we are to know and that prodigy
of our knowing which is ever half the very beauty of
the atmosphere of authenticity; from the moment the
reporters are thus multiplied from pitch to pitch the
tone of each, especially as "rendered" by his precursor
in the series, becomes for the prime poet of all an immense question—these circumferential tones having

not only to be such individually separate notes, but to keep so clear of the others, the central, the numerous and various voices of the agents proper, those expressive of the action itself and in whom the objectivity resides. We usually escape the worst of this difficulty of a tone *about* the tone of our characters, our projected performers, by keeping it single, keeping it "down" and thereby comparatively impersonal or, as we may say, inscrutable; which is what a creative force, in its blest fatuity, likes to be. But the omniscience, remaining indeed nameless, though constantly active, which sets Marlow's omniscience in motion from the very first page, insisting on a reciprocity with it throughout, this original omniscience invites consideration of itself only in a degree less than that in which Marlow's own invites it; and Marlow's own is a prolonged hovering flight of the subjective over the outstretched ground of the case exposed. We make out this ground but through the shadow cast by the flight, clarify it though the real author visibly reminds himself again and again that he must—all the more that, as if by some tremendous forecast of future applied science, the upper aeroplane causes another, as we have said, to depend from it and that one still another; these dropping shadow after shadow, to the no small menace of intrinsic colour and form and whatever, upon the passive expanse. What shall we most call Mr. Conrad's method accordingly but his attempt to clarify *quand même*—ridden as he has been, we perceive at the end of fifty pages of "Chance," by such a danger of steeping his matter in perfect eventual obscuration as we recall no other artist's consenting to with an equal grace. This grace, which presently comes over us as the sign of the whole business, is Mr.

Conrad's gallantry itself, and the shortest account of
the rest of the connection for our present purpose is
that his gallantry is thus his success. It literally strikes
us that his volume sets in motion more than anything
else a drama in which his own system and his combined eccentricities of recital represent the protagonist
in face of powers leagued against it, and of which the
dénouement gives us the system fighting in triumph,
though with its back desperately to the wall, and laying the powers piled up at its feet. This frankly has
been *our* spectacle, our suspense and our thrill; with
the one flaw on the roundness of it all the fact that the
predicament was not imposed rather than invoked,
was not the effect of a challenge from without, but that
of a mystic impulse from within.

Of an exquisite refinement at all events are the
critical questions opened up in the attempt, the question in particular of by what it exactly is that the experiment is crowned. Pronouncing it crowned and
the case saved by sheer gallantry, as we did above, is
perhaps to fall just short of the conclusion we might
reach were we to push further. "Chance" *is* an example of objectivity, most precious of aims, not only
menaced but definitely compromised; whereby we are
in presence of something really of the strangest, a
general and diffused lapse of authenticity which an
inordinate number of common readers—since it always
takes this and these to account encouragingly for
"editions"—have not only condoned but have emphatically commended. They can have done this but
through the bribe of some authenticity other in kind,
no doubt, and seeming to them equally great if not
greater, which gives back by the left hand what the

right has, with however dissimulated a grace, taken away. What Mr. Conrad's left hand gives back then is simply Mr. Conrad himself. We asked above what would become, by such a form of practice, of indispensable "fusion" or, to call it by another name, of the fine process by which our impatient material, at a given moment, shakes off the humiliation of the handled, the fumbled state, puts its head in the air and, to its own beautiful illusory consciousness at least, simply runs its race. Such an amount of handling and fumbling and repointing has it, on the system of the multiplied "putter into marble," to shake off! And yet behold, the sense of discomfort, as the show here works out, *has* been conjured away. The fusion has taken place, or at any rate *a* fusion; only it has been transferred in wondrous fashion to an unexpected, and on the whole more limited plane of operation; it has succeeded in getting effected, so to speak, not on the ground but in the air, not between our writer's idea and his machinery, but between the different parts of his genius itself. His genius is what is left over from the other, the compromised and compromising quantities—the Marlows and their determinant inventors and interlocutors, the Powells, the Franklins, the Fynes, the tell-tale little dogs, the successive members of a cue from one to the other of which the sense and the interest of the subject have to be passed on together, in the manner of the buckets of water for the improvised extinction of a fire, before reaching our apprehension: all with whatever result, to this apprehension, of a quantity to be allowed for as spilt by the way. The residuum has accordingly the form not of such and such a number of images discharged and ordered, but that rather of a wandering, circling, yearning imaginative *faculty*, encountered in its habit as it lives and diffusing itself as a presence or a tide, a noble sociability of vision. So we have as the force that fills the cup just the high-water mark of a beautiful and generous mind at play in conditions comparatively thankless — thoroughly, unweariedly, yet at the same time ever so elegantly at play, and doing more for itself than it succeeds in getting done for it. Than which nothing could be of a greater reward to critical curiosity were it not still for the wonder of wonders, a new page in the record altogether —the fact that these things are apparently what the common reader has seen and understood. Great then would seem to be after all the common reader!

IV

We must not fail of the point, however, that we have made these remarks not at all with an eye to the question of whether "Chance" has been well or ill inspired as to its particular choice of a way of really attending to itself among all the possible alternatives, but only on the ground of its having compared, selected and held on; since any alternative that might have been preferred and that should have been effectively adopted would point our moral as well—and this even if it is of profit none the less to note the most striking of Mr. Conrad's compositional consequences. There is one of these that has had most to do with making his pages differ in texture, and to our very first glance, from that straggle of ungoverned verbiage which leads us up and down those of his fellow fabulists in general on a vain hunt for some projected mass of truth, some solidity of substance, as to which the deluge of "dialogue," the flooding report of things said, or at least of words pretendedly spoken, shall have learned the art of being merely illustrational. What first springs from any form of real attention, no matter which, we on a comparison so made quickly perceive to be a practical challenge of the preposterous pretension of this most fatuous of the luxuries of looseness to acquit itself with authority of the structural and compositional office. Infinitely valid and vivid as illustration, it altogether depends for dignity and sense upon our state of possession of its historic preliminaries, its promoting conditions, its supporting ground; that is upon our waiting occupancy of the chamber it proposes to light and which, when no other source of effect is more indicated, it doubtless quite inimitably fills with life. Then its relation to what encloses and confines and, in its sovereign interest, finely compresses it, offering it constituted aspects, surfaces, presences, faces and figures of the matter we are either generally or acutely concerned with to play over and hang upon, then this relation gives it all its value: it has flowered from the soil prepared and sheds back its richness into the field of cultivation. It is interesting, in a word, only when nothing else is equally so, carrying the vessel of the interest with least of a stumble or a sacrifice; but it is of the essence that the sounds so set in motion (it being as sound above all that they undertake to convey sense,) should have something to proceed from, in their course, to address themselves to and be affected by, with all the sensibility of sounds. It is of the essence that they should live in a medium, and in a medium only, since it takes a medium to give them an identity, the intenser the better, and that the medium should subserve them by enjoying in a like degree the luxury of an existence. We need of course scarce expressly note that the play,

as distinguished from the novel, lives exclusively on
the spoken word—not on the report of the thing said
but, directly and audibly, on that very thing; that it
thrives by its law on the exercise under which the
novel hopelessly collapses when the attempt is made
disproportionately to impose it. There is no danger
for the play of the cart before the horse, no disaster
involved in it; that form being *all* horse and the
interest itself mounted and astride, and not, as that
of the novel, dependent in the first instance on wheels.
The order in which the drama simply says things gives
it all its form, while the story told and the picture
painted, as the novel at the pass we have brought it
to embraces them, reports of an infinite diversity of
matters, gathers together and gives out again a hundred sorts, and finds its order and its structure, its
unity and its beauty, in the alternation of parts and
the adjustment of differences. It is no less apparent
that the novel may be fundamentally *organised*—such
things as "The Egoist" and "The Awkward Age" are
there to prove it; but in this case it adheres uncon-
fusedly to that logic and has nothing to say to any
other. Were it not for a second exception, one at this
season rather pertinent, "Chance" then, to return to
it a moment, would be as happy an example as we
might just now put our hand on of the automatic
working of a scheme unfavourable to that treatment
of the colloquy by endless dangling strings which
makes the current "story" in general so figure to us
a porcupine of extravagant yet abnormally relaxed
bristles.

The exception we speak of would be Mrs. Wharton's
"Custom of the Country," in which, as in this lady's

other fictions, we recognise the happy fact of an abuse
of no one of the resources it enjoys at the expense of
the others; the whole series offering as general an
example of dialogue flowering and not weeding, illustrational and not itself starved of illustration, or
starved of referability and association, which is the
same thing, as meets the eye in any glance that leaves
Mr. Wells at Mr. Wells's best-inspired hour out of our
own account. The truth is, however, that Mrs. Wharton is herself here out of our account, even as we
have easily recognised Mr. Galsworthy and Mr. Maurice Hewlett to be; these three authors, with whatever differences between them, remaining essentially
votaries of selection and intention and being embodi-
ments thereby, in each case, of some state over and
above that simple state of possession of much evidence, that confused conception of what the "slice"
of life must consist of, which forms the text of our
remarks. Mrs. Wharton, *her* conception of the "slice"
so clarified and cultivated, would herself of course
form a text in quite another connection, as Mr. Hewlett and Mr. Galsworthy would do each in his own,
which we abstain from specifying; but there are two
or three grounds on which the author of "Ethan
Frome," "The Valley of Decision" and "The House
of Mirth," whom we brush by with reluctance, would
point the moral of the treasure of amusement sitting
in the lap of method with a felicity peculiarly her own.
If one of these is that she too has clearly a saturation
—which it would be ever so interesting to determine
and appreciate—we have it from her not in the crude
state but in the extract, the extract that makes all
the difference for our sense of an artistic economy.
If the extract, as would appear, is the result of an

artistic economy, as the latter is its logical motive, so we find it associated in Mrs. Wharton with such appeals to our interest, for instance, as the fact that, absolutely sole among our students of this form, she suffers, she even encourages, her expression to flower into some sharp image or figure of her thought when that will make the thought more finely touch us.   Her step, without straying, encounters the living analogy, which she gathers, in passing, without awkwardness of pause, and which the page then carries on its breast as a trophy plucked by a happy adventurous dash, a token of spirit and temper as well as a proof of vision. We note it as one of the *kinds* of proof of vision that most fail us in that comparative desert of the inselective where our imagination has itself to hunt out or call down (often among strange witnessed flounderings or sand-storms) such analogies as may mercifully "put" the thing.   Mrs. Wharton not only owes to her cultivated art of putting it the distinction enjoyed when some ideal of expression has the *whole* of the case, the case once made its concern, in charge, but might further act for us, were we to follow up her exhibition, as lighting not a little that question of "tone," the author's own intrinsic, as to which we have just seen Mr. Conrad's late production rather tend to darken counsel.   "The Custom of the Country" is an eminent instance of the sort of tonic value most opposed to that baffled relation between the subject-matter and its emergence which we find constituted by the circumvalations of "Chance."   Mrs. Wharton's reaction in presence of the aspects of life hitherto, it would seem, mainly exposed to her is for the most part the ironic—to which we gather that these particular aspects have so much ministered that, were we to pursue the quest, we might recognise in them precisely the saturation as to which we a moment ago reserved our judgment. "The Custom of the Country" is at any rate consistently, almost scientifically satiric, as indeed the satiric light was doubtless the only one in which the elements engaged could at all be focussed together. But this happens directly to the profit of something that, as we read, becomes more and more one with the principle of authority at work; the light that gathers is a dry light, of great intensity, and the effect, if not rather the very essence, of its dryness is a particular fine asperity. The usual "creative" conditions and associations, as we have elsewhere languished among them, are thanks to this ever so sensibly altered; the general authoritative relation attested becomes clear —we move in an air purged at a stroke of the old sentimental and romantic values, the perversions with the maximum of waste of perversions, and we shall not here attempt to state what this makes for in the way of esthetic refreshment and relief; the waste having kept us so dangling on the dark esthetic abyss. A shade of asperity may be in such fashion a security against waste, and in the dearth of displayed securities we should welcome it on that ground alone. It helps at any rate to constitute for the talent manifest in "The Custom" a rare identity, so far should we have to go to seek another instance of the dry, or call it perhaps even the hard, intellectual touch in the soft, or call it perhaps even the humid, temperamental air; in other words of the masculine conclusion tending so to crown the feminine observation.

If we mentioned Mr. Compton Mackenzie at the beginning of these reflections only to leave him waiting for some further appreciation, this is exactly because his case, to the most interesting effect, is no simple one, like two or three our others, but on the contrary mystifying enough almost to stand by itself. What would be this striking young writer's state of acquaintance and possession, and should we find it, on our recognition of it, to be all he is content to pitch forth, without discriminations or determinants, without motives or lights? Do "Carnival" and "Sinister Street" proceed from the theory of the slice or from the conception of the extract, "the extract flasked and fine," the chemical process superseding the mechanical? Mr. Compton Mackenzie's literary aspect, though decidedly that of youth, or that of experience, a great deal of young experience, in its freshness, offers the attraction of a complexity defiant of the prompt conclusion, really charms us by giving us something to wonder about. We literally find it not easy to say if there may not lurk in "Carnival," for example, a selective sense more apprehensible, to a push of inquiry, than its overflooded surface, a real invitation to wade and upon which everything within the author's ken appears poured out, would at first lead us to suspect. The question comes up in like fashion as to the distinctly more developed successor of that work, before which we in fact find questions multiply to a positive quickening of critical pleasure. We ask ourselves what "Sinister Street" may mean as a whole in spite of our sense of being brushed from the first by a hundred subordinate purposes, the succession and alternation of which seem to make after a fashion a plan, and which, though full of occasional design, yet fail to gather themselves for application or to converge to an idea. Any idea will serve, ever, that has held up its candle to composition—and it is perhaps because composition proposes itself under Mr. Compton Mackenzie's energy on a scale well-nigh of the most prodigious that we must wait to see whither it tends. The question of what he may here mean "on the whole," as we just said, is doubtless admonished to stand back till we be possessed of the whole. This interesting volume is but a first, committed up to its eyes to continuity and with an announced sequel to follow. The recital exhibits at the point we have reached the intimate experience of a boy at school and in his holidays, the amplification of which is to come with his terms and their breaks at a university; and the record will probably form a more squared and extended picture of life equally conditioned by the extremity of youth than we shall know where else to look for. Youth clearly has been Mr. Mackenzie's saturation, as it has been Mr. Hugh Walpole's, but we see this not as a subject (youth in itself is no specific subject, any more than age is,) but as matter for a subject and as requiring a motive to redeem it from the merely passive state of the slice. We are sure throughout both "Sinister Street" and "Carnival" of breathing the air of the extract, as we contentiously call it, only in certain of the rounded episodes strung on the loose cord as so many vivid beads, each of its chosen hue, and the series of which, even with differences of price between them, we take for a lively gage of performance to come. These episodes would be easy to cite; they are handsomely numerous and each strikes us as giving in its turn great salience to its motive; besides which each is in its turn "done" with an eminent sense and a remarkably straight hand for doing. They may well be cited together as both signally and finely symptomatic, for the literary gesture

and the *bravura* breadth with which such frequent
medallions as the adventure on the boy's part of the
Catholic church at Bournemouth, as his experiment of
the Benedictine house in Wiltshire, as his period of
acquaintance with the esthetic *cénacle* in London, as
his relation with his chosen school friend under the
intensity of boyish choosing, are ornamentally hung
up, differ not so much in degree as in kind from any
play of presentation that we mostly see elsewhere offered us. To which we might add other like matters
that we lack space to enumerate, the scene, the aspect,
the figure in motion tending always, under touches
thick and strong, to emerge and flush, sound and strike,
catch us in its truth. We have read "tales of school
life" in which the boys more or less swarmed and
sounded, but from which the masters have practically
been quite absent, to the great weakening of any picture of the boyish consciousness, on which the magis-
terial fact is so heavily projected. If that is less true
for some boys than for others, the "point" of Michael
Fane is that for him it is truest. The types of masters have in "Sinister Street" both number and salience, rendered though they be mostly as grotesques—
which effect we take as characterising the particular
turn of mind of the young observer and discoverer
commemorated.

That he *is* a discoverer is of the essence of his interest, a successful and resourceful young discoverer,
even as the poor ballet-girl in "Carnival" is a tragically baffled and helpless one; so that what each of
the works proposes to itself is a recital of the things
discovered. Those thus brought to our view in the
boy's case are of much more interest, to our sense,
than like matters in the other connection, thanks to

his remarkable and living capacity; the heroine of
"Carnival" is frankly too minute a vessel of experience for treatment on the scale on which the author
has honoured her—she is done assuredly, but under
multiplications of touch that become too much, in the
narrow field, monotonies; and she leaves us asking almost as much what she exhibitionally means, what application resides in the accumulation of facts concerning her, as if she too were after all but a slice, or at
the most but a slice *of* a slice, and her history but one
of the aspects, on her author's part, of the condition
of repleteness against the postulate of the entire adequacy of which we protest. So far as this record does
affect us as an achieved "extract," to reiterate our
term, that result abides in its not losing its centre,
which is its fidelity to the one question of her dole-
fully embarrassed little measure of life. We know to
that extent with some intensity what her producer
would be at, yet an element of the arbitrary hangs for
us about the particular illustration—illustrations leaving us ever but half appreciative till we catch that one
bright light in which they give out all they contain.
This light is of course always for the author to set
somewhere. Is it set then so much as it should be
in "Sinister Street," and is our impression of the
promise of this recital one with a dawning divination
of the illustrative card that Mr. Mackenzie may still
have up his sleeve and that our after sense shall recognise as the last thing left on the table? By no means,
we can as yet easily say, for if a boy's experience has
ever been given us for its face value simply, for what
it is worth in mere recovered intensity, it is so given
us here. Of all the saturations it can in fact scarce
have helped being the most sufficient in itself, for it

is exactly, where it is best, from beginning to end the remembered and reported thing, that thing alone, that thing existent in the field of memory, though gaining value too from the applied intelligence, or in other words from the lively talent, of the memoriser. The memoriser helps, he contributes, he completes, and what we have admired in him is that in the case of each of the pearls fished up by his dive—though indeed these fruits of the rummage are not all pearls—his mind has had a further iridescence to confer. It is the fineness of the iridescence that on such an occasion matters, and this appeal to our interest is again and again on Mr. Compton Mackenzie's page of the happiest and the brightest. It is never more so than when we catch him, as we repeatedly do, in the act of positively caring for his expression as expression, positively providing for his phrase as a fondly foreseeing parent for a child, positively loving it in the light of what it may do for him—meeting revelations, that is, in what it may do, and appearing to recognise that the value of the offered thing, its whole relation to us, is created by the breath of language, that on such terms exclusively, for appropriation and enjoyment, we know it, and that any claimed independence of "form" on its part is the most abject of fallacies. Do these things mean that, moved by life, this interesting young novelist is even now uncontrollably on the way to style? We might cite had we space several symptoms, the very vividest, of that possibility; though such an appearance in the field of our general survey has against it presumptions enough to bring us surely back to our original contention—the scant degree in which that field has ever had to reckon with criticism.

DUMAS THE YOUNGER

1895

ONE of the things that most bring home his time of life to a man of fifty is the increase of the rate at which he loses his friends. Some one dies every week, some one dies every day, and if the rate be high among his coevals it is higher still in the generation that, on awaking to spectatorship, he found in possession of the stage. He begins to feel his own world, the world of his most vivid impressions, gradually become historical. He is present, and closely present, at the process by which legend grows up. He sees the friends in question pictured as only death can picture them— a master superior to the Rembrandts and Titians. They have been of many sorts and many degrees, they have been private and public, but they have had in common that they were the furniture of this first fresh world, the world in which associations are formed. That one by one they go is what makes the main difference in it. The landscape of life, in foreground and distance, becomes, as the painters say, another composition, another subject; and quite as much as the objects directly under our eyes we miss the features that have educated for us our sense of proportion.

Among such features for the author of these lines the younger Dumas, who has just passed away, was in the public order long one of the most conspicuous. Suffused as he is already with the quick historic haze, fixed, for whatever term, in his ultimate value, he appeals to me, I must begin by declaring, as a party to one of these associations that have the savour of the prime. I knew him only in his work, but he is the object of an old-time sentiment for the beginning of which I have to go back absurdly far. He arrived early—he was so loudly introduced by his name. I am tempted to say that I knew him when he was young, but what I suppose I mean is that I knew him when I myself was. I knew him indeed when we both were, for I recall that in Paris, in distant days and undeveloped conditions, I was aware with perhaps undue and uncanny precocity of his first successes. There emerges in my memory from the night of time the image of a small boy walking in the Palais Royal with innocent American girls who were his cousins and wistfully hearing them relate how many times (they lived in Paris) they had seen Madame Doche in "La Dame aux Camélias" and what floods of tears she had made them weep. It was the first time I had heard of pockethandkerchiefs as a provision for the play. I had no remotest idea of the social position of the lady of the expensive flowers, and the artless objects of my envy had, in spite of their repeated privilege, even less of one; but her title had a strange beauty and her story a strange meaning—things that ever after were to accompany the name of the author with a faint yet rich echo. The younger Dumas, after all, was then not only relatively but absolutely young; the American infants, privileged and unprivileged, were only somewhat younger; the former going with their *bonne*, who must have enjoyed the adventure, to the "upper boxes" of the old Vaudeville of the Place de la Bourse, where later on I remember thinking Madame Fargueil divine. He was quite as fortunate moreover in his own designation as in that of his heroine; for it emphasised that bloom of youth (I don't say bloom of innocence—a very different matter) which was the signal-note of the work destined, in the world at large, to bring him nine-tenths of his celebrity.

Written at twenty-five "La Dame aux Camélias" remains in its combination of freshness and form, of the feeling of the springtime of life and the sense of the conditions of the theatre, a singular, an astonishing production. The author has had no time to part with his illusions, but has had full opportunity to master the most difficult of the arts. Consecrated as he was to this mastery he never afterwards showed greater adroitness than he had then done in keeping his knowledge and his *naïveté* from spoiling each other. The play has been blown about the world at a fearful rate, but it has never lost its happy juvenility, a charm that nothing can vulgarise. It is all champagne and tears—fresh perversity, fresh credulity, fresh passion, fresh pain. We have each seen it both well done and ill done, and perhaps more particularly the latter—in strange places, in barbarous tongues, with Marguerite Gautier fat and Armand Duval old. I remember ages ago in Boston a version in which this young lady and this young gentleman were represented as "engaged": that indeed for all I know may still be the form in which the piece most enjoys favour with the Anglo-Saxon public. Nothing makes any difference—it carries with it an April air: some tender young man and some coughing young woman have only to speak the lines to give it a great place among the love-stories of the world. I recollect coming out of the Gymnase one night when Madame Pierson had been the Marguerite—this was very long since—and giving myself up on the boulevard to a fine critical sense of what in such a composition was flimsy and what was false. Somehow, none the less, my fine critical sense never prevented my embracing the next opportunity to expose it to the same irritation; for I have been, I am happy to think to-day, a playgoer who, whatever else he may have had on his conscience, has never had the neglect of any chance to see this dramatist acted. Least of all, within a much shorter period, has it undermined one's kindness to have had occasion to admire in connection with the piece such an artist for instance as Eleonora Duse. We have seen Madame Duse this year or two in her tattered translation, with few advantages, with meagre accessories and with one side of the character of the heroine scarcely touched at all—so little indeed that the Italian version joins hands with the American and the relation of Marguerite and Armand seems to present itself as a question of the consecrated even if not approved "union." For this interesting actress, however, the most beautiful thing. is always the great thing, and her performance—if seen on a fortunate evening—lives in the mind as a fine vindication of the play. I am not sure indeed that it is the very performance Dumas intended; but he lived long enough to have forgotten perhaps what that performance was. He might on some sides, I think, have accepted Madame Duse's as a reminder.

If I have stopped to be myself so much reminded, it is because after and outside of "La Dame aux Camélias" Dumas really never figured among us all again— a circumstance full of illustration of one of the most striking of our peculiarities, the capacity for granting a prodigious ear to some one manifestation of an author's talent and caring nothing whatever for the others. It is solely the manifestation and never the talent that interests us, and nothing is stranger than the fact that no critic has ever explained on our behalf the system by which we hurl ourselves on a writer to-day and stare at him to-morrow as if we had never heard of him. It gives us the air of perpetually awaking from mistakes, but it renders obscure all our canons of judgment. A great force makes a great success, but a great force is furthermore no less a great force on Friday than on Monday. Was the reader a sorry dupe on the first day, or is the writer a wanton sacrifice on the second? That the public is intelligent on both occasions is a claim it can scarcely make: it can only choose between having its acuteness impugned or its manners condemned. At any rate if we have in England and the United States only the two alternatives of the roar of the market and the silence of the tomb the situation is apt to be different in France, where the quality that goes into a man's work and gives it an identity is the source of the attention excited. It happens that the interest in the play of the genius is greater there than the "boom" of the particular hit, the concern primarily for the author rather than the subject, instead of, as among ourselves, primarily for the subject rather than the author. Is this because the French have been acute enough to reflect that authors comprehend subjects, but that subjects can unfortunately not be said to comprehend authors? Literature would be a merry game if the business were arranged in the latter fashion. However such a question may be answered, Dumas was in his own country, to the end, the force that, save in connection with his first play, he failed to become elsewhere; and if he was there much the most original worker in his field one of the incidental signs of his originality was that, despite our inveterate practice, in theatrical matters, of helping ourselves from our neighbour's plate, he was inveterately not a convenience to us. We picked our morsels from the plates of smaller people— we never found on that of the author of "Le Fils Naturel" any we could swallow. He was not to our poor purpose, and I cannot help thinking that this helps a little to give his artistic measure. It would be a bad note for him now if we had found him amenable to that graceless game of which we show signs to-day of having grown ashamed, but which flourished for years in two imperturbable communities as the art of theatrical adaptation. A Dumas adaptable is a Dumas inconceivable; and in point of fact he was touched by the purveyors of the English-speaking stage only to prove fatal to them. If the history of so mean a traffic as the one here glanced at were worth writing it would throw light on some odd conceptions of the delicacy in the abused name of which it was carried on. It is all to the honour of our author's seriousness that he was, in such conditions, so unmanageable; though one must of course hasten to add that this seriousness was not the only reason of it. There were several others, not undiscoverable, and the effect of the whole combination was, in view of the brilliant fortune of his productions at home and the eager foraging of English and American speculators, to place him on a footing all his own. He was of active interest among us only to individual observers —simply as one of the most devoted of whom I trace these few pages of commemoration.

It takes some analysis, yet is not impossible, to explain why among the men of his time to whom the creative gift had been granted his image, for sundry such admirers, always presented him as somehow the happiest consciousness. They were perhaps not always aware of it, but now that he is gone they have a revelation of the place he occupied in the envious mind. This envy flowed doubtless, to begin with, from the sense of his extraordinarily firm grasp of his hard refractory art; the grasp that had put him into possession of it without fumblings or gropings made him canter away on the back of it the moment he had touched the stirrup. He had the air through all his career of a man riding a dangerous horse without ever being thrown. Every one else had a fall—he alone never really quitted the saddle, never produced a play that was not to stay to be revived and in the case of his comparative failures enjoy some sort of revenge, even to that of travelling in the repertory of great actresses round the globe. Such travels, moreover, much as they may please his shade, are far from having been the only felicities of his long career. The others strike me as so numerous that I scarcely indeed know where to begin to reckon them. Greatly even if oddly auspicious for instance was just his stark sonship to his prodigious father, his having been launched with that momentum into the particular world in which he was to live. It was a privilege to make up for the legal irregularity attaching to his birth; we think of it really almost to wonder that it didn't lift him on a still higher wave. His limitations, which one encounters with a sort of violence, were not to be overlooked; it expresses them in some degree to say that he was bricked up in his hard Parisianism, but it is also incontestable that some of them were much concerned in producing his firm and easy equilibrium. We understand, however, the trap they set for him when we reflect that a certain omniscience, a great breadth of horizon, may well have seemed to him to be transmitted, in his blood, from such a boundless fountain of life. What mattered to him the fact of a reach of reference that stopped at the *banlieue*, when experience had sat at his cradle in the shape not at all of a fairy godmother but of an immediate progenitor who was at once fabulous and familiar? He had been encompassed by all history in being held in such arms—it was an entrance into possession of more matters than he could even guess what to do with. The profit was all the greater as the son had the luxury of differing actively from the father, as well as that of actively admiring and, in a splendid sense, on all the becoming sides, those of stature, strength and health, vividly reproducing him. He had in relation to his special gift, his mastery of the dramatic form, a faculty of imagination as contracted as that of the author of "Monte Cristo" was boundless, but his moral sense on the other hand, as distinguished from that of his parent, was of the liveliest, was indeed of the most special and curious kind. The moral sense of the parent was to be found only in his good humour and his good health—the moral sense of a musketeer in love. This lack of adventurous vision, of the long flight and the joy of motion, was in the younger genius quite one of the conditions of his strength and luck, of his fine assurance, his sharp edge, his high emphasis, his state untroubled above all by things not within his too irregularly conditioned ken. The things close about him were the things he saw—there were alternatives, differences, opposites, of which he lacked so much as the suspicion. Nothing contributes more to the prompt fortune of an artist than some such positive and exclusive temper, the courage of his convictions, as we usually call it, the power to neglect something thoroughly, to abound aggressively in his own sense and express without reserve his own saturation. The saturation of the author of "Le Demi-Monde" was never far to seek. He was as native to Paris as a nectarine to a south wall. He would have fared ill if he had not had a great gift and Paris had not been a great city.

It was another element of the happy mixture that he came into the world at the moment in all our time that was for a man of letters the most amusing and beguiling—the moment exactly when he could see the end of one era and the beginning of another and join hands luxuriously with each. This was an advantage to which it would have taken a genius more elastic to do full justice, but which must have made him feel himself both greatly related and inspiringly free. He sprang straight from the lap of full-grown romanticism; he was a boy, a privileged and initiated youth, when his father, when Victor Hugo, when Lamartine and Musset and Scribe and Michelet and Balzac and George Sand were at the high tide of production. He saw them all, knew them all, lived with them and made of them his profit, tasting just enough of the old concoction to understand the proportions in which the new should be mixed. He had above all in his father, for the purpose that was in him, a magnificent springboard—a background to throw into relief, as a ruddy sunset seems to make a young tree doubly bristle, a profile of another type. If it was not indispensable it was at any rate quite poetic justice that the successor to the name should be, in his conditions, the great casuist of the theatre. He had seen the end of an age of imagination, he had seen all that could be done and shown in the way of mere illustration of the passions. That the passions are always with us is a fact he had not the smallest pretension to shut his eyes to —they were to constitute the almost exclusive subject of his study. But he was to study them not for the pleasure, the picture, the poetry they offer; he was to study them in the interest of something quite outside of them, about which the author of "Antony" and "Kean," about which Victor Hugo and Musset, Scribe and Balzac and even George Sand had had almost nothing to say. He was to study them from the point of view of the idea of the right and the wrong, of duty and conduct, and he was to this end to spend his artistic life with them and give a new turn to the theatre. He was in short to become, on the basis of a determined observation of the manners of his time and country, a professional moralist.

There can scarcely be a better illustration of differences of national habit and attitude than the fact that while among his own people this is the character, as an operative force, borne by the author of "Le Demi-Monde" and "Les Idées de Madame Aubray," so among a couple of others, in the proportion in which his reputation there has emerged from the vague, his most definite identity is that of a mere painter of indecent people and indecent doings. There are, as I have hinted, several reasons for the circumstance already noted, the failure of the attempt to domesti-

cate him on the English-speaking stage; but one states
the case fairly, I think, in saying that what accounts
for half of it is our passion, in the presence of a work
of art, for confounding the object, as the philosophers
have it, with the subject, for losing sight of the idea
in the vehicle, of the intention in the fable. Dumas
is a dramatist as to whom nine playgoers out of ten
would precipitately exclaim: "Ah, but you know,
isn't he dreadfully immoral?" Such are the lions in
the path of reputation, such the fate, in an alien air,
of a master whose main reproach in his native clime
is the importunity and the rigour of his lesson. The
real difference, I take it, is that whereas we like to be
good the French like to be better. We like to be
moral, they like to moralise. This helps us to understand the number of our innocent writers—writers innocent even of reflection, a practice of course essentially
indelicate, inasmuch as it speedily brings us face to
face with scandal and even with evil. It accounts
doubtless also for the number of writers on the further side of the Channel who have made the journey
once for all and to whom, in the dangerous quarter
they have reached, it appears of the very nature of
scandal and evil to be inquired about. The whole
undertaking of such a writer as Dumas is, according
to his light, to carry a particular, an esthetic form of
investigation as far as it will stretch—to study, and
study thoroughly, the bad cases. These bad cases
were precisely what our managers and adapters, our
spectators and critics would have nothing to do with.
It defines indeed the separation that they should have
been, in the light in which he presented them, precisely what made them for his own public exceptionally edifying. One of his great contentions is, for
instance, that seduced girls should under all circum-

stances be married—by somebody or other, failing the
seducer. This is a contention that, as we feel, barely
concerns us, shut up as we are in the antecedent conviction that they should under no circumstances be seduced. He meets all the cases that, as we see him, we
feel to have been spread out before him; meets them
successively, systematically, at once with a great earnestness and a great wit. He is exuberantly sincere:
his good faith sometimes obscures his humour, but
nothing obscures his good faith. So he gives us in
their order the unworthy brides who must be de-
nounced, the prenuptial children who must be adopted,
the natural sons who must be avenged, the wavering
ladies who must be saved, the credulous fiancés who
must be enlightened, the profligate wives who must be
shot, the merely blemished ones who must be forgiven,
the too vindictive ones who must be humoured, the
venal young men who must be exposed, the unfaithful
husbands who must be frightened, the frivolous fa-
thers who must be pulled up and the earnest sons who
must pull them. To enjoy his manner of dealing with
such material we must grant him in every connection
his full premise: that of the importunity of the phenomenon, the ubiquity of the general plight, the plight
in which people are left by an insufficient control of their
passions. We must grant him in fact for his didactic
and dramatic purpose a great many things. These
things, taken together and added to some others, constitute the luxurious terms on which I have spoken of
him as appearing to the alien admirer to have practised his complicated art.

When we speak of the passions in general we really
mean, for the most part, the first of the number, the
most imperious in its action and the most interesting

in its consequences, the passion that unites and divides the sexes. It is the passion, at any rate, to which Dumas as dramatist and pamphleteer mainly devoted himself: his plays, his prefaces, his manifestos, his few tales roll exclusively on the special relation of the man to the woman and the woman to the man, and on the dangers of various sorts, even that of ridicule, with which this relation surrounds each party. This element of danger is what I have called the general plight, for when our author considers the sexes as united and divided it is with the predominance of the division that he is principally struck. It is not an unfair account of him to say that life presented itself to him almost wholly as a fierce battle between the woman and the man. He sides now with one and now with the other; the former combatant, in her own country, however, was far from pronouncing him sympathetic. His subject at all events is what we of English race call the sexes and what they in France call the sex. To talk of love is to talk, as we have it, of men and women; to talk of love is, as the French have it, to *parler femmes*. From every play of our author's we receive the impression that to *parler femmes* is its essential and innermost purpose. It is not assuredly singular that a novelist, a dramatist *should* talk of love, or even should talk of nothing else: what, in addition to his adroitness and his penetration, makes the position special for Dumas is that he talks of it— and in the form of address most associated with pure diversion—altogether from the anxious point of view of the legislator and the citizen.

"Diane de Lys," which immediately followed "La Dame aux Camélias," is, so far as I can recall it, a picture pure and simple, a pretty story, as we say, sufficiently romantic and rather long-winded; but with "Le Demi-Monde" began his rich argumentative series, concluding only the other day with "Denise" and "Francillon," the series in which every theme is a proposition to be established and every proposition a form of duty to be faced. The only variation that I can recollect in the list is the disinterested portraiture of "Le Père Prodigue," with its remarkable presentation, in the figure of Albertine de la Borde, of vice domesticated and thrifty, keeping early hours and books in double-entry, and its remarkable illustration, I may further add, of all that was the reverse of infallible in the author's power to distinguish between amiable infirmities and ugly ones. The idea on which "Le Père Prodigue" rests belongs more distinctively to the world of comedy than almost any other situation exhibited in the series; but what are we to say of the selection, for comic effect, of a fable of which the principal feature is a son's not unfounded suspicion of the attitude of his own father to his own wife? The father is the image of a nature profusely frivolous, but we scent something more frivolous still in the way his frivolity is disposed of. At the time the play was produced the spectator thought himself warranted in recognising in this picture the personal character (certainly not the personal genius) of the elder Dumas. If the spectator *was* so warranted, that only helps, I think, to make "Le Père Prodigue" a stumbling-block for the critic—make it, I mean, an exhibition of the author off his guard and a fact to be taken into account in an estimate of his moral reach; a moral reach, for the rest, at all events, never impugned by any obliquity in facing that conception of the duty imposed which it is the main source of the writer's interest in the figured circumstances that they may be held to impose it, and which he was apt to set forth more dogmatically, or at least more excitedly, in an occasional and polemical pamphlet. These pamphlets, I may parenthetically say, strike me as definitely compromising to his character as artist. What shines in them most is the appetite for a discussion, or rather the appetite for a conclusion, and the passion for a simplified and vindictive justice. But I have never found it easy to forgive a writer who, in possession of a form capable of all sorts of splendid application, puts on this resource the slight of using substitutes for it at will, as if it is good but for parts of the cause. If it is good for anything it is good for the whole demonstration, and if it is not good for the whole demonstration it is good for nothing—nothing that *he* is concerned with. If the picture of life doesn't cover the ground what in the world *can* cover it? The fault can only be the painter's. Woe, in the esthetic line, to any example that requires the escort of precept. It is like a guest arriving to dine accompanied by constables. Our author's prefaces and treatises show a mistrust of disinterested art. He would have declared probably that his art was not disinterested; to which our reply would be that it had then no right to put us off the scent and prepare deceptions for us by coming within an ace of being as good as if it were.

The merits of the play—that is of the picture, in these hands—are sometimes singularly independent of the lesson conveyed. The merits of the lesson conveyed are in other cases much more incontestable than those of the picture, than the production of the air of

life or the happiest observance of the conditions of
the drama. The conclusion, the prescription, of "Denise" strikes me (to give an instance) as singularly fine,
but the subject belongs none the less to the hapless
order of those that fail to profit by the dramatic form
though they have sacrificed the highest advantages of
the literary. A play—even the best—pays so tremendously by what it essentially can not do for the
comparatively little it practically can, that a mistake
in the arithmetic of this positive side speedily produces a wide deviation. In other words the spectator,
and still more the reader, sees such a theme as that
of "Denise," which may be described as the evolution of a view, presented most in accordance with its
nature when the attempt is not made to present it in
accordance with the nature of the theatre. It is the
nature of the theatre to give its victims, in exchange
for melancholy concessions, a vision of the immediate
not to be enjoyed in any other way; and consequently
when the material offered it to deal with is not the
immediate, but the contingent, the derived, the hypo-
thetic, our melancholy concessions have been made in
vain and the inadequacy of the form comes out. In
"Francillon," partly perhaps because the thing has
nothing to do with anybody's duty—least of all with
the heroine's, which would be surely to keep off the
streets—the form happens to be remarkably adequate.
The question is of the liberty of the protagonist, the
right of a wronged and indignant wife to work out her
husband's chastisement in the same material as his
sin, work it out moreover on the spot, as a blow is
repaid by a blow, exacting an eye for an eye and a
tooth for a tooth. The play has all the kinds of life
that the theatre can achieve, because in the first place

Dumas, though acting as the wife's advocate, has had the intelligence to give us a solution which is only a scenic sequence and not a real, still less a "philosophic," one; and because in the second it deals with emotions and impulses, which can be shown by the short measure, and not with reflections and aspirations, which can be shown but by the long.

I am not pretending to take things in turn, but a critic with a generous memory of the spell of Dumas should not, however pressed, neglect to strain a point for "Le Demi-Monde." I doubt my competence, however, to consider that admirable work scientifically—I find myself too condemned to consider it sentimentally. A critic is lost, as a critic, from the moment his feeling about the worse parts of the matter he investigates fails to differ materially from his feeling about the better. That is an attitude even less enlightened than being unconscious of the blemishes; all the same it must serve me for the present case. I am perfectly aware that Olivier de Jalin is a man of no true delicacy; in spite of which I take when I see them represented the liveliest interest in his proceedings. I am perfectly aware that Madame d'Ange, with her *calme infernal*, as George Sand calls it, is tainted and tortuous; in spite of which my imagination quite warms to Madame d'Ange. Perhaps I should indeed rather say that this interest and this sympathy have for their object the great total of the play. It is the member of the series in which Dumas first took up the scales in one hand and the sword in the other, and it is a wonderful piece of work, wonderful in kind of maturity, for a man of thirty. It has all the easy amplitude we call authority. I won't pretend to say what

I think, here, of the author's justice, and if I happen
to think ill of it I won't pretend to care. I see the
thing through too many old memories, old echoes, old
charms. In the light of the admirable acting of ancient days, of the faded image of the exquisite Des-
clée, of a dim recollection even of the prehistoric Rose
Chéri and of Mademoiselle Delaporte, it represents too
many of the reasons why I saw him always ideally
triumphant. To practise an art which for its full, its
rich effect depended on interpretation, and to be able
to do one's work with an eye on interpretation of that
quality—this had in common with supreme bliss the
element at any rate of being attainable only by the
elect. It partook of a peace the world cannot give.
To be a moralist with the aid of Croizette, a philosopher with the aid of Delaunay, an Academician, even,
with the aid of Bartet—such things suggested an almost equivocal union of virtue and success. One had
never seen virtue so agreeable to one's self, nor success so useful to others. One had never seen a play
that was a model so alive in spite of it. Models in
the theatre were apt to be dead and vivacities vulgar.
One had never above all seen on the stage a picture
so conformable to deep pictorial art, a drama so liberally, gradually, scientifically flushed with its action.
Beautiful in "Le Demi-Monde" is the way the subject quietly, steadily, strongly expands from within.

It was always the coercive force that his tone gave
one the strongest sense of life, and it remains the interesting thing that this element in Dumas abounds
in spite of not being fed from the source that we usually assume to be the richest. It was not fed from the
imagination, for his imagination, by no means of the

great plastic sort, has left us a comparatively small
heritage of typical figures. His characters are all
pointed by observation, they are clear notes in the
concert, but not one of them has known the little in-
visible push that, even when shyly and awkwardly administered, makes the puppet, in spite of the string,
walk off by himself and quite "cut," if the mood take
him, that distant relation his creator. They are always formal with this personage and thoroughly conscious and proud of him; there is a charm of mystery and poetry and oddity, a glory of unexpectedness,
that they consistently lack. Their life, and that, in
each case, of the whole story (quite the most wonderful part of this) is simply the author's own life, his
high vitality, his very presence and temperament and
voice. They do more for him even than they do for
the subject, and he himself is at last accordingly the
most vivid thing in every situation. He keeps it at
arm's length because he has the instinct of the dramatist and the conscience of the artist, but we feel all the
while that his face is bigger than his mask. Nothing
about his work is more extraordinary than this manner in which his personality pervades without spoiling
it the most detached and most impersonal of literary
forms. The reasons for such an impunity are first
that his precautions, the result of a great intelligence,
were so effective, and second that his personality, the
result of a great affiliation, was so robust. It may be
said that the precautions were not effective if the
man himself was what one most enjoyed in the play.
The only answer to that can be that I speak merely
for myself and for the fresher sensibility of the happy
time. Other admirers found certainly other things;
what I found most was a tall figure in muscular mo-

tion and the sense of a character that had made admirably free with life. If it was mainly as an unabashed observer that he had made free, and if the life supplied was much of it uncommonly queer, that never diminished the action of his hard masculinity and his fine intellectual brutality. There was an easy competence in it all, and a masterful experience, and a kind of vicarious courage. In particular there was a real genius for putting all persons—especially all bad ones—very much in their place. Then it was all, for another bribe, so copious and so close, so sustained and so quiet, with such fascinating unities and complex simplicities and natural solutions. It was the breath of the world and the development of an art.

All the good, however, that I recollect thinking of Dumas only reminds me how little I desired that my remarks in general should lead me into vain discriminations. There are some indeed that are not vain— at least they help us to understand. He has a noble strain of force, a fulness of blood that has permitted him to be tapped without shrinking. We must speak of him in the present tense, as we always speak of the masters. The theatre of his time, wherever it has been serious, has on the ground of general method lived on him; wherever it has not done so it has not lived at all. To pretend to be too shocked to profit by him was a way of covering up its levity, but there was no escaping its fate. He was the kind of artistic influence that is as inevitable as a medical specific: you may decline it from black bottle to-day—you will take it from a green bottle to-morrow. The energy that went forth blooming as Dumas has come back grizzled as Ibsen, and would under the latter form, I

am sure, very freely acknowledge its debt. A critic
whose words meet my eyes as I write very justly says
that: "Just as we have the novel before Balzac and
the novel after Balzac, the poetry that preceded Victor
Hugo and the poetry that followed him, so we have
the drama before Alexandre Dumas and the drama
after him." He has left his strong hand upon it; he
remodelled it as a vehicle, he refreshed it as an art.
His passion for it was obviously great, but there would
be a high injustice to him in not immediately adding
that his interest in the material it dealt with, in his
subject, his question, his problem, was greater still
than this joy of the craftsman. That might well be,
but there are celebrated cases in which it has not
been. The largest quality in Dumas was his immense
concern about life—his sense of human character and
human fate as commanding and controllable things.
To do something on their behalf was paramount for
him, and *what* to do in his own case clear: what else
but act upon the conscience as violently as he could,
and with the remarkable weapons that Providence had
placed within his grasp and for which he was to show
his gratitude by a perfectly intrepid application?
These weapons were three: a hard rare wit, not lam-
bent like a flame, but stiff and straight like an arrow
from a crossbow; a perception not less rare of some
of the realities of the particular human tendency about
which most falsities have clustered; and lastly that
native instinct for the conditions of dramatic presentation without which any attempt to meet them is a
helpless groping.

It must always be remembered of him that he was
the observer of a special order of things, the moralist

of a particular relation as the umpire of a yacht-race
is the legislator of a particular sport. His vision and
his talent, as I have said, were all for the immediate,
for the manners and the practices he himself was
drenched with: he had none of the faculty that scents
from afar, that wings away and dips beyond the horizon. There are moments when a reader not of his
own race feels that he simplifies almost absurdly.
There are too many things he didn't after all guess,
too many cases he didn't after all provide for. He
has a certain odour of bad company that almost im-
perils his distinction. This was doubtless the deepest of the reasons why among ourselves he flourished
so scantly: we felt ourselves to be of a world in which
the elements were differently mixed, the proportions
differently marked, so that the tables of our law would
have to be differently graven. His very earnestness
was only a hindrance—he might have had more to
say to us if he had consented to have less application.
This produced the curious dryness, the obtrusive economy of his drama—the hammered sharpness of every
outline, the metallic ring of every sound. His terrible knowledge suggested a kind of uniform—gilt but-
tons, a feathered hat and a little official book; it was
almost like an irruption of the police. The most general masters are the poets, with all the things they
blessedly don't hold for so very certain and all the
things they blessedly and preferably invent. It is
true that Dumas was splendid, in his way, exactly
because he was not vague: his concentration, all confidence and doctrine and epigram, is the explanation of
his extraordinary force. That force is his abiding
quality: one feels that he was magnificently a man—
that he stands up high and sees straight and speaks

loud. It is his great temperament, undiminished by what it lacks, that endears him to his admirers. It made him still of the greater race and played well its part in its time—so well that one thinks of him finally as perhaps not, when all is said, of the very happiest group, the group of those for whom in the general affection there is yet more to come. He had an immense reverberation—he practised the art that makes up for being the most difficult by being the most acclaimed. There is no postponed poetic justice for those who have had everything. He was seconded in a manner that must have made success a double delight. There are indications that the dramatist of the future will be less and less elated. He may well become so if he is to see himself less and less interpreted.

THE NOVEL IN "THE RING AND THE
BOOK" [1]

1912

IF on such an occasion as this—even with our natural
impulse to shake ourselves free of reserves—some sharp
choice between the dozen different aspects of one of
the most copious of our poets becomes a prime necessity, though remaining at the same time a great difficulty, so in respect to the most voluminous of his
works the admirer is promptly held up, as we have
come to call it; finds himself almost baffled by alternatives. "The Ring and the Book" is so vast and so
essentially gothic a structure, spreading and soaring
and branching at such a rate, covering such ground,
putting forth such pinnacles and towers and brave excrescences, planting its transepts and chapels and por-
ticos, its clustered hugeness or inordinate muchness,
that with any first approach we but walk vaguely and
slowly, rather bewilderedly, round and round it, wondering at what point we had best attempt such entrance as will save our steps and light our uncertainty,
most enable us to reach our personal chair, our indicated chapel or shrine, when once within. For it is to
be granted that to this inner view the likeness of the
literary monument to one of the great religious gives

[1] Address delivered before the Academic Committee of the Royal Society
of Literature in Commemoration of the Centenary of Robert Browning,
May 7, 1912.

385

way a little, sustains itself less than in the first, the
affronting mass; unless we simply figure ourselves,
under the great roof, looking about us through a splendid thickness and dimness of air, an accumulation of
spiritual presences or unprofaned mysteries, that makes
our impression heavily general—general only—and
leaves us helpless for reporting on particulars. The
particulars for our purpose have thus their identity
much rather in certain features of the twenty faces—
either of one or of another of these—that the structure turns to the outer day and that we can, as it
were, sit down before and consider at our comparative
ease. I say comparative advisedly, for I cling to the
dear old tradition that Browning is "difficult"—which
we were all brought up on and which I think we should,
especially on a rich retrospective day like this, with
the atmosphere of his great career settling upon us as
much as possible, feel it a shock to see break down
in too many places at once. Selecting my ground, by
your kind invitation, for sticking in and planting before you, to flourish so far as it shall, my little sprig
of bay, I have of course tried to measure the quantity
of ease with which our material may on that noted
spot allow itself to be treated. There are innumerable things in "The Ring and the Book"—as the
comprehensive image I began with makes it needless
I should say; and I have been above all appealed to
by the possibility that one of these, pursued for a
while through the labyrinth, but at last overtaken and
then more or less confessing its identity, might have
yielded up its best essence as a grateful theme under
some fine strong economy of *prose* treatment. So here
you have me talking at once of prose and seeking
that connection to help out my case.

From far back, from my first reading of these volumes, which took place at the time of their disclosure
to the world, when I was a fairly young person, the
sense, almost the pang, of the novel they might have
constituted sprang sharply from them; so that I was
to go on through the years almost irreverently, all but
quite profanely if you will, thinking of the great loose
and uncontrolled composition, the great heavy-hanging
cluster of related but unreconciled parts, as a fiction
of the so-called historic type, that is as a suggested
study of the manners and conditions from which our
own have more or less traceably issued, just tragically
spoiled—or as a work of art, in other words, smothered in the producing. To which I hasten to add my
consciousness of the scant degree in which such a
fresh start from our author's documents, such a re-
projection of them, wonderful documents as they can
only have been, may claim a critical basis. Conceive
me as simply astride of my different fancy, my other
dream, of the matter—which bolted with me, as I have
said, at the first alarm.

Browning worked in this connection literally *upon*
documents; no page of his long story is more vivid and
splendid than that of his find of the Book in the litter
of a market-stall in Florence and the swoop of practised perception with which he caught up in it a treasure. Here was a subject stated to the last ounce of
its weight, a living and breathing record of facts pitiful
and terrible, a mass of matter bristling with revelations and yet at the same time wrapped over with
layer upon layer of contemporary appreciation; which
appreciation, in its turn, was a part of the wealth to
be appreciated. What our great master saw was his

situation founded, seated there in positively packed and congested significance, though by just so much as it was charged with meanings and values were those things undeveloped and unexpressed. They looked up at him, even in that first flush and from their market-stall, and said to him, in their compressed compass, as with the muffled rumble of a slow-coming earthquake, "Express us, express us, immortalise us as we'll immortalise *you!*"—so that the terms of the understanding were so far cogent and clear. It was an understanding, on their side, with the poet; and since that poet had produced "Men and Women," "Dramatic Lyrics," "Dramatis Personæ" and sundry plays—we needn't even foist on him "Sordello"—he could but understand in his own way. That way would have had to be quite some other, we fully see, had he been by habit and profession not just the lyric, epic, dramatic commentator, the extractor, to whatever essential potency and redundancy, of the moral of the fable, but the very fabulist himself, the inventor and projector, layer down of the postulate and digger of the foundation. I doubt if we have a precedent for this energy of appropriation of a deposit of *stated* matter, a block of sense already in position and requiring not to be shaped and squared and caused any further to solidify, but rather to suffer disintegration, be pulled apart, melted down, hammered, by the most characteristic of the poet's processes, to powder—dust of gold and silver, let us say. He was to apply to it his favourite system—that of looking at his subject from the point of view of a curiosity almost sublime in its freedom, yet almost homely in its method, and of smuggling as many more points of view together into that one as the fancy might take him to smuggle, on a scale on which even he had never before applied it; this with a courage and a confidence that, in presence of all the conditions, conditions many of them arduous and arid and thankless even to defiance, we can only pronounce splendid, and of which the issue was to be of a proportioned monstrous magnificence.

The one definite forecast for this product would have been that it should figure for its producer as a poem—as if he had simply said, "I embark at any rate for the Golden Isles"; everything else was of the pure incalculable, the frank voyage of adventure. To what extent the Golden Isles were in fact to be reached is a matter we needn't pretend, I think, absolutely to determine; let us feel for ourselves and as we will about it—either see our adventurer, disembarked bag and baggage and in possession, plant his flag on the highest eminence within his circle of sea, or, on the other hand, but watch him approach and beat back a little, tack and turn and stand off, always fairly in sight of land, catching rare glimpses and meeting strange airs, but not quite achieving the final *coup* that annexes the group. He returns to us under either view all scented and salted with his measure of contact, and that for the moment is enough for us—more than enough for me at any rate, engaged for your beguilement in this practical relation of snuffing up what he brings. He brings, however one puts it, a detailed report, which is but another word for a story; and it is with his story, his offered, not his borrowed one—a very different matter—that I am concerned. We are probably most of us so aware of its general content that if I sum this up I may do so briefly. The Book of the Florentine rubbish-heap is the full account (as full accounts were

conceived in those days) of the trial before the Roman
courts, with inquiries and judgments by the Tuscan
authorities intermixed, of a certain Count Guido Franceschini of Arezzo, decapitated, in company with four
confederates—these latter hanged—on February 22,
1698, for the murder of his young wife Pompilia Comparini and her ostensible parents, Pietro and Violante
of that ilk.

The circumstances leading to this climax were primarily his marriage to Pompilia, some years before, in
Rome—she being then but in her thirteenth year—
under the impression, fostered in him by the elder pair,
that she was their own child and on this head heiress
to moneys settled on them from of old in the event of
their having a child. They had in fact had none, and
had, in substitution, invented, so to speak, Pompilia,
the luckless base-born baby of a woman of lamentable
character easily induced to part with her for cash.
They bring up the hapless creature as their daughter,
and as their daughter they marry her, in Rome, to the
middle-aged and impecunious Count Guido, a rapacious and unscrupulous fortune-seeker by whose superior social position, as we say, dreadfully *decaduto*
though he be, they are dazzled out of all circumspec-
tion. The girl, innocent, ignorant, bewildered, scared
and purely passive, is taken home by her husband to
Arezzo, where she is at first attended by Pietro and
Violante and where the direst disappointment await
the three. Count Guido proves the basest of men and
his home a place of terror and of torture, from which at
the age of seventeen, and shortly prior to her giving
birth to an heir to the house, such as it is, she is res-
cued by a pitying witness of her misery, Canon Capon-

sacchi, a man of the world and adorning it, yet in holy
orders, as men of the world in Italy might then be, who
clandestinely helps her, at peril of both their lives, back
to Rome, and of whom it is attested that he has had
no other relation with her but this of distinguished and
all-disinterested friend in need. The pretended parents
have at an early stage thrown up their benighted game,
fleeing from the rigour of their dupe's domestic rule,
disclosing to him vindictively the part they have played
and the consequent failure of any profit to him through
his wife, and leaving him in turn to wreak his spite,
which has become infernal, on the wretched Pompilia.
He pursues her to Rome, on her eventual flight, and
overtakes her, with her companion, just outside the
gates; but having, by the aid of the local powers, re-
achieved possession of her, he contents himself for the
time with procuring her sequestration in a convent,
from which, however, she is presently allowed to emerge
in view of the near birth of her child. She rejoins
Pietro and Violante, devoted to her, oddly enough,
through all their folly and fatuity; and under their
roof, in a lonely Roman suburb, her child comes into
the world. Her husband meanwhile, hearing of her
release, gives way afresh to the fury that had not at
the climax of his former pursuit taken full effect; he
recruits a band of four of his young tenants or farm-
labourers and makes his way, armed, like his companions, with knives, to the door behind which three
of the parties to all the wrong done him, as he holds,
then lurk. He pronounces, after knocking and waiting, the name of Caponsacchi; upon which, as the
door opens, Violante presents herself. He stabs her
to death on the spot with repeated blows—like her
companions she is off her guard; and he throws him-

self on each of these with equal murderous effect. Pietro, crying for mercy, falls second beneath him; after which he attacks his wife, whom he literally hacks to death. She survives, by a miracle, long enough, in spite of all her wounds, to testify; which testimony, as may be imagined, is not the least precious part of the case. Justice is on the whole, though deprecated and delayed, what we call satisfactory; the last word is for the Pope in person, Innocent XII. Pignatelli, at whose deliberation, lone and supreme, on Browning's page, we splendidly assist; and Count Guido and his accomplices, bloodless as to the act though these appear to have been, meet their discriminated doom.

That is the bundle of facts, accompanied with the bundle of proceedings, legal, ecclesiastical, diplomatic and other, *on* the facts, that our author, of a summer's day, made prize of; but our general temptation, as I say—out of which springs this question of the other values of character and effect, the other completeness of picture and drama, that the confused whole might have had for us—is a distinctly different thing. The difference consists, you see, to begin with, in the very breath of our poet's genius, already, and so inordinately, at play on them from the first of our knowing them. And it consists in the second place of such an extracted sense of the whole, which becomes, after the most extraordinary fashion, bigger by the extraction, immeasurably bigger than even the most cumulative weight of the mere crude evidence, that our choice of how to take it all is in a manner determined for us: we can only take it as tremendously interesting, interesting not only in itself but with the great added interest, the dignity and authority and beauty, of Browning's general perception of it. We can't not accept this, and little enough on the whole do we want not to: it sees us, with its tremendous push, that of its poetic, esthetic, historic, psychologic shoulder (one scarce knows how to name it), so far on our way. Yet all the while we are in presence not at all of an achieved form, but of a mere preparation for one, though on the hugest scale; so that, you see, we are no more than decently attentive with our question: "Which of them all, of the various methods of casting the wondrously mixed metal, is he, as he goes, preparing?" Well, as he keeps giving and giving, in immeasurable plenty, it is in our selection from it all and our picking it over that we seek, and to whatever various and unequal effect find, our account. He works over his vast material, and we then work *him* over, though not availing ourselves, to this end, of a grain he himself doesn't somehow give us; and there we are.

I admit that my faith in my particular contention would be a degree firmer and fonder if there didn't glimmer through our poet's splendid hocus-pocus just the hint of one of those flaws that sometimes deform the fair face of a subject otherwise generally appealing or promising—of such a subject in especial as may have been submitted to us, possibly even with the pretension to impose it, in too complete a shape. The idea but half hinted—when it is a very good one— is apt to contain the germ of happier fruit than the freight of the whole branch, waved at us or dropped into our lap, very often proves. This happens when we take over, as the phrase is, established data, take

them over from existing records and under some involved obligation to take them as they stand. That
drawback rests heavily for instance on the so-called
historic fiction—so beautiful a case it is of a muddle-
ment of terms—and is just one of the eminent reasons
why the embarrassed Muse of that form, pulled up
again and again, and the more often the fine intelligence invokes her, by the need of a superior harmony
which shall be after all but a superior truth, catches
up her flurried skirts and makes her saving dash for
some gap in the hedge of romance. Now the flaw on
this so intensely expressive face, that of the general
donnée of the fate of Pompilia, is that amid the variety of forces at play about her the unity of the situation isn't, by one of those large straight ideal ges-
tures on the part of the Muse, handed to us at a stroke.
The question of the whereabouts of the unity of a
group of data subject to be wrought together into a
thing of art, the question in other words of the point
at which the various implications of interest, no matter how many, *most* converge and interfuse, becomes
always, by my sense of the affair, quite the first to be
answered; for according to the answer shapes and fills
itself the very vessel of that beauty—the beauty, exactly, *of* interest, of maximum interest, which is the
ultimate extract of any collocation of facts, any picture of life, and the finest aspect of any artistic work.
Call a novel a picture of life as much as we will; call
it, according to one of our recent fashions, a slice, or
even a chunk, even a "bloody" chunk, of life, a rough
excision from that substance as superficially cut and
as summarily served as possible, it still fails to escape
this exposure to appreciation, or in other words to
criticism, that it has had to be selected, selected under

some sense for something; and the unity of the exhibition should meet us, does meet us if the work be
done, at the point at which that sense is most patent.
If the slice or the chunk, or whatever we call it, if *it*
isn't "done," as we say—and as it so often declines
to be—the work itself of course isn't likely to be; and
there we may dismiss it.

The first thing we do is to cast about for some centre in our field; seeing that, for such a purpose as
ours, the subject might very nearly go a-begging with
none more definite than the author has provided for
it. I find that centre in the embracing consciousness
of Caponsacchi, which, coming to the rescue of our
question of treatment, of our search for a point of
control, practically saves everything, and shows itself
moreover the only thing that *can* save. The more
we ask of any other part of our picture that it shall
exercise a comprehensive function, the more we see
that particular part inadequate; as inadequate even
in the extraordinarily magnified range of spirit and
reach of intelligence of the atrocious Franceschini as
in the sublime passivity and plasticity of the childish
Pompilia, educated to the last point though she be
indeed by suffering, but otherwise so untaught that
she can neither read nor write. The magnified state
is in this work still more than elsewhere the note of
the intelligence, of any and every faculty of thought, imputed by our poet to his creatures; and it takes a great
mind, one of the greatest, we may at once say, to make
these persons express and confess themselves to such
an effect of intellectual splendour. He resorts primarily to *their* sense, their sense of themselves and of
everything else they know, to exhibit them, and has

for this purpose to keep them, and to keep them persistently and inexhaustibly, under the fixed lens of his prodigious vision. He thus makes out in them boundless treasures of truth—truth even when it happens to be, as in the case of Count Guido, but a shining wealth of constitutional falsity. Of the extent to which he may after this fashion unlimitedly draw upon them his exposure of Count Guido, which goes on and on, though partly, I admit, by repeating itself, is a wondrous example. It is not too much to say of Pompilia—Pompilia pierced with twenty wounds, Pompilia on her death-bed, Pompilia but seventeen years old and but a fortnight a mother—that she *acquires* an intellectual splendour just by the fact of the vast covering charity of imagination with which her recording, our commemorated, avenger, never so as in this case an avenger of the wronged beautiful things of life, hangs over and breathes upon her. We see her come out to him, and the extremely remarkable thing is that we see it, on the whole, without doubting that it might just have been. Nothing could thus be more interesting, however it may at moments and in places puzzle us, than the impunity, on our poet's part, of most of these overstretchings of proportion, these violations of the immediate appearance. Browning is deep down below the immediate with the first step of his approach; he has vaulted over the gate, is already far afield and never, so long as we watch him, has occasion to fall back. We wonder, for, after all, the real is his quest, the very ideal of the real, the real most finely mixed with life, which *is* in the last analysis the ideal; and we know, with our dimmer vision, no such reality as a Franceschini fighting for his life, fighting for the vindication of his baseness, embodying his squalor, with an audacity of wit, an

intensity of colour, a variety of speculation and illustration, that represent well-nigh the maximum play
of the human mind.   It is in like sort scarce too much
to say of the exquisite Pompilia that on her part intelligence and expression are disengaged to a point at
which the angels may well begin to envy her; and all
again without our once wincing so far as our consistently liking to see and hear and believe is concerned.
Caponsacchi regales us, of course, with the rarest fruit
of a great character, a great culture and a great case;
but Caponsacchi is acceptedly and naturally, needfully and illustratively, splendid.   He *is* the soul of
man at its finest—having passed through the smoky
fires of life and emerging clear and high.   Greatest of
all the spirits exhibited, however, is that of the more
than octogenarian Pope, at whose brooding, pondering, solitary vigil, by the end of a hard grey winter
day in the great bleak waiting Vatican—"in the plain
closet where he does such work"—we assist as intimately as at every other step of the case, and on
whose grand meditation we heavily hang.   But the
Pope strikes us at first—though indeed perhaps only
at first—as too high above the whole connection functionally and historically for us to place him within it
dramatically.   Our novel faces provisionally the question of dispensing with him, as it dispenses with the
amazing, bristling, all too indulgently presented Roman
advocates on either side of the case, who combine to
put together the most formidable monument we possess to Browning's active curiosity and the liveliest
proof of his almost unlimited power to give on his
readers' nerves without giving on his own.

What remains with us all this time, none the less,
is the effect of magnification, the exposure of each of

these figures, in its degree, to that iridescent wash of personality, of temper and faculty, that our author ladles out to them, as the copious share of each, from his own great reservoir of spiritual health, and which makes us, as I have noted, seek the reason of a perpetual anomaly. Why, bristling so with references to *him* rather than with references to each other or to any accompanying set of circumstances, do they still establish more truth and beauty than they sacrifice, do they still, according to their chance, help to make "The Ring and the Book" a great living thing, a great objective mass? I brushed by the answer a moment ago, I think, in speaking of the development in Pompilia of the resource of expression, which brings us round, it seems to me, to the justification of Browning's method. To express his inner self—his outward was a different affair!—and to express it utterly, even if no matter how, was clearly, for his own measure and consciousness of that inner self, to *be* poetic; and the solution of all the deviations and disparities or, speaking critically, monstrosities, in the mingled tissue of this work, is the fact that whether or no by such convulsions of soul and sense life got delivered for him, the garment of life (which for him was poetry and poetry alone) got disposed in its due and adequate multitudinous folds. We move with him but in images and references and vast and far correspondences; we eat but of strange compounds and drink but of rare distillations; and very soon, after a course of this, we feel ourselves, however much or however little to our advantage we may on occasion pronounce it, in the world of Expression at any cost. That, essentially, *is* the world of poetry—which in the cases known to our experience where it seems to us to differ from

Browning's world does so but through this latter's
having been, by the vigour and violence, the bold
familiarity, of his grasp and pull at it, moved several
degrees nearer us, so to speak, than any other of the
same general sort with which we are acquainted; so
that, intellectually, we back away from it a little, back
down before it, again and again, as we try to get off
from a picture or a group or a view which is too much
upon us and thereby out of focus.   Browning is "upon"
us, straighter upon us always, somehow, than anyone
else of his race; and we thus recoil, we push our chair
back, from the table he so tremendously spreads, just
to see a little better what is on it.   This makes a
relation with him that it is difficult to express; as if
he came up against us, each time, on the same side
of the street and not on the other side, across the
way, where we mostly see the poets elegantly walk,
and where we greet them without danger of concussion.
It is on this same side, as I call it, on *our* side, on
the other hand, that I rather see our encounter with
the novelists taking place; we being, as it were, more
mixed with them, or they at least, by their desire and
necessity, more mixed with us, and our brush of them,
in their minor frenzy, a comparatively muffled encounter.

We have in the whole thing, at any rate, the element of action which is at the same time constant picture, and the element of picture which is at the same
time constant action; and with a fusion, as the mass
moves, that is none the less effective, none the less
thick and complete, from our not owing it in the
least to an artful economy.   Another force pushes its
way through the waste and rules the scene, making

wrong things right and right things a hundred times more so—that breath of Browning's own particular matchless Italy which takes us full in the face and remains from the first the felt rich coloured air in which we live. The quantity of that atmosphere that he had to give out is like nothing else in English poetry, any more than in English prose, that I recall; and since I am taking these liberties with him, let me take one too, a little, with the fruit of another genius shining at us here in association—with that great placed and timed prose fiction which we owe to George Eliot and in which *her* projection of the stage and scenery is so different a matter. Curious enough this difference where so many things make for identity— the quantity of talent, the quantity of knowledge, the high equality (or almost) of culture and curiosity, not to say of "spiritual life." Each writer drags along a far-sweeping train, though indeed Browning's spreads so considerably furthest; but his stirs up, to my vision, a perfect cloud of gold-dust, while hers, in "Romola," by contrast, leaves the air about as clear, about as white, and withal about as cold, as before she had benevolently entered it. This straight saturation of our author's, this prime assimilation of the elements for which the name of Italy stands, is a single splendid case, however; I can think of no second one that is not below it—if we take it as supremely expressed in those of his lyrics and shorter dramatic monologues that it has most helped to inspire. The Rome and Tuscany of the early 'fifties had become for him so at once a medium, a bath of the senses and percep- tions, into which he could sink, in which he could unlimitedly soak, that wherever he might be touched afterwards he gave out some effect of that immersion.

This places him to my mind quite apart, makes the rest of our poetic record of a similar experience comparatively pale and abstract. Shelley and Swinburne —to name only his compeers—are, I know, a part of the record; but the author of "Men and Women," of "Pippa Passes," of certain of the Dramatic Lyrics and other scattered felicities, not only expresses and reflects the matter; he fairly, he heatedly, if I may use such a term, exudes and perspires it. Shelley, let us say in the connection, is a light and Swinburne, let us say, a sound; Browning alone of them all is a temperature. We feel it, we are in it at a plunge, with the very first pages of the thing before us; to which, I confess, we surrender with a momentum drawn from fifty of their predecessors, pages not less sovereign, elsewhere.

The old Florence of the late spring closes round us; the hand of Italy is at once, with the recital of the old-world litter of Piazza San Lorenzo, with that of the great glare and of the great shadow-masses, heavy upon us, heavy with that strange weight, that mixed pressure, which is somehow, to the imagination, at once a caress and a menace. Our poet kicks up on the spot and at short notice what I have called his cloud of gold-dust. I can but speak for myself at least— something that I want to feel both as historic and esthetic truth, both as pictorial and moral interest, something that will repay my fancy tenfold if I can but feel it, hovers before me, and I say to myself that, whether or no a great poem is to come off, I will be hanged if one of the vividest of all stories and one of the sharpest of all impressions doesn't. I beckon these things on, I follow them up, I so desire and need them that I of course, by my imaginative collaboration, contribute to them—from the moment, that is, of my finding myself really in relation to the great points. On the other hand, as certainly, it has taken the author of the first volume, and of the two admirable chapters of the same—since I can't call them cantos— entitled respectively "Half-Rome" and "The Other Half-Rome," to put me in relation; where it is that he keeps me more and more, letting the closeness of my state, it must be owned, occasionally drop, letting the finer call on me even, for bad quarters-of-an-hour, considerably languish, but starting up before me again in vivid authority if I really presume to droop or stray. He takes his wilful way with me, but I make it my own, picking over and over as I have said, like some lingering talking pedlar's client, his great unloosed pack; and thus it is that by the time I am settled with Pompilia at Arezzo I have lived into all the conditions. They press upon me close, those wonderful dreadful beautiful particulars of the Italy of the eve of the eighteenth century—Browning himself moving about, darting hither and thither in them, at his mighty ease: beautiful, I say, because of the quantity of romantic and esthetic tradition from a more romantic and esthetic age still visibly, palpably, in solution there; and wonderful and dreadful through something of a similar tissue of matchless and ruthless consistencies and immoralities. I make to my hand, as this infatuated reader, *my* Italy of the eve of the eighteenth century—a vast painted and gilded rococo shell roofing over a scenic, an amazingly figured and furnished earth, but shutting out almost the whole of our own dearly-bought, rudely-recovered spiritual sky. You see I have this right, all the while, if I recognise my suggested material, which keeps coming and coming in the measure of my need, and my duty to which *is* to recognise it, and as handsomely and actively as possible. The great thing is that I have such a group of figures moving across so constituted a scene—figures so typical, so salient, so reeking with the old-world character, so impressed all over with its manners and its morals, and so predestined, we see, to this particular horrid little drama. And let me not be charged with giving it away, the idea of the latent prose fiction, by calling it little and horrid; let me not—for with my contention I can't possibly afford to—appear to agree with those who speak of the Franceschini-Comparini case as a mere vulgar criminal anecdote.

It might have been such but for two reasons—counting only the principal ones; one of these our fact that we see it so, I repeat, in Browning's inordinately-coloured light, and the other—which is indeed perhaps but another face of the same—that, with whatever limitations, it gives us in the rarest manner three characters of the first importance. I hold three a great many; I could have done with it almost, I think, if there had been but one or two; our rich provision shows you at any rate what I mean by speaking of our author's performance as above all a preparation for something. Deeply he felt that with the three—the three built up at us each with an equal genial rage of reiterative touches—there couldn't eventually not be something done (artistically done, I mean) if someone would only do it. There they are in their old yellow Arezzo, that miniature milder Florence, as sleepy to my recollection as a little En-

glish cathedral city clustered about a Close, but dream-
ing not so peacefully nor so innocently; there is the
great fretted fabric of the Church on which they are
all swarming and grovelling, yet after their fashion
interesting parasites, from the high and dry old Arch-
bishop, meanly wise or ignobly edifying, to whom
Pompilia resorts in her woe and who practically pushes
her away with a shuffling velvet foot; down through
the couple of Franceschini cadets, Canon Girolamo
and Abate Paul, mere minions, fairly in the vermin-
ous degree, of the overgrown order or too-rank organism; down to Count Guido himself and to Canon
Caponsacchi, who have taken the tonsure at the
outset of their careers, but none too strictly the vows,
and who lead their lives under some strangest pro-
fanest pervertedest clerical category. There have been
before this the Roman preliminaries, the career of the
queer Comparini, the adoption, the assumption of the
parentship, of the ill-starred little girl, with the sordid cynicism of her marriage out of hand, conveying
her presumptive little fortune, her poor handful of
even less than contingent cash, to hungry middle-
aged Count Guido's stale "rank"; the many-toned
note or turbid harmony of all of which recurs to us
in the vivid image of the pieties and paganisms of
San Lorenzo in Lucina, that banal little church in the
old upper Corso—banal, that is, at the worst, with
the rare Roman *banalité;* bravely banal, or banal
with style—that we have all passed with a sense of
its reprieve to our sight-seeing, and where the bleeding bodies of the still-breathing Pompilia and her extinct companions are laid out on the greasy marble
of the altar-steps. To glance at these things, however, is fairly to be tangled, and at once, in the au-

thor's complexity of suggestion, to which our own
thick-coming fancies respond in no less a measure;
so that I have already missed my time to so much
even as name properly the tremendous little chapter
we should have devoted to the Franceschini interior
as revealed at last to Comparini eyes; the sinister
scene or ragged ruin of the Aretine "palace," where
pride and penury and, at once, rabid resentment show
their teeth in the dark and the void, and where Pompilia's inspired little character, clear silver hardened,
effectually beaten and battered, to steel, begins to
shine at the blackness with a light that fairly outfaces
at last the gleam of wolfish fangs—the character that
draws from Guido, in his, alas, too boundless harangue
of the fourth volume, some of the sharpest specifica-
tions into which that extraordinary desert, that indescribable waste of intellectual life, as I have hinted
at its being, from time to time flowers.

> "None of your abnegation of revenge!
> Fly at me frank, tug where I tear again!
> Away with the empty stare!   Be holy still,
> And stupid ever!   Occupy your patch
> Of private snow that's somewhere in what world
> May now be growing icy round your head,
> And aguish at your foot-print—freeze not me!"

I have spoken of the enveloping consciousness—or
call it just the struggling, emerging, comparing, at last
intensely living conscience—of Caponsacchi as the indicated centre of our situation or determinant of our
form, in the matter of the excellent novel; and know
of course what such an indication lets me in for, re-
sponsibly speaking, in the way of a rearrangement of
relations, in the way of liberties taken.   To lift our

subject out of the sphere of anecdote and place it in
the sphere of drama, liberally considered, to give it
dignity by extracting its finest importance, causing its
parts to flower together into some splendid special
sense, we supply it with a large lucid reflector, which
we find only, as I have already noted, in that mind
and soul concerned in the business that have at once
the highest sensibility and the highest capacity, or
that are, as we may call it, most admirably agitated.
There is the awkward fact, the objector may say, that
by our record the mind and soul in question are not
concerned till a given hour, when many things have
already happened and the climax is almost in sight;
to which we reply, at our ease, that we simply don't
suffer that fact to be awkward. From the moment
I am taking liberties I suffer *no* awkwardness; I should
be very helpless, quite without resource and without
vision, if I did. I said it to begin with: Browning
works the whole thing over—the whole thing as originally given him—and we work *him;* helpfully, artfully, boldly, which is our whole blest basis. We
therefore turn Caponsacchi on earlier, ever so much
earlier; turn him on, with a brave ingenuity, from
the very first—that is in Rome if need be; place him
there in the field, at once recipient and agent, vaguely
conscious and with splendid brooding apprehension,
awaiting the adventure of his life, awaiting his call,
his real call (the others have been such vain shows
and hollow stopgaps), awaiting, in fine, his terrible
great fortune. His direct connection with Pompilia
begins certainly at Arezzo, only after she has been
some time hideously mismated and has suffered all
but her direst extremity—that is of the essence; we
take it; it's all right. But his indirect participation

is another affair, and we get it—at a magnificent stroke
—by the fact that his view of Franceschini, his fellow-
Aretine sordidly "on the make," his measure of un-
desired, indeed of quite execrated contact with him,
brushed against in the motley hungry Roman traffic,
where and while that sinister soul snuffs about on the
very vague or the very foul scent of *his* fortune, may
begin whenever we like. We have only to have it
begin right, only to make it, on the part of two men,
a relation of strong irritated perception and restless
righteous convinced instinct in the one nature and of
equally instinctive hate and envy, jealousy and latent
fear, on the other, to see the indirect connection, the
one with Pompilia, as I say, throw across our page
as portentous a shadow as we need. Then we get
Caponsacchi as a recipient up to the brim—as an
agent, a predestined one, up to the hilt. I can scarce
begin to tell you what I see him give, as we say, or
how his sentient and observational life, his fine reactions in presence of such a creature as Guido, such
a social type and image and lurid light, as it were,
make him comparatively a modern man, breathed
upon, to that deep and interesting agitation I have
mentioned, by more forces than he yet reckons or
knows the names of.

The direct relation—always to Pompilia—is made,
at Arezzo, as we know, by Franceschini himself; preparing his own doom, in the false light of his debased
wit, by creating an appearance of hidden dealing between his wife and the priest which shall, as promptly
as he likes—if he but work it right—compromise and
overwhelm them. The particular deepest damnation
he conceives for his weaker, his weakest victim is that

she shall take the cleric Caponsacchi for her lover, he indubitably willing—to Guido's apprehension; and that her castigation at his hands for this, sufficiently proved upon her, shall be the last luxury of his own baseness. He forges infernally, though grossly enough, an imputed correspondence between them, a series of love-letters, scandalous scrawls, of the last erotic intensity; which we in the event see solemnly weighed by his fatuous judges, all fatuous save the grave old Pope, in the scale of Pompilia's guilt and responsibility. It is this atrocity that at the *dénouement* damns Guido himself most, or well-nigh; but if it fails and recoils, as all his calculations do—it is only his rush of passion that doesn't miss—this is by the fact exactly that, as we have seen, his wife and her friend are, for our perfect persuasion, characters of the deepest dye. There, if you please, is the finest side of our subject; such sides come up, such sides flare out upon us, when we get such characters in such embroilments. Admire with me therefore our felicity in this first-class value of Browning's beautiful critical genial vision of his Caponsacchi—vision of him as the tried and tempered and illuminated *man*, a great round smooth, though as yet but little worn gold-piece, an embossed and figured ducat or sequin of the period, placed by the poet in my hand. He gives me that value to spend for him, spend on all the strange old experience, old sights and sounds and stuffs, of the old stored Italy—so we have at least the wit to spend it to high advantage; which is just what I mean by our taking the liberties we spoke of. I see such bits we can get with it; but the difficulty is that I see so many more things than I can have even dreamed of giving you a hint of. I see the Arezzo life and the

Arezzo crisis with every "i" dotted and every circumstance presented; and when Guido takes his wife, as a possible trap for her, to the theatre—the theatre of old Arezzo: share with me the tattered vision and inhale the musty air!—I am well in range of Pompilia, the tragically exquisite, in her box, with her husband not there for the hour but posted elsewhere; I look at her in fact over Caponsacchi's shoulder and that of his brother-canon Conti, while this light character, a vivid recruit to our company, manages to toss into her lap, and as coming in guise of overture from his smitten friend, "a papertwist of comfits." There is a particular famous occasion at the theatre in a work of more or less contemporary fiction—at a petty provincial theatre which isn't even, as you might think, the place where Pendennis had his first glimpse of Miss Fotheringay. The evening at the Rouen playhouse of Flaubert's "Madame Bovary" has a relief not elsewhere equalled—it is the most *done* visit to the play in all literature—but, though "doing" is now so woefully out of favour, my idea would be to give it here a precious *pendant;* which connection, silly Canon Conti, the old fripperies and levities, the whole queer picture and show of manners, is handed over to us, expressly, as inapt for poetic illustration.

What is equally apt for poetic or for the other, indeed, is the thing for which we feel "The Ring and the Book" preponderantly done—it is at least what comes out clearest, comes out as straightest and strongest and finest, from Browning's genius—the exhibition of the great constringent relation between man and woman at once at its maximum and as the relation most worth while in life for either party; an exhibi-

tion forming quite the main substance of our author's
message. He has dealt, in his immense variety and
vivacity, with other relations, but on this he has
thrown his most living weight; it remains the thing
of which his own rich experience most convincingly
spoke to him. He has testified to it as charged to
the brim with the burden of the senses, and has testified to it as almost too clarified, too liberated and sublimated, for traceable application or fair record; he
has figured it as never too much either of the flesh or
of the spirit for him, so long as the possibility of both
of these is in each, but always and ever as the thing
absolutely most worth while. It is in the highest and
rarest degree clarified and disengaged for Caponsacchi and Pompilia; but what their history most con-
cludes to is how ineffably it was, whatever happened,
worth while. Worth while most then for them or for
us is the question? Well, let us say worth while assuredly for us, in this noble exercise of our imagination. Which accordingly shows us what we, for all
our prose basis, would have found, to repeat my term
once more, prepared for us. There isn't a detail of
their panting flight to Rome over the autumn Apen-
nines—the long hours when they melt together only
not to meet—that doesn't positively plead for our perfect prose transcript. And if it be said that the mere
massacre at the final end is a lapse to passivity from
the high plane, for our pair of protagonists, of constructive, of heroic vision, this is not a blur from the
time everything that happens happens most effectively
to Caponsacchi's life. Pompilia's is taken, but she is
none the less given; and it is in his consciousness and
experience that she most intensely flowers—with all
her jubilation for doing so. So that *he* contains the

whole—unless indeed after all the Pope does, the Pope whom I was leaving out as too transcendent for *our* version. Unless, unless, further and further, I see what I have at this late moment no right to; see, as the very end and splendid climax of all, Caponsacchi sent for to the Vatican and admitted alone to the Papal presence. *There* is a scene if we will; and in the mere mutual confrontation, brief, silent, searching, recognising, consecrating, almost as august on the one part as on the other. It rounds us off; but you will think I stray too far. I have wanted, alas, to say such still other fond fine things—it being of our poet's great nature to prompt them at every step—that I almost feel I have missed half my points; which will doubtless therefore show you these remarks in their nakedness. Take them and my particular contention as a pretext and a minor affair if you will only feel them at the same time as at the worst a restless refinement of homage. It has been easy in many another case to run to earth the stray prime fancy, the original anecdote or artless tale, from which a great imaginative work, starting off after meeting it, has sprung and rebounded again and soared; and perhaps it is right and happy and final that one should have faltered in attempting by a converse curiosity to clip off or tie back the wings that once have spread. You will agree with me none the less, I feel, that Browning's great generous wings are over us still and even now, more than ever now; and also that they shake down on us his blessing.

AN AMERICAN ART–SCHOLAR: CHARLES ELIOT NORTON
1908

I GLADLY embrace the occasion to devote a few words to the honoured memory of my distinguished friend the late Charles Eliot Norton, who, dying at Cambridge, Massachusetts, on the 21st of October last, after having reached his eightieth year, had long occupied—and with an originality of spirit and a beneficence of effect all his own—the chair of the History of the Fine Arts at Harvard University, as well as, in the view of the American world surrounding that seat of influence, the position of one of the most accomplished of scholars and most efficient of citizens. This commemorative page may not disclaim the personal tone, for I can speak of Charles Norton but in the light of an affection which began long years ago, even though my part in our relation had to be, for some time, markedly that of a junior; of which tie I was to remain ever after, despite long stretches of material separation, a conscious and grateful beneficiary. I can speak of him therefore as I happened myself to see and know him—with interest and sympathy acting, for considerable periods together, across distances and superficial differences, yet with the sense of his extremely individual character and career suffering no abatement, and indeed with my impression of the fine consistency and exemplary value of these things clear as never before.

I find this impression go back for its origin very far—to one autumn day when, an extremely immature aspirant to the rare laurel of the critic, I went out from Boston to Cambridge to offer him a contribution to the old, if I should not rather say the then middle-aged, "North American Review," of which he had recently undertaken the editorship. I already knew him a little, enough to have met casual kindness at his hands; but my vision of his active presence and function, in the community that had happily produced and that was long to enjoy him, found itself, I think, completely constituted at that hour, with scarce an essential touch to be afterwards added. He largely developed and expanded as time went on; certain more or less local reserves and conservatisms fell away from him; but his temper and attitude, all his own from the first, were to give a singular unity to his life. This intensity of perception on his young visitor's part may perhaps have sprung a little from the fact that he accepted on the spot, as the visitor still romantically remembers, a certain very first awkward essay in criticism, and was to publish it in his forthcoming number; but I little doubt whether even had he refused it the grace of the whole occasion would have lost anything to my excited view, and feel sure that the interest in particular would have gained had he charmingly put before me (as he would have been sure to do) the ground of his discrimination. For his eminent character as a "representative of culture" announced itself exactly in proportion as one's general sense of the medium in which it was to be exerted was strong; and I seem verily to recall that even in the comparative tenderness of that season I had grasped the idea of the precious, the quite far-reaching part such an exemplar might play. Charles Norton's distinction and value—this was still some years before his professorate had taken form—showed early and above all the note and the advantage that they were to be virtues of American application, and were to draw their life from the signal American opportunity; to that degree that the detailed record of his influence would be really one of the most interesting of American social documents, and that his good work is best lighted by a due acquaintance with the conditions of the life about him, indispensable for a founded recognition of it. It is not too much to say that the representative of culture—always in the high and special sense in which he practised that faith —had before him in the United States of those days a great and arduous mission, requiring plentiful courage as well as plentiful knowledge, endless good humour as well as assured taste.

What comes back to me then from the early day I have glanced at is exactly that prompt sense of the clustered evidence of my friend's perfect adaptation to the civilising mission, and not least to the needfully dauntless and unperturbed side of it. His so pleasant old hereditary home, with its ample acres and numerous spoils—at a time when acres merely marginal and, so to speak, atmospheric, as well as spoils at all felicitously gathered, were rare in the United States—seemed to minister to the general assurance, constituting as they did such a picture of life as one vaguely supposed recognisable, right and left, in an old society, or, otherwise expressed, in that "Europe" which was always, roundabout one, the fond alternative of the cultivated imagination, but of which the possible American copy ever seemed far to seek. To put it in a nutshell, the pilgrimage to the Shady Hill of those years had, among the "spoils," among pictures and books, drawings and medals, memories and relics and anecdotes, things of a remote but charming reference, very much the effect of a sudden rise into a finer and clearer air and of a stopgap against one's own coveted renewal of the more direct experience. If I allude to a particular, to a personal yearning appreciation of those matters, it is with the justified conviction—this justification having been all along abundantly perceptible—that appreciation of the general sort only waited to be called for, though to be called for with due authority. It was the sign of our host, on the attaching spot, and almost the principal one, that he spoke, all round and with the highest emphasis, as under the warrant of authority, and that at a time when, as to the main matter of his claim and his discourse, scarce anyone pretended to it, he carried himself valiantly under that banner. The main matter of his discourse offered itself just simply as the matter of *civilisation*—the particular civilisation that a young roaring and money-getting democracy, inevitably but almost exclusively occupied with "business success," most needed to have brought home to it. The New England air in especial was no natural conductor of any appeal to an esthetic aim, but the interest of Professor Norton's general work, to say nothing of the interest of his character for a closer view, is exactly that the whole fruitful enterprise was to prove intimately a New England adventure; illustrating thus at the same time and once more the innate capacity of New England for leavening the great American mass on the finer issues.

To have grown up as the accomplished man at large was in itself at that time to have felt, and even in some degree to have suffered, this hand of differentiation; the only accomplished men of the exhibited New England Society had been the ministers, the heads of the congregations—whom, however, one docks of little of their credit in saying that their accomplishments and their earnestness had been almost wholly in the moral order. The advantage of that connection was indeed what Norton was fundamentally to have enjoyed in his descent, both on his father's and his mother's side (pre-eminently on the latter, the historic stock of the Eliots) from a long line of those stalwart pastoral worthies who had notably formed the aristocracy of Massachusetts. It was largely, no doubt, to this heritage of character and conscience that he owed the strong and special strain of confidence with which he addressed himself to the business of perfect candour toward his fellow-citizens—his pupils in particular; they, to whom this candour was to become in the long run the rarest and raciest and most endearing of "treats," being but his fellow-citizens in the making. This view of an urgent duty would have been a comparatively slight thing, moreover, without the special preoccupations, without the love of the high humanities and curiosities and urbanities in themselves, without the conception of science and the ingrained studious cast of mind, which had been also an affair of heredity with him and had opened his eyes betimes to educative values and standards other than most of those he saw flourish near at hand. He would defer to dilettantism as little as to vulgarity, and if he ultimately embraced the fine ideal of taking up the work that lay close to him at home, and of irrigating

the immediate arid tracts and desert spaces, it was
not from ignorance of the temptation to wander and
linger where the streams already flowed and the soil
had already borne an abiding fruit.

He had come to Italy and to England early in life;
he had repeated his visits to these countries with infinite relish and as often as possible—though never, as
a good New Englander, without certain firm and,
where they had to be, invidious discriminations; he
was attached to them by a hundred intellectual and
social ties; but he had been from the first incapable
of doubting that the best activity and the liveliest
interest lay where it always, given certain conditions,
lies in America—in a measure of response to intellectual and esthethic "missionary" labour more traceable and appreciable, more distinguishably attested
and registered, more directly and artlessly grateful, in
a word, than in the thicker elemental mixture of Europe. On the whole side of taste and association his
choice was thus betimes for conscious exile and for a
considerably, though doubtless not altogether irreme-
diably, deprived state; but it was at the same time
for a freedom of exhortation and a play of ironic comment less restricted, after all, in the clear American
air, than on ground more pretentiously enclosed—less
restricted, that is, from the moment personal conviction might be absolute and indifference to every form
of provincial bewilderment equally patient and complete. The incontestable *crânerie* of his attitude—a
thing that one felt to be a high form of sincerity—
always at last won success; the respect and affection
that more and more surrounded him and that finally
made his situation sole of its kind and pre-eminently

happy, attest together the interesting truth that unqualified confidence in one's errand, the serenest acceptance of a responsibility and the exercise of a critical authority never too apt to return critically upon
itself, only require for beneficent action that they be
attended at once with a fund of illustration and a
fund of good humour.

Professor Norton's pre-eminent work in the interpretation of Dante—by which I mean his translation,
text and notes, of the "Divine Comedy" and the
"New Life," an achievement of infinite piety, patience
and resource; his admirable volume on Church-Build-
ing in the Middle Ages (to say nothing of his charming earlier one, "Study and Travel in Italy," largely
devoted to the cathedral of Orvieto); his long and intimate friendship with Ruskin, commemorated by his
publication, as joint-executor to Ruskin's will, of the
best fruits of the latter's sustained correspondence
with him; his numerous English friendships, in especial—to say nothing of his native—all with persons
of a highly representative character: these things give
in part the measure of his finest curiosities and of his
appetite, in all directions, for the best sources and examples and the best company. But it is probable
that if his Harvard lectures are in form for publication, and if his general correspondence, and above all
his own easily handsomest show in it, comes to be
published, as most emphatically it should be, they
will testify not in the least to any unredeemed con-
traction of life, but to the largest and happiest and
most rewarded energy. An exhilarated invocation of
close responsibility, an absolute ease of mind about
one's point of view, a thorough and never-failing in-

tellectual wholeness, are so far from weakening the
appeal to young allegiances that, once they succeed
at all, they succeed the better for going all their length.
So it was that, with admirable urbanity of form and
uncompromising straightness of attack, the Professor
of the History of the Fine Arts at Harvard for a quarter of a century let himself go; thinking no trouble
wasted and no flutter and no scandal other than auspicious if only he might, to the receptive and aspiring
undergraduate mind, brand the ugly and the vulgar
and the inferior wherever he found them, tracking
them through plausible disguises and into trumpery
strongholds; if only he might convert young products
of the unmitigated American order into material for
men of the world in the finer sense of that term; if
only in short he might render more supple their view,
liable to obfuscation from sights and sounds about
them, of the true meaning of a liberal education and
of the civilised character and spirit in the civilised
State.

What it came to thus was that he availed himself
to the utmost of his free hand for sowing and planting ideals—ideals that, though they might after all be
vague and general things, lacking sometimes a little
the clearer connections with practice, were yet a new
and inspiring note to most of his hearers, who could
be, trusted, just so far as they were intelligent and
loyal, not to be heavily embarrassed by them, not to
want for fields of application. It was given him,
quite unprecedentedly, to be popular, to be altogether loved and cherished, even while "rubbing it
into" whomever it might concern that such unfortunates were mainly given over to mediocrity and vul-

garity, and that half the crude and ugly objects and aspects, half the low standards and loose ends surrounding them and which they might take for granted with a facility and a complacency alike deplorable, represented a platitude of imagination that dishonoured the citizen on whom a University worthy of the name should have left its stamp. Happy, it would thus in fact seem, beyond any other occasion for educative influence, the immense and delightful opportunity he enjoyed, the clear field and long reach attached to preaching an esthetic crusade, to pleading for the higher amenities in general, in a new and superficially tutored, yet also but superficially prejudiced, country, where a consequently felt and noted rise of the tide of manners may be held to have come home to him, or certainly to have visited his dreams. His effect on the community at large, with allowances of time, was ever indubitable—even though such workers have everywhere to take much on trust and to remember that bushels of doctrine, and even tons of example, make at the most ounces and grains of responsive life. It can only be the very general and hopeful view that sustains and rewards—with here and there, at wide intervals, the prized individual instance of the sown seed actively emerging and flowering.

If not all ingenious disciples could give independent proof, however, all could rally and feel the spirit; all could crowd to a course of instruction which, largely elective and optional, yet united more listeners than many others put together, and in which the subject itself, the illustration of European artistic endeavour at large, or in other words the record of man's most comprehensive sacrifice to organised beauty, tended so to take up on familiar ground the question of manners, character, conscience, tone, to bristle with questions addressed to the actual and possible American scene. That, I hasten to add, was of course but one side of the matter; there were wells of special science for those who chose to draw from them, and an inner circle of pupils whose whole fruitful relation to their philosopher and friend—the happy and easy privilege of Shady Hill in general, where other charming personal influences helped, not counting as least in this —can scarce have failed to prepare much practical evidence for observation still to come. The ivory tower of study would ever, by his natural bent, I think, have most solicited Charles Norton; but he liked, as I say, he accepted without a reserve, the function of presiding over young destinies; he believed in the personal and the social communication of light, and had a gift for the generous and personal relation that perhaps found its best issue, as I have already hinted, in his admirable letters. These were not of this hustled and hustling age, but of a cooler and steadier sphere and rhythm, and of a charming mannerly substantial type to which he will have been, I think, among correspondents truly animated by the social spirit and a due cosmopolite ideal, one of the last systematically to sacrifice. With the lapse of years I ceased to be, I admit, a near spectator of his situation; but my sense of his activity—with more intimate renewals, besides, occasionally taking place— was to be, all along, so constantly fed by echo and anecdote and all manner of indirect glimpses, that I find myself speak quite with the confidence and with all the attachment of a continuous "assistant."

With which, if I reflect on this, I see how interesting a *case* above all my distinguished friend was ever to remain to me—a case, I mean, of such a mixture of the elements as would have seemed in advance, critically speaking, quite anomalous or at least highly incalculable. His interest was predominantly in Art, as the most beneficial of human products; his ostensible plea was for the esthetic law, under the wide wing of which we really move, it may seem to many of us, in an air of strange and treacherous appearances, of much bewilderment and not a little mystification; of terribly fine and complicated issues in short, such as call for the highest interpretative wisdom. But if nothing was of a more delightful example than Professor Norton's large and nourished serenity in all these connections, a serenity seasoned and tempered, as it were, by infinite interest in his "subject," by a steadying faith in exact and extensive knowledge, so to a fond and incorrigible student of character the case, as I have called it, and the long and genial career, may seem to shine in the light of quite other importances, quite other references, than the presumed and the nominal. Nothing in fact *can* be more interesting to a haunter of other intellectual climes and a worshipper at the esthetic shrine *quand même* than to note once more how race and implanted quality and association always in the end come by their own; how for example a son of the Puritans the most intellectually transmuted, the most liberally emancipated and initiated possible, could still plead most for substance when proposing to plead for style, could still try to lose himself in the labyrinth of delight while keeping tight hold of the clue of duty, tangled even a little in his feet; could still address himself all consistently to the moral conscience while speaking as by his office for our imagination and our free curiosity. All of which vision of him, however, is far from pointing to a wasted effort. The great thing, whatever turn we take, is to find before us perspectives and to have a weight to throw; in accordance with which wisdom the world he lived in received for long no firmer nor more gallant and generous impress than that of Charles Eliot Norton.

LONDON NOTES

January 1897

I AM afraid the interest of the world of native letters is not at this moment so great as to make us despise mere translation as an aid to curiosity. There is indeed no reason why we should forbear to say in advance what we are certain, every time, to say after (after the heat has cooled I mean:) namely, that nothing is easier to concede than that Ibsen—contentious name!—would be much less remarked if he were one of a dozen. It is impossible, in London at least, to shut one's eyes to the fact that if to so many ingenious minds he is a kind of pictorial monster, a grotesque on the sign of a side-show, this is at least partly because his form has a monstrous rarity. It is one of the odd things of our actual esthetics that the more theatres multiply the less any one reads a play—the less any one cares, in a word, for the text of the adventure. That no one ever *does* read a play has long been a commonplace of the wisdom of booksellers. Ibsen, however, is a text, and Ibsen is read, and Ibsen contradicts the custom and confounds the prejudice; with the effect thereby, in an odd way, of being doubly an exotic. His violent substance imposes, as it were, his insidious form; it is not (as would have seemed more likely) the form that imposes the substance. Mr. William Archer has just published his version of "John Gabriel Borkman," of which, moreover, French and German versions reach us at the same moment. There are therefore all the elements of a fresh breeze in the wind—one has already a sense as of a cracking of whips and a girding of loins. You may by this time be terribly tired of it all in America; but, as I mentioned a fortnight ago, we have had very recent evidence that languor here, in this connection, is by no means as yet the dominant note. It is not the dispute itself, however, that most interests me: let me pay it, for what it has been and what it still may be, the mere superficial tribute of saying that it constitutes one of the very few cases of contagious discussion of a matter not political, a question not of mere practice, of which I remember to have felt, in a heavy air, the engaging titillation. In London generally, I think, the wandering breath of criticism is the stray guest at the big party—the shy young man whom nobody knows. In this remarkable instance the shy young man has ventured to pause and hover, has lighted on a topic, introduced himself and, after a gasp of consternation in the company, seen a little circle gather round him. I can only speak as one of the little circle, testifying to my individual glee.

The author who at the age of seventy, a provincial of provincials, turns out "John Gabriel" is frankly for me so much one of the peculiar pleasures of the day, one of the current strong sensations, that, erect as he seems still to stand, I deplore his extreme maturity and, thinking of what shall happen, look round in vain for any other possible source of the same kind of emotion. For Ibsen strikes me as an extraordinary curiosity, and every time he sounds his note the miracle to my perception is renewed. I call it a miracle because it is a result of so dry a view of life, so indifferent a vision of the comedy of things. His idea of the thing represented is never the comic idea, though this is evidently what it often only can be for many of his English readers and spectators. Comedy moreover is a product mainly of observation, and I scarcely know what to say of his figures except that they haven't the *signs*. The answer to that is doubtless partly that they haven't the English, but have the Norwegian. In such a case one of the Norwegian must be in truth this very lack of signs.

They have no tone but their moral tone. They are highly animated abstractions, with the extraordinary, the brilliant property of becoming when represented at once more abstract and more living. If the spirit is a lamp within us, glowing through what the world and the flesh make of us as through a ground-glass shade, then such pictures as Little Eyolf and John Gabriel are each a *chassez-croisez* of lamps burning, as in tasteless parlours, with the flame practically exposed. There are no shades in the house, or the Norwegian ground-glass is singularly clear. There is a positive odour of spiritual paraffin. The author nevertheless arrives at the dramatist's great goal—he arrives for all his meagreness at intensity. The meagreness, which is after all but an unconscious, an admirable economy, never interferes with that: it plays straight into the hands of his rare mastery of form. The contrast between this form—so difficult to have reached, so "evolved," so civilised—and the bareness and bleakness of his little northern democracy is the source of half the hard frugal charm that he puts forth. In the cold fixed light of it the notes we speak of as deficiencies take a sharp value in the picture. There is no small-talk, there are scarcely any manners. On the other hand there is so little vulgarity that this of itself has almost the effect of a deeper, a more lonely provincialism. The background at any rate is the sunset over the ice. Well in the very front of the scene lunges with extraordinary length of arm the Ego against the Ego, and rocks in a rigour of passion the soul against the soul—a spectacle, a movement, as definite as the relief of silhouettes in black paper or of a train of Eskimo dogs on the snow. Down from that desolation the sturdy old symbolist comes this time with a supreme example of his method. It is a high wonder and pleasure to welcome such splendid fruit from sap that might by now have shown something of the chill of age. Never has he juggled more gallantly with difficulty and danger than in this really prodigious "John Gabriel," in which a great span of tragedy is taken between three or four persons—a trio of the grim and grizzled—in the two or three hours of a winter's evening; in which the whole thing throbs with an actability that fairly shakes us as we read; and in which, as the very flower of his artistic triumph, he has given us for the most beautiful and touching of his heroines a sad old maid of sixty. Such "parts," even from the vulgarest point of view, are Borkman and Ella Rentheim.

LONDON NOTES

June 1897

I AM afraid there are at this moment only two notes
for a communication from London to strike.   One is
that of the plunge into the deep and turbid waters of
the Jubilee; the other is that of the inevitable retreat
from them—the backward scramble up the bank and
scurry over its crest and out of sight.   London is in a
sorry state;   nevertheless I judge that the number of
persons about to arrive undaunted will not fall substantially short of the number of horror-stricken fugi-
tives.   Not to depart is practically to arrive;   for there
is little difference in the two kinds of violence, the
shock you await or the shock that awaits you.   Let
me hasten, however, to declare that—to speak for the
present only of the former of these—the prospect is
full of suggestion, the affair promises a rare sort of
interest.   It began a fortnight since to be clear—and
the certitude grows each day—that we are to be
treated to a revelation really precious, the domestic
or familiar vision, as it were, the back-stairs or under-
side view, of a situation that will rank as celebrated.
Balzac's image of *l'envers de l'histoire contemporaine*
is in fact already under our nose, already offered us
in a big bouncing unmistakable case.   We brush with
an irreverent hand the back of the tapestry—we crawl
on unabashed knees under the tent of the circus.   The
commemoration of the completed sixtieth year of her
Majesty's reign will figure to the end of time in the

roll of English wonders and can scarcely fail to hold
its own as an occasion unparalleled. And yet we
touch it as we come and go—we feel it mainly as a
great incommodity. It has already so intimate, so
ugly, so measurable a side that these impressions begin
to fall into their place with a kind of representative
force, to figure as a symbol of the general truth that
the principal pomps and circumstances of the historic
page have had their most intense existence as material
and social arrangements, disagreeable or amusing accidents, affecting the few momentary mortals at that
time in the neighbourhood. The gross defacement of
London, the uproarious traffic in seats, the miles of
unsightly scaffolding between the West End and the
City, the screaming advertisements, the sordid struggle, the individual questions—"Haven't we been
cheated by the plausible wretch?" or "How the devil
shall we get *to* our seats after paying such a lot, hey?"
—these things are actually the historic page. If we
are writing that page every hour let us at any rate
commend ourselves for having begun betimes, even
though this early diligence be attended with extraordinary effects. The great day was a week ago still a
month off, but what we even then had full in view,
was, for the coming stretch of time, a London reduced
to such disfigurement as might much better seem to
consort with some great national penance or mourn-
ing. The show, when the show comes off, is to last
but a couple of hours; and nothing so odd surely ever
occurred in such a connection as so huge a disproportion between the discipline and the joy. If this be
honour, the simple may well say, give us, merciful
powers, the rigour of indifference! From Hyde Park
Corner to the heart of the City and over the water

to the solid south the long line of thoroughfares is masked by a forest of timber and smothered in swaggering posters and catchpenny bids, with all of which and with the vociferous air that enfolds them we are to spend these next weeks in such comfort as we may. The splendour will have of course to be great to wash down the vulgarity—and infinitely dazzling no doubt it will be; yet even if it falls short I shall still feel that, let the quantity of shock, as I have ventured to call it, be what it must, it will on the whole be exceeded by what I have ventured to call the quantity of suggestion. This, to be frank, has even now rolled up at such a rate that to deal with it I should scarce know where to take it first. Let me not therefore pretend to deal, but only glance and pass.

The foremost, the immense impression is of course the constant, the permanent, the ever-supreme—the impression of that greatest glory of our race, its passionate feeling for trade. I doubt if the commercial instinct be not, as London now feels it throb and glow, quite as striking as any conceivable projection of it that even our American pressure of the pump might, at the highest, produce. That is the real tent of the circus—that is the real back of the tapestry. There have long, I know, been persons ready to prove by book that the explanation of the "historical event" has always been somebody's desire to make money; never, at all events, from the near view, will that explanation have covered so much of the ground. No result of the fact that the Queen has reigned sixty years—no sort of sentimental or other association with it—begins to have the air of coming home to the London conscience like this happy consequence of the

chance in it to sell something dear.   As yet that chance
is the one sound that fills the air, and will probably
be the only note audibly struck till the plaudits of the
day itself begin to substitute, none too soon, a more
mellifluous one.   When the people are all at the windows and in the trees and on the water-spouts, house-
tops, scaffolds and other ledges and coigns of vantage
set as traps for them by the motive power, *then* doubtless there will be another aspect to reckon with—then
we shall see, of the grand occasion, nothing but what
is decently and presentably historic.   All I mean is
that, pending the apotheosis, London has found in
this particular chapter of the career of its aged sovereign only an enormous selfish advertisement.   It
came to me the other day in a quoted epigram that
the advertisement shows as far off as across the Channel and all the way to Paris, where one of the reflections it has suggested—as it must inevitably suggest
many—appears to be that, in contrast, when, a year
ago, the Russian sovereigns were about to arrive no
good Parisian thought for a moment of anything but
how he could most work for the adornment of his
town.   I dare say that in fact from a good Parisian
or two a window or a tree was to be hired; but the
echo is at least interesting *as* an echo, not less than
as a reminder of how we still wait here for the outbreak of the kind of enthusiasm that shall take the
decorative form.   The graceful tip of its nose has, it
must be admitted, yet to show.   But there are other
sides still, and one of them immense—the light we
may take as flooding, I mean, the whole question of
the solidity of the throne.   It is impossible to live
long in England without feeling that the monarchy
is—below-ground, so to speak, in particular—a rock;

but it was reserved for these days to accentuate the
immobility of even that portion of the rock which
protrudes above the surface. It is being tested in a
manner by fire, and it resists with a vitality nothing
short of prophetic. The commercial instinct, as I say,
perches upon it with a security and a success that
banish a rival from the field. It is the biggest of all
draws for the biggest of all circuses; it will bring more
money to more doors than anything that can be imagined in its place. It will march through the ages
unshaken. The coronation of a new sovereign is an
event, at the worst, well within the compass of the
mind, and what will that bring with it so much as a
fresh lively market and miles of new posters and new
carpentry? Then, who knows?—coronations will, for
a stretch and a change perhaps, be more frequent than
anniversaries; and the bargains struck over the last
will, again at the worst, carry an hilarious country
well on to the next. Has not the monarchy moreover
—besides thus periodically making trade roar—the
lively merit, for such an observer as I fancy considering these things, of helping more than anything else the
answers to the questions into which our actual curiosity most overflows; the question for instance of whether
in the case before us the triumph of vulgarity be not
precisely the flushed but muscular triumph of the inevitable? If vulgarity thrones now on the house-tops,
"blown" and red in the face, is it not because it has
been pushed aloft by deep forces and is really after
all itself the show? The picturesque at any rate has
to meet the conditions. We miss, we regret the old
"style" of history; but the style would, I think, be
there if we let it: the age has a manner of its own that
disconcerts, that swamps it. The age is the loudest

thing of all. What has altered is simply the conditions. Poor history has to meet them, these conditions; she must accommodate herself. She must accept vulgarity or perish. Some day doubtless she *will* perish, but for a little while longer she remembers and struggles. She becomes indeed, as we look up Piccadilly in the light of this image, perhaps rather more dramatic than ever—at any rate more pathetic, more noble in her choked humiliation. Then even as we pity her we try perhaps to bring her round, to make her understand a little better. We try to explain that if we are dreadful to deal with it is only, really, a good deal because we so detestably grow and grow. There is so horribly much of us—that's where *our* style breaks down. Small crowds and paltry bargains didn't matter, and a little vulgarity—just a very little—could in other times manage to pass. Our shame, alas, is our quantity.

I have no sooner, none the less, qualified it so ungraciously than I ask myself what after all we should do without it. If we have opened the floodgates we have at least opened them wide, and it is our very quantity that perhaps in the last resort will save us. It cuts both ways, as the phrase is—it covers all the ground; it helps the escape as well as produces the assault. If retreat for instance at the present juncture is, as I began by hinting, urgently imposed, it is thanks to our having so much of everything that we find a bridge for our feet. We hope to get off in time, but meanwhile even on the spot there are blessed alternatives and reliefs. I have been trying a number very hard, but I have expatiated so on the complaint that I have left little room for the remedy.

London reminds one of nothing so often as of the help she gives one to forget her. One of the forms actually taken by this happy habit is the ingenious little exhibition, at the Grafton Galleries, of so-called Dramatic and Musical Art. The name is rather a grand one and the show has many gaps; but it profits, as such places in London so often profit, by the law that makes you mostly care less what you get into than what you get out of. With its Hogarths and Zoffanys —none too many, I admit—its other last-century portraits and relics, its numerous ghosts of Garrick, its old play-bills and prints, its echoes of dead plaudits and its very thin attendance, it happens to be for the moment a quiet bower in the bear-garden. It is a "scratch" company, but only—and I can scarce say why—in the portion in which the portraits of the day prevail is the impression vulgar. Even there indeed this suspicion receives a grand lift from Mr. Whistler's exquisite image of Henry Irving as the Philip of Tennyson's "Queen Mary." To pause before such a work is in fact to be held to the spot by just the highest operation of the charm one has sought there—the charm of a certain degree of melancholy meditation. Meditation indeed forgets Garrick and Hogarth and all the handsome heads of the Kembles in wonder reintensified at the attitude of a stupid generation toward an art and a taste so rare. Wonder is perhaps after all not the word to use, for how *should* a stupid generation, liking so much that it does like and with a faculty trained to coarser motions, recognise in Mr. Whistler's work one of the finest of all distillations of the artistic intelligence? To turn from his picture to the rest of the show—which, of course, I admit, is not a collection of masterpieces—is to drop from the world of distinction, of perception, of beauty and mystery and perpetuity, into—well, a very ordinary place. And yet the effect of Whistler at his best is exactly to give to the place he hangs in—or perhaps I should say to the person he hangs for—something of the sense, of the illusion, of a great museum. He isolates himself in a manner all his own; his presence is in itself a sort of implication of a choice corner. Have we in this a faint foresight of the eventual turn of the wheel—of one of the nooks of honour, those innermost rooms of great collections, in which our posterity shall find him? Look at him at any rate on any occasion, but above all at his best, only long enough, and hallucination sets in. We are in the presence of one of the prizes marked with two stars in the guidebook; the polished floor is beneath us and the rococo roof above; the great names are ranged about, and the eye is aware of the near window, in its deep recess, that overhangs old gardens or a celebrated square.

LONDON NOTES

July 1897

I CONTINUED last month to seek private diversion, which I found to be more and more required as the machinery of public began to work. Never was a better chance apparently for the great anodyne of art. It was a supreme opportunity to test the spell of the magician, for one felt one was saved if a fictive world would open. I knocked in this way at a dozen doors, I read a succession of novels; with the effect perhaps of feeling more than ever before my individual liability in our great general debt to the novelists. The great thing to say for them is surely that at any given moment they offer us another world, another consciousness, an experience that, as effective as the dentist's ether, muffles the ache of the actual and, by helping us to an interval, tides us over and makes us face, in the return to the inevitable, a combination that may at least have changed. What we get of course, in proportion as the picture lives, is simply another actual—the actual of other people; and I no more than any one else pretend to say *why* that should be a relief, a relief as great, I mean, as it practically proves. We meet in this question, I think, the eternal mystery—the mystery that sends us back simply to the queer constitution of man and that is not in the least lighted by the plea of "romance," the argument that relief depends wholly upon the quantity, as it were, of fable. It depends, to my sense, on the quantity of nothing but art—in which the material, fable or fact or whatever it be, falls so into solution, is so reduced and transmuted, that I absolutely am acquainted with no receipt whatever for computing its proportion and amount.

The only amount I can compute is the force of the author, for that is directly registered in my attention, my submission. A hundred things naturally go to make it up; but he knows so much better than I what they are that I should blush to give him a glimpse of my inferior account of them. The anodyne is not the particular picture, it is our own act of surrender, and therefore most, for each reader, what he most surrenders to. This latter element would seem in turn to vary from case to case, were it not indeed that there are readers prepared, I believe, to limit their surrender in advance. With some, we gather, it declines for instance to operate save on an exhibition of "high life." In others again it is proof against any solicitation but that of low. In many it vibrates only to "adventure"; in many only to Charlotte Brontë; in various groups, according to affinity, only to Jane Austen, to old Dumas, to Miss Corelli, to Dostoievsky or whomever it may be. The readers easiest to conceive, however, are probably those for whom, in the whole impression, the note of sincerity in the artist is what most matters, what most reaches and touches. That, obviously, is the relation that gives the widest range to the anodyne.

I am afraid that, profiting by my license, I drag forward Mr. George Gissing from an antiquity of several weeks. I blow the dust of oblivion from M.

Pierre Loti and indeed from all the company—they have been published for days and days. I foresee, however, that I must neglect the company for the sake of the two members I have named, writers—I speak for myself—always in order, though not, I admit, on quite the same line. Mr. Gissing would have been particularly in order had he only kept for the present period the work preceding his latest; all the more that "In the Year of Jubilee" has to my perception some points of superiority to "The Whirlpool." For this author in general, at any rate, I profess, and have professed ever since reading "The New Grub Street," a persistent taste—a taste that triumphs even over the fact that he almost as persistently disappoints me. I fail as yet to make out why exactly it is that going so far he so sturdily refuses to go further. The whole business of distribution and composition he strikes me as having cast to the winds; but just this fact of a question about him is a part of the wonder—I use the word in the sense of enjoyment—that he excites. It is not every day in the year that we meet a novelist about whom there is a question. The circumstance alone is almost sufficient to beguile or to enthrall; and I seem to myself to have said almost everything in speaking of something that Mr. Gissing "goes far" enough to do. To go far enough to do anything is, in the conditions we live in, a lively achievement.

"The Whirlpool," I crudely confess, was in a manner a grief to me, but the book has much substance, and there is no light privilege in an emotion so sustained. This emotion perhaps it is that most makes me, to the end, stick to Mr. Gissing—makes me with an almost nervous clutch quite cling to him. I shall

not know how to deal with him, however, if I withhold the last outrage of calling him an interesting case.
He seems to me above all a case of saturation, and it
is mainly his saturation that makes him interesting—
I mean especially in the sense of making him singular.
The interest would be greater were his art more complete; but we must take what we can get, and Mr.
Gissing has a way of his own. The great thing is that
his saturation is with elements that, presented to us
in contemporary English fiction, affect us as a product of extraordinary oddity and rarity: he reeks with
the savour, he is bowed beneath the fruits, of contact
with the lower, with the lowest middle-class, and that
is sufficient to make him an authority—*the* authority
in fact—on a region vast and unexplored.

The English novel has as a general thing kept so
desperately, so nervously clear of it, whisking back
compromised skirts and bumping frantically against
obstacles to retreat, that we welcome as the boldest
of adventurers a painter who has faced it and survived. We have had low life in plenty, for, with its
sores and vices, its crimes and penalties, misery has
colour enough to open the door to any quantity of
artistic patronage. We have shuddered in the dens
of thieves and the cells of murderers, and have dropped
the inevitable tear over tortured childhood and purified sin. We have popped in at the damp cottage with
my lady and heard the quaint rustic, bless his simple
heart, commit himself for our amusement. We have
fraternised on the other hand with the peerage and
the county families, staying at fine old houses till
exhausted nature has, for this source of intoxication,
not a wink of sociability left. It has grown, the source

in question, as stale as the sweet biscuit with pink en-
hancements in that familiar jar of the refreshment
counter from which even the attendant young lady in
black, with admirers and a social position, hesitates
to extract it. We have recognised the humble, the
wretched, even the wicked; also we have recognised
the "smart." But save under the immense pressure
of Dickens we have never done anything so dreadful
as to recognise the vulgar. We have at the very most
recognised it as the extravagant, the grotesque. The
case of Dickens was absolutely special; he dealt intensely with "lower middle," with "lowest" middle,
elements, but he escaped the predicament of showing
them as vulgar by showing them only as prodigiously
droll. When his people are not funny who shall dare
to say what they are? The critic may draw breath
as from a responsibility averted when he reflects that
they almost always *are* funny. They belong to a walk
of life that we may be ridiculous but never at all
serious about. We may be tragic, but that is often but
a form of humour. I seem to hear Mr. Gissing say:
"Well, dreariness for dreariness, let us try Brondes-
bury and Pinner; especially as in the first place I
know them so well; as in the second they are the
essence of England; and as in the third they are, artistically speaking, virgin soil. Behold them glitter
in the morning dew."

So he *is* serious—almost imperturbably—about them,
and, as it turns out, even quite manfully and admirably sad. He has the great thing: his saturation
(with the visible and audible common) can project
itself, let him get outside of it and walk round it. I
scarcely think he stays, as it were, outside quite as

much as he might; and on the question of form he
certainly strikes me as staying far too little. It is
form above all that is talent, and if Mr. Gissing's
were proportionate to his knowledge, to what may be
called his possession, we should have a larger force to
reckon with. That—not to speak of the lack of intensity in his imagination—is the direction in which
one would wish him to go further. Our Anglo-Saxon
tradition of these matters remains surely in some respects the strangest. After the perusal of such a book
as "The Whirlpool" I feel as if I had almost to explain that by "these matters" I mean the whole question of composition, of foreshortening, of the proportion and relation of parts. Mr. Gissing, to wind up
my reserves, overdoes the ostensible report of spoken
words; though I hasten to add that this abuse is so
general a sign, in these days, of the English and the
American novel as to deprive a challenge of every
hope of credit. It is attended visibly—that is visibly
to those who can see—with two or three woeful results.
If it had none other it would still deserve arraignment
on the simple ground of what it crowds out—the
golden blocks themselves of the structure, the whole
divine exercise and mystery of the exquisite art of
presentation.

The ugliest trick it plays at any rate is its effect
on that side of the novelist's effort—the side of most
difficulty and thereby of most dignity—which consists in giving the sense of duration, of the lapse and
accumulation of time. This is altogether to my view
the stiffest problem that the artist in fiction has to
tackle, and nothing is more striking at present than
the blankness, for the most part, of his indifference to

it. The mere multiplication of quoted remarks is the last thing to strengthen his hand. Such an expedient works exactly to the opposite end, absolutely minimising, in regard to time, our impression of lapse and passage. That is so much the case that I can think of no novel in which it prevails as giving at all the sense of the gradual and the retarded—the stretch of the years in which developments really take place. The picture is nothing unless it be a picture of the conditions, and the conditions are usually hereby quite omitted. Thanks to this perversity everything dealt with in fiction appears at present to occur simply on the occasion of a few conversations about it; there is no other constitution of it. A few hours, a few days seem to account for it. The process, the "dark backward and abysm," is really so little reproduced. We feel tempted to send many an author, to learn the rudiments of this secret, back to his Balzac again, the most accomplished master of it. He will learn also from Balzac while he is about it that nothing furthermore, as intrinsic effect, so much discounts itself as this abuse of the element of colloquy.

"Dialogue," as it is commonly called, is singularly suicidal from the moment it is not directly illustrative of something given us by another method, something constituted and presented. It is impossible to read work even as interesting as Mr. Gissing's without recognising the impossibility of making people both talk "all the time" and talk with the needful differences. The thing, so far as we have got, is simply too hard. There is always at the best the author's voice to be kept out. It can be kept out for occasions, it can not be kept out always. The solution therefore is to leave it its function, for it has the supreme one. This function, properly exercised, averts the disaster of the blight of the colloquy really in place—illustrative and indispensable. Nothing is more inevitable than such a blight when antecedently the general effect of the process has been undermined. We then want the report of the spoken word—want that only. But, proportionately, it doesn't come, doesn't count. It has been fatally cheapened. There is no effect, no relief.

I am writing a treatise when I meant only to give a glance; and it may be asked if the best thing I find in Mr. Gissing is after all then but an opportunity to denounce. The answer to that is that I find two other things—or should find them rather had I not deprived myself as usual of proper space. One of these is the pretext for speaking, by absolute rebound, as it were, and in the interest of vivid contrast, of Pierre Loti; the other is a better occasion still, an occasion for the liveliest sympathy. It is impossible not to be affected by the frankness and straightness of Mr. Gissing's feeling for his subject, a subject almost always distinctly remunerative to the ironic and even to the dramatic mind. He has the strongest deepest sense of common humanity, of the general struggle and the general grey grim comedy. He loves the real, he renders it, and though he has a tendency to drift too much with his tide, he gives us, in the great welter of the savourless, an individual manly strain. If he only had distinction he would make the suburbs "hum." I don't mean of course by his circulation there—the effect Ibsen is supposed to have on them; I mean objectively and as a rounded whole, as a great theme treated.

I am ashamed of having postponed "Ramuntcho," for "Ramuntcho" is a direct recall of the beauty of "Pêcheur d'Islande" and "Mon Frère Yves"—in other words a literary impression of the most exquisite order. Perhaps indeed it is as well that a critic *should* postpone—and quite indefinitely—an author as to whom he is ready to confess that his critical instinct is quite suspended. Oh the blessing of a book, the luxury of a talent, that one is only anxious not to reason about, only anxious to turn over in the mind and to taste! It is a poor business perhaps, but I have nothing more responsible to say of Loti than that I adore him. I love him when he is bad—and heaven knows he has occasionally been so—more than I love other writers when they are good. If therefore he is on the whole quite at his best in "Ramuntcho" I fear my appreciation is an undertaking too merely active for indirect expression. I can give it no more coherent form than to say that he makes the act of partaking one of the joys that, as things mainly go, a reader must be pretty well provided to be able not to jump at. And yet there are readers, apparently, who *are* so provided. There are readers who don't jump and are cocksure they can do without it. My sense of the situation is that they are wrong—that with famine stalking so abroad literally no one can. I defy it not to tell somewhere—become a gap one can immediately "spot."

It is well to content one's self, at all events, with affection; so stiff a job, in such a case, is understanding or, still more, explanation. There is a kind of finality in Loti's simplicity—if it even *be* simplicity. He performs in an air in which, on the part of the

spectator, analysis withers and only submission lives.
Has it anything to do with literature? Has it anything to do with nature? It must be, we should suppose, the last refinement either of one or of the other.
Is it all emotion, is it all calculation, is it all truth, is
it all humbug? All we can say as readers is that it
is for ourselves all experience, and of the most personal intensity. The great question is whether it be
emotion "neat" or emotion rendered and reduced. If
it be resolved into art why hasn't it more of the chill?
If it be sensibility pure why isn't it cruder and clum-
sier? What is exquisite is the contact of sensibility
made somehow so convenient—with only the beauty
preserved. It is not too much to say of Loti that
his sensibility begins where that of most of those who
use the article ends. If moreover in effect he represents the triumph of instinct, when was instinct ever
so sustained and so unerring? It keeps him unfailingly, in the matter of "dialogue," out of the overflow and the waste. It is a joy to see how his looseness is pervaded after all by proportion.

LONDON NOTES

August 1897

I SHRINK at this day from any air of relapsing into reference to those Victorian saturnalia of which the force may now be taken as pretty well spent; and if I remount the stream for an instant it is but with the innocent intention of plucking the one little flower of literature that, while the current roared, happened— so far at least as I could observe—to sprout by the bank. If it was sole of its kind moreover it was, I hasten to add, a mere accident of the Jubilee and as little a prominent as a preconcerted feature. What it comes to therefore is that if I gathered at the supreme moment a literary impression, the literary impression had yet nothing to do with the affair; nothing, that is, beyond the casual connection given by a some-what acrid aftertaste, the vision of the London of the morrow as I met this experience in a woeful squeeze through town the day after the fair. It was the sin-gular fate of M. Paul Bourget, invited to lecture at Oxford under university patronage and with Gustave Flaubert for his subject, to have found his appear-ance arranged for June 23. I express this untoward-ness but feebly, I know, for those at a distance from the edge of the whirlpool, the vast concentric eddies that sucked down all other life.

I found, on the morrow in question—the great day had been the 22nd—the main suggestion of a journey

from the south of England up to Waterloo and across
from Waterloo to Paddington to be that of one of
those deep gasps or wild staggers, losses of wind and
of balance, that follow some tremendous effort or some
violent concussion. The weather was splendid and
torrid and London a huge dusty cabless confusion of
timber already tottering, of decorations already stale,
of *badauds* already bored. The banquet-hall was by
no means deserted, but it was choked with mere echoes
and candle-ends; one had heard often enough of a
"great national awakening," and this was the greatest it would have been possible to imagine. Millions
of eyes, opening to dust and glare from the scenery
of dreams, seemed slowly to stare and to try to recollect. Certainly at that distance the omens were poor
for such concentration as a French critic might have
been moved to count upon, and even on reaching Oxford I was met by the sense that the spirit of that
seat of learning, though accustomed to intellectual
strain, had before the afternoon but little of a margin
for pulling itself together. Let me say at once that
it made the most of the scant interval and that when
five o'clock came the bare scholastic room at the Taylorian offered M. Bourget's reputation and topic, in
the hot dead Oxford air, an attention as deep and as
many-headed as the combination could ever have
hoped to command.

For one auditor of whom I can speak, at all events,
the occasion had an intensity of interest transcending
even that of Flaubert's strange personal story—which
was part of M. Bourget's theme—and of the new and
deep meanings that the lecturer read into it. Just the
fact of the occasion itself struck me as having well-

nigh most to say, and at any rate fed most the all but
bottomless sense that constitutes to-day my chief re-
ceptacle of impressions; a sense which at the same time
I fear I cannot better describe than as that˙ of the
way we are markedly going. No undue eagerness to
determine whether this be well or ill attaches to the
particular consciousness I speak of, and I can only
give it frankly for what, on the whole, it most, for
beguilement, for amusement, for the sweet thrill of
perception, represents and achieves—the quickened
notation of our "modernity." I feel that I can pay
this last-named lively influence no greater tribute than
by candidly accepting as an aid to expression its convenient name. To do that doubtless is to accept with
the name a host of other things. From the moment,
at any rate, the quickening I speak of sets in it is wonderful how many of these other things play, by every
circumstance, into the picture.

That the day should have come for M. Bourget to
lecture at Oxford, and should have come by the same
stroke for Gustave Flaubert to be lectured about, filled
the mind to a degree, and left it in an agitation of
violence, which almost excluded the question of what
in especial one of these spirits was to give and the
other to gain. It was enough of an emotion, for the
occasion, to live in the circumstance that the author
of "Madame Bovary" could receive in England a
public baptism of such peculiar solemnity. With the
vision of that, one could bring in all the light and
colour of all the rest of the picture and absolutely see,
for the instant, something momentous in the very act
of happening, something certainly that might easily
become momentous with a little interpretation. Such

are the happy chances of the critical spirit, always yearning to interpret, but not always in presence of the right mystery.

There was a degree of poetic justice, or at least of poetic generosity, in the introduction of Flaubert to a scene, to conditions of credit and honour, so little to have been by himself ever apprehended or estimated: it was impossible not to feel that no setting or stage for the crowning of his bust could less have appeared familiar to him, and that he wouldn't have failed to wonder into what strangely alien air his glory had strayed. So it is that, as I say, the whole affair was a little miracle of our breathless pace, and no corner from which another member of the craft could watch it was so quiet as to attenuate the small magnificence of the hour. No novelist, in a word, worth his salt could fail of a consciousness, under the impression, of his becoming rather more of a novelist than before. Was it not, on the whole, just the essence of the matter that had for the moment there its official recognition? were not the blest mystery and art ushered forward in a more expectant and consecrating hush than had ever yet been known to wait upon them?

One may perhaps take these things too hard and read into them foolish fancies; but the hush in question was filled to my imagination—quite apart from the listening faces, of which there would be special things to say that I wouldn't for the world risk—with the great picture of all the old grey quads and old green gardens, of all the so totally different traditions and processions that were content at last, if only for the drowsy end of a summer afternoon, to range them-

selves round and play at hospitality. What it appeared possible to make out was a certain faint convergence: that was the idea of which, during the whole
process, I felt the agreeable obsession. From the moment it brushed the mind certainly the impulse was
to clutch and detain it: too doleful would it have
been to entertain for an instant the fear that M. Bourget's lecture could leave the two elements of his case
facing each other only at the same distance at which
it had found them. No, no; there was nothing for it
but to assume and insist that with each tick of the
clock they moved a little nearer together. That was
the process, as I have called it, and none the less interesting to the observer that it may not have been,
and may not yet be, rapid, full, complete, quite easy
or clear or successful. It was the seed of contact that
assuredly was sown; it was the friendly beginning
that in a manner was made. The situation was handled and modified—the day was a date. I shall perhaps remain obscure unless I say more expressly and
literally that the particular thing into which, for the
perfect outsider, the occasion most worked was a lively
interest—so far as an outsider could feel it—in the
whole odd phenomenon and spectacle of a certain usual
positive *want* of convergence, want of communication
between what the seat and habit of the classics, the
famous frequentation and discipline, do for their victims in one direction and what they do not do for
them in another. Was the invitation to M. Bourget
not a dim symptom of a bridging of this queerest of
all chasms? I can only so denominate—as a most
anomalous gap—the class of possibilities to which we
owe its so often coming over us in England that the
light kindled by the immense academic privilege is apt

suddenly to turn to thick smoke in the air of contemporary letters.

There are movements of the classic torch round modern objects—strange drips and drops and wondrous waverings—that have the effect of putting it straight out. The range of reference that I allude to and that is most the fashion draws its credit from being an education of the taste, and it doubtless makes on the prescribed lines and in the close company of the ancients tremendous tests and triumphs for that principle. Nothing, however, is so singular as to see what again and again becomes of it in the presence of examples for which prescription and association are of no avail. I am speaking here of course not of unexpected reserves, but of unexpected raptures, bewildering revelations of a failure of the sense of perspective. This leads at times to queer conjunctions, strange collocations in which Euripides gives an arm to Sarah Grand and Octave Feuillet harks back to Virgil. It is the breath of a madness in which one gropes for a method—probes in vain the hiatus and sighs for the missing link. I am far from meaning to say that all this will find itself amended by the discreet dose administered the other day at the Taylorian of even so great an antidote as Flaubert; but I come back to my theory that there is after all hope for a world still so accessible to salutary shocks. That was apparent indeed some years ago. Was it not at the Taylorian that Taine and Renan successively lectured? Oxford, wherever it was, heard them even then to the end. It is for the Taines, Renans and Bourgets very much the salting of the tail of the bird: there must be more than one try.

It is possible to have glanced at some of the odd
estimates that the conversation of the cultivated throws
to the surface and yet to say quite without reserve
that the world of books has suffered no small shrinkage by the recent death of Mrs. Oliphant. She had
long lived and worked in it, and from no individual
perhaps had the great contemporary flood received a
more copious tribute. I know not if some study of
her remarkable life, and still more of her remarkable
character, be in preparation, but she was a figure that
would on many sides still lend itself to vivid portraiture. Her success had been in its day as great as her
activity, yet it was always present to me that her
singular gift was less recognised, or at any rate less
reflected, less reported upon, than it deserved: unless
indeed she may have been one of those difficult cases
for criticism, an energy of which the spirit and the
form, straggling apart, never join hands with that effect of union which in literature more than anywhere
else is strength.

Criticism, among us all, has come to the pass of
being shy of difficult cases, and no one, for that matter, practised it more in the hit-or-miss fashion and
on happy-go-lucky lines than Mrs. Oliphant herself.
She practised it, as she practised everything, on such
an inordinate scale that her biographer, if there is to
be one, will have no small task in the mere drafting
of lists of her contributions to magazines and journals
in general and to "Blackwood" in particular. She
wrought in "Blackwood" for years, anonymously and
profusely; no writer of the day found a *porte-voix*
nearer to hand or used it with an easier personal lati-
tude and comfort. I should almost suppose in fact
that no woman had ever, for half a century, had her

personal "say" so publicly and irresponsibly. Her facilities of course were of her own making, but the
wonder was that once made they could be so applied.

The explanation of her extraordinary fecundity was
a rare original equipment, an imperturbability of courage, health and brain, to which was added the fortune
or the merit of her having had to tune her instrument
at the earliest age. That instrument was essentially
a Scotch one; her stream flowed long and full without
losing its primary colour. To say that she was organised highly for literature would be to make too light
of too many hazards and conditions; but few writers
of our time have been so organised for liberal, for—
one may almost put it—heroic production. One of the
interesting things in big persons is that they leave us
plenty of questions, if only about themselves; and
precisely one of those that Mrs. Oliphant suggests is
the wonder and mystery of a love of letters that could
be so great without ever, on a single occasion even,
being greater. It was of course not a matter of mere
love; it was a part of her volume and abundance that
she understood life itself in a fine freehanded manner
and, I imagine, seldom refused to risk a push at a subject, however it might have given pause, that would
help to turn her wide wheel. She worked largely from
obligation—to meet the necessities and charges and
pleasures and sorrows of which she had a plentiful
share. She showed in it all a sort of sedentary dash
—an acceptance of the day's task and an abstention
from the plaintive note from which I confess I could
never withhold my admiration.

Her capacity for labour was infinite—for labour of
the only sort that, with the fine strain of old Scotch

pride and belated letterless toryism that was in her,
she regarded as respectable. She had small patience
with new-fangled attitudes or with a finical conscience.
What was good enough for Sir Walter was good enough
for her, and I make no doubt that her shrewd unfil-
tered easy flow, fed after all by an immensity of reading as well as of observation and humour, would have
been good enough for Sir Walter. If this had been
the case with her abounding history, biography and
criticism, it would have been still more the case with
her uncontrolled flood of fiction. She was really a
great *improvisatrice*, a night-working spinner of long,
loose, vivid yarns, numberless, pauseless, admirable,
repeatedly, for their full, pleasant, reckless rustle over
depths and difficulties—admirable indeed, in any case
of Scotch elements, for many a close engagement with
these. She showed in no literary relation more acuteness than in the relation—so profitable a one as it has
always been—to the inexhaustible little country which
has given so much, yet has ever so much more to give,
and all the romance and reality of which she had at
the end of her pen. Her Scotch folk have a wealth of
life, and I think no Scotch talk in fiction less of a
strain to the patience of the profane. It may be less
austerely veracious than some—but these are esoteric
matters.

Reading since her death "Kirsteen"—one of the
hundred, but published in her latest period and much
admired by some judges—I was, though beguiled, not
too much beguiled to be struck afresh with that elu-
sive fact on which I just touched, the mixture in the
whole thing. Such a product as "Kirsteen" has life—
is full of life, but the critic is infinitely baffled. It

may of course be said to him that he has nothing to
do with compositions of this order—with such wares
altogether as Mrs. Oliphant dealt in. But he can accept that retort only with a renunciation of some of
his liveliest anxieties. Let him take some early day
for getting behind, as it were, the complexion of a
talent that could care to handle a thing to the tune
of so many pages and yet not care more to "do" it.
There is a fascination in the mere spectacle of so serene an instinct for the middle way, so visible a conviction that to reflect is to be lost.

Mrs. Oliphant was never lost, but she too often
saved herself at the expense of her subject. I have
no space to insist, but so much of the essence of the
situation in "Kirsteen" strikes me as missed, dropped
out without a thought, that the wonder is all the
greater of the fact that in spite of it the book does in
a manner scramble over its course and throw up a
fresh strong air. This was certainly the most that
the author would have pretended, and from her scorn
of precautions springs a gleam of impertinence quite
in place in her sharp and handsome physiognomy,
that of a person whose eggs are not all in one basket,
nor all her imagination in service at once. There is
scant enough question of "art" in the matter, but
there is a friendly way for us to feel about so much
cleverness, courage and humanity. We meet the case
in wishing that the timid talents were a little more
like her and the bold ones a little less.

THE END